SQL Server 2016 High Availability

UNLEASHED

Unleashed Series

Visit informit.com/unleashed for a complete list of available products.

Unleashed takes you beyond the basics, providing an exhaustive, technically sophisticated reference for professionals who need to exploit a technology to its fullest potential. It's the best resource for practical advice from the experts and the most in-depth coverage of the latest technologies.

Make sure to connect with us!
informit.com/socialconnect

Paul Bertucci

SQL Server 2016 High Availability

UNLEASHED

SAMS | 800 East 96th Street, Indianapolis, Indiana 46240 USA

SQL Server 2016 High Availability Unleashed

ISBN-13: 978-0-672-33776-5

ISBN-10: 0-672-33776-2

Library of Congress Cataloging-in-Publication Data: 2017942001

Printed in the United States of America

1   17

Trademarks

All terms mentioned in this book that are known to be trademarks or service marks have been appropriately capitalized. Sams Publishing cannot attest to the accuracy of this information. Use of a term in this book should not be regarded as affecting the validity of any trademark or service mark.

Warning and Disclaimer

Every effort has been made to make this book as complete and as accurate as possible, but no warranty or fitness is implied. The information provided is on an "as is" basis. The authors and the publisher shall have neither liability nor responsibility to any person or entity with respect to any loss or damages arising from the information contained in this book.

Special Sales

For information about buying this title in bulk quantities, or for special sales opportunities (which may include electronic versions; custom cover designs; and content particular to your business, training goals, marketing focus, or branding interests), please contact our corporate sales department at corpsales@pearsoned.com or (800) 382-3419.

For government sales inquiries, please contact governmentsales@pearsoned.com.

For questions about sales outside the U.S., please contact intlcs@pearson.com.

Editor-in-chief
Greg Wiegand

Editor
Trina MacDonald

Managing Editor
Sandra Schroeder

Development Editor
Mark Renfrow

Project Editor
Lori Lyons

Production Manager
Dhayanidhi

Copy Editor
Catherine D. Wilson

Indexer
Lisa Stumpf

Proofreader
H. S. Rupa

Technical Editor
J. Boyd Nolan

Editorial Assistant
Courtney Martin

Cover Designer
Chuti Prasertsith

Compositor
codeMantra

Contents at a Glance

Table of Contents

About the Author

Paul Bertucci is the founder of Data by Design (www.dataXdesign.com) a database consulting firm with offices in the United States and Paris, France. He has more than 30 years of experience with database design, data modeling, data architecture, data replication, performance and tuning, distributed data systems, big data/Hadoop, data integration, high availability, disaster recovery/business continuity, master data management/data quality, and system architectures for numerous Fortune 500 companies, including Intel, Coca-Cola, Symantec, Autodesk, Apple, Toshiba, Lockheed, Wells Fargo, Merrill-Lynch, Safeway, Texaco, Charles Schwab, Wealth Front, Pacific Gas and Electric, Dayton Hudson, Abbott Labs, Cisco Systems, Sybase, and Honda, to name a few. He has written numerous articles, company and international data standards, and high-profile courses such as "Performance and Tuning" and "Physical Database Design" for Sybase and "Entity Relationship Modeling" courses for Chen & Associates (Dr. Peter P. Chen). Other Sams books that he has authored include the highly popular *Microsoft SQL Server Unleashed* series (SQL Server 2000, 2005, 2008 R2, 2012, and 2014), *ADO.NET in 24 Hours*, and *Microsoft SQL Server High Availability*.

He has deployed numerous traditional database systems with MS SQL Server, Sybase, DB2, and Oracle database engines, big data databases with Hadoop, and non-SQL databases (value pair) such as Oracle's NoSQL and Cassandra NoSQL. He has designed/architected several commercially available tools in the database, data modeling, performance and tuning, data integrity, data integration, and multidimensional planning spaces.

Paul is also an experienced leader of global enterprise architecture teams for multi-billion-dollar companies and lead global teams in data warehousing/BI, big data, master data management, identity management, enterprise application integration, and collaboration systems. He has held positions such as chief data architect for Symantec, chief architect and director of Shared Services for Autodesk, CTO for Diginome, and CTO for both LISI and PointCare. Paul speaks regularly at many conferences and gatherings worldwide, such as SQL Saturday's, Ignite, TechEd, MDM Summit, Oracle World, Informatica World, SRII, MIT Chief Data Officer symposium, and many others.

Paul received his formal education in computer science and electrical engineering from UC Berkeley (Go, Bears!). He lives in the beautiful Pacific Northwest (Oregon) with the three children who still live at home (Donny, Juliana, and Nina) and lives near the other two, "working" adult children, Marissa and Paul Jr., who live in Portland.

Paul can be reached at pbertucci@dataXdesign.com.

Contributing Author

Raju Shreewastava is a leading expert in data warehousing, business intelligence, and big data for numerous companies around the globe. He is based out of Silicon Valley, supporting several high-profile big data implementations. He previously led the data warehouse/business intelligence and big data teams while working for Paul at Autodesk. His big data and Azure contributions of content and examples represent the bulk of Chapter 11, "High Availability and Big Data Options." He has more than 20 years of experience with database design, data integration, and deployments. Raju can be reached at raju.shreewastava@gmail.com.

Dedication

*Successes are hard to achieve without hard work, fortitude,
support, inspiration, and guidance. The daily examples
of how to succeed I owe to my parents, Donald and Jane Bertucci,
and my inspiration comes to me easily from wanting to be the
best father I can be for my children and helping them become
successful in their own lives. But I find even greater inspiration
and amazing support from my loving life partner, Michelle,
to whom I dedicate this book. Infinity!*

Acknowledgments

All my writing efforts require a huge sacrifice of time to properly research, demonstrate, and describe leading-edge subject matter. The brunt of the burden usually falls on those many people who are near and very dear to me. With this in mind, I desperately need to thank my family for allowing me to encroach on many months of what should have been my family's "quality time."

However, with sacrifice also comes reward, in this case in the form of technical excellence and solid business relationships. Many individuals were involved in this effort, both directly and indirectly. Thanks to my technology leaders network, Yves Moison, Jose Solera, Anthony Vanlandingham, Jack McElreath, Paul Broenen, Jeff Brzycki, Walter Kuketz, Steve Luk, Bert Haberland, Peter P. Chen, Gary Dunn, Martin Sommer, Raju Shreewastava, Mark Ginnebaugh, Christy Foulger, Suzanne Finley, and G. "Morgan" Watkins.

Thanks also for the technology environment, setup, and testing help from Ryan McCarty and for the big data and Azure content and examples that form the bulk of Chapter 11, "High Availability and Big Data options," from Raju Shreewastava.

Thanks, guys!

Many good suggestions and comments came from the technical and copy editors at Pearson, yielding an outstanding effort.

We Want to Hear from You!

As the reader of this book, *you* are our most important critic and commentator. We value your opinion and want to know what we're doing right, what we could do better, what areas you'd like to see us publish in, and any other words of wisdom you're willing to pass our way.

We welcome your comments. You can email or write to let us know what you did or didn't like about this book—as well as what we can do to make our books better.

Please note that we cannot help you with technical problems related to the topic of this book.

When you write, please be sure to include this book's title and author as well as your name and email address. We will carefully review your comments and share them with the author and editors who worked on the book.

Email: consumer@samspublishing.com

Mail: Sams Publishing
ATTN: Reader Feedback
800 East 96th Street
Indianapolis
IN 46240 USA

Reader Services

Register your copy of *SQL Server 2016 High Availability Unleashed* at www.informit.com for convenient access to downloads, updates, and corrections as they become available. To start the registration process, go to www.informit.com/register and log in or create an account*. Enter the product ISBN 9780672337765 and click Submit. When the process is complete, you will find any available bonus content under Registered Products.

*Be sure to check the box that you would like to hear from us to receive exclusive discounts on future editions of this product.

Introduction

"Always on, always ready is not just a business goal but a competitive requirement for any company that wants to compete in the cloud space. Highly available technologies—deployed in the right architectures—allow for nonstop delivery of value to your customers."

—Jeff Brzycki, Chief Information Officer, Autodesk, March 2017

Five 9s

Downtime (system unavailability) directly translates to loss of profit, productivity, your ability to deliver to your customers, and customer goodwill—plain and simple. If your current or planned applications are vulnerable to downtime problems—or if you are unsure of the potential downtime issues—then this book is for you. Is your business at or nearing a requirement to be "highly available" or "continually available" in order to protect the previously mentioned profit, productivity, and customer goodwill? Again, this book is for you.

Helping you understand the high availability (HA) solutions available to you and choosing the high availability approach that maximizes benefit and minimizes cost is our primary goal. This book provides a roadmap to design and implement these high availability solutions. The good news is that software and hardware vendors in general, and Microsoft specifically, have come a long way in supporting high availability needs and will move even further toward achieving 99.999% availability (herein referred to as "five 9s") in the near future. A 24×7 application that aspires to achieve five 9s would tolerate only a yearly total of 5.26 minutes of downtime. Knowing how to design for such high availability is crucial.

This book even touches on some alternatives for "always available" systems (100% availability). These capabilities, coupled with a formal methodology for designing high availability solutions, will allow you to design, install, and maintain systems to maximize availability while minimizing development and platform costs.

The success or failure of your company may well be influenced, if not driven, by your ability to understand the essential elements that comprise a high availability environment, the business requirements driving the proper high availability approach, and the cost considerations affecting the ROI (return on investment) of a high availability solution. It is likely that a company's most critical applications demand some type of high availability solution. For example, if a global online ordering system went down and remained down for any length of time, millions of dollars would be lost, along with the public's goodwill toward that company. The stakes are high indeed!

This book outlines how you can "design in" high availability for new applications and "upgrade" current applications to improve availability. In all cases, a crucial consideration will be the business drivers influencing a proposed application's uptime requirements, factoring in the dollar cost, productivity cost, and the goodwill cost of *not* having that system available to the end users for any period of time.

This book highlights current Microsoft capabilities and options that allow you to achieve high availability systems. These include, among others, Microsoft Cluster Services, Microsoft SQL Server 2016 SQL Clustering, SQL Data Replication, Log Shipping, Database Mirroring/Snapshots, AlwaysOn Availability Groups, and built-in architectures on Azure for Big Data and Azure SQL.

Most importantly, this book presents a set of business scenarios that reflect actual companies' high availability requirements. These business scenarios guide you through the design process, show you how to determine the high availability approach best suited for a particular business scenario, and help specify a roadmap to implement the business scenario with a specific technical solution.

This book may feel more like a cookbook or a Google Maps route suggestion than a typical technical manual—and that is the intention. It is one thing to describe technical syntax, but it is much more important to actually explain why you choose a particular approach to meet a particular business or application requirement. This book focuses on the later. The business scenarios introduced and implemented in this book come from live customer implementations. It does not reveal the names of these customers for obvious nondisclosure reasons. However, these business scenarios should allow you to correlate your own business requirements to these high availability situations. This book also includes examples using the infamous AdventureWorks database provided by Microsoft. Utilizing the AdventureWorks database will allow you to replicate some of the solutions quickly and easily in your own sandbox.

Several tools, scripts, documents, and references to help you jump-start your next high availability implementation are available at the book's website at

www.informit.com/title/9780672337765.

Who This Book Is For

The material in this book is intended for intermediate- to advanced-level users, in roles such as system designer/architect, system administrator, data architect, database administrator, SQL programmer, and even managerial types, such as chief information officer (CIO) or chief technology officer (CTO). In addition, the justifications, alternatives, and ROI considerations might be beneficial for a chief financial officer (CFO), since many of the issues and ramifications translate into lost profit, productivity, and goodwill. A motivated CFO who understands the benefits, complexities, and capabilities of achieving high availability can rest easier knowing that the company is in good hands with a well-designed high availability solution protecting the bottom line.

How This Book Is Organized

This book is divided into three parts:

▶ **Part I, "Understanding High Availability"**—Chapters 1 and 2 establish a definition of high availability, introduce high availability business scenarios that are typically found in the real world, and describe the various hardware and software options in the Microsoft family of products that directly address high availability.

▶ **Part II, "Choosing the Right High Availability Approaches"**—Chapter 3 explicitly defines a formal design approach to be used as a roadmap to navigate the appropriate high availability solution for each business scenario introduced.

▶ **Part III, "Implementing High Availability"**—Chapters 4–17 describe the architecture, design, implementation steps, and techniques needed for each high availability solution. Each business scenario will be driven to its "complete" implementation. Then, a summary of the overall approach is provided, along with a look into the future of high availability.

This book also looks at big data options because more and more organizations are expanding their footprint to include big data and also requiring high availability for this massive volume of data.

This "soup-to-nuts" approach should yield ample clarity for you—from inception of the business requirements to the complete implementation of a high availability solution for the given business and service-level requirements.

Conventions Used in This Book

Names of commands and stored procedures are presented in a special `monospaced` computer typeface. We have tried to be consistent in our use of uppercase and lowercase for keywords and object names. However, because the default installation of SQL Server doesn't make a distinction between upper- and lowercase for SQL keywords or object names and data, you might find some of the examples presented in either upper- or lowercase.

Notes cover any design or architecture idea that is related to the topic being discussed. They are meant to supplement the discussed idea or to help guide design. For example, a note might provide some additional insight into what type of disk RAID levels are appropriate for the different types of data accesses a database is used for. This would be considered above and beyond the normal RAID level explanation but is great to consider when building SQL Server databases.

Setting Your Goals High

As with any other system you have ever touched, it is critical to establish and document the system's availability expectations with your end users (business). For systems aspiring to very high availability, these expectations must be very precise. The stakes are truly higher in HA systems. A well-grounded and time-tested HA methodology such as the ones described in this book balances costs and benefits and reduces the likelihood of poor or uninformed decisions on the high availability options available with current technology. Lots of things must be done right to achieve the proper level of current and future application high availability. This book—plain and simple—will show you how to understand, cost justify, and achieve these high availability goals and minimize your company's exposure to downtime. You might also find that this book is a great companion book to Sams Publishing's *Microsoft SQL Server 2014 Unleashed.*

CHAPTER 1

Understanding High Availability

Knowing clearly what essential elements comprise a high availability environment and completely understanding the business requirements that are driving you to think about high availability solutions may well determine the success or failure of your company. More times than not, a company's most critical application demands some type of high availability solution. Having high availability is often termed having "resilience"—the ability to recover or fail over quickly. In today's competitive marketplace, if a global online ordering system goes down (that is, is unavailable for any reason) and remains down for any length of time, millions of dollars may be lost, along with the public's goodwill toward that company. Profit margins are thin enough, without having to add your system's downtime into the equation of whether your company makes a profit. The impact of unplanned or even planned downtime may be much greater than you realize.

Overview of High Availability

Unplanned outages are very expensive, and the cost of downtime is rising, according to a 2013 survey from the Ponemon Institute (see www.datacenterknowledge.com/archives/2013/12/03/study-cost-data-center-downtime-rising). The average cost per minute of unplanned down time was reported as $7,900, up 41% from 2010. In that same survey, the average reported incident length was 86 minutes, which calculates to an average cost per incident of approximately $690,200. (In 2010, it was 97 minutes at approximately $505,500.)

Another recent survey from Eagle Rock Alliance (ERP; see www.eaglerockltd.com) that focused on the cost of downtime by industry sector indicated significantly high per-hour cost of downtime, especially in some industry sectors. Consider the following examples of per-hour dollar losses:

▶ **Airline reservation system**—$150,000–$200,000/hour loss

▶ **ATM service fees**—$12,000–$17,000/hour loss

▶ **Stock brokerage (retail)**—$5.6–$7.3 million/hour loss

The results of these studies indicate an average annual cost exceeding billions of dollars for downtime globally—and perhaps even more.

The stakes are high in building rock-solid applications to run your business. The trick is to pour your applications into architectures and systems that can fulfill your availability needs from the start. If you have existing applications that should have been deployed with a high availability solution, you are possibly putting your company at risk, and you will need to accelerate getting your high availability solution into place at almost any cost as quickly as you can go (without making mistakes). If you are building a new application, you need to take into account the proper high availability solution by integrating various high availability considerations into your current development methodology.

This chapter defines many high availability terms, describes an availability percentage calculation, identifies the different categories of availability, shows you which critical pieces of information are needed for a complete high availability requirement (perhaps *your* high availability requirement), and describes a few common business scenarios that are candidates for high availability. Later chapters show you how to match your high availability requirements to a particular high availability solution, with a focus on Microsoft-based options. Today you can take advantage of on-premises options, cloud options, and various hybrid options that include both on-premises and cloud options. Although fairly new, there are now full platform as a service (PaaS) options available from Microsoft for application and database tiers that take much of the administration and management out of the picture. These options feature Azure SQL databases and configurations that can cover various high availability solutions.

As shown in Figure 1.1, how highly available a system becomes is actually a combination of several elements. This figure illustrates many of the potential system components, including on-premises, cloud, and hybrid options. From a high availability point of view, your application will only be as good as the weakest link in this complex stack.

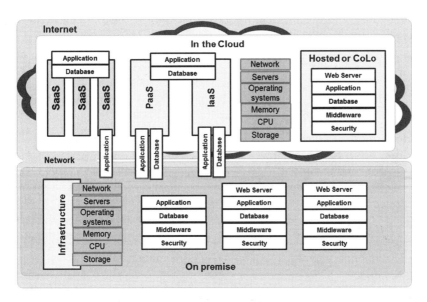

FIGURE 1.1   System stack, showing each system hardware and software component that can fail.

Your application might be on the cloud as a software as a service (SaaS) application, in which case you are relying on that SaaS vendor for your availability, and you only need to worry about connectivity over the Internet and network. Perhaps you have built your application using a PaaS environment in the cloud. Again, you must rely on the PaaS vendor for your availability. Many other combinations of cloud and hosted options are being used these days, as you can also see in Figure 1.1. This includes using infrastructure as a service (IaaS), fully hosted infrastructure (hardware you rent), and colocation (CoLo; your servers on someone else's racks).

As you can also see in Figure 1.1, each system component (network, application, middleware, database, and the operating system) has its own vulnerability and may also affect the other layers of the stack.

If the OS fails or must be brought down for maintenance, the rest of the stack is affected. In the outermost part of the stack is the network. If the network fails, the application is probably not affected (that is, the application is still running). However, because the application cannot be accessed by a user via the network, it is essentially "down."

Embedded throughout this stack are all the physical hardware (infrastructure) components, which have their own failure issues. With a move toward more cloud-based or hybrid application solutions, the emphasis of your high availability focus may also be refocused. And, to top things off, there is a human error aspect running through all these components as well. If you reduce or eliminate human errors (bringing a database (DB) offline accidentally, deleting a table's data in error, and so on), you increase your system's availability greatly. (There are standard ways to combat these human error issues, but discussing them is slightly outside the realm of this book.)

As the availability tree in Figure 1.2 shows, continuous application availability (or high availability) involves three major variables:

▶ **Uptime**—The time during which your application is up, running, and available to the end users.

▶ **Planned downtime**—The time during which IT makes one or more of the system stacks unavailable for planned maintenance, upgrades, so on.

▶ **Unplanned downtime**—The time during which the system is unavailable due to failure—human error, hardware failure, software failure, or natural disaster (earthquake, tornado, and so on).

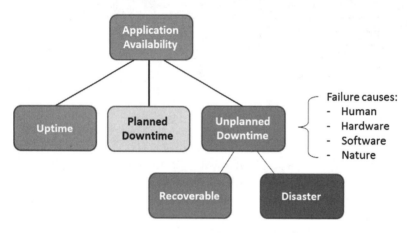

FIGURE 1.2   Availability tree depicting the different aspects of availability.

As you may already know from your own personal experience, the planned downtime comprises the lion's share of unavailability on most systems. It involves things such as hardware upgrades; OS upgrades (such as from Windows 2010 to Windows 2014); and application of service packs to the DB, OS, or applications. However, there is a steady trend to adopt hardware and software platforms that allow for this element to be minimized (and, often, completely eliminated). For instance, many vendors offer systems whose hardware components, such as CPUs, disk drives, and even memory, are "hot swappable." But the price of these systems tends to be high. We'll talk about the cost and ROI of high availability systems in Chapter 3, "Choosing High Availability."

The uptime variable is what you are typically measured against. You want it to be constantly moving closer and closer to a "continuously available" level for the applications that require it. Any downtime, planned or unplanned, is factored into your overall requirements of what *you* need for a high availability system. You can "design in" uptime to your overall system stack and application architectures by using basic distributed data techniques, basic backup and recovery practices, and basic application clustering techniques, as well as by leveraging hardware solutions that are almost completely resilient to failures.

Unplanned downtime usually takes the form of memory failures, disk drive failures, database corruptions (both logical and physical), data integrity breakdowns, virus breakouts, application errors, OS failures, network failures, natural disasters, and plain and simple human errors. There are basically two types of unplanned downtime:

▶ **Downtime that is "recoverable" by normal recovery mechanisms**—This includes downtime caused by things like swapping in a new hard drive to replace a failed one and then bringing the system back up.

▶ **Downtime that is "not recoverable" and that makes your system completely unavailable and unable to be recovered locally**—This includes things such as a natural disaster or any other unplanned downtime that affects hardware. (Those of us who live in California are frequently reminded of things such as earthquakes and forest fires that contribute to downtime and nonrecoverable failures in many systems.)

In addition, a good disaster recovery plan is paramount to any company's critical application implementation and should be part of your high availability planning.

If you simply apply a standard high availability technique to all your applications, you will probably sacrifice something that may turn out to be equally important (such as performance or recovery time). So, be very cautious with a blanket approach to high availability. I found a perfect example of this type of poorly formed template high availability approach at a major auto manufacturer (which will remain nameless). Figure 1.3 shows that company's common SQL clustering environment for *all* of its B2C applications.

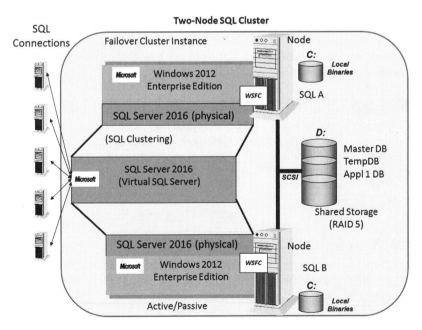

FIGURE 1.3   A poorly formed high availability template approach.

At the outset, the company had the right idea—to use SQL clustering. Then it wondered why some of these applications ran so slowly and why all of them had a fairly long recovery time when failures occurred. Starting with RAID 5 shared storage for all applications was the company's first mistake. RAID 5 is best suited for read-only applications, but for typical OLTP applications, twice the number of disk I/Os occur, which directly translates to poorer performance overall. In addition, only full database backups were being done on a nightly basis (no backups of any kind during the day), and these OLTP-oriented applications were running "at risk" during the day (with no up-to-the-minute recovery). The company needed to quickly start doing incremental transaction log backups on these volatile data applications. This was just the tip of the iceberg.

Calculating Availability

Calculating what the availability of a system has been (or needs to be) is actually quite simple. You simply subtract the "time unavailable" from the "mean time between unavailability" and then divide this by the same "mean time between unavailability." This is the formula:

$$\text{Availability percentage} = ((MBU - TU) / MBU) \times 100$$

where:

MBU is mean time between unavailability

TU is time unavailable (planned/unplanned downtime)

It's important to use a common time factor as the basis of this calculation (for example, minutes). The "time available" is the actual time if you're calculating what has already happened, and it is the estimated time if you're doing this for the future. In addition, it is here that you add in all unplanned and planned downtime. The "mean time between unavailability" is the time since the last unavailability occurred.

> **NOTE**
>
> For a system that needs to be up 24 hours per day, 7 days a week, 365 days per year, you would measure against 100% of the minutes in the year. For a system that is only supposed to be available 18 hours per day, 7 days a week, you would measure against 75% of the minutes in the year. In other words, you measure your availability against the planned hours of operation, not the total number of minutes in a year (unless your planned hours of operation are 24×7×365).

Availability Example: A 24×7×365 Application

Say that an application had an unplanned failure on March 1 that took 38 minutes to recover from (in this example, a database had to be restored from a full database backup due to an application software error). Planned downtime on April 15 lasted 68 minutes (to run software upgrades to fix some Microsoft security holes and other server issues).

Another planned downtime lasted 442 minutes on April 20 (hardware upgrades of memory and disks). You would calculate this system's availability as follows:

Availability (from February 14 through February 28):

Mean time between unavailability was 20,160 minutes
[MBU = (15 days × 24 hours × 60 minutes)]

Time unavailable was 38 minutes [TU = 38 minutes]

This is the calculation:

((MBU – TU) / MBU) × 100 = Availability %

or

((20,160 minutes – 38 minutes)/20,160 minutes) × 100 = **99.81%**

Availability (from March 1 through April 15):

Mean time between unavailability was 66,240 minutes
[MBU = (46 days × 24 hours × 60 minutes)]

Time unavailable was 68 minutes [TU = 68 minutes]

This is the calculation:

((MBU – TU) / MBU) × 100 = Availability %

or

((66,240 minutes – 68 minutes)/ 66,240 minutes) × 100 = **99.90%**

Availability (from April 16 through April 20):

Mean time between unavailability was 7,200 minutes
[MBU = (5 days × 24 hours × 60 minutes)]

Time unavailable was 442 minutes [TU = 442 minutes]

This is the calculation:

((MBU – TU) / MBU) × 100 = Availability %

or

((7,200 minutes – 442 minutes)/7,200 minutes) × 100 = **93.86%**

Figure 1.4 shows these availability percentages mapped against the time of planned operation by month. A 95% availability was the targeted goal for this application.

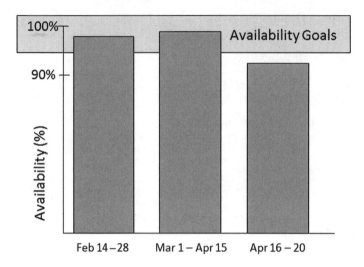

FIGURE 1.4   Availability percentages charted across planned operation.

As you can see, the availability goals were easily met for February and March, but availability dipped below these goals in April.

Overall, between February 14 and April 20, the availability averaged 99.42% (95,640 of planned operation time and 548 minutes of total downtime, yielding an average of 99.42% availability). This sustained average may or may not be acceptable, depending on the cost of the downtime to the business during those isolated downtime intervals.

The Availability Continuum

The continuum in Figure 1.5 shows a general classification of availability based on the amount of downtime an application will tolerate without impact to the business. You would write your service level agreements (SLAs) to support and try to achieve one of these continuum categories.

Topping the chart is the category extreme availability, so named to indicate that this is the least tolerant category and is essentially a zero (or near zero) downtime requirement (sustained 99.5% to 100% availability). Next is the high availability category, which depicts a minimal tolerance for downtime (sustained 95% to 99.4% availability). Most "critical" applications would fit into this category of availability need. Then comes the standard availability category, with a more normal type of operation (sustained 83% to 94% availability). The acceptable availability category is for applications that are deemed "noncritical" to the business, such as online employee benefits self-service applications. These can tolerate much lower availability ranges (sustained 70% to 82% availability). Finally, the marginal availability category is for "nonproduction" custom applications, such as marketing mailing label applications that can tolerate significant downtime (sustained 0% to 69% availability). Again remember that availability is measured based on the planned operation times of the application.

	Characteristic	Availability Range
Extreme Availability	Zero, or near zero downtime!	**(99.5%–100%)**
High Availability	Minimal downtime	**(95%–99.4%)**
Standard Availability	With some downtime tolerance	**(83%–94%)**
Acceptable Availability	Non-critical Applications	**(70%–82%)**
Marginal Availability	Non-production Applications	**(up to 69%)**

Availability Range **describes the percentage of time relative to the "planned" hours of operations**

8,760 hours/year | 168 hours/week | 24 hours/day
525,600 minutes/year | 7,200 minutes/week | 1,440 minutes/day

FIGURE 1.5   Availability continuum.

The mythical five 9s (a sustained 99.999% availability) falls directly in the extreme availability category. In general, the computer industry calls this "high availability," but I push this type of near-zero downtime requirement into its own "extreme" category, all by itself. Most applications can only dream about this level of availability because of the costs involved, the high level of operational support required, the specialized hardware that must be in place, and many other extreme factors.

As you recall, downtime can be either unplanned or planned. Figure 1.6 shows how the availability continuum categories lay out over these aspects.

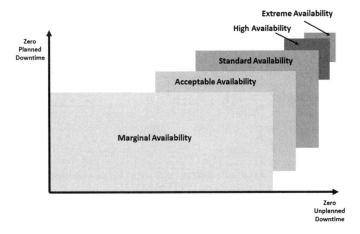

FIGURE 1.6   Planned and unplanned availability.

As you can see, having extreme availability places you in the far upper-right quadrant of both near-zero planned downtime and near-zero unplanned downtime.

Figure 1.7 shows the same unplanned/planned availability axis and availability categories but includes several common types of applications in the industry and places them in their approximate areas of availability need.

Leading the way might be a financial institution's automated teller machines (ATMs). Having this type of system available 100% of the time can be crucial to a company's customer service perception in this highly competitive industry. A 911 emergency tracking system is another slightly different application that again demands some extreme availability need. In the next plateau are systems such as e-commerce applications (online ordering systems). These types of systems tolerate some limited downtime but clearly need to be very highly available (minimal downtime) because of the potentially high dollar loss if the ordering system is not available to take orders. Other types of applications, such as email systems and inventory management tend to require only a standard level of availability, while many human resources and accounting systems can operate just fine in a lower (acceptable availability) mode. Marginally available applications are typically applications such as marketing mailing label runs or other one-off, nonproduction applications that can be scheduled to run whenever it is convenient or within some predefined range of availability.

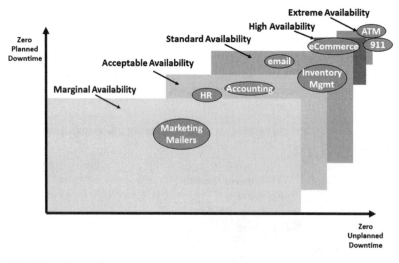

FIGURE 1.7   Application types and availability.

Availability Variables

The following are the primary variables that help you determine what high availability path you should be going down:

▶ **Uptime requirement**—This is the goal (from 0% to 100%) of what you require from your application for its planned hours of operation. This is above 95% for a typical highly available application.

▶ **Time to recover**—This is a general indication (from long to short) of the amount of time required to recover an application and put it back online. This could be stated in minutes, hours, or just in terms of long, medium, or short amount of time to recover. The more precise the better, though. For example, a typical time to recover for an OLTP (online transaction processing) application might be 5 minutes. This is fairly short but can be achieved with various techniques.

▶ **Tolerance of recovery time**—You need to describe what the impact might be (from high to low tolerance) of extended recovery times needed to resynchronize data, restore transactions, and so on. This is mostly tied to the time-to-recover variable but can vary widely, depending on who the end users of the system are. For example, internal company users of a self-service HR application may have a high tolerance for downtime (because the application doesn't affect their primary work). However, the same end users might have a very low tolerance for downtime of the conference room scheduling/meeting system.

▶ **Data resiliency**—You need to describe how much data you are willing to lose and whether it needs to be kept intact (that is, have complete data integrity, even in failure). This is often described in terms of low to high data resiliency. Both hardware and software solutions are in play for this variable—mirrored disk, RAID levels, database backup/recovery options, and so on.

▶ **Application resiliency**—You need an application-oriented description of the behavior you are seeking (from low to high application resiliency). In other words, should your applications (programs) be able to be restarted, switched to other machines without the end user having to reconnect, and so on? Very often the term *application clustering* is used to describe applications that have been written and designed to fail over to another machine without the end users realizing they have been switched. The .NET default of using "optimistic concurrency" combined with SQL clustering often yields this type of end-user experience very easily.

▶ **Degree of distributed access/synchronization**—For systems that are geographically distributed or partitioned (as are many global applications), it is critical to understand how distributed and tightly coupled they must be at all times (indicated from low to high degree of distributed access and synchronization required). A low specification of this variable indicates that the application and data are very loosely coupled and can stand on their own for periods of time. Then they can be resynchronized at a later date.

▶ **Scheduled maintenance frequency**—This is an indication of the anticipated (or current) rate of scheduled maintenance required for the box, OS, network, application software, and other components in the system stack. This may vary greatly, from often to never. Some applications may undergo upgrades, point releases, or patches very frequently (for example, SAP and Oracle applications).

▶ **Performance/scalability**—This is a firm requirement of the overall system performance and scalability needed for the application (from low- to high-performance need). This variable will drive many of the high availability solutions that you end up with because high-performance systems often sacrifice many of the other variables mentioned here (such as data resilience).

▶ **Cost of downtime ($ lost/hour)**—You need to estimate or calculate the dollar (or euro, yen, and so forth) cost for every minute of downtime (from low to high cost). You will usually find that the cost is not a single number, like an average cost per minute. In reality, short downtimes have lower costs, and the costs (losses) grow exponentially for longer downtimes. In addition, I usually try to measure the "good-will" cost (or loss) for B2C type of applications. So, this variable might have a sub-variable for you to specify.

▶ **Cost to build and maintain the high availability solution ($)**—This last variable may not be known initially. However, as you near the design and implementation of a high availability system, the costs come barreling in rapidly and often trump certain decisions (such as throwing out that RAID 10 idea due to the excessive cost of a large number of mirrored disks). This variable is also used in the cost justification of the high availability solution, so it must be specified or estimated as early as possible.

As you can see in Figure 1.8, you can think of each of these variables as an oil gauge or a temperature gauge. In your own early depiction of your high availability requirements, simply place an arrow along the gauge of each variable to estimate the approximate "temperature," or level, of a particular variable. As you can see, I have specified all the variables of a system that will fall directly into being highly available. This one is fairly tame, as highly available systems go, because there is a high tolerance for recovery time, and application resilience is moderately low. Later in this chapter, I describe four business scenarios, each of them including a full specification of these primary variables. In addition, starting in Chapter 3, an ROI calculation is included to provide the full cost justification of a particular HA solution.

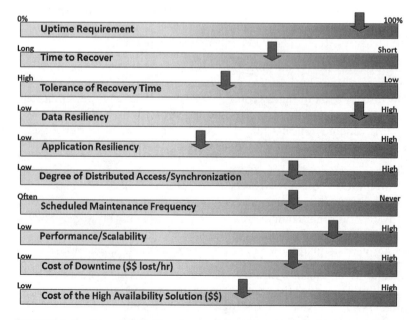

FIGURE 1.8   Primary variables for understanding your availability needs.

General Design Approach for Achieving High Availability

A good overall approach for achieving high availability for any application can be accomplished by doing the following:

▶ **Shoring up your "software" system stack from the center out (operating system, database, middleware, antivirus, and so on, in this order)**—This includes upgrading to the latest OS levels and other software component releases and putting into place all the support service contracts for them. This is extremely important for being able to get a quick fix for a bug that brings your system down.

▶ **Shoring up your hardware devices (redundant network cards, ECC memory, RAID disk arrays, disk mirroring, clustered servers, and so on)**—Be careful with the RAID levels because they will vary depending on your applications' characteristics.

▶ **Reducing human errors**—This involves implementing strict system controls, standards, procedures, extensive QA testing, and other application insulation techniques. Human errors account for many systems being unavailable.

▶ **Defining the primary variables of a potential highly available system**—This should also include defining your applications' service level requirements along with defining a solid disaster recovery plan.

Figure 1.9 shows a one-two punch approach that blends all these areas into two basic steps that need to be taken to achieve high availability for an application.

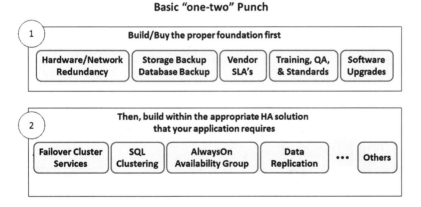

FIGURE 1.9   One-two punch for achieving high availability.

The basic premise is to build the proper foundation first (or use a PaaS/IaaS foundation that has this built into it already) followed by applying the appropriate Microsoft HA solution(s) that matches your applications' needs.

The proper foundation consists of the following:

▶ Building the proper hardware/network redundancies

▶ Putting into place all software and upgrades at the highest release levels possible, including antivirus software and so on

▶ Designing/deploying disk backups and DB backups that best service your application platforms

▶ Establishing the necessary vendor service level agreements/contracts

▶ Ensuring comprehensive end-user, administrator, and developer training, including extensive QA testing of all applications and rigid programming, system, and database standards

You must then gather the details of the high availability requirements for your application. Start with the HA primary variables and go from there. Then, based on the software available, the hardware available, and the high availability requirements, you can match and build out the appropriate HA solution on top of this solid foundation.

This book emphasizes the following types of high availability solutions:

▶ Failover cluster services

▶ SQL clustering

▶ AlwaysOn availability groups

▶ Data Replication

▶ Extending your deployment into the cloud (IaaS on Microsoft Azure)

▶ Utilizing Azure SQL databases in the cloud (PaaS on Microsoft Azure)

NOTE

This book discusses something called "application clustering" in concept and not in any technical detail, since it is programming oriented and really would require a complete programming book to give it the proper treatment.

Development Methodology with High Availability Built In

Figure 1.10 shows a traditional "waterfall" software development methodology. As you can see, understanding and gathering information that will yield the proper high availability designs for your application can start as early as the initial assessment and scoping phase (phase 0).

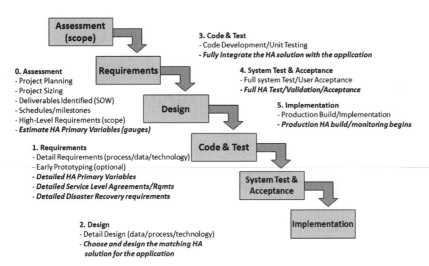

FIGURE 1.10   Development methodology with high availability built in.

The general software development phases and the corresponding high availability tasks within each phase are as follows:

▶ Phase 0: Assessment (scope)

Project planning

Project sizing

Deliverables identified (statement of work)

Schedules/milestones

High-level requirements (scope)

Estimate the high availability primary variables (gauges)

▶ Phase 1: Requirements

Detail requirements (process/data/technology)

Early prototyping (optional)

Detailed high availability primary variables

Detailed service level agreements/requirements

Detailed disaster recovery requirements

▶ Phase 2: Design

Detail design (data/process/technology)

Choose and design the matching high availability solution for the application

▶ Phase 3: Coding and testing

Code development/unit testing

Fully integrate the high availability solution with the application

▶ Phase 4: System testing and acceptance

Full system test/user acceptance

Full high availability testing/validation/acceptance

▶ Phase 5: Implementation

Production build/implementation

Production high availability build/monitoring begins

For those following a rapid development, "iterative" life cycle (commonly referred to as a rapid/spiral or Agile methodology), Figure 1.11 lays out the same type of high availability elements within this iterative development approach.

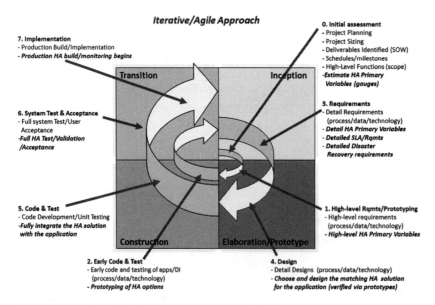

FIGURE 1.11   Spiral/rapid development methodology.

Assessing Existing Applications

If you haven't integrated high availability into your development methodology, or if you are retrofitting your existing applications for high availability, a more focused mini-assessment project can be launched that will yield all the right answers and point you to the high availability solution that best matches your existing applications' needs. I call this Phase 0 high availability assessment (aka the "weakest link assessment").

Essentially, you must quickly answer the following questions:

- ▶ What are the current and future characteristics of your application?
- ▶ What are your service level requirements?
- ▶ What is the impact (cost) of downtime?
- ▶ What are your vulnerabilities (hardware, software, human errors, and so on)?
- ▶ What is your timeline for implementing a high availability solution?
- ▶ What is your budget for a high availability solution?

These types of assessments can be crunched out in 5 to 7 days, which is an extremely short amount of time, considering the potential impact on your company's bottom line and the goodwill of the public toward your company. Completing a Phase 0 high availability assessment will also provide you with the proper staging platform for the next several steps, including defining your formal service level requirements, selecting the right high availability solution, building it, testing it, and implementing it—oh, and enjoying the comfort of having a rock-solid highly available solution in place (that works!).

If you have time, make sure you include as much detail as possible in the following areas:

- ▶ Analysis of the current state/future state of the application
- ▶ Hardware configuration/options available
- ▶ Software configuration/options available
- ▶ Backup/recovery procedures used
- ▶ Standards/guidelines used
- ▶ Testing/QA process employed
- ▶ Assessing who are the Personnel administering systems
- ▶ Assessing who are the Personnel developing systems

One deliverable from this assessment should be the complete list of primary variables for high availability. This list will be one of your main decision-making tools for choosing a high availability solution that matches your application.

What Is a Service Level Agreement?

Service level agreements (or requirements) have been mentioned over and over in this chapter. Determining what they are and whether they are needed is essential to understanding a high availability need.

Basically, a *service level agreement* (SLA) is a contract between an application owner (custodian) and an application user. For example, an employee of a company is the application user of a self-service benefits application, and the HR department is the application owner. The HR department signs up (via an internal SLA) to have this application be available to employees during normal business hours. This is what the HR department is held to (measured against). Then, in turn, the HR department might have its own SLA with the IT department that administers and maintains the application. An SLA has the following basic elements:

1. Application owner

2. Application user

3. Application description

4. Application hours of operation/availability

5. Agreement terms, including the following:

   ▶ Duration of agreement (often yearly)

   ▶ Levels of response time (to failures, application enhancements, so on)

   ▶ Procedures/steps to follow

   ▶ Penalties (very often monetary) if levels are not met

Describing penalties is especially important if you want this kind of agreement to have "teeth," as it should have. Companies such as application service providers (ASPs) probably have the most comprehensive and most severe SLAs on the planet. Of course, their livelihood depends on meeting their SLAs, and perhaps they get huge bonuses when they exceed their SLAs as well.

High Availability Business Scenarios

In the following sections I present four high availability business scenarios that have been hand selected based on their clear need for some type of high availability solution. Each of the following sections provides a short summary of a business scenario, followed by a much more in-depth description as each business scenario is identified and matched to a particular high availability solution. For each one I describe a complete software and system stack depiction, along with the specification of the high availability primary variables (gauge). Your company may have business scenarios similar to these and, at the very least, you should be able to correlate these high availability solutions to ones that will fit your applications' high availability needs. All these business scenarios are Microsoft-based applications with various high availability/fault tolerant hardware configurations in place.

The downtime costs and other variables for each scenario are fully described in Chapter 3, which matches each scenario with the appropriate high availability solution. These four business scenarios demonstrate how you can use a business scenario's requirements to determine the proper high availability solution.

An Application Service Provider

The first business scenario/application centers on a very real application service provider (ASP) and its operating model. This ASP houses (and develops) numerous global, web-based online order entry systems for several major beauty and health product companies in the world. Its customer base is truly global; as the earth turns, the user base accessing the system shifts with it. The company is headquartered in California (Silicon Valley—where else?), and this ASP guarantees 99.00% uptime to its customers. In this case, the customers are sales associates and their sales managers. If the ASP achieves these guarantees, it gets significant bonuses. If it falls below certain thresholds, it is liable for specific penalties. The processing mix of activity is approximately 65% online order entry and approximately 35% reporting.

Availability:

- ▶ 24 hours per day

- ▶ 7 days per week

- ▶ 365 days per year

Planned downtime: 0.25% (less than 1%)

Unplanned downtime: 0.25% (less than 1%) will be tolerable

Availability possible category: Extreme availability

Worldwide Sales and Marketing—Brand Promotion

A major chip manufacturer created a highly successful promotion and branding program that results in billions of dollars in advertising being rebated back to its worldwide sales channel partners. These sales channel partners must enter their complete advertisement copy (whether it is for newspaper, radio, TV, or other media) and is measured against ad compliance and logo usage and placements. If a sales channel partner is in compliance, it receives up to 50% of the cost of its advertisement back from this chip manufacturer. The dollars being exchanged on a minute-by-minute basis are enormous. There are three major advertising regions: Far East, Europe, and North America. Any other advertisements outside these three are lumped into an "Other Regions" bucket. Each region produces a huge daily load of new advertisement information that is processed instantaneously for compliance. Each major region deals only with that region's advertisements but receives the compliance rules and compliance judgment from the chip manufacturer's headquarters. Application mix is approximately 75% online entry of advertisement events and 25% management and compliance reporting.

Availability:

- ▶ 24 hours per day

- ▶ 7 days a week

- ▶ 365 days a year

Planned downtime: 3%

Unplanned downtime: 2% will be tolerable

Availability possible category: High availability

Investment Portfolio Management

An investment portfolio management application is housed in a major server farm in the heart of the world's financial center: New York. Serving North American customers only, this application provides the ability to do full trading of stocks and options in all financial markets (United States and international), along with full portfolio holdings assessment, historical performance, and holdings valuation. Primary users are investment managers for their large customers. Stock purchasing/selling comprise 90% of the daytime activity, with massive assessment, historical performance, and valuation reporting done after the markets have closed. Three major peaks occur each weekday, driven by the three major trading markets of the world (United States, Europe, and the Far East). During the weekends, the application is used for the long-range planning reporting and front-loading stock trades for the coming week.

Availability:

▶ 20 hours per day

▶ 7 days per week

▶ 365 days per year

Planned downtime: 4%

Unplanned downtime: 1% will be tolerable

Availability possible category: High availability

Call-Before-You Dig Call Center

A tri-state underground construction call center has an application that determines within 6 inches the likelihood of hitting any underground gas mains, water mains, electrical wiring, phone lines, or cables that might be present on a proposed dig site for construction. Law requires that a call be placed to this center to determine whether it is safe to dig and to identify the exact location of any underground hazard *before* any digging has started. This is a "life at risk"–classified application and must be available nearly 100% of the time during common construction workdays (Monday through Saturday). Each year more than 25 people are killed nationwide digging into unknown underground hazards. Application mix is 95% query only with 5% devoted to updating images, geospatial values, and various pipe and cable location information provided by the regional utility companies.

Availability:

▶ 15 hours per day (5:00 a.m.–8:00 p.m.)

▶ 6 days per week (closed Sunday)

▶ 312 days per year

Planned downtime: 0%

Unplanned downtime: 0.5% (less than 1%) will be tolerable

Availability possible category: Extreme availability

Microsoft Technologies That Yield High Availability

As you will see in the coming chapters, several mainline technology offerings from Microsoft allow you to design a tailored high availability solution that best matches your company's availability needs. As mentioned earlier, this book focuses on the most viable and production-worthy options, including the following:

▶ **Windows Server Failover Clustering (WSFC)**—WSFC provides the functionality to provide local high availability at the server instance level, basically allowing multiple nodes (server instances) to be linked together in active/active and active/passive modes that fail over to each other if one node becomes unavailable. A failover cluster instance (FCI) is a single SQL Server instance that is installed across WSFC nodes and possibly across multiple subnets. WSFC allows for up to 64 nodes to be clustered (on Hyper-V), with some restrictions. Typically between 2 and 4 nodes are clustered to provide both the power and availability needed for an application. Each node in the cluster is made aware of each other node in such a way that if one fails, the other takes over its resources (such as its shared disk). An application needs to be "cluster aware" in order to take advantage of this capability. An example of a cluster-aware application is SQL Server. This is considered to be a foundation requirement to many high available solutions, such as SQL clustering and the AlwaysOn availability groups configurations. (See Chapter 4, "Failover Clustering.")

▶ **SQL clustering**—You can define between two and eight SQL Servers running on different machines to act as points of failover if the "active" SQL Server ever fails. Typically run in an active/passive mode (but not limited to that), this cluster-aware capability guarantees, via the creation of a virtual SQL Server, that a client application can connect to and do work on this virtual SQL Server nearly all the time. (See Chapter 5, "SQL Server Clustering.")

▶ **AlwaysOn availability groups**—Now considered the flagship product configuration for SQL Server high availability and disaster recovery, the AlwaysOn capability builds on FCS across nodes and provides a powerful synchronous or asynchronous option for a database and the instances to be highly available with almost no downtime. Failover times are often measured in seconds rather than minutes or hours. This option can create numerous options for HA and distributed processing. With SQL 2016, as many as eight secondaries can be created as a part of a single availability group. (Chapter 6, "SQL Server AlwaysOn and Availability Groups," dives into the options and configurations for this major innovation from Microsoft.)

▶ **Database Snapshots**—You can use the point-in-time database snapshot capabilities to create milestones when doing production mass updates, inserts, or deletions. This method provides a point to which to recover your data in case there is an issue *without* having to restore the database or bring it offline, thus maintaining your application's availability. (See Chapter 7, "SQL Server Database Snapshots.")

▶ **Data Replication**—SQL Server offers a highly efficient mechanism to distribute data to other locations for the purpose of maximizing availability and mitigating risk of failures. Data Replication identifies a publisher, distributor, and subscriber model to distribute data (replicate it) to another location with a full data integrity guarantee. Thus, a separate location can have an exact image of the primary database to be used as a failover point or as a location to maximize regional availability. (See Chapter 8, "SQL Server Data Replication.")

▶ **Log Shipping**—SQL Server provides a mechanism that allows the transaction log of a primary database to be applied to a secondary copy of that same database. The end result is a hot spare, or at least a reasonably "warm" spare (only as hot as the last transaction log that got applied to it). It is available as a failover point, if needed, or as a place to consider isolating read-only processing away from the primary server for performance and availability factors. (See Chapter 9, "SQL Server Log Shipping.")

▶ **Other hybrid or complete options**—Other options are available, such as dynamically stretching warm and cold data to Azure (the cloud) with Stretch Database and availability groups, deploying big data options (on Azure), full Azure SQL database deployments, and a few other HA options in the cloud. (See Chapters 10, "High Availability Options in the Cloud," and 11, "High Availability and Big Data Options.")

Summary

This chapter discusses several primary variables of availability that should help capture your high availability requirements cleanly and precisely. These variables include a basic uptime requirement, time to recovery, tolerance of recovery, data resiliency, application resiliency, performance and scalability, and the costs of downtime (loss). You can couple this information with your hardware/software configurations, several Microsoft-based technology offerings, and your allowable upgrade budget to fairly easily determine exactly which high availability solution will best support your availability needs. A general one-two punch approach of establishing a proper high availability foundation in your environment should be done as soon as possible to at least get your "at risk" applications out of that tenuous state. Once this is complete, you can serve the knock-out punch that fully matches the proper high availability solution to all your critical applications—and get it right the first time.

The following sections delve into the critical needs surrounding disaster recovery and business continuity. Many of the SQL Server options covered in this book also lend themselves to disaster recovery configurations with minimal time and data loss (see Chapter 13, "Disaster Recovery and Business Continuity"). But first, let's move on to a more complete discussion of the Microsoft high availability capabilities in Chapter 2, "Microsoft High Availability Options."

Microsoft High Availability Options

Understanding your high availability requirements is only the first step in implementing a successful high availability solution. Knowing what available technical options exist is equally important. Then, by following a few basic design guidelines, you can match your requirements to a suitable high availability technical solution. This chapter introduces you to the fundamental HA options, such as RAID disk arrays, redundant network connectors (NICs), and Windows Server Failover Clustering (WSFC), as well as other more high-level options, such as AlwaysOn availability groups, SQL clustering, SQL Server Data Replication, and some Microsoft Azure and SQL Azure options that can help you create a solid high availability foundation.

Getting Started with High Availability

Remember that the hardware/software stack presented in Chapter 1, "Understanding High Availability," outlines the major components and shows that if one component fails, the others may also be affected. With this in mind, the best approach for moving into supporting high availability is to work on shoring up the basic foundation components first (as suggested in the one-two punch approach in Chapter 1). Figure 2.1 shows the initial foundation components to target.

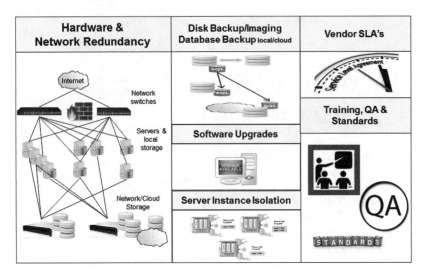

FIGURE 2.1   Initial foundation components for HA.

By addressing these components first, you add a significant amount of stability and high availability capability across your hardware/system stack. In other words, addressing these components allows you to move up to the level from which you should start before you completely jump into a particular high availability solution. If you do nothing further from this point, you will have already achieved a portion of your high availability goals. Figure 2.1 shows the following initial foundation components that get you headed in the right high availability direction:

- ▶ **Hardware**—To get to a foundation level with high availability, start by addressing your basic hardware issues for high availability and fault tolerance. This includes redundant power supplies, UPSs, redundant network connections, and ECC (error correcting code) memory. Also available are hot-swappable components, such as disks, CPUs, and memory. In addition, servers use multiple CPUs, fault-tolerant disk systems like RAID disk arrays, mirrored disks, storage area networks (SANs), network attached storage (NAS), redundant fans, and so on. Cost may drive the full extent of what you choose to build out, but you should start with the following:

  - ▶ Redundant power supplies (and UPSs)

  - ▶ Redundant fan systems

  - ▶ Fault-tolerant disks—RAID disk arrays (1 through 10), preferably hot swappable

  - ▶ ECC memory

  - ▶ Redundant Ethernet connections

- ▶ **Backup**—Next look at the basic techniques for and frequency of disk backups and database backups. Often this is way behind in what it needs to be to guarantee recoverability and even the basic level of high availability. I've lost track of the number of times I've walked into a customer site and found out that the database backups were not being run, were corrupted, or weren't even considered necessary. You would be shocked by the list of Fortune 1000 companies where this occurs.

▶ **Software upgrades**—You need to ensure that all upgrades to your OS are applied and that the configurations of all options are correct. This includes making sure you have antivirus software installed (if applicable) along with the appropriate firewalls for external-facing systems. This should be further extended to your other application and DB tiers. Make sure you are applying service packs and point releases of these other major components on a timely basis.

▶ **Vendor agreements**—These agreements include software licenses, software support agreements, hardware service agreements, and both hardware and software service level agreements. Essentially, you need to make sure you can get all software upgrades and patches for your OS and for your application software at any time, as well as get software support, hardware support agreements, and both software and hardware SLAs in place to guarantee a level of service within a defined period of time.

> **NOTE**
>
> In the past 10 or 15 years, I've put in place countless SLAs, and I've never lost a job by doing this. However, I know of people who didn't bother to put these types of agreements in place and did lose their jobs. Implementing SLAs provides a good insurance policy.

▶ **Training**—Training can be for software developers to guarantee that the code they write is optimal, for system administrators who need to administer your applications, and even for the end users to make sure they use the system correctly. All these types of training play into the ultimate goals of achieving high availability.

▶ **Quality assurance**—Testing as much as possible and doing it in a very formal way is a great way to guarantee a system's availability. I've seen dozens of studies over the years which clearly show that the more thoroughly you test (and the more formal your QA procedures), the fewer software problems you will have. To this day, I'm not sure why people skimp on testing. It has such a huge impact on system reliability and availability.

▶ **Standards/procedures**—In addition to training and QA, coding standards, code walkthroughs, naming standards, formal system development life cycles, protection to ensure that tables are not dropped, use of governors, and other standards/procedures contribute to more stable and potentially more highly available systems.

▶ **Server instance isolation**—By design, you may want to isolate applications (for example SQL Server applications and their databases) from each other in order to mitigate the risk of one of these applications causing another to fail. Never put other applications in each other's way if you don't have to. The only things that might force you to load up a single server with all your applications would be expensive licensing costs for each server's software, and perhaps hardware scarcity (that is strict limitations on the number of servers available for all applications). We explore this in more detail later in this chapter.

Creating a Fault-Tolerant Disk: RAID and Mirroring

When it comes to creating a fault-tolerant disk subsystem, you can do basic "vanilla" mirroring of a disk or varying RAID disk array configurations. These are tried and true methods, but determining which one to use can be tricky. The problem is that you often need to thoroughly understand significant implementation aspects such as the performance impact, complexity of administration, and cost. Let's look at disk mirroring first.

Basically, disk mirroring is a technique that involves writing data to two duplicate disks simultaneously (or three, with triple mirroring) as part of a single logical disk write operation. In other words, when you write a piece of data to a disk that has been mirrored, it is automatically written to the primary disk *and* to the mirrored (duplicate) disk at the same time. Both disks in the mirror are usually the same size and have the same technical specification. If the primary disk fails for any reason, the mirrored (duplicate) disk is automatically used as the primary. The application that was using the disk never knows that a failure has occurred, thus greatly enhancing your application's availability. At some point, you can swap in a new disk and re-mirror it, and off you go again, without missing a beat. Figure 2.2 illustrates the basic disk-mirroring concept of data being written simultaneously.

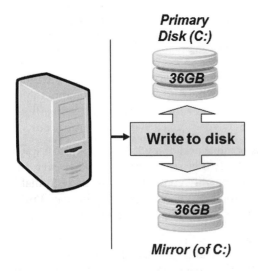

Primary Disk (C:)

36GB

Write to disk

36GB

Mirror (of C:)

FIGURE 2.2   Mirrored disk—simultaneous writes.

Of course, the downside of disk mirroring is that the mirrored disk drives are not directly usable, and you are effectively burning up double the number of disk drives. This can be costly because many servers don't have the sheer space within their physical rack footprint to house numerous mirrored disks. Very often, separate external disk drive rack systems (with separate power supplies) solve this problem.

What should be mirrored? In many high availability systems, the first disk drive that is targeted for mirroring is the one that contains the OS. This one mirroring choice instantly increases the availability of the system by some factor and is considered a fundamental cornerstone for high availability. For non-RAID systems, you can selectively choose critical pieces of your application and its underlying databases as candidates for mirrored disk. Figure 2.3 illustrates a Microsoft SQL Server 2016–based ERP system that has been laid out within a mirrored disk configuration.

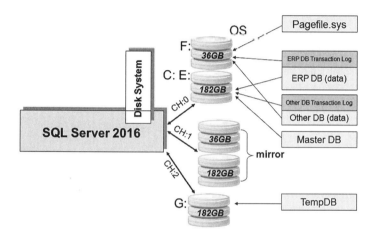

FIGURE 2.3   ERP system (Microsoft SQL Server 2016 based)—mirrored disk.

The use of disk mirroring has also been integrated into various RAID level configurations, as explained in the next section.

Increasing System Availability with RAID

Perhaps the most popular method of increasing system availability is by implementing various redundant array of independent disks (RAID) configurations. RAID, by definition, makes the underlying disk subsystem much more stable and available, with less susceptibility to disk failures. Using certain RAID configurations can be an important part of your foundation for high availability. Let's look at what RAID really is.

RAID has several levels of configurations that yield different capabilities. The primary goal of RAID is to decrease disk subsystem failures. Some configurations are highly redundant and incorporate disk mirroring. Some use sophisticated algorithms for spreading out data over several disks so that if any one disk fails, the others can continue processing. In addition, the data that was on the failed disk can be recovered from what is stored on the other disks (RAID 5). This is almost like magic. But where there is magic, there is cost (both in performance and in hardware). Table 2.1 summarizes the common RAID level configurations.

TABLE 2.1   RAID Levels

Level	Characteristic/Behavior
RAID 0	Striping (without parity)
RAID 1	Mirroring (with duplexing if available)
RAID 2	Bit-level striping with hamming code ECC
RAID 3	Byte-level striping with dedicated parity
RAID 4	Block-level striping with dedicated parity
RAID 5	Block-level striping with distributed parity
RAID 6	Block-level striping with dual distributed parity
RAID 7	Asynchronous, cached striping with dedicated parity
RAID 0+1, 01, 0/1	Mirrored stripes
RAID 1+0, 10, 1/0	Stripe of mirrors
RAID 50, 0/5	Striped set of RAID 5 arrays
RAID 53, 3/5	Striped set of RAID 3 arrays

Disk controller manufacturers and disk drive manufacturers sell various types of disk controllers for these RAID arrays that may also have different amounts of cache (memory) built in. These product offerings give you a great deal of flexibility in regard to defining the RAID level configurations that best suit your needs. Since many of the defined RAID levels are not commercially viable (or available), this chapter describes only the ones that are best suited for a company's high availability solution (in terms of cost, management, and fault tolerance). These are RAID levels 0, 1, 5, and 1+0 (10).

RAID 0: Striping (Without Parity)
RAID 0 is simply a disk array that consists of one or more physical disks that have no parity checking (error checking of disk writes/reads) at all. This is really just a series of disk drives sitting on the operating system, without any redundancy or error checking whatsoever—no fault tolerance. The disk striping comes from the ability to spread *segments* (*data blocks*) across more than one physical disk for performance. Figure 2.4 shows this basic RAID level configuration and how data blocks can be striped across multiple disks. A piece of data (A) is broken down into data block A1 (on Disk W) and data block A2 (on Disk X). The payoff comes when you need to retrieve the data. On average, because of the striping, the data is stored more shallowly and is readily retrieved (as compared to normal nonstriped data storage retrieval). In other words, you don't have to seek as deep into an individual disk to retrieve a piece of data; it is, on average, located higher up on multiple disks and assembled more quickly. This translates into faster retrieval times. For the best performance, you can have one disk drive per controller, or at the very least one disk drive per channel (as shown in Figure 2.4).

Disks

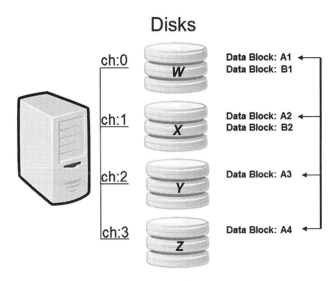

FIGURE 2.4   RAID level 0.

RAID 0 is often configured to support file access that doesn't need to be protected from failure but does need to be fast (that is, no additional overhead). You would be surprised at the number of things that meet this type of requirement. RAID 0 is also used in combination with both RAID 1+0 (10) and RAID 0+1 (01) to produce much more robust availability. These levels are described later in this chapter.

RAID 1: Mirroring (with Duplexing)

RAID 1 is the first RAID level that handles disk failures and therefore is truly fault tolerant. RAID 1 is mirroring for one or more disks at a time. In other words, if you configure five disks with RAID 1 (mirroring), you need five additional redundant disks for their mirror. Think of this as "mirrored pairs." As described earlier, when writes occur to this RAID 1 configuration, they are simultaneously written to the redundant (mirrored) disks. If a failure of any primary disk ever occurs, the mirrored disk is instantly activated. Most mirrored configurations read from either the mirrored or primary disk for data; it doesn't matter because the disks are identical, and this read traffic is managed by the disk controller. However, for every logical disk write, there are two separate physical disk writes—the primary and the mirror. Duplexing is achieved by adding a redundant disk controller card for additional fault tolerance. Figure 2.5 illustrates a RAID 1 configuration.

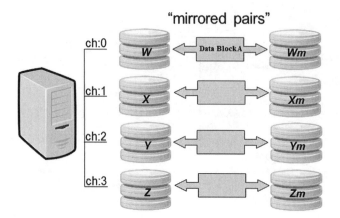

FIGURE 2.5   RAID level 1.

This RAID configuration offers good results for folks who need a certain level of write fault tolerance but can withstand the slight performance impact of the additional physical writes. To reestablish a mirrored pair after a disk failure has occurred, you just pop in a replacement disk, re-copy the good disk's data to the new disk, and off you go.

RAID 5: Block-Level Striping with Distributed Parity

The notion of parity is first introduced with RAID 3. *Parity* means that there will be a data parity value generated (and stored) for a piece of data (or block of data) when it is written, and this parity is checked when it is read (and corrected, if necessary). RAID 5 distributes the parity storage across all the disks in the array in such a way that any piece of data can be recovered from the parity information on all the other disks. Figure 2.6 shows this striped, distributed parity technique.

To put this another way, if the disk containing data blocks A is lost, the data can be recovered from the parity values that are stored on all the other disks. Notice that a data block never stores its own parity values. This makes RAID 5 a good fault-tolerant option for applications that need this type of availability.

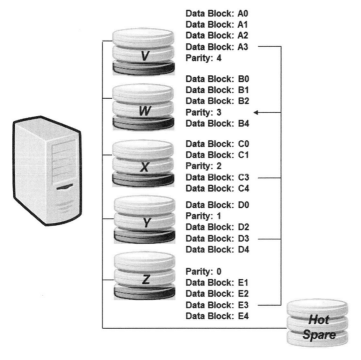

FIGURE 2.6   RAID level 5.

In most RAID 5 implementations, a hot spare is kept online and can be used automatically when a failure has occurred. This hot spare gets rebuilt with data blocks (and parity) dynamically from all the surviving disks. You usually notice this via RAID failure alarms, and there is a huge disk subsystem slowdown during this rebuild. When this is complete, you are back in a fault-tolerant state. However, RAID 5 configurations cannot sustain two disk failures at one time because this would not allow the complete parity values that are needed to rebuild a single disk's data blocks to be accessed. RAID 5 requires that there be up to four (or more) physical disk writes for every logical write that is done (one write to each parity storage). This translates to poor performance for write- and update-intensive applications but ample performance for read-intensive applications.

RAID 0+1, 01, 0/1: Mirrored Stripes

RAID 0+1 is implemented as a mirrored array (RAID 1) whose segments are RAID 0 arrays. This is not the same as RAID 1+0 (10), as you will see in the next section. RAID 0+1 has the same fault tolerance as RAID 5. It also has the same overhead for fault tolerance as mirroring alone. Fairly high read/write rates can be sustained due to the multiple stripe segments of the RAID 0 portion.

The downside of RAID 0+1 is that when a single drive fails, the whole array deteriorates to a RAID level 0 array because of this approach used of mixing striping with mirroring. Figure 2.7 shows how this mirrored stripe configuration is achieved.

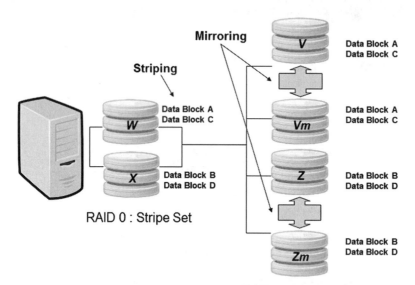

FIGURE 2.7   RAID level 0+1 (0/1).

RAID 1+0, 10, 1/0: Stripe of Mirrors

▶ RAID 1+0 is implemented as a striped array (RAID 0) whose segments are mirrored arrays (RAID 1). This is more favorable in regard to failures than non-mirrored approaches. Basically, RAID 1+0 has the same fault tolerance as RAID level 1 (mirroring). The failure of a single disk does not put any other mirrored segments in jeopardy. It is considered to be better than RAID 0+1 in this regard. And, to the delight of many a system designer, RAID 1+0 can sustain very high read/write rates because of the striping (from RAID 0). Figure 2.8 shows the subtleties of this RAID 1+0 configuration.

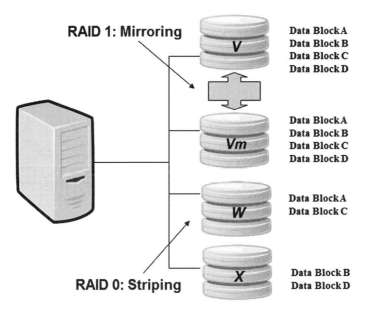

RAID 1: Mirroring

V
Data Block A
Data Block B
Data Block C
Data Block D

Vm
Data Block A
Data Block B
Data Block C
Data Block D

W
Data Block A
Data Block C

X
Data Block B
Data Block D

RAID 0: Striping

FIGURE 2.8   RAID level 1+0 (10).

> **NOTE**
>
> Building your systems/servers with at least RAID 1, RAID 5, and RAID 1+0 is critical to achieving a highly available system along with a high-performing system. RAID 5 is better suited for read-only applications that need fault tolerance and high availability, while RAID 1 and RAID 1+0 are better suited for OLTP or moderately high-volatility applications. RAID 0 by itself can help boost performance for any data allocations that don't need the fault tolerance of the other RAID configurations but need to be high performing.

Mitigating Risk by Spreading Out Server Instances

Server instance isolation was briefly touched on in a prior section of this chapter but needs to be expanded on because it is so critical and because application isolation should become a part of your fundamental design principles. As mentioned earlier, by design, you should try to isolate applications (such as SQL Server's applications and their associated databases) from each other in order to mitigate the risk of one of these applications causing another to fail. A classic example of this is when a company loads up a single SQL Server instance with between two and eight applications and their associated databases. The problem is that the applications are sharing memory, CPUs, and internal work areas such as TempDB. Figure 2.9 shows a loaded up SQL Server instance that is being asked to service four major applications (Appl 1 DB through Appl 4 DB).

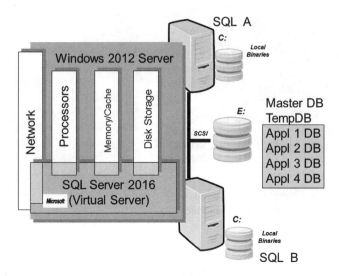

FIGURE 2.9   Applications sharing a single SQL Server 2000 instance.

This single SQL Server instance is sharing memory (cache) and critical internal working areas such as TempDB with all four major applications. Everything runs along fine until one of these applications submits a runaway query, and all other applications being serviced by that SQL Server instance come to a grinding halt. Most of this built-in risk could have been avoided by simply putting each application (or perhaps two applications) onto its own SQL Server instance, as shown in Figure 2.10. This fundamental design approach greatly reduces the risk of one application affecting another.

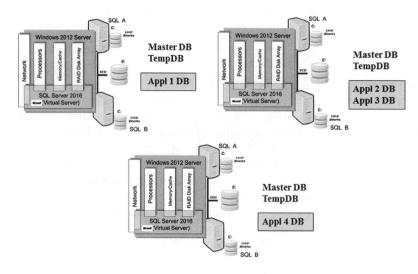

FIGURE 2.10   Isolating applications from each other—SQL Server 2016.

I've lost count of the number of companies that have made this very fundamental sharing error. The trouble is that they keep adding new applications to their existing server instance without having a full understanding of the shared resources that underpin the environment. It is very often too late when they finally realize that they are hurting themselves "by design." You have now been given proper warning of the risks. If other factors such as cost or hardware availability dictate otherwise, then at least you can make a calculated risk that you enter into knowingly (and properly documented as well).

Microsoft Options for Building an HA Solution

Once you have the proper foundation in place, you can build a tailored software-driven high availability solution much more easily and "match" one or more high availability options to your requirements. Remember that different high availability solutions yield different results. The focus of this book is on the Microsoft offerings because they are potentially already available in your company's software stack. Figure 2.11 identifies the current Microsoft options that can be drawn upon together or individually.

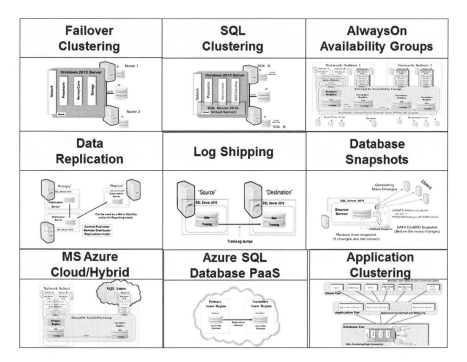

FIGURE 2.11   Building with various Microsoft high availability options.

With the exception of application clustering (which is available as part of a particular application's capabilities—as with some application server technologies), all of these options are readily available "out-of-the-box" from Microsoft in the Windows Server family of products and in Microsoft SQL Server 2016, and we are seeing increased coverage for HA and DR in the Microsoft Azure cloud space.

It is important to understand that one or more of these options can be used together, but not all go together. For example, you could use Windows Server Failover Clustering (WSFC) along with Microsoft SQL Server 2016's SQL clustering to implement a SQL clustering database configuration or build out the AlwaysOn availability groups configuration. We will get into much more detailed explanations on these in the next few chapters. The following sections provide a brief overview of each of these options.

First up is a critical foundation capability called Windows Server Failover Clustering. WSFC could actually be considered a part of the basic foundation components that we described earlier, except that it's possible to build a high availability system without it (one that uses numerous redundant hardware components and disk mirroring or RAID for its disk subsystem, for example). Microsoft has made WSFC the cornerstone of its clustering capabilities, and WSFC is now used by many applications that are "cluster enabled." A couple good examples of cluster-enabled technologies are Microsoft SQL Server instances and Reporting Services.

Windows Server Failover Clustering (WSFC)

A *server failover cluster* is a group of two or more physically separate servers running WSFC and working collectively as a single system. The server failover cluster, in turn, provides high availability, scalability, and manageability for resources and applications. In other words, a group of servers is physically connected via communication hardware (network), shares storage (via SCSI or Fibre Channel connectors), and uses WSFC software to tie them all together into managed resources.

Server failover clusters can preserve client access to applications and resources during failures and planned outages. This is server instance-level failover. If one of the servers in a cluster is unavailable due to failure or maintenance, resources and applications move (fail over) to another available cluster node.

> **NOTE**
>
> Prior to Windows Server 2008 R2, clustering was done with Microsoft Cluster Services (MSCS). If you are running an older OS version, refer to *SQL Server 2008 R2 Unleashed* to see how to set up SQL clustering on this older operating system.

Clusters use an algorithm to detect a failure, and they use failover policies to determine how to handle the work from a failed server. These policies also specify how a server is to be restored to the cluster when it becomes available again.

Although clustering doesn't guarantee continuous operation, it does provide availability sufficient for most mission-critical applications and is a building block in numerous high-availability solutions. WSFC can monitor applications and resources to automatically recognize and recover from many failure conditions. This capability provides great flexibility in managing the workload within a cluster, and it improves the overall availability of the system. Technologies that are cluster aware—such as SQL Server, Microsoft Message

Queuing (MSMQ), Distributed Transaction Coordinator (DTC), and file shares—have already been programmed to work within (that is, under the control of) WSFC.

WSFC still has some hardware and software compatibility to worry about, but it now includes the Cluster Validation Wizard, which helps you see whether your configuration will work. You can also still refer to Microsoft's support site for server clustering (see http://support.microsoft.com/kb/309395). In addition, SQL Server Failover Cluster Instances (FCI) is not supported where the cluster nodes are also domain controllers.

Let's look a little more closely at a two-node active/passive cluster configuration. At regular intervals, known as time slices, the failover cluster nodes look to see if they are still alive. If the active node is determined to be failed (not functioning), a failover is initiated, and another node in the cluster takes over for the failed node. Each physical server (node) uses separate network adapters for its own network connection. (Therefore, there is always at least one network communication capability working for the cluster at all times, as shown in Figure 2.12.)

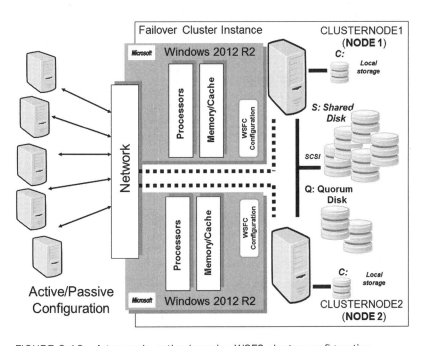

FIGURE 2.12 A two-node active/passive WSFC cluster configuration.

You will see exactly how this is done in Chapter 4. (Hint: It's not magic.)

SQL Clustering

If you want a SQL Server instance to be clustered for high availability, you are essentially asking that this SQL Server instance (and the database) be completely resilient to a server

failure and completely available to the application without the end user ever even notic-
ing that there was a failure. Microsoft provides this capability through the SQL clustering
option in SQL Server 2016. SQL clustering builds on top of MSCS for its underlying detection of a failed server and for its availability of the databases on the shared disk (which is
controlled by MSCS). SQL Server is a cluster-aware/cluster-enabled technology. You can
create a "virtual" SQL Server that is known to the application (the constant in the equation) and two physical SQL Servers that share one set of databases. Only one SQL Server
is active at a time, and it just goes along and does its work. If that server fails (and with it
the physical SQL Server instance), the passive server (and the physical SQL Server instance
on that server) takes over instantaneously. This is possible because cluster services also
controls the shared disk where the databases are. The end user (and application) pretty
much never know which physical SQL Server instance they are on or whether one failed.
Figure 2.13 illustrates a typical SQL clustering configuration that is built on top of MSCS.

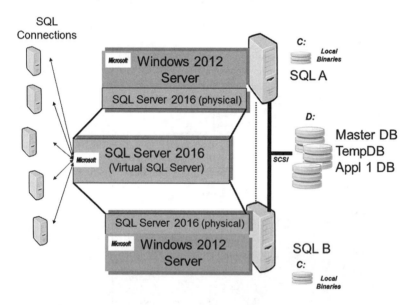

FIGURE 2.13   SQL clustering basic configuration.

Setup and management of this type of configuration is much easier than you might
realize. More and more, SQL clustering is the method chosen for most high availability
solutions. Later on, you will see that other methods may also be viable for achieving high
availability, depending on the application's HA requirements. (Chapter 5, "SQL Server
Clustering," describes SQL clustering in detail.) Extending the clustering model to include
network load balancing (NLB) pushes this particular solution into even higher availability. Figure 2.14 shows a four-host NLB cluster architecture that acts as a virtual server to
handle the network traffic.

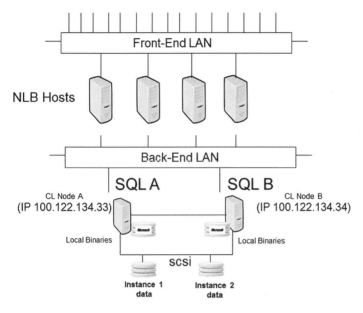

FIGURE 2.14   An NLB host cluster with a two-node server cluster.

The NLB hosts work together among the four hosts to distribute the work efficiently. NLB automatically detects the failure of a server and repartitions client traffic among the remaining servers.

AlwaysOn Availability Groups

Built on WSFC, the SQL Server AlwaysOn configuration leverages the tried-and-true experience and technology components of SQL clustering and database mirroring under the covers (and repackaged). AlwaysOn Failover Cluster Instances (FCI) is the server-level instance portion of the AlwaysOn HA capability. Figure 2.15 shows this availability group capability.

Availability groups are focused on database-level failover and availability by utilizing a data redundancy approach. Again borrowing from the database mirroring experience (and underlying technologies), a transactionally consistent secondary replica is made that can be used for both read-only access (active for use at all times) and for failover if the primary database (primary replica) fails for any reason. Also in Figure 2.15, you can see a SQL Server AlwaysOn availability group being used for HA and even for distributing the read-only workload off the primary SQL Server instance to the secondary replica. You can have up to four secondary replicas in an availability group, with the first secondary replica being used for automatic failover (using the synchronous-commit mode) and then other secondary replicas available for workload distribution and manual failover use. Remember that this is storing data redundantly, and you can burn up a lot of disk storage fast. When in synchronous-commit mode, that secondary replica can also be used to make database backups because it is completely consistent with the primary replica.

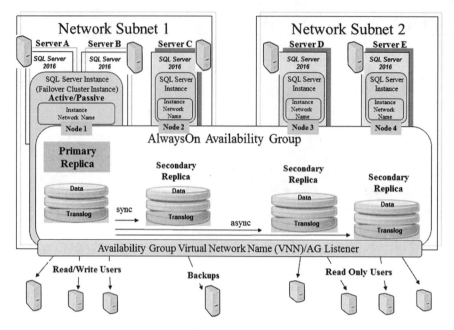

FIGURE 2.15   AlwaysOn availability group configuration for HA.

Data Replication

Data replication is a technology option that can be utilized to achieve high availability. Originally, data replication was created to offload processing from a very busy server (such as an OLTP application that must also support a big reporting workload) or to distribute data for different, very distinct user bases (such as worldwide geographic-specific applications). As data replication (transactional replication) became more stable and reliable, it started to be used to create "warm," almost "hot," standby SQL Servers that could also be used to fulfill basic reporting needs. If the primary server ever failed, the reporting users would still be able to work (hence a higher degree of availability achieved for them), and the replicated reporting database could be utilized as a substitute for the primary server, if needed (hence a warm standby SQL Server). When doing transactional replication in the "instantaneous replication" mode, all data changes are replicated to the replica servers extremely quickly. This may fit some companies' availability requirements and also fulfill their distributed reporting requirements as well. Figure 2.16 shows a typical SQL data replication configuration that serves as a basis for high availability and also fulfills a reporting server requirement at the same time.

The downside comes into play if ever the replicate is needed to become the primary server (that is, take over the work from the original server). It takes a bit of administration that is *not* transparent to the end user. Connection strings have to be changed, ODBC data sources need to be updated, and so on. However, this may take minutes as opposed to hours of database recovery time, and it may well be tolerable to end users. In addition, there is a risk of not having all the transactions from the primary server. Often, however, a company is willing to live with this small risk in favor of availability. Remember that this replicated database is a mirror image of the primary database (up to the point of the last update), which makes it very attractive as a warm standby. For databases that are primarily read-only, this is a great way to distribute the load and mitigate the risk of any one server failing. Configuration options such as peer-to-peer and central publisher models can be created based on your individual HA needs. (See Chapter 8, "SQL Server Data Replication.")

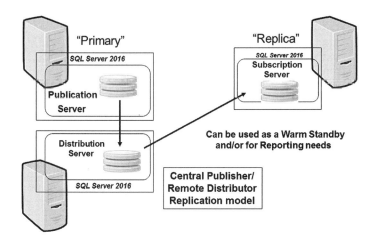

FIGURE 2.16   Data replication basic configuration for HA.

In the same family as data replication is change data capture (CDC). CDC capabilities have become much more stable and more tightly integrated into SQL Server. Basically, a change process is running that reads any change transactions from the transaction log and pushes them to a series of change tables. CDC does require that table objects and some CDC stored procedures be added to the SQL Server instance that is a source of data to be replicated. The CDC process and change table activity also adds overhead to the source SQL Server. Another CDC process (invoked via the SQL agent) reads, transforms, and writes the table changes to another SQL Server database (target). This target can then be used for reporting or as a warm standby for HA. The data in that target (replica) is as recent as the last transaction set written from the change tables (usually quite current). Potential exists for some data loss, but CDC is yet another tool for replicating data both for distributed workload and to achieve HA.

Log Shipping

Another, more direct method of creating a completely redundant database image is Log Shipping. Microsoft certifies Log Shipping as a method of creating an "almost hot" spare. Some folks even use log shipping as an alternative to data replication (it has been referred to as "the poor man's data replication"). Keep in mind that log shipping does three primary things:

▶ Makes an exact image copy of a database on one server from a database dump

▶ Creates a copy of that database on one or more other servers from that dump

▶ Continuously applies transaction log dumps from the original database to the copy

In other words, log shipping effectively replicates the data of one server to one or more other servers via transaction log dumps. Figure 2.17 shows a source/destination SQL Server pair that has been configured for log shipping.

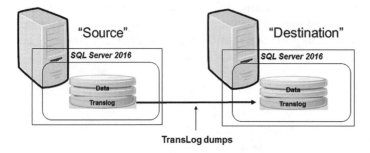

FIGURE 2.17   Log shipping in support of high availability.

This is a great solution when you have to create one or more failover servers. It turns out that, to some degree, log shipping fits the requirement of creating a read-only subscriber as well. The following are the gating factors for using log shipping as the method of creating and maintaining a redundant database image:

▶ Time exists between the transaction log dumps on the source database and when these dumps get applied to the destination DBs; this is called data latency.

▶ Sources and destinations must be the same SQL Server version.

▶ Data is read-only on the destination SQL Server until the log shipping pairing is broken (as it should be to guarantee that the translogs can be applied to the destination SQL Server).

The data latency restrictions might quickly disqualify log shipping as a foolproof high availability solution. However, log shipping might be adequate for certain situations. If a failure ever occurs on the primary SQL Server, a destination SQL Server that was created and maintained via log shipping can be swapped into use at a moment's notice. It would contain exactly what was on the source SQL Server (right down to every user ID, table, index, and file allocation map, except for any changes to the source database that occurred after the last log dump was applied). This directly achieves a level of high availability. It is still not completely transparent, though, because the SQL Server instance names are different, and the end user may be required to log in again to the new server instance.

Database Snapshots

In SQL Server 2016, Database Snapshots is still supported and can be combined with Database Mirroring (which *will* be deprecated in the next release of SQL Server) to offload reporting or other read-only access to a secondary location, thus enhancing both performance and availability of the primary database. In addition, as shown in Figure 2.18, database snapshots can aid high availability by utilizing features that restore a database back to a point in time rapidly if things like mass updates are applied to the primary database but the subsequent results are not acceptable. This can have a huge impact on recovery time objectives and can directly affect HA.

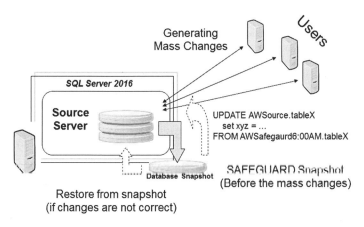

FIGURE 2.18   Database snapshots in support of high availability.

Microsoft Azure Options and Azure SQL Databases

AlwaysOn availability groups provide high availability for groups of databases by adding secondary replicas. These replicas can be an intricate part of your high availability and failover strategy. In addition, these secondary replicas are often used to offload read-only workloads or backup tasks. You can fairly easily extend your on-premises availability groups to Microsoft Azure. To do so, you must provision one or more Azure VMs with SQL Server and then add them as replicas to your on-premises availability groups configuration. Figure 2.19 illustrates what an on-premises SQL Server AlwaysOn with availability groups configuration would look like when extended to a Microsoft Azure infrastructure as a service (IaaS) virtual machine.

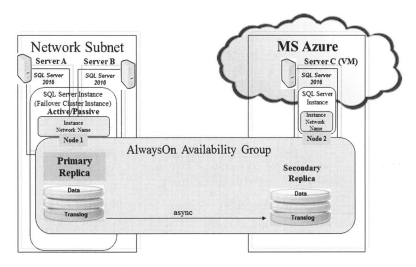

FIGURE 2.19   Extending AlwaysOn availability groups to Azure.

If you are considering using Azure virtual machines, make sure you take into account the ongoing maintenance effort required to patch, update, and manage your VM environments.

Another option that leverages Microsoft Azure and can enhance your high availability and performance requirements is Stretch Database. In simple terms, the Stretch Database capability introduced in SQL Server 2016 can enable you to move less-used data at both the database and table levels to Microsoft Azure seamlessly. You do this by enabling the Stretch Database feature in your SQL Server 2016 database and linking (via linked server functionality) to Microsoft Azure. Moving historical data or less frequently accessed data to this remote storage (linked) location in Azure can not only help preserve high performance of the active data portion of your database but can safely offload data for recovery and availability purposes. Figure 2.20 shows how data from within an on-premises database can be earmark "eligible data" for remote storage at Azure (on the cloud). A linked server secure connection is established that moves this eligible data to the remote data endpoint in Azure.

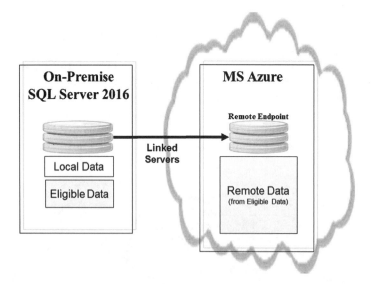

FIGURE 2.20   Stretching an on-premises database to Microsoft Azure with Stretch Database.

Queries against tables with Stretch Database enabled automatically run against both the local database and the remote endpoint. Stretch Database leverages processing power in Azure to run queries against remote data by rewriting the query.

Finally, as you can see in Figure 2.21, if you opt to fully deploy an application on Microsoft's Azure platform as a service (PaaS) offering, you can use the various Azure SQL Database options for both high availability and disaster recovery. Azure SQL Database is a relational database service in the cloud, based on the Microsoft SQL Server engine but with mission-critical capabilities. Azure SQL Database delivers predictable performance and scalability with virtually no downtime, and it can service your business continuity and data protection needs as well. Azure SQL Database supports existing SQL Server tools, libraries, and APIs, which makes it easier for you to move and extend an application to the cloud. Just focusing on the database tier via Azure SQL Database, a standard SQL database is incorporated into your application the same way as it would be if you were supporting it on-premises with SQL Server 2016. This standard configuration automatically provides you some level of database backup (to geo regions—other locations in the Microsoft data center regional footprint) and allows you to recover data from these backups via a Geo-Restore command.

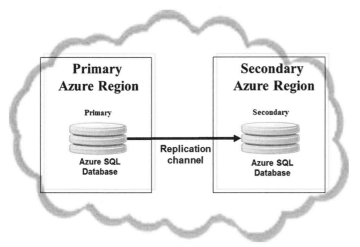

FIGURE 2.21   Azure SQL Database primary and secondary configuration for HA.

A more advanced configuration with much less data loss potential is shown in Figure 2.21. This configuration creates a direct secondary replica of your SQL database in another geo region (via a replication channel and geo-replication). You can fail over to this secondary replica in case the primary SQL database (in one region) is lost. This is done without having to worry about managing availability groups and other HA nuances (in the case where you have rolled your own high availability solution). There are, however, a number of downsides to this approach, such as manual client string changes, some data loss, and other critical high availability restrictions. (We discuss the pros and cons of using this configuration in Chapter 10, "High Availability Options in the Cloud.")

Application Clustering

As described earlier, high availability of an application is across all of its technology tiers (web, application, database, infrastructure). Many techniques and options exist at each tier. One major approach has long been to create scalability and availability at the application server tier. Large applications such as SAP's ERP offering have implemented application clustering to guarantee that the end user is always able to be served by the application, regardless of whether data is needed from the data tier. If one application server fails or becomes oversaturated from too much traffic, another application server is used to pick up the slack and service the end user without missing a beat. This is termed *application clustering*. Often even the state of the logical work transaction can be recovered and handed off to the receiving clustered application server. Figure 2.22 shows a typical multitiered application with application clustering and application load balancing which ensures that the end user (regardless of what client tier device or endpoint the user accesses the application from) is serviced at all times.

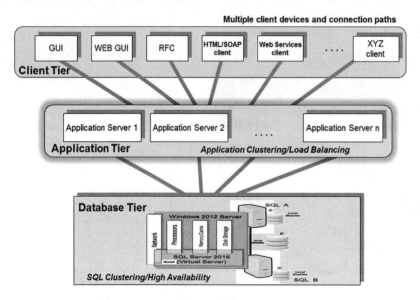

FIGURE 2.22   Application clustering at the application tier of a multitiered HA solution.

Remember that your application is available only if you are functioning on all the tiers (web, app, and data).

Summary

This chapter introduces many of the principal high availability options available in the Microsoft software stack and with hardware components. You need to build a solid foundation on which to build your highly available systems. As you completely define an applications' high availability requirements, a proper high availability solution can be matched that will serve you well for years to come. As you have seen, Microsoft can support your on-premises, cloud, and various hybrid combinations that span both.

Chapter 3, "Choosing High Availability," outlines the complex process of matching your high availability requirements to the proper high availability solution. You may need to select two or more options to use together to meet your needs. For this reason, a step-by-step approach (that you can repeat) is presented in Chapter 3.

Choosing High Availability

Chapters 1, "Understanding High Availability," and 2, "Microsoft High Availability Options," describe most of the essential elements that need to be defined in order to properly assess an application's likeliness of being built utilizing a high availability configuration of some kind. This chapter describes a rigorous process you can step through to determine exactly what HA solution is right for you. It begins with a Phase 0 high availability assessment. Formally conducting a Phase 0 HA assessment ensures that you consider the primary questions that need to be answered *before* you go off and try to throw some type of HA solution at your application. but the four-step process described in this chapter helps you determine which solution is the best one for your situation.

A Four-Step Process for Moving Toward High Availability

In order to make the best possible decision about which high availability solution matches your business requirements, you can follow a simple four-step process.

1. Step 1 is a typically brief Phase 0 HA assessment to gather all the needed information as quickly and as accurately as possible. It may not be brief, however, if decide to drill down a bit further in each requirement area.

2. Step 2 requires involves gauging the high availability primary variables as completely and accurately as possible. This gauge is actually a deliverable of the Phase 0 HA assessment, but it is worth calling out individually as a separate step because it can be used as a

high-level depiction of your application's HA requirements and is easily understood by management-level folks in an organization (refer to Figure 1.8 in Chapter 1).

3. Step 3 involves using the assessment and the gauge information to determine the optimal high availability solution that technically and fiscally matches your business needs. A hybrid decision-tree selection method can help in this step.

4. As an added bonus, this chapter runs through a basic return on investment (ROI) calculation as an optional Step 4 of this high availability decision process. The ROI calculation is optional because most folks don't bother with it; they are already losing so much money and goodwill during downtime that the return on their investment can be overwhelming. Very often, the ROI cannot be clearly measured, and no financial impact can be calculated.

This four-step process is, in effect, a mini-methodology designed to yield a specific high availability answer that best matches your needs.

NOTE

This chapter describes a fairly simple and straightforward method of calculating the ROI when deploying a specific high availability solution. Your calculations will vary because ROI is extremely unique for any company. However, in general, ROI can be calculated by adding up the incremental costs of the new HA solution and comparing them against the complete cost of downtime for a period of time (I suggest using a 1-year time period). This ROI calculation includes the following:

Maintenance cost (for a 1-year period):

+ system admin personnel cost (additional time for training of these personnel)

+ software licensing cost (of additional HA components)

Hardware cost (add +):

+ hardware cost (of additional HW in the new HA solution)

Deployment/assessment cost:

+ deployment cost (develop, test, QA, production implementation of the solution)

+ HA assessment cost (be bold and go ahead and throw the cost of the assessment into this to be a complete ROI calculation)

Downtime cost (for a 1-year period):

If you kept track of last year's downtime record, use that number; otherwise, produce an estimate of planned and unplanned downtime for this calculation.

+ Planned downtime hours × cost of hourly downtime to the company (revenue loss/productivity loss/goodwill loss [optional])

+ Unplanned downtime hours × cost of hourly downtime to the company (revenue loss/ productivity loss/goodwill loss [optional])

If the HA costs (above) are more than the downtime costs for 1 year, then extend it out another year, and then another until you can determine how long it will take to get the ROI.

In reality, most companies will have achieved the ROI within 6 to 9 months in the first year.

Step 1: Launching a Phase 0 HA Assessment

The hardest part of getting a Phase 0 HA assessment started is rounding up the right resources to pull it off well. This effort is so critical to your company's existence that you are going to want to use your best folks. In addition, timing is everything. It would be nice to launch a Phase 0 HA assessment before you have gotten too far down the path on a new system's development. Or, if this is after the fact, put all the attention you can on completing this assessment as accurately and completely as possible.

Resources for a Phase 0 HA Assessment

For a Phase 0 HA assessment, you need to assemble between two and three resources (professionals) with the ability to properly understand and capture the technical components of your environment, along with the business drivers behind the application being assessed. Again, these should be some of the best folks you have. If your best folks don't have enough bandwidth to take this on, then get outside help; don't settle for less skilled employees. The small amount of time and budget that this assessment will cost will be minimal compared to the far-reaching impact of its results. These are the types of people and their skill sets you should include in the Phase 0 assessment:

- ▶ **A system architect/data architect (SA/DA)**—You want someone with both extensive system design and data design experience who will be able to understand the hardware, software, and database aspects of high availability.

- ▶ **A very senior business analyst (SBA)**—This person must be completely versed in development methodologies and the business requirements that are being targeted by the application (and by the assessment).

- ▶ **A part-time senior technical lead (STL)**—You want a software engineer type with good overall system development skills so that he or she can help in assessing the coding standards that are being followed, the completeness of the system testing tasks, and the general software configuration that has been (or will be) implemented.

The Phase 0 HA Assessment Tasks

After you have assembled a team, you can start on the assessment, which is broken down into several tasks that will yield the different critical pieces of information needed to determine the correct high availability solution. Some tasks are used when you are assessing existing systems; these tasks might not apply to a system that is brand new.

The vast majority of Phase 0 HA assessments are conducted for existing systems. What this seems to indicate is that most folks are retrofitting their applications to be more highly available after they have been implemented. Of course, it would have been best to have identified and analyzed the high availability requirements of an application during development in the first place.

A few of the tasks that described here may not be needed in determining the correct HA solution. However, I have included them here for the sake of completeness, and they often help form a more complete picture of the environment and processing that is being implemented. Remember, this type of assessment becomes a valuable depiction of what you were trying to achieve based on what you were being asked to support. Salient points within each task are outlined as well. Let's dig into these tasks:

▶ **Task 1**—Describe the current state of the application. This involves the following points:

NOTE

If this is a new application, skip Task 1!

 ▶ Data (data usage and physical implementation)

 ▶ Process (business processes being supported)

 ▶ Technology (hardware/software platform/configuration)

 ▶ Backup/recovery procedures

 ▶ Standards/guidelines used

 ▶ Testing/QA process employed

 ▶ Service level agreement (SLA) currently defined

 ▶ Level of expertise of personnel administering system

 ▶ Level of expertise of personnel developing/testing system

▶ **Task 2**—Describe the future state of the application. This involves the following points:

 ▶ Data (data usage and physical implementation, data volume growth, data resilience)

 ▶ Process (business processes being supported, expanded functionality anticipated, and application resilience)

 ▶ Technology (hardware/software platform/configuration, new technology being acquired)

 ▶ Backup/recovery procedures being planned

 ▶ Standards/guidelines used or being enhanced

 ▶ Testing/QA process being changed or enhanced

 ▶ SLA desired from here on out

 ▶ Level of expertise of personnel administering system (planned training and hiring)

 ▶ Level of expertise of personnel developing/testing system (planned training and hiring)

▶ **Task 3**—Describe the unplanned downtime reasons at different intervals (past 7 days, past month, past quarter, past 6 months, past year).

If this is a new application, Task 3 is to create an estimate of the future month, quarter, 6-month, and 1-year intervals.

▶ **Task 4**—Describe the planned downtime reasons at different intervals (past 7 days, past month, past quarter, past 6 months, past year).

If this is a new application, Task 4 is to create an estimate of the future month, quarter, 6 month, and 1 year intervals.

▶ **Task 5**—Calculate the availability percentage across different time intervals (past 7 days, past month, past quarter, past 6 months, past year). (Refer to Chapter 1 for this complete calculation.)

If this is a new application, Task 5 is to create an estimate of the future monthly, quarter, 6-month, and 1-year intervals.

▶ **Task 6**—Calculate the loss of downtime. This involves the following points:

  ▶ **Revenue loss (per hour of unavailability)**—For example, in an online order entry system, look at any peak order entry hour and calculate the total order amounts for that peak hour. This will be your revenue loss per hour value.

  ▶ **Productivity dollar loss (per hour of unavailability)**—For example, in an internal financial data warehouse that is used for executive decision support, calculate the length of time that this data mart/warehouse was not available within the past month or two and multiply this by the number of executives/ managers who were supposed to be querying it during that period. This is the "productivity effect." Multiply this by the average salary of these execs/managers to get a rough estimate of productivity dollar loss. This does not consider the bad business decisions they might have made without having their data mart/warehouse available and the dollar loss of those bad business decisions. Calculating a productivity dollar loss might be a bit aggressive for this assessment, but there needs to be something to measure against and to help justify the return on investment. For applications that are not productivity applications, this value will not be calculated.

  ▶ **Goodwill dollar loss (in terms of customers lost per hour of unavailability)**— It's extremely important to include this component. Goodwill loss can be measured by taking the average number of customers for a period of time (such as last month's online order customer average) and comparing it with a period of processing following a system failure (where there was a significant amount of downtime). Chances are that there was a drop-off of the same amount that can be rationalized as goodwill loss (that is, the online customer didn't come back to you, they went to the competition). You must then take that percentage drop-off (for example, 2%) and multiply it by the peak order amount averages for the defined period. This period loss number is like a repeating loss overhead value that should be included in the ROI calculation for every month.

> **NOTE**
>
> If this is a new application, Task 6 is to create an estimate of the losses.

The loss of downtime might be difficult to calculate but will help in any justification process for purchase of HA-enabling products and in the measurement of ROI.

Once you have completed these tasks, you are ready to move on to step 2: gauging the HA primary variables.

Step 2: Gauging HA Primary Variables

It is now time to properly place your arrows (as relative value indications) on the primary variable gauges (refer to Figure 1.8). You should place the assessment arrow on each of the 10 variables as accurately as possible and as rigorously as possible. Each variable continuum should be evenly divided into a scale of some kind, and an exact value should be determined or calculated to help place the arrow. For example, the cost of the downtime (per hour) variable could be a scale from $0/hr at the bottom (left) to $500,000/hr at the top (right) for Company X. The $500,000/hr top scale value would represent what might have been the peak order amounts ever taken in by the online order entry system for Company X and thus would represent the known dollar amount being lost for this period. Remember that everything is relative to the other systems in your company and to the perceived value of each of these variables. In other words, some companies won't place much value on the end-user tolerance of downtime variable if the application is for internal employees. So, adjust accordingly.

For each of the primary variable gauges, you need to follow these steps:

1. Assign relative values to each primary variable (based on your company's characteristics).

2. Place an arrow on the perceived (or estimated) point in each gauge that best reflects the system being assessed.

As another example, let's look at the first HA primary variable, total uptime requirement percentage. If you are assessing an ATM system, the placement of the assessment arrow would be at a percentage of 98% or higher. Remember that five 9s means a 99.999% uptime percentage. Also remember that this uptime requirement is for the "planned" time ot operation, not the total time in a day (or a year)—except, ot course, it the system is a 24×7×365 system. Very often the service level agreement that is defined for this application will spell out the uptime percentage requirement. Figure 3.1 shows the placement of the assessment arrow at 99.999% for the ATM application example—at the top edge of extreme availability (at least from an uptime percentage point of view).

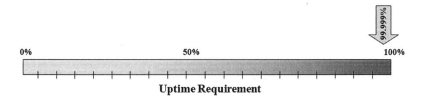

FIGURE 3.1   HA primary variables gauge—ATM uptime percentage example.

Step 3: Determining the Optimal HA Solution

Once you have completed step 1 and step 2, the hard part is over, and you probably have enough information to make a *very* good high availability solution choice. If your information from these two steps was spotty and incomplete, the decision you make will probably be somewhat suspect. But, in general, it may be good enough to get you mostly what you are trying to achieve.

Step 3 draws on a formal deterministic approach that combines the assessment results and gauge information to yield the right HA solution for your requirements.

A Hybrid High Availability Selection Method

Many potential selection methods could be used to help in selecting the best HA solution. There are scoring methods, decision-tree methods, and simple estimation methods. I like a hybrid decision-tree method that uses the primary variable answers to guide you to an HA solution.

With any selection method for determining an HA solution, you will get several possible high availability answers, one of which will be that *no* high availability solution is needed. The general cost and administrative complexity of each solution are also described. As new HA solutions are identified in the industry (or by a particular vendor, such as Microsoft), this list can be expanded. But, for now, this book focuses on the following (see Figure 3.2):

▶ **Disk methods**—Disk methods include disk mirroring, RAID, and so on. Characteristics: Medium cost and low administration complexity.

▶ **Other hardware**—Other hardware includes redundant power supplies, fans, CPUs, and so on (many of which are hot swappable). Characteristics: Medium cost and low administration complexity.

▶ **Failover clustering**—Windows Server Failover Clustering allows two (or more) systems to fail over to each other in a passive/active or active/active mode. Characteristics: Medium cost and moderate administration complexity.

▶ **SQL clustering**—SQL clustering fully enables a Microsoft SQL Server instance to fail over to another system using WSFC (because SQL Server 2016 is cluster aware). Characteristics: Medium cost and moderate administration complexity.

▶ **AlwaysOn availability groups (AVG)**—AlwaysOn provides database-level failover and availability by utilizing a data redundancy approach. Primary and up to eight secondary replicas are created and synchronized to form a robust high availability configuration and a work offloading option. Characteristics: High cost (due to Microsoft licensing for required Enterprise Edition) and moderate administration complexity.

▶ **Data replication**—You can use transactional replication to redundantly distribute transactions from one SQL Server database to another instantaneously. Both SQL Server databases (on different servers) can be used for workload balancing as well. Some limitations exist but are very manageable. Characteristics: Low cost and moderate administration complexity.

▶ **Log shipping**—You can directly apply SQL Server database transaction log entries to a warm standby copy of the same SQL Server database. There are some limitations with this technique. Characteristics: Low cost and low administration complexity.

▶ **DB Snapshots**—You can allow database-level creation of point-in-time data access for reporting users, mass update protection, and testing advantages. This is often used in conjunction with database mirroring to make the mirror available for read-only access for other pools of end users. Characteristics: Low cost and moderate administration complexity.

▶ **Microsoft Azure availability groups**—This is an extension of the on-premises capability of availability groups for failover and secondary replicas to the cloud (Microsoft Azure). Characteristics: Medium cost and moderate administration complexity.

▶ **Microsoft Azure Stretch Database**—You can move, at the database and table levels, less-accessed (eligible) data to Microsoft Azure remote storage (remote endpoint/ remote data). Characteristics: Medium cost and moderate administration complexity.

▶ **Microsoft Azure SQL database**—You can create both standard and advanced cloud-based SQL databases that allow for database backups to be geo-distributed and secondary SQL databases to be created as secondary failovers and usable replicas. Characteristics: Moderate cost and moderate administration complexity.

▶ **No high availability solution needed**

Figure 3.2 illustrates the options that are typically valid together or by themselves. Any options that has an X in an intersection with another means that these options are often used together; they either need to be built on top of an option or can be additive to this option for more a more effective high availability solution. For example, you could use disk methods, other HW, failover clustering, and SQL clustering.

	Disk Methods	Other Hardware	Failover Clustering	SQL Clustering	AlwaysOn AVG	Data Replication	Log Shipping	DB Snapshots	MS Azure AVG	MS Azure Stretch DB	Azure SQL Database
Disk Methods		X	X	X	X	X	X	X		X	
Other Hardware	X		X	X	X	X	X	X		X	
Failover Clustering	X	X		X	X	X		X		X	
SQL Clustering	X	X	X		X	X				X	
AlwaysOn AVG	X	X	X	X		X			X	X	
Data Replication	X	X	X	X	X			.			
Log Shipping	X	X						X		X	
DB Snapshots	X	X	X	X	X	X			X	X	
MS Azure AVG			X	X	X			X			
MS Azure Stretch DB			X	X	X			X	X		X
Azure SQL Database										X	X

FIGURE 3.2   Valid high availability options and combinations.

As pointed out earlier, some of these possible solutions actually include others (for example, SQL clustering is built on top of failover clustering). This needs to be factored into the results of the selection.

The Decision-Tree Approach for Choosing an HA Solution

The decision-tree approach involves taking the high availability information garnered in the Phase 0 assessment and traversing down a particular path (decision tree) to an appropriate HA solution. In this case, I have chosen a hybrid decision-tree technique that uses Nassi-Shneiderman charts, which fit well with depicting complex questions and yield very specific results. (I don't show the use of all the Nassi-Shneiderman chart techniques; only the conditional/question part.) As Figure 3.3 shows, a Nassi-Shneiderman chart includes the following:

▶ **Condition/question**—For which you need to decide an answer.

▶ **Cases**—Any number of known cases (answers) that the question might have (Case A, Case B,...Case *n*).

▶ **Action/result**—The specific result or action to be followed, depending on the case chosen (Result A, Result B,...,Result *n*).

Each question is considered in the context of all the questions answered before it. You are essentially navigating your way down a complex tree structure that will yield a definitive HA solution.

The questions are ordered so that they will clearly flesh out specific needs and push you in a specific high availability direction. Figure 3.4 illustrates an example of a question put into the Nassi-Shneiderman construct. The question is "What percentage of availability must your application have (for its scheduled time of operation)?" If you have completed enough of the Phase 0 assessment, answering this question should be easy. Answering this question is also a good audit or validation of your Phase 0 assessment.

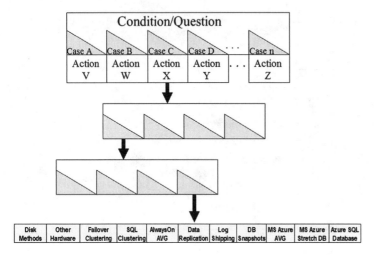

FIGURE 3.3   Hybrid decision tree using Nassi-Shneiderman charts.

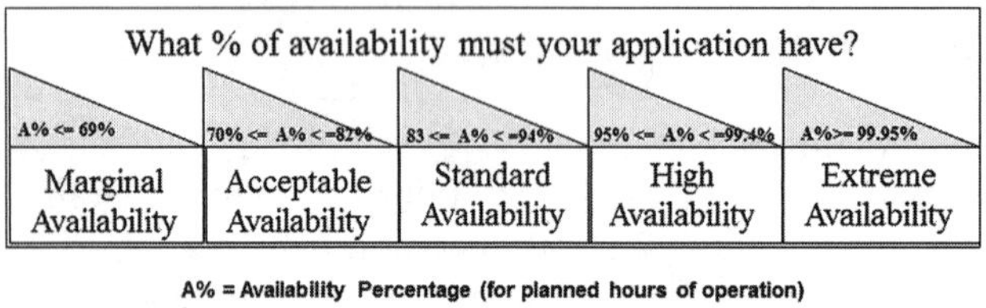

What % of availability must your application have?				
A% <= 69%	70% <= A% < =82%	83 <= A% < =94%	95% <= A% < =99.4%	A%>= 99.95%
Marginal Availability	Acceptable Availability	Standard Availability	High Availability	Extreme Availability

A% = Availability Percentage (for planned hours of operation)

FIGURE 3.4   Nassi-Shneiderman question example.

In the normal course of events, you start with the most critical aspects of high availability. Then, depending on the answer to each question, you proceed down a specific path with a new question. As each high availability characteristic is considered, the path (actions followed) lead you to a specific HA solution. The series of questions that need to be answered are taken from the HA primary variables gauge but are expanded slightly to make them conditional in nature. They are as follows:

▶ What percentage of time must the application remain up during its scheduled time of operation? (The goal!)

▶ How much tolerance does the end user have when the system is not available (planned or unplanned unavailability)?

▶ What is the per-hour cost of downtime for this application?

▶ How long does it take to get the application back online following a failure (of any kind)? (Worst case!)

▶ How much of the application is distributed and will require some type of synchronization with other nodes before all nodes are considered to be 100% available?

▶ How much data inconsistency can be tolerated in favor of having the application available?

▶ How often is scheduled maintenance required for this application (and environment)?

▶ How important are high performance and scalability?

▶ How important is it for the application to keep its current connection alive with the end user?

▶ What is the estimated cost of a possible high availability solution? What is the budget?

NOTE

An important factor that may come into play is your timeline for getting an application to become highly available. If the timeline is very short, your solution may exclude costs as a barrier and may not even consider hardware solutions that take months to order and install. In this case, it would be appropriate expand the primary variables gauge to include this question (and any others) as well. This particular question could be "What is the timeline for making your application highly available?"

However, this book assumes that you have a reasonable amount of time to properly assess your application.

It is also assumed that if you have written (or are planning to write) an application that will be cluster aware, you can leverage WSFC. This would be considered to be an implementation of application clustering (that is, an application that is cluster aware). As mentioned earlier, SQL Server is a cluster-aware program. However, I don't consider it to be application clustering in the strictest sense; it is, rather, database clustering.

Scenario 1: Application Service Provider (ASP) Assessment

To drive home the decision-tree method, this section walks you through a complete path (decision tree) for the application service provider (ASP) business scenario first mentioned in Chapter 1. This section shows how to answer the questions based on an already completed Phase 0 HA assessment for the ASP. As you recall, this scenario involves a very real ASP and its operating model. This ASP houses and develops numerous global, web-based online order entry systems for several major beauty and health products companies around the world. Its customer base is truly global. The company is headquartered in California, and this ASP guarantees 99.95% uptime to its customers. In this case, the customers are sales associates and their sales managers. If the ASP achieves these guarantees, it gets significant bonuses; if it falls below certain thresholds, it is liable for specific penalties. The processing mix of activity is approximately 65% online order entry and approximately 35% reporting.

Availability:

▶ 24 hours per day

▶ 7 days per week

▶ 365 days per year

Planned downtime: 0.25% (less than 1%)

Unplanned downtime: 0.25% (less than 1%) will be tolerable

Figure 3.5 shows the first three questions in the decision tree and their corresponding responses (actions). Remember that the questions are cumulative. Each new question carries along the responses of the preceding questions. The responses, taken together, determine the HA solution that best fits. The following pages proceed through the ASP business scenario depiction to give you a feel for how this works.

HA assessment (decision tree):

1. What percentage of time must the application remain up during its scheduled time of operation? (The goal!)

   Response: **E: 99.95%**—Extreme availability goal.

2. How much tolerance does the end user have when the system is not available (planned or unplanned unavailability)?

   Response: **E: Very low tolerance of downtime**—Extremely critical.

3. What is the per-hour cost of downtime for this application?

   Response: **D: $15k/hour cost of downtime**—High cost.

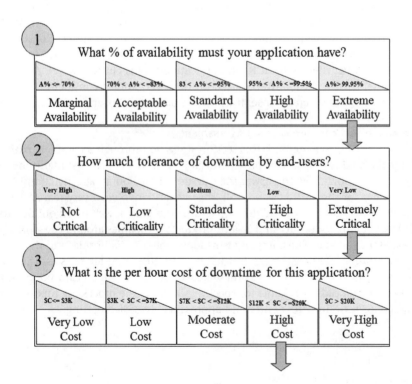

FIGURE 3.5   Decision tree for the ASP, questions 1–3.

Remember that all questions are additive. After going through just three questions, you can see that this ASP business scenario has a pretty high cost per hour when it is not available (a 0.5% per-hour cost [total gross revenues of $3 billion]). This, coupled with high uptime goals and extremely low end-user tolerance for downtime (because of the nature of the ASP business), will drive this application to a particular type of HA solution very quickly. You could easily just stop now and jump to an HA solution of maximum hardware redundancy, RAID, WSFC, and SQL clustering in order to fulfill the HA requirement goals; however, there are still several aspects of the requirement, such as distributed data processing requirements and budget available for the HA solution, that could easily change this outcome. You should always complete the entire set of questions for clarity, consistency, completeness, and cost justification purposes.

Figure 3.6 forges ahead with the next set of questions and answers.

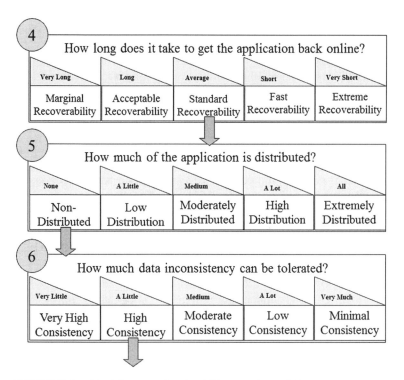

FIGURE 3.6   Decision tree for the ASP, questions 4–6.

4. How long does it take to get the application back online following a failure (of any kind)? (Worst case!)

Response: **C: Average**—Standard amount of time to recover (that is, to get back online). Accomplished via standard DB recovery mechanisms (incremental transaction log dumps done every 15 minutes). Faster recovery times would be beneficial, but data integrity is of huge importance.

5. How much of the application is distributed and will require some type of synchronization with other nodes before all nodes are considered to be 100% available?

Response: **A: None**—There aren't any components of this application that are distributed (nondistributed). This simplifies the data synchronization aspects to consider but does not necessarily mean that a distributed HA solution won't better serve the overall application. If the application has a heavy reporting component, some type of data replication architecture could serve it well. This will be addressed in the performance/scalability question later.

6. How much data inconsistency can be tolerated in favor of having the application available?

Response: **B: A little**—A high degree of data consistency must be maintained at all times. This gives little room for any HA option that would sacrifice data consistency in favor of availability.

For systems with primarily static data, complete images of the application databases could be kept at numerous locations for instantaneous access any time they are needed, with little danger of having data inconsistent (in administered properly). For systems with a lot of data volatility, the answer on this one question may well dictate the HA option to use. Very often the HA option best suited for high data consistency needs is SQL clustering and log shipping, coupled with RAID at the disk subsystem level.

Another short pause in the path to an HA solution finds you not having to support a complex distributed environment but having to make sure you keep the data consistent as much as possible. In addition, you can plan on typical recovery times to get the application back online in case of failures. (The ASP's service level agreement probably specified this.) However, if a faster recovery mechanism is possible, it should be considered because it will have a direct impact on the total amount of unplanned downtime and could potentially allow the ASP to get some uptime bonuses (that might also be in the SLA).

Now, let's venture into the next set of questions, as illustrated in Figure 3.7. These focus on planned downtime, performance, and application connectivity perception.

7. How often is scheduled maintenance required for this application (and environment)?

Response: **C: Average**—A reasonable amount of downtime is needed to service operating system patches/upgrades, hardware changes/swapping, and application patches/upgrades. For 24×7 systems, this will cut into the availability time directly. For systems with downtime windows, the pressure is much less in this area.

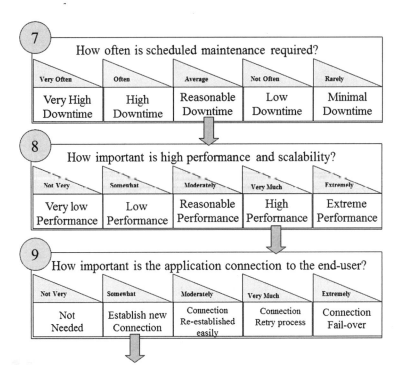

FIGURE 3.7   Decision tree for the ASP, questions 7–9.

8. How important are high performance and scalability?

Response: **D: Very much**—The ASP considers all of its applications to be high-performance systems that must meet strict performance numbers and must be able to scale to support large number of users. These performance thresholds would be spelled out clearly in the service level agreement. Any HA solution must therefore be a scalable solution as well.

9. How important is it for the application to keep its current connection alive with the end user?

Response: **B: Somewhat**—At the very least, the ability to establish a new connection to the application within a short amount of time will be required. No client connection failover is required. This was partially made possible by the overall transactional approach of "optimistic concurrency" used by the applications. This approach puts much less pressure on holding a connection for long periods of time (to hold/lock rows).

As you can see in Figure 3.8, the estimated cost of a potential HA solution would be between $100k and $250k. Budget for HA should be estimated to be a couple of full days' worth of downtime cost. For the ASP example, this would be roughly about $720k. The ROI calculation will show how quickly this will be recovered.

NOTE

A bit later in this chapter, you will work though a complete ROI calculation so that you can fully understand where these values come from.

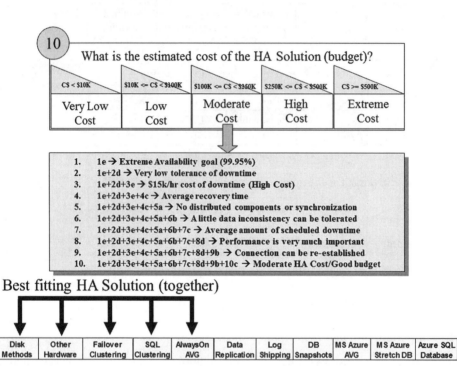

FIGURE 3.8   Decision tree for the ASP, question 10 and HA solution.

10. What is the estimated cost of a possible high availability solution? What is the budget?

Response: C: **$100k <= C$ < $250k**—This is a moderate amount of cost for potentially a huge amount of benefit. These estimates are involved:

▶ Five new multi-core servers with 64GB RAM at $30k per server

▶ Five Microsoft Windows 2012 licenses

▶ Five shared SCSI disk systems with RAID 10 (50 drives)

▶ Five days of additional training costs for personnel

▶ Five SQL Server Enterprise Edition licenses

The HA Solution for Scenario 1

Figure 3.8 shows the final selection of hardware redundancy, shared disk RAID arrays, failover clustering, SQL clustering for the primary server instance, a secondary replication in synchronous mode for instantaneous failover, and two more asynchronous secondary replicas for heavy load balancing of online read-only access and reporting needs. There is little doubt about the needs being met well by this particular set of HA solutions. It clearly meets all of the most significant requirements of uptime, tolerance, performance, and costs. The ASP's SLA allows for brief amounts of downtime to service all OS, hardware, and application upgrades, but due to the availability group configuration, all these are handled with rolling updates and zero downtime for the applications. Figure 3.9 shows the live HA solution technical architecture, with a budget allowing for a larger amount of hardware redundancy to be utilized.

The ASP actually put this HA solution in place and then achieved nearly five 9s for extended periods of time (exceeding its original goals of 99.95% uptime). One additional note is that the ASP also employs a spreading out of the risk strategy to further reduce downtime created from application and shared hardware failures. It will put at most two to three applications on a particular clustered solution. (Refer to Figure 2.10 in Chapter 2 for a more complete depiction of this risk mitigation approach.)

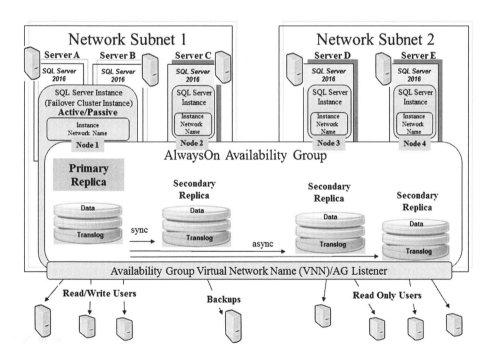

FIGURE 3.9   ASP HA solution technical architecture.

The decision-tree approach can also be illustrated in a slightly different way. Figure 3.10 shows an abbreviated bubble chart technique of this decision-tree path traversal.

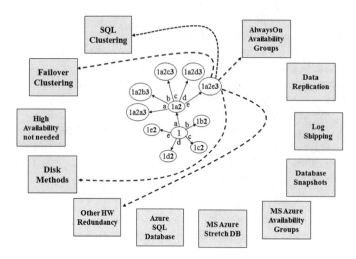

FIGURE 3.10   Bubble chart decision-tree path traversal.

Remember that each question takes into context all questions before it. The result is a specific HA solution that best meets your business requirements.

Scenario 2: Worldwide Sales and Marketing (Brand Promotion) Assessment

Recall that Scenario 2 features a major chip manufacturer that has created a highly successful promotion and branding program, which results in billions of dollars in advertising dollars being rebated back to the company's worldwide sales channel partners. These sales channel partners must enter in their complete advertisements (newspaper, radio, TV, other) and be measured against ad compliance and logo usage and placements. If a sales channel partner is in compliance, it will receive up to 50% of the cost of its advertisement back from this chip manufacturer. There are three major advertising regions: Far East, Europe, and North America. Any other advertisements outside these first three are lumped into an "Other Regions" bucket. Each region produces a huge daily load of new advertisement information that is processed instantaneously for compliance. Each major region deals only with that region's advertisements but receives the compliance rules and compliance judgment from the chip manufacturer's headquarters. Application mix is approximately 75% online entry of advertisement events and 25% management and compliance reporting.

Availability:

▶ 24 hours per day

▶ 7 days a week

▶ 365 days a year

Planned downtime: 3%

Unplanned downtime: 2% will be tolerable

HA assessment (decision tree):

1. What percentage of time must the application remain up during its scheduled time of operation? (The goal!)

   Response: D: 95.0%—High availability goal. This, however, is not a super-critical application in terms of keeping the company running (as an order entry system would be).

2. How much tolerance does the end user have when the system is not available (planned or unplanned unavailability)?

   Response: C: **Medium tolerance of downtime**—Standard criticality.

3. What is the per-hour cost of downtime for this application?

   Response: B: **$5k/hour cost of downtime**—Low cost.

   As you can see so far, this sales and marketing application is nice to have available, but it can tolerate some downtime without hurting the company very much. Sales are not lost; work just gets backed up a bit. In addition, the cost of downtime is reasonably low, at $5k/hr. This is roughly the rate at which advertisement staff can't be working on marketing materials.

4. How long does it take to get the application back online following a failure (of any kind)? (Worst case!)

   Response: C: **Average**—Standard amount of time to recover (that is, to get back online). Accomplished via standard DB recovery mechanisms (incremental transaction log dumps done every 15 minutes).

5. How much of the application is distributed and will require some type of synchronization with other nodes before all nodes are considered to be 100% available?

   Response: D: **High distribution**—This is a global application that relies on data being created and maintained at headquarters from around the world (OLTP activity) but must also support heavy regional reporting (reporting activity) that doesn't interfere with the performance of the OLTP activity.

6. How much data inconsistency can be tolerated in favor of having the application available?

   Response: B: **A little**—A high degree of data consistency must be maintained at all times. This gives little room for any HA option that would sacrifice data consistency in favor of availability. This is regionally sensitive, in that when data is being updated by Europe, the Far East doesn't need to get data updates right away.

7. How often is scheduled maintenance required for this application (and environment)?

Response: **C: Average**—A reasonable amount of downtime will occur to service operating system patches/upgrades, hardware changes/swapping, and application patches/upgrades.

8. How important is high performance and scalability?

Response: **D: Very much**—Performance (and scalability) are very important for this application. Ideally, an overall approach of separating the OLTP activity from the reporting activity will pay big dividends toward this.

9. How important is it for the application to keep its current connection alive with the end user?

Response: **B: Somewhat**—At the very least, the ability to establish a new connection to the application within a short amount of time will be required. No client connection failover is required. In fact, for the worst-case scenario of the headquarters database becoming unavailable, the OLTP activity could easily be shifted to any other full copy of the database that is being used for reporting and is being kept current (as will be seen in the HA solution for this scenario).

10. What is the estimated cost of a possible high availability solution? What is the budget?

Response: **B: $10k <= C$ < $100k**—This is a pretty low amount of cost for potentially a huge amount of benefit. These estimates are involved:

▶ Five new multi-core servers with 32GB RAM at $10k per server

▶ Five new Microsoft Windows 2012 Server licenses

▶ Five SCSI disk systems with RAID 10 (25 drives)

▶ Two days of additional training costs for personnel

▶ Five new SQL Server licenses (remote distributor, three subscribers)

The HA Solution for Scenario 2

Figure 3.11 shows that a basic hardware/disk redundancy approach on each server should be used, along with SQL Server's robust "transactional" data replication implementation, to create three regional reporting images of the primary marketing database (MktgDB). These distributed copies will try to alleviate the major reporting burden against the OLTP (primary) database and also can serve as a warm standby copy of the database in the event of a major database problem at headquarters. Overall, this distributed architecture is easy to maintain and keep in sync and is highly scalable, as shown in Figure 3.12.

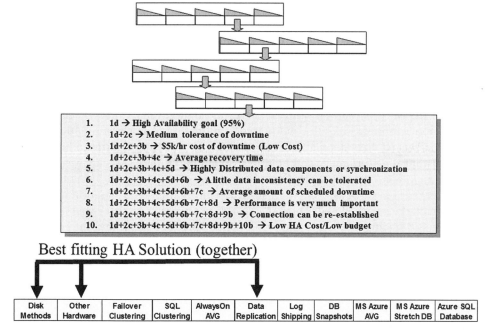

FIGURE 3.11   Sales/marketing decision-tree summary plus HA solution.

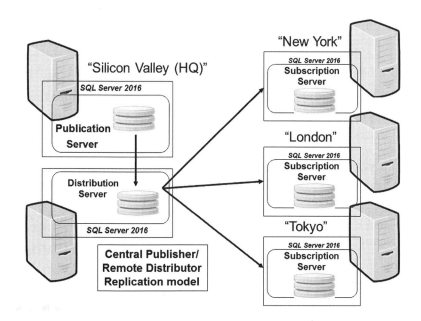

FIGURE 3.12   Sales/marketing HA solution technical architecture.

After building this HA solution, the uptime goal was achieved for most of the time. Occasionally, there were some delays in resyncing the data at each regional site (subscribers). But, in general, the users were extremely happy with performance, availability, and minimal costs.

Scenario 3: Investment Portfolio Management Assessment

An investment portfolio management application will be housed in a major server farm in the heart of the world's financial center: New York. Serving North American customers only, this application provides the ability to do full trading of stocks and options in all financial markets (United States and international), along with full portfolio holdings assessment, historical performance, and holdings valuation. Primary users are investment managers for their large customers. Stock purchasing and selling comprise 90% of the daytime activity, and massive assessment, historical performance, and valuation reporting occur after the markets have closed. Three major peaks occur each weekday that are driven by the three major trading markets of the world (United States, Europe, and the Far East). During the weekends, the application is used for the long-range planning reporting and front-loading stock trades for the coming week.

Availability:

▶ 20 hours per day

▶ 7 days per week

▶ 365 days per year

Planned downtime: **4%**

Unplanned downtime: **1%** will be tolerable

HA assessment (decision tree):

1. What percentage of time must the application remain up during its scheduled time of operation? (The goal!)

   Response: **D: 95.0%**—High availability goal. This particular financial institution (one of the largest on the planet) tends to allow for a small percentage of "built-in" downtime (planned or unplanned). A smaller, more nimble financial institution would probably have slightly more aggressive uptime goals (for example, five 9s). Time is money, you know.

2. How much tolerance does the end user have when the system is not available (planned or unplanned unavailability)?

   Response: **D: Low tolerance of downtime**—High criticality due to market timings (selling and buying stocks within market windows).

3. What is the per-hour cost of downtime for this application?

   Response: **E: $150k/hour cost of downtime**—Very high cost. However, this is the worse-case scenario. When the markets are closed, the cost of downtime is marginal.

4. How long does it take to get the application back online following a failure (of any kind)? (Worst case!)

Response: **E: Very short recovery**—This application's time to recover should be a very short amount of time (that is, to get back online).

5. How much of the application is distributed and will require some type of synchronization with other nodes before all nodes are considered to be 100% available?

Response: **C: Medium distribution**—This moderately distributed application has a large OLTP requirement and a large report processing requirement.

6. How much data inconsistency can be tolerated in favor of having the application available?

Response: **A: Very little**—A very high degree of data consistency must be maintained at all times because this is financial data.

7. How often is scheduled maintenance required for this application (and environment)?

Response: **C: Average**—A reasonable amount of downtime will occur to service operating system patches/upgrades, hardware changes/swapping, and application patches/upgrades.

8. How important is high performance and scalability?

Response: **D: Very much**—Performance (and scalability) are very important for this application.

9. How important is it for the application to keep its current connection alive with the end user?

Response: **B: Somewhat**—At the very least, the ability to establish a new connection to the application within a short amount of time will be required. No client connection failover is required.

10. What is the estimated cost of a possible high availability solution? What is the budget?

Response: **C: $100k <= C$ < $250k**—This is a moderate amount of cost for potentially a huge amount of benefit. These estimates are involved:

  ▶ Two new multi-core servers with 64GB RAM at $50k per server

  ▶ Three Microsoft Windows 2012 Server licenses

  ▶ Three SQL Server Enterprise Edition licenses

  ▶ $1,000/month Microsoft Azure IaaS fees

  ▶ Two shared SCSI disk systems with RAID 10 (30 drives)

  ▶ Twelve days of additional training costs for personnel

The company budgeted $1.25 million for all HA costs. A solid HA solution won't even approach those numbers coming way under the budgeted amount.

Figure 3.13 shows the overall summary of the decision-tree results, along with the HA solution for the portfolio management scenario.

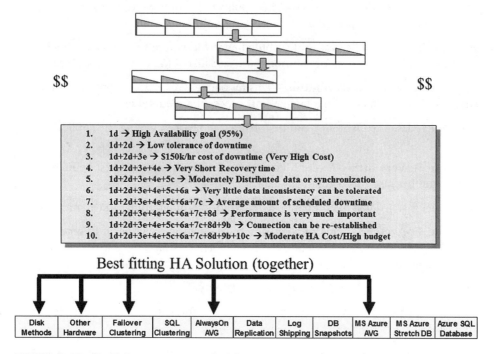

FIGURE 3.13   Portfolio management decision-tree summary plus HA solution.

The HA Solution for Scenario 3

As identified in Figure 3.13, the company opted for the basic hardware/disk redundancy approach on each server, with an AlwaysOn availability group asynchronous secondary replica for failover, offloading of DB backups, and a reporting workload on both the local secondary replica and the Microsoft Azure secondary replica. In fact, most of the reporting was eventually directed to the Microsoft Azure secondary replica; data was only about 10 seconds behind the primary replica, on average. There is now plenty of risk mitigation with this technical architecture, and it is not difficult to maintain (as shown in Figure 3.14).

Once this HA solution was put together, it exceeded the high availability goals on a regular basis. Great performance has also resulted due to the splitting out of the OLTP from the reporting; this is very often a solid design approach.

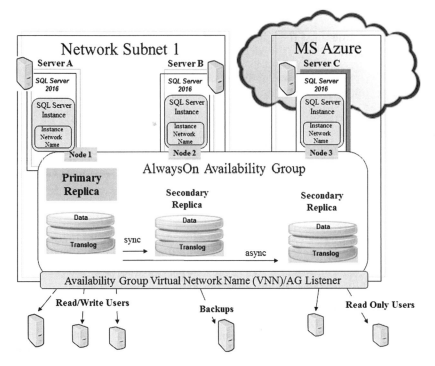

FIGURE 3.14   Portfolio management HA solution technical architecture.

Scenario 4: Call Before You Dig Assessment

Recall from Chapter 1 that at a tri-state underground construction call center, an application must determine within 6 inches the likelihood of hitting any underground gas mains,
water mains, electrical wiring, phone lines, or cables that might be present on a proposed
dig site for construction. Law requires that a call be placed to this center to determine
whether it is safe to dig and identify the exact location of any underground hazard *before*
any digging has started. This application is classified as "life at risk" and must be available
very nearly 100% of the time during common construction workdays (Monday through
Saturday). Each year more than 25 people are killed nationwide digging into unknown
underground hazards. The application mix is 95% query only with 5% devoted to updating images, geospatial values, and various pipe and cable location information provided
by the regional utility companies.

Availability:

▶ 15 hours per day (5:00 a.m.–8:00 p.m.)

▶ 6 days per week (closed on Sunday)

▶ 312 days per year

Planned downtime: **0%**

Unplanned downtime: **0.5%** (less than 1%) will be tolerable

HA assessment (decision tree):

1. What percentage of time must the application remain up during its scheduled time of operation? (The goal!)

   Response: **E: 99.95%**—Extreme availability goal. This is a "life critical" application. Someone may be killed if information cannot be obtained from this system during its planned time of operation.

2. How much tolerance does the end user have when the system is not available (planned or unplanned unavailability)?

   Response: **E: Very low tolerance of downtime**—In other words, this has extreme criticality from the end user's point of view.

3. What is the per-hour cost of downtime for this application?

   Response: **A: $2k/hour cost of downtime**—Very low dollar cost. Very high life cost. This one question is very deceiving. There is no limit to the cost of loss of life. However, you must go with the original dollar costing approach. So, bear with me on this one. Hopefully, the outcome will be the same.

4. How long does it take to get the application back online following a failure (of any kind)? (Worst case!)

   Response: **E: Very short recovery**—This application's time to recover should be a very short amount of time (that is, to get back online).

5. How much of the application is distributed and will require some type of synchronization with other nodes before all nodes are considered to be 100% available?

   Response: **A: None**—There is no data distribution requirement for this application.

6. How much data inconsistency can be tolerated in favor of having the application available?

   Response: **A: Very little**—A very high degree of data consistency must be maintained at all times. This data must be extremely accurate and up to date due to the life-threatening aspects to incorrect information.

7. How often is scheduled maintenance required for this application (and environment)?

   Response: **C: Average**—A reasonable amount of downtime will occur to service operating system patches/upgrades, hardware changes/swapping, and application patches/upgrades. This system has a planned time of operation of 15×6×312, yielding plenty of time for this type of maintenance. Thus, it will have 0% planned downtime but an average amount of scheduled maintenance.

8. How important are high performance and scalability?

   Response: **C: Moderate performance**—Performance and scalability aren't paramount for this application. The accuracy and availability to the information are most important.

9. How important is it for the application to keep its current connection alive with the end user?

   Response: **B: Somewhat**—At the very least, the ability to establish a new connection to the application within a short amount of time will be required. No client connection failover is required.

10. What is the estimated cost of a possible high availability solution? What is the budget?

    ▶ Response: **B: $10k <= C$ < $100k**—This is a pretty low cost. These estimates are involved: Four new multi-core servers with 64GB RAM at $30k per server

    ▶ Four new Microsoft Windows 2012 Server licenses

    ▶ One shared SCSI disk system with RAID 5 (10 drives)—this is primarily a read-only system (95% reads)

    ▶ One SCSI disk system RAID 5 (5 drives)

    ▶ $750/month Microsoft Azure IaaS fees

    ▶ Five days of additional training costs for personnel

    ▶ Four new SQL Server Enterprise Edition licenses

    The budget for the whole HA solution is somewhat limited to under $100k as well.

The HA Solution for Scenario 4

Figure 3.15 summarizes the decision-tree answers for the call before digging application. As you have seen, this is a very critical system during its planned hours of operation, but it has low performance goals and a low cost of downtime (when it is down). Regardless, it is highly desirable for this system to be up and running as much as possible. The HA solution that best fits this particular application's needs is a combination that yields maximum redundancy (hardware, disk, and database) with the additional insurance policy of maintaining a SQL clustered primary as a part of a high availability group that has a failover secondary replica and a Microsoft Azure secondary replica in case the whole SQL cluster configuration fails. This is a pretty extreme attempt at always having a valid application up and running to support the loss-of-life aspect of this application.

After building this HA solution, the uptime goal was achieved easily. Performance has been exceptional, and this application continuously achieves its availability goals. Figure 3.16 shows the technical HA solution employed.

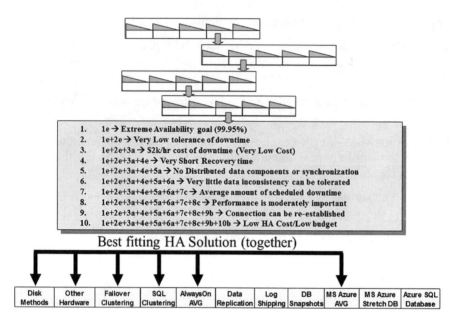

FIGURE 3.15   Call before digging decision-tree summary plus HA solution.

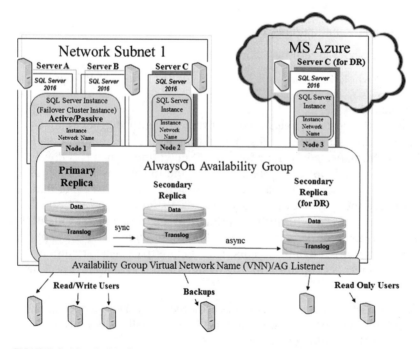

FIGURE 3.16   Call before you dig HA solution technical architecture.

Step 4: Justifying the Cost of a Selected High Availability Solution

If money doesn't grow on trees in your organization or if the cost of downtime isn't a huge dollar amount per hour, it might be necessary for you to justify the cost of a high availability solution that you are about to build. If yours is like most other organizations, any new change to a system or an application must be evaluated on its value to the organization, and a calculation of how soon it will pay for itself must be done. ROI calculations provide the cost justification behind a proposed solution.

ROI Calculation

As stated earlier, ROI can be calculated by adding up the incremental costs (or estimates) of the new HA solution and comparing them against the complete cost of downtime for a period of time (such as 1 year). This section uses the ASP business from Scenario 1 as the basis for a ROI calculation. Recall that for this scenario, the costs are estimated to be between **$100k and $250k** and include the following:

▶ Five new multi-core servers with 64GB RAM at $30k per server

▶ Five Microsoft Windows 2012 Server licenses

▶ Five shared SCSI disk systems with RAID 10 (50 drives)

▶ Five days of additional training costs for personnel

▶ Five SQL Server Enterprise Edition licenses

These are the incremental costs:

▶ Maintenance cost (for a 1-year period):

    ▶ **$20k (estimate)**—System admin personnel cost (additional time for training of these personnel)

    ▶ **$35k (estimate)**—Software licensing cost (of additional HA components)

▶ Hardware cost:

    ▶ **$100k hardware cost**—The cost of additional HW in the new HA solution

▶ Deployment/assessment cost:

    ▶ **$20k deployment cost**—The costs for development, testing, QA, and production implementation of the solution

    ▶ **$10k HA assessment cost**—Be bold and go ahead and throw the cost of the assessment into this estimate to get a complete ROI calculation

▶ Downtime cost (for a 1-year period):

    ▶ If you kept track of last year's downtime record, use that number; otherwise, produce an estimate of planned and unplanned downtime for this calculation. For this scenario, the estimated cost of downtime/hour is be **$15k/hour.**

▶ Planned downtime cost (revenue loss cost) = Planned downtime hours × cost of hourly downtime to the company:

a. 0.25% × 8,760 hours in a year = 21.9 hours of planned downtime

b. 21.9 hours × $15k/hr = $328,500/year cost of planned downtime.

▶ Unplanned downtime cost (revenue loss cost) = Unplanned downtime hours × cost of hourly downtime to the company:

a. 0.25% × 8,760 hours in a year = 21.9 hours of unplanned downtime

b. 21.9 hours × $15k/hr = $328,500/year cost of unplanned downtime.

ROI totals:

▶ Total of the incremental costs = $185,000 (for the year)

▶ Total of downtime cost = $657,000 (for the year)

The incremental cost is 0.28 of the downtime cost for 1 year. In other words, the investment of the HA solution will pay for itself in 0.28 year, or 3.4 months!

In reality, most companies will have achieved the ROI within 6 to 9 months.

Adding HA Elements to Your Development Methodology

Most of the high availability elements identified in the Phase 0 HA assessment process and the primary variables gauge can be cleanly added (extended) to your company's current system development life cycle. By adding the HA-oriented elements to your standard development methodology, you ensure that this information is captured and can readily target new applications to the correct technology solution. Figure 3.17 highlights the high availability tasks that could be added to a typical waterfall development methodology. As you can see, HA starts from early on in the assessment phase and is present all the way through the implementation phase. Think of this as extending your development capability. It truly guarantees that all your applications are properly evaluated and designed against their high availability needs, if they have any.

Summary

This chapter introduces a fairly formal approach to assessing and choosing a high availability solution for your applications. In reality, most folks who are attempting to do this Phase 0 HA assessment are really retrofitting their existing application for high availability. That's okay because this Phase 0 assessment directly supports the retrofitting process. The key to success is doing as complete a job as you can on the assessment and using some of your best folks to do it. They will interpret the technology and the business needs with the most accuracy. You have a lot riding on the proper assessment—potentially your company's existence. If you cannot free up your best folks to do this Phase 0 assessment, then hire some professionals who do this every day to do it for you. You will recoup the relatively small cost of this short effort very quickly.

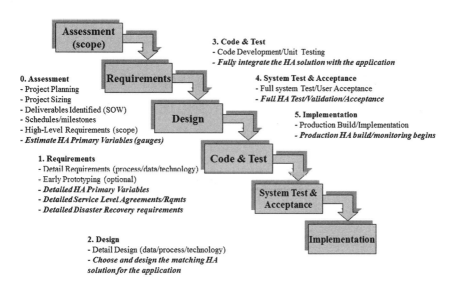

FIGURE 3.17   Development methodology with high availability built in.

It is no small task to understand an application's HA requirement, time to recovery, tolerance of recovery, data resiliency, application resiliency, performance/scalability, and costs of downtime (loss). Then, you must couple this information with your hardware/software configurations, several Microsoft-based technology offerings, and your allowable upgrade budget. The cost of *not* doing this upgrade will have a much greater impact, and if you are going to move to a high availability solution, getting the right one in place to start with will save tons of time and money in and of itself—and potentially your job.

Chapters 4 through 10 describe the Microsoft solutions that can be used to create a high availability solution (or component) and show exactly how to implement them. Those chapters provide a cookbook-type approach that will take you through the complete setup of something such as WSFC, SQL Clustering, Log Shipping, Data Replication, Availability Groups, or even a Stretch Database configuration using Microsoft Azure.

So, hold on to your hat, here we go.

CHAPTER 4
Failover Clustering

In today's fast-paced businesses environments, enterprise computing requires that the entire set of technologies used to develop, deploy, and manage mission-critical business applications be highly reliable, scalable, and resilient. The technology scope includes the network, the entire hardware or cloud technology stack, the operating systems on the servers, the applications you deploy, the database management systems, and everything in between.

An enterprise must now be able to provide a complete solution with regard to the following:

▶ **Scalability**—As organizations grow, so does the need for more computing power. The systems in place must enable an organization to leverage existing hardware and quickly and easily add computing power as needs demand.

▶ **Availability**—As organizations rely more on information, it is critical that the information be available at all times and under all circumstances. Downtime is not acceptable. Moving to five 9s reliability (that is, 99.999% uptime) is a must, not a dream.

▶ **Interoperability**—As organizations grow and evolve, so do their information systems. It is impractical to think that an organization will not have many heterogeneous sources of information. It is becoming increasingly important for applications to get to all the information, regardless of its location.

▶ **Reliability**—An organization is only as good as its data and information. It is critical that the systems providing that information be bulletproof.

It is assumed that you are already using or acquiring a certain level of foundational capa-bilities with regard to network, hardware, and operating system resilience. However, there are some further foundational operating system components that can be enabled to raise your high availability bar even higher. Central to many HA features on Windows servers is Windows Server Failover Clustering (WSFC). This has been around for quite some time and, as you will see in the next few chapters, it is used at the foundation level to build out other more advanced and integrated features for SQL Server and high availability. The tried-and-true HA solution using WSFC is SQL clustering, which creates redundant SQL Server instances (for server resilience) and shares storage between the servers. This shared storage is usually mirrored storage of one kind or another (for storage resilience). You can use SQL clustering for local server instance resilience and then include that with a larger HA topology using AlwaysOn availability groups across several nodes.

For SQL clustering, a failover cluster instance (FCI) is created; it is essentially an instance of SQL Server that is installed across WSFC nodes and, possibly, across multiple subnets. On the network, an FCI appears to be an instance of SQL Server running on a single com-puter; however, the FCI provides failover from one WSFC node to another if the current (active) node becomes unavailable. You can achieve many of your enterprise's high avail-ability demands easily and inexpensively by using WSFC, network load balancing (NLB), SQL Server failover clustering, and AlwaysOn availability groups (or combinations of them).

Variations of Failover Clustering

WSFC provides the core clustering functionality for SQL Server clustering (covered in Chapter 5, "SQL Server Clustering"). WSFC simplifies providing SQL instance-level resil-ience and is also an important part of the high availability options of AlwaysOn FCIs and AlwaysOn availability groups (when also including database-level failover). Chapter 6, "SQL Server AlwaysOn Availability Groups," covers the core SQL AlwaysOn availability groups feature. Other items worth noting include the following:

▶ **Multisite failover clustering**—With Windows Server 2008 and later, you can cre-ate a multisite failover cluster configuration that includes nodes that are dispersed across multiple physical sites or data centers. Multisite failover clusters are referred to as geographically dispersed failover clusters, stretch clusters, or multi-subnet clus-ters. Multisite failover clustering enables you to create a SQL Server multisite failover cluster.

▶ **WSFC requirement for SQL clustering and AlwaysOn**—When you want to con-figure SQL Server failover clustering (without AlwaysOn), AlwaysOn FCIs, and AlwaysOn availability groups, you must first create a WSFC cluster that embraces these servers. The good news is that it is simpler than ever before to do this, thanks to the Create Cluster Wizard in the Failover Cluster Manager.

▶ **Reduction in the hardware limitations and constraints**—Previously, you had to know what hardware and software limitations you had to deal with when con-figuring SQL clustering configurations. With WSFC and SQL Server 2016, many of these limitations have been eliminated, such as nodes not having to be exactly the same anymore. You must still check the compatibility list, but the list is really short now.

▶ **No need to have a dedicated network interface card (NIC) between nodes**—With WSFC improvements, a dedicated network connection between the nodes in the cluster is no longer required. You only need to have a valid network path from each node that is used to monitor the nodes in the cluster; it doesn't have to be dedicated, thus simplifying the hardware needed and the configuration process. You can still use a dedicated network connection for something called the heartbeat.

▶ **Easier SQL Clustering Installations**—Some slight changes have been made to the SQL installation and options in the SQL installer to more clearly address SQL clustering setup and completion steps. For example, you can configure SQL clustering setup for each node first and then use the Advanced Wizard to complete the SQL Server clustering configuration.

These features and enhancements combine to make setting up SQL Server failover clustering and AlwaysOn availability groups an easy high availability proposition. They take much of the implementation risk out of the equation and make this type of installation available to a broader installation base.

How Clustering Works

Put simply, clustering allows you to think of two or more servers as one unit of computing capability that have multiple-node high availability resilience. Clustering is an immensely powerful tool for achieving higher availability virtually transparently to whatever you are placing on the cluster.

There are two approaches to implementing failover clustering: active/passive and active/ active modes.

In an active/passive configuration, one of the nodes in the failover cluster is the active node. Another node is idle until, for whatever reason, a failover occurs (to the passive node). With a failover situation, the secondary node (the passive node) takes control of all the managed resources without the end user ever knowing that a failover has occurred. The only exception to this is that the end user (a SQL client, for example) might experience a brief transactional interruption because failover clustering cannot take over in-flight transactions. However, the end user (client) doesn't ever have to worry about the different nodes. Figure 4.1 shows a typical two-node failover clustering configuration in an active/passive mode, in which Node 2 is idle (that is, passive). This type of configuration is perfect for creating the SQL Server–based clustering and other clustering configurations. Remember that SQL Server is just an application that will run within this type of clustering configuration and is *cluster aware*. In other words, SQL Server becomes a "resource" within failover clustering that can take advantage of the failover clustering resilience.

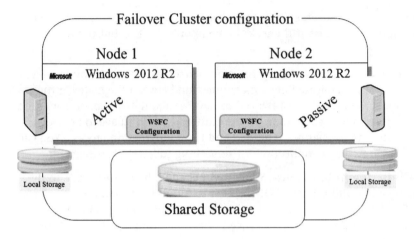

FIGURE 4.1   A typical two-node active/passive failover clustering configuration.

In an active/active configuration, you can have both nodes active at the same time and put separate SQL Server instances, doing different jobs, on each. This really isn't a true Oracle RAC-like capability; rather, it simply uses both nodes for processing power of different workloads. This gives organizations with more constrained hardware availability a chance to use a clustering configuration that can fail over to or from any node, without having to set aside idle hardware, but it introduces a load issue on each node individually if failovers occur. So, be careful with this idea.

As previously mentioned, SQL Server failover clustering is actually created within (on top of) WSFC. WSFC, not SQL Server, is capable of detecting hardware or software failures and automatically shifting control of the managed resources to a healthy node. SQL Server 2016 utilizes failover clustering based on the clustering features of WSFC. As mentioned previously, SQL Server is a fully cluster-aware application and becomes a set of resources managed by WSFC. The failover cluster shares a common set of cluster resources such as clustered storage (that is, shared storage).

> **NOTE**
>
> You can install SQL Server on as many servers as you want; the number is limited only by the operating system license and SQL Server edition you have purchased. However, you should not overload WSFC with more than 10 or so SQL Servers to manage if you can help it.

Understanding WSFC

A *server failover cluster* is a group of two or more physically separate servers running WSFC and working collectively as a single system. The server failover cluster, in turn, provides high availability, scalability, and manageability for resources and applications. In other words, a group of servers is physically connected via communication hardware (network), shares storage (via SCSI or Fibre Channel connectors), and uses WSFC software to tie them all together into managed resources.

Server failover clusters can preserve client access to applications and resources during failures and planned outages. They provide server instance–level failover. If one of the servers in a cluster is unavailable due to failure or maintenance, resources and applications move (fail over) to another available cluster node.

Clusters use an algorithm to detect a failure, and they use failover policies to determine how to handle the work from a failed server. These policies also specify how a server is to be restored to the cluster when it becomes available again.

Although clustering doesn't guarantee continuous operation, it does provide availability sufficient for most mission-critical applications and is a building block of numerous high availability solutions. WSFC can monitor applications and resources and automatically recognize and recover from many failure conditions. This capability provides great flexibility in managing the workload within a cluster, and it improves the overall availability of the system. Technologies that are cluster aware—such as SQL Server, Microsoft Message Queuing (MSMQ), Distributed Transaction Coordinator (DTC), and file shares—have already been programmed to work within WSFC.

WSFC still has some hardware and software compatibility to worry about, but the built-in Cluster Validation Wizard allows you to see whether your configuration will work. In addition, SQL Server FCIs are not supported where the cluster nodes are also domain controllers.

Let's look a little more closely at a two-node active/passive cluster configuration. At regular intervals, known as *time slices*, the failover cluster nodes look to see if they are still *alive*. If the active node is determined to be failed (not functioning), a failover is initiated, and another node in the cluster takes over for the failed node. Each physical server (node) uses separate network adapters for its own network connection. (Therefore, there is always at least one network communication capability working for the cluster at all times, as shown in Figure 4.2.)

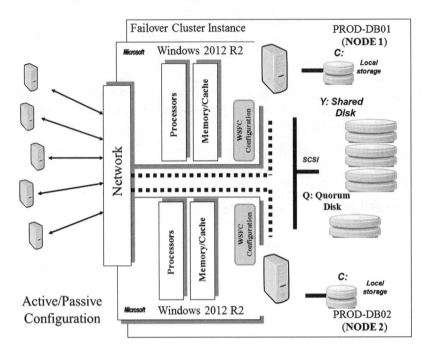

FIGURE 4.2   A two-node active/passive WSFC cluster configuration.

The *shared disk* array is a collection of physical disks (SCSI RAID or Fibre Channel–connected disks) that the cluster accesses and controls as resources. WSFC supports *shared nothing* disk arrays, in which only one node can own a given resource at any given moment. All other nodes are denied access until they own the resource. This protects the data from being overwritten when two computers have access to the same drives concurrently.

The *quorum drive* is a logical drive designated on the shared disk array for WSFC. This continuously updated drive contains information about the state of the cluster. If this drive becomes corrupt or damaged, the cluster installation also becomes corrupt or damaged.

> **NOTE**
>
> In general (and as part of a high availability disk configuration), the quorum drive should be isolated to a drive all by itself and should be mirrored to guarantee that it is available to the cluster at all times. Without it, the cluster doesn't come up at all, and you cannot access your SQL databases.

The WSFC architecture requires a single quorum resource in the cluster that is used as the tie-breaker to avoid split-brain scenarios. A *split-brain scenario* happens when all the network communication links between two or more cluster nodes fail. In such cases, the cluster may be split into two or more partitions that cannot communicate with each other. WSFC guarantees that even in these cases, a resource is brought online on only one node.

If the different partitions of the cluster each brought a given resource online, this would violate what a cluster guarantees and potentially cause data corruption. When the cluster is partitioned, the quorum resource is used as an arbiter. The partition that owns the quorum resource is allowed to continue. The other partitions of the cluster are said to have "lost quorum," and WSFC and any resources hosted on nodes that are not part of the partition that has quorum are terminated.

The quorum resource is a storage-class resource and, in addition to being the arbiter in a split-brain scenario, is used to store the definitive version of the cluster configuration. To ensure that the cluster always has an up-to-date copy of the latest configuration information, you should deploy the quorum resource on a highly available disk configuration (using mirroring, triple-mirroring, or RAID 10, at the very least).

The notion of quorum as a single shared disk resource means that the storage subsystem has to interact with the cluster infrastructure to provide the illusion of a single storage device with very strict semantics. Although the quorum disk itself can be made highly available via RAID or mirroring, the controller port may be a single point of failure. In addition, if an application inadvertently corrupts the quorum disk or an operator takes down the quorum disk, the cluster becomes unavailable.

This situation can be resolved by using a majority node set option as a single quorum resource from a WSFC perspective. In this set, the cluster log and configuration information are stored on multiple disks across the cluster. A new majority node set resource ensures that the cluster configuration data stored on the majority node set is kept consistent across the different disks.

The disks that make up the majority node set could, in principle, be local disks physically attached to the nodes themselves or disks on a shared storage fabric (that is, a collection of centralized shared storage area network [SAN] devices connected over a switched-fabric or Fibre Channel–arbitrated loop SAN). In the majority node set implementation that is provided as part of WSFC in Windows Server 2008 and later, every node in the cluster uses a directory on its own local system disk to store the quorum data, as shown in Figure 4.3.

Node Majority - Quorum option

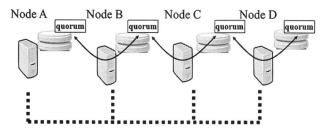

FIGURE 4.3   A node majority.

If the configuration of the cluster changes, the change is reflected across the different disks. The change is considered to have been committed (that is, made persistent) only if the change is made to a majority of the nodes (that is, [Number of nodes configured in the cluster]/2) + 1). In this way, a majority of the nodes have an up-to-date copy of the quorum data. WSFC itself starts up only if a majority of the nodes currently configured as part of the cluster are up and running.

If there are fewer nodes, the cluster is said not to have quorum, and therefore WSFC waits (trying to restart) until more nodes try to join. Only when a majority (or quorum) of nodes are available does WSFC start up and bring the resources online. This way, because the up-to-date configuration is written to a majority of the nodes, regardless of node failures, the cluster always guarantees that it starts up with the most up-to-date configuration.

With Windows 2008 and later, a few more quorum drive configurations are possible that address various voting strategies and also support geographically separated cluster nodes, as follows:

▶ **Node Majority**—With this configuration, more than one-half of the voting nodes in the cluster must vote affirmatively for the cluster to be healthy.

▶ **Node and File Share Majority**—This configuration is like Node Majority, but a remote file share is also configured as a voting witness, and connectivity from any node to that share is also counted as an affirmative vote. More than one-half of the possible votes must be affirmative for the cluster to be healthy.

▶ **Node and Disk Majority**—This configuration is like Node Majority quorum mode, except that a shared disk cluster resource is also designated as a voting witness, and connectivity from any node to that shared disk is also counted as an affirmative vote.

▶ **Disk Only**—With this configuration, a shared disk cluster resource is designated as a witness, and connectivity by any node to that shared disk is counted as an affirmative vote.

Extending WSFC with NLB

You can use a critical technology called network load balancing (NLB) to ensure that a server is always available to handle requests. NLB works by spreading incoming client requests among a number of servers linked together to support a particular application. A typical example is to use NLB to process incoming visitors to your website. As more visitors come to your site, you can incrementally increase capacity by adding servers. This type of expansion is often referred to as *software scaling*, or *scaling out*. Figure 4.4 illustrates this extended clustering architecture with NLB.

WSFC with Network Load Balancing

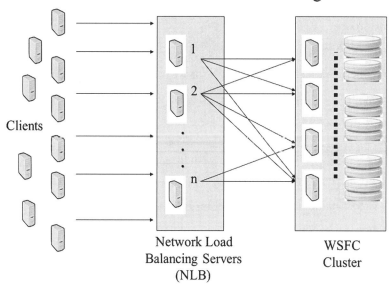

FIGURE 4.4   An NLB configuration.

By using WSFC and NLB clustering technologies together, you can create an *n*-tier infrastructure. For instance, you can create an *n*-tiered e-commerce application by deploying NLB across a front-end web server farm and use WSFC clustering on the back end for your line-of-business applications, such as clustering your SQL Server databases. This approach gives you the benefits of near-linear scalability without server- or application-based single points of failure. This, combined with industry-standard best practices for designing high availability networking infrastructures, can ensure that your Windows-based, Internet-enabled business will be online all the time and can quickly scale to meet demand. Other tiers could be added to the topology, such as an application-center tier that uses component load balancing. This further extends the clustering and scalability reach for candidate applications that can benefit from this type of architecture.

How WSFC Sets the Stage for SQL Server Clustering and AlwaysOn

Good setup practices include documenting all the needed Internet Protocol (IP) addresses, network names, domain definitions, and SQL Server references to set up a two-node SQL Server failover clustering configuration (configured in an active/passive mode) or an AlwaysOn availability groups configuration *before* you physically set up your clustering configuration.

You first identify the servers (nodes), such as PROD-DB01 (the first node) and PROD-DB02 (the second node), and the cluster group name, DXD_Cluster.

The cluster controls the following resources:

▶ Physical disks (`Cluster Disk 1` is for the quorum disk, `Cluster Disk 2` is for the shared disks, and so on)

▶ The cluster IP address (for example, 20.0.0.242)

▶ The cluster name (network name) (for example, `DXD_Cluster`)

▶ The DTC (optional)

▶ The domain name (for example, `DXD.local`)

You need the following for SQL clustering documentation:

▶ The SQL Server virtual IP address (for example, 192.168.1.211)

▶ The SQL Server virtual name (network name) (for example, `VSQL16DXD`)

▶ SQL Server instance (for example, `SQL16DXD_DB01`)

▶ SQL Server agents

▶ SQL Server SSIS services (if needed)

▶ The SQL Server full-text search service instances (if needed)

You need the following for AlwaysOn availability groups documentation:

▶ The availability group listener IP address (for example, 20.00.243)

▶ The availability group listener name (for example, `DXD_LISTENER`)

▶ The availability group name (for example, `DXD_AG`)

▶ SQL server instances (for example, `SQL16DXD_DB01`, `SQL16DXD_DB02`, `SQL16DXD_DR01`)

▶ SQL server agents

▶ SQL Server SSIS services (if needed)

▶ The SQL Server full-text search service instances (if needed)

After you have successfully installed, configured, and tested your failover cluster (in WSFC), you can add the SQL Server components as resources that will be managed by WSFC. You will learn about the installation of SQL clustering and AlwaysOn availability groups in Chapter 5, "SQL Server Clustering," and Chapter 6, "SQL Server AlwaysOn Availability Groups."

Installing Failover Clustering

On your Windows 2012 or later R2 server, you need to fire up Windows Server Manager and install the failover clustering feature on the local instances to be used. Follow these steps:

1. In the Windows Server Manager, select Add Roles and Features from the Tasks drop-down in the lower-right corner (see Figure 4.5).

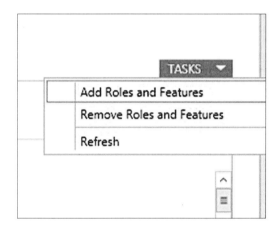

FIGURE 4.5   Using Windows 2012 R2 Server Manager to add failover clustering to a local server.

2. In the next dialog box in the Add Roles and Features Wizard, select either a role-based or feature-based installation. You don't need remote installation. When you're done making selections (typically feature-based), click Next.

3. Choose the correct target (destination) server and then click Next.

4. In the dialog that appears, scroll down until you find the Failover Clustering option and check it, as shown in Figure 4.6.

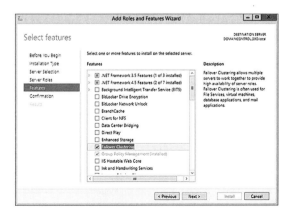

FIGURE 4.6   Using Windows 2012 R2 Server Manager to select Failover Clustering.

Figure 4.7 shows the final installation confirmation dialog box that appears before the feature is enabled. Once it is installed, you need to do the same thing on the other nodes (servers) that will be part of the cluster. When you have completed this, you can fire up the Failover Cluster Manager and start configuring clustering with these two nodes.

FIGURE 4.7   Failover Clustering feature installation confirmation dialog.

With the Failover Clustering feature installed on your server, you are ready to use the Validate a Configuration Wizard (see Figure 4.8) to specify all the nodes that will be a part of the two-node cluster and check whether it is viable to use.

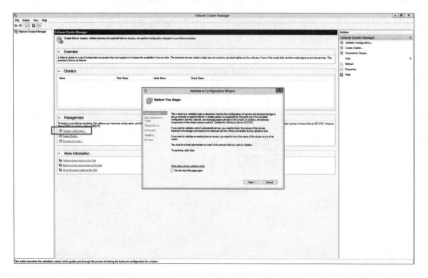

FIGURE 4.8   Failover Cluster Manager Validate a Configuration Wizard.

The cluster must pass all validations. When the validation is complete, you can create the cluster, name it, and bring all nodes and resources online to the cluster. Follow these steps:

1. On the first dialog in the wizard, specify the servers to use in the cluster. To do so, click the Browse button to the right of the Enter Name box and specify the two server nodes you want: PROD-DB01 and PROD-DB02 (see Figure 4.9). Then click OK.

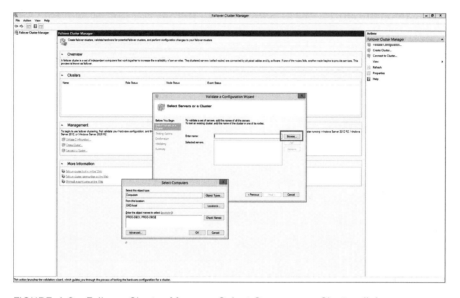

FIGURE 4.9   Failover Cluster Manager Select Servers or a Cluster dialog.

2. In the dialog that appears, specify to run all validation tests to guarantee that you don't miss any issues in this critical validation process. Figure 4.10 shows the successful completion of the failover clustering validation for the two-node configuration. Everything is labeled "Validated."

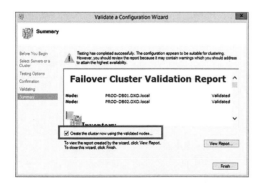

FIGURE 4.10   Failover Cluster Manager failover cluster validation summary.

3. As shown in Figure 4.10, check the Create the Cluster Now Using the Validated Nodes box and click Finish. The Create Cluster Wizard (yes, another wizard!) now appears. This wizard will gather the access point for administering the cluster, confirm the components of the cluster, and create the cluster with the name you specify.

4. As shown in Figure 4.11, enter DXD_CLUSTER as the cluster name. A default IP address is assigned to this cluster, but you can change it later to the IP address that you prefer to use. Remember that this wizard knows about the two nodes you just validated, and it automatically includes them in this cluster. As you can see in Figure 4.12, both nodes are included in the cluster.

FIGURE 4.11   Creating the cluster name in the Create Cluster Wizard.

5. Ask that all eligible disk storage be added by checking the Add All Eligible Storage to the Cluster box.

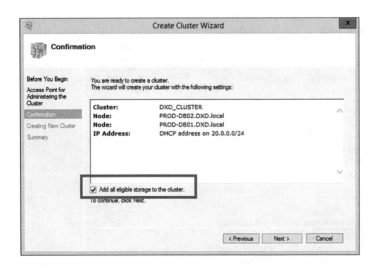

FIGURE 4.12   Creating a cluster with validated nodes and the eligible disk option checked.

6. In the summary dialog that appears, review what will be done, including what eligible storage will be included. Go ahead and click Finish. Figure 4.13 shows a completed cluster configuration for the two-node cluster, including the cluster network, cluster storage, and the two nodes (PROD-DB01 and PROD-DB02).

FIGURE 4.13   The new DXD_CLUSTER cluster.

Figure 4.14 shows you the node view of the cluster. As you can see, both nodes are up and running. Figure 4.14 also shows the disks that are in this cluster. One disk is used as the quorum drive (for cluster decisions), and the other is the main available storage drive that will be used for databases and such. Don't forget to specify (via the properties of the clustered disks) both nodes as possible owners for the disks. This is essential because the disks are shared between these two nodes.

You now have a fully functional failover cluster with a shared disk ready to be used for things like SQL Server clustering. A good setup practices is to documents all the needed IP addresses, network names, domain definitions, and SQL Server references to set up a two-node SQL Server failover cluster.

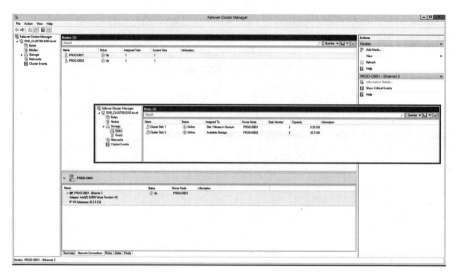

FIGURE 4.14   Failover Cluster Manager view of both nodes and the disks in the cluster.

A SQL Clustering Configuration

Installing SQL clustering on Windows continues to get easier and easier. Most of it can be done from one node now. Figure 4.15 shows a two-node cluster configuration like the one described in Figure 4.1 but now with all the SQL Server and WSFC components identified. This virtual SQL Server is the only thing the end user will ever see. As you can also see in Figure 4.15, the virtual server name is VSQL16DXD, and the SQL Server instance name is SQL16DXD_DB01. This figure also shows the other cluster group resources that will be part of the SQL Server clustering configuration: DTC (now optional), SQL Agent, SQL Server Full-Text Search, and the shared disk where the databases and the quorum will live.

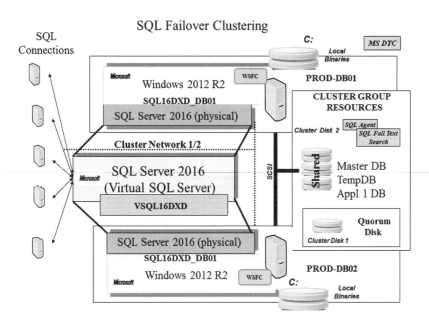

FIGURE 4.15   A basic two-node SQL Server failover clustering configuration.

SQL Server Agent is installed as part of the SQL Server installation process, and it is associated with the SQL Server instance for which it is installed. The same is true for SQL Server Full-Text Search; it is associated with the particular SQL Server instance that it is installed to work with. The SQL Server installation process completely installs all software on all nodes you designate (see Chapter 5).

An AlwaysOn Availability Group Configuration

Creating an AlwaysOn availability group configuration is very different from creating a SQL clustering configuration, but it still starts from the failover clustering foundation. However, there is typically no shared storage, and separate SQL Server instances are installed on each node. Figure 4.16 shows a configuration that includes a primary SQL Server (on the first node), a secondary replica SQL Server for failover (on the second node), and another secondary replica SQL Server (on a third node) that will be a disaster recovery node. The primary and secondary replicas are referenced by way of the availability group, thus insulating the end user from the physical SQL Server instance name (see Chapter 6).

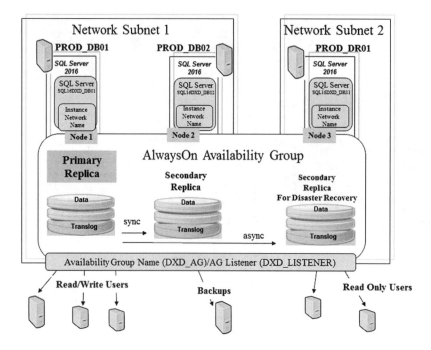

FIGURE 4.16   An AlwaysOn availability group SQL Server configuration.

Configuring SQL Server Database Disks

Before you go too much further, we need to talk about how you should lay out a SQL Server implementation on the shared disks managed by the failover cluster. The overall usage intent of a particular SQL Server instance dictates how you might choose to configure your shared disk and how it might be best configured for scalability and availability.

In general, RAID 0 is great for storage that doesn't need fault tolerance; RAID 1 or RAID 10 is great for storage that needs fault tolerance but doesn't have to sacrifice too much performance (as with most online transaction processing [OLTP] systems); and RAID 5 is great for storage that needs fault tolerance but where data doesn't change much (that is, low data volatility, as in many decision support systems [DSSs]/read-only systems).

There is a time and place to use each of the different fault-tolerant disk configurations. Table 4.1 provides recommendations to follow in deciding which SQL Server database file types should be placed on which RAID level disk configurations. (These recommendations apply whether the RAID disk array is part of a SQL Server cluster or not.) If you are using NAS or SAN, you will have different levels of resilience automatically built into those devices. Still, separation to separate LUNs is advised so you can better manage things at the channel levels.

TABLE 4.1   SQL Server Clustering Disk Fault-Tolerance Recommendations

Device	Description	Fault Tolerance
Quorum drive	The quorum drive used with WSFC should be isolated to a drive by itself (often mirrored as well, for maximum availability).	RAID 1 or RAID 10
OLTP SQL Server database files	For OLTP systems, the database data/index files should be placed on a RAID 10 disk system.	RAID 10
DSS SQL Server database files	For DSSs that are primarily read-only, the database data/index files should be placed on a RAID 5 disk system.	RAID 5
tempdb	This is a highly volatile form of disk I/O (when not able to do all its work in the cache).	RAID 10
SQL Server transaction log files	The SQL Server transaction log files should be on their own mirrored volume for both performance and database protection. (For DSSs, this could be RAID 5 also.)	RAID 10 or RAID 1

Summary

Failover clustering is the cornerstone of both SQL Server clustering and the AlwaysOn availability groups high availability configurations. As described in this chapter, there can be shared resources such as storage, nodes, even SQL Servers. These are cluster-aware resources that inherit the overall quality of being able to be managed within a cluster as if they were one working unit. If any of the core resources (such as a node) ever fails, the cluster is able to fail over to the other node, thus achieving high availability at the server (node) level. In Chapter 5, you will see how SQL Server failover clustering allows you to get SQL Server instance-level failover with shared storage. Then, in Chapter 6, you will see how AlwaysOn availability groups can give you SQL Server instance and database high availability through redundancy of both the SQL Server and the databases.

CHAPTER 5

SQL Server Clustering

As described in Chapter 4, "Failover Clustering," WSFC is capable of detecting hardware or software failures and automatically shifting control of a failed server (node) to a healthy node. SQL Server clustering implements SQL Server instance-level resilience built on top of this core foundational clustering feature.

As mentioned previously, SQL Server is a fully cluster-aware application. The failover cluster shares a common set of cluster resources, such as clustered (shared) disk drives, networks, and, yes, SQL Server itself.

SQL Server allows you to fail over and fail back to or from another node in a cluster. In an active/passive configuration, an instance of SQL Server actively services database requests from one of the nodes in a SQL cluster (active node). Another node is idle until, for whatever reason, a failover occurs. With a failover situation, the secondary node (the passive node) takes over all SQL resources (databases) without the end user ever knowing that a failover has occurred. The end user might experience some type of brief transactional interruption because SQL clustering cannot take over in-flight transactions. However, the end user is still just connected to a single (virtual) SQL Server and truly doesn't know which node is fulfilling requests. This type of application transparency is a highly desirable feature that has made SQL clustering fairly popular over the past 15 years.

In an active/active configuration, SQL Server runs multiple servers simultaneously with different databases, allowing organizations with more constrained hardware requirements (that is, no designated secondary systems) to enable failover to or from any node without having to set aside (idle) hardware. There can also be multisite SQL clustering across data centers (sites), further enhancing the high availability options that SQL Server clustering can fulfill.

Installing SQL Server Clustering Within WSFC

For SQL Server clustering, you must install a new SQL Server instance within a minimum two-node cluster. You should not move a SQL Server instance from an unclustered configuration to a clustered configuration. If you already have SQL Server installed in an unclustered environment, you need to make all the necessary backups (or detach databases) first and then uninstall the unclustered SQL Server instance. Some upgrade paths and migration paths are possible from prior versions of SQL Server and Windows Server. You must also specify the same product key on all the nodes that you are preparing for the same failover cluster. You also should make sure to use the same SQL Server instance ID for all the nodes that are prepared for the failover cluster.

With all WSFC resources running and in the online state, you run the SQL Server 2014 Setup program from the node that is online (for example, PROD-DB01). You are asked to install all software components required prior to installing SQL Server (.NET Framework 3.5 or 4.0, Microsoft SQL Native Client, and the Microsoft SQL Server 2016 Setup support files). Make sure that you have the proper permissions to do a SQL Server install!

It has gotten easier and easier to install and configure SQL Server clustering in each SQL Server version.

SQL Server failover cluster installation consists of the following steps:

1. **Install a new SQL Server failover cluster**—Create and configure an initial SQL Server failover cluster instance to be used in the SQL Server failover cluster.

2. **Add a node to a SQL Server failover cluster**—Add additional node to the SQL Server failover cluster and complete the high availability configuration.

Almost all of this multinode SQL installation and configuration can now be done from the primary (active) node. Figure 5.1 shows the two-node SQL Server clustering configuration that you will set up in this chapter.

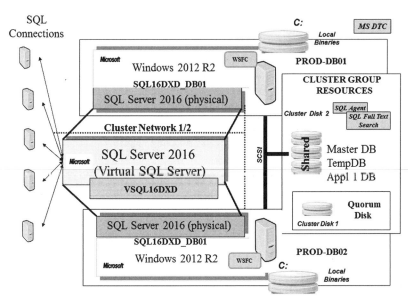

FIGURE 5.1   A two-node SQL Server failover clustering configuration in an active/passive mode.

You begin by selecting New SQL Server Failover Cluster Installation from the SQL Server Installation Center Installation for the PROD-DB01 node (see Figure 5.2).

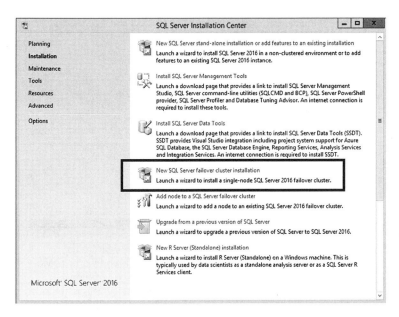

FIGURE 5.2   Launching the Install a SQL Server Failover Cluster Wizard from the Installation Center.

The Install a SQL Server Failover Cluster Wizard opens, starting with a rule check of the node in the cluster (PROD-DB01).

Figure 5.3 shows the Install Failover Cluster Rules dialog and the results of a successful initial failover cluster rules check for the PROD-DB01 node. Because WSFC is already set up, this wizard also checks on the other available node, PROD-DB02, for many of the same minimum installation requirements (DTC, DNS settings, Cluster Remote Access, so on).

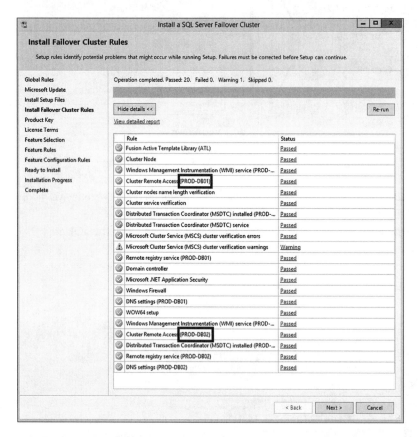

FIGURE 5.3   SQL failover cluster rules verifications for nodes.

> **NOTE**
>
> SQL Server failover clustering is available with SQL Server 2016 Standard Edition, Enterprise Edition, and Developer Edition. However, Standard Edition supports only a two-node cluster. If you want to configure a cluster with more than two nodes, you need to upgrade to SQL Server 2016 Enterprise Edition, which has no limitations on the number of clusters.

If this check fails, you must resolve the warnings before you continue. After product key and licensing terms dialogs are completed, the install setup files are loaded.

You are then prompted to proceed to the SQL Server feature installation portion of the setup in the Feature Selection dialog, shown in Figure 5.4. Next, a set of feature rules validation checks must be passed for things like cluster supported for this edition and product update language compatibility.

FIGURE 5.4 The Feature Selection dialog for a SQL Server failover cluster installation.

Next, you need to specify of the SQL Server network name (the name of the new SQL Server failover cluster, which is essentially the virtual SQL Server name). You also need to specify a named instance for the physical SQL Server itself (SQL16DXD_DB01 in this example) on the PROD-DB01 node (as shown in Figure 5.5).

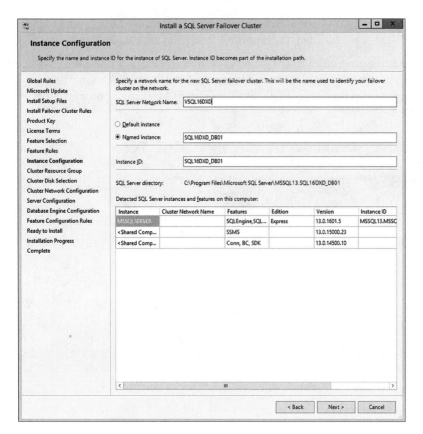

FIGURE 5.5   Specifying the SQL Server network name (VSQL16DXD) and instance name
(SQL16DXD_DB01).

When an application attempts to connect to an instance of SQL Server 2016 that is running on a failover cluster, the application must specify both the virtual server name and
the instance name (if an instance name was used), such as VSQL16DXD\SQL16DXD_DB01 (virtual server name\SQL Server instance name other than the default) or VSQL16DXD (just the
virtual SQL Server name, without the default SQL Server instance name). The virtual server
name must be unique on the network.

Next comes the cluster resource group specification for your SQL cluster, followed by
the selection of the disks to be clustered. This is where the SQL Server resources are
placed within WSFC. For this example, you can use the SQL Server resource group name
(SQL16DXD_DB01) and click Next (see Figure 5.6). After you assign the resource group, you
need to identify which clustered disks are to be used on the Cluster Disk Selection dialog,
also shown in Figure 5.6. It contains a Cluster Disk 2 disk option (which was the shared
drive volume) and a Cluster Disk 1 disk option (which was the quorum drive location).
You simply select the available drive(s) where you want to put your SQL database files (the
Cluster Disk 2 disk drive option in this example). As you can also see, the only "qualified"
disk is the Cluster Disk 2 drive. If the quorum resource is in the cluster group you have

selected, a warning message is issued, informing you of this fact. A general rule of thumb is to isolate the quorum resource to a separate cluster group.

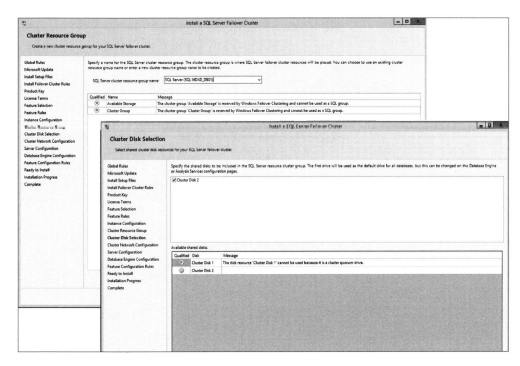

FIGURE 5.6   Cluster resource group specification and cluster disk selection.

The next thing you need to do for this new virtual server specification is to identify an IP address and which network it should use. As you can see in the Cluster Network Configuration dialog, shown in Figure 5.7, you simply type in the IP address (in this example, 20.0.0.222) that is to be the IP address for this virtual SQL Server for the available networks known to this cluster configuration (in this example, for the Cluster Network 1 network). If the IP address being specified is already in use, an error occurs.

> **NOTE**
>
> Keep in mind that you are using a separate IP address for the virtual SQL Server failover cluster that is completely different from the cluster IP addresses themselves. In an unclustered installation of SQL Server, the server can be referenced using the machine's IP address. In a clustered configuration, you do not use the IP addresses of the physical servers; instead, you use this separately assigned IP address for the "virtual" SQL Server.

You then need to specify the server configuration service accounts for the SQL Server Agent, Database Engine, so on. These should be the same for both nodes you will be including in the SQL Server cluster configuration (as you can see in Figure 5.8, SQL Server Agent account name and SQL Server Database Engine account name).

FIGURE 5.7   Specifying the virtual SQL Server IP address and which network to use.

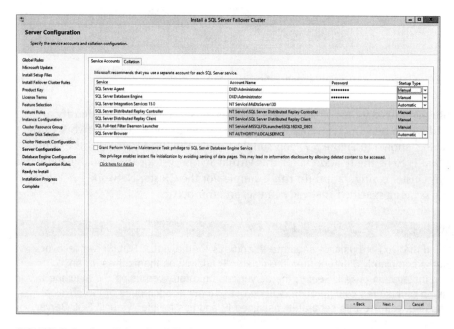

FIGURE 5.8   Specifying the SQL Server service accounts and passwords for the SQL Server failover cluster.

You then see the Database Engine Configuration dialog with all the standard things you usually must specify: authentication mode, data directories, TempDB, and filestream options. At this point, you have worked your way down to the feature configuration rules check to determine whether everything specified to this point is correct. The next dialog shows a summary of what is about to be done in this installation and the location of the configuration file (and path) that can be used later if you are doing command-line installations of new nodes in the cluster (see Figure 5.9).

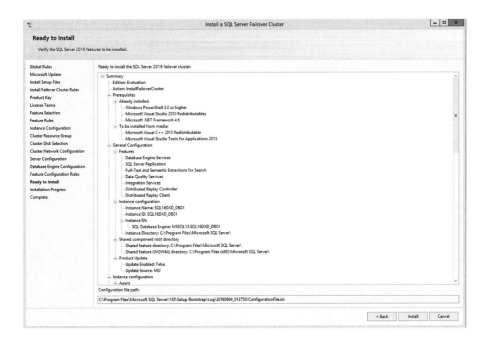

FIGURE 5.9   Ready to install the SQL Server failover cluster.

Figure 5.10 shows the complete SQL server installation for this node.

Before moving on to the next part of the SQL Server failover cluster node installation, you can take a quick peek at what the Failover Cluster Manager has set up so far by opening the Roles node in the failover cluster. Figure 5.11 shows the SQL Server instance up and running within the failover cluster, the server name (VSQL16DXD), and the other clustered resources, including the SQL Server instance and the SQL Server Agent for that instance. All are online and being managed by the failover cluster now. However, there is no second node yet. If this SQL Server instance failed right now, it would not have anything to fail over to.

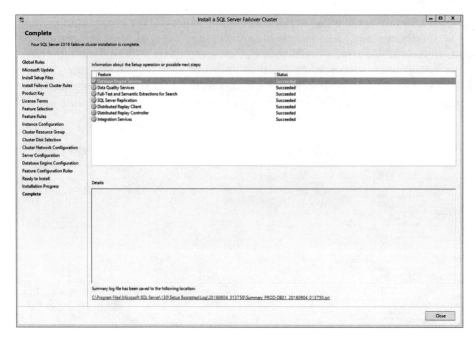

FIGURE 5.10   The SQL Server 2016 failover cluster preparation and install is complete for this node.

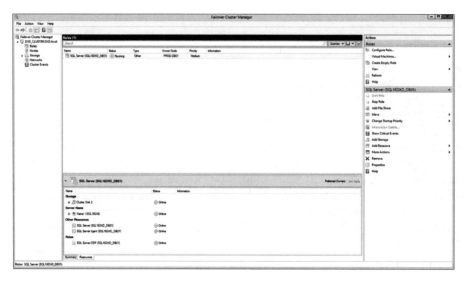

FIGURE 5.11   The Failover Cluster Manager, showing the newly created SQL Server instance and other clustered resources.

Now you must take care of the second node that is to be in the SQL Server cluster (PROD-DB02 in this example). You can add as many nodes to a SQL Server cluster configuration as needed, but here you'll stick to two for the active/passive configuration. For the second node, you must select Add Node to a SQL Server Failover Cluster, as shown in Figure 5.12.

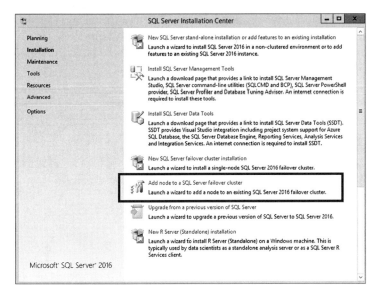

FIGURE 5.12   The Add Node to a SQL Server Failover Cluster option in SQL Server Installation Center.

The Add a Failover Cluster Node Wizard first does a brief global rules check and looks for any critical Microsoft Windows updates and SQL Server product updates the installation may need. It is always a good idea to install the most up-to-date code possible. In Figure 5.13, you can see that a critical update for SQL Server has been identified.

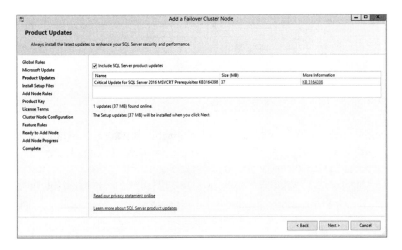

FIGURE 5.13   Microsoft Windows and SQL Server Product Updates dialog.

All product updates and setup files are added for the installation. The next step in the wizard is the Add Node Rules dialog, which runs some preliminary rules checking, captures the product key and license terms, deals with the cluster node configuration, handles the setup of the service accounts, and then adds the new node to the cluster. This is sort of the same steps you did for the original node, but from the second node's perspective (as you can see in Figure 5.14). This includes verification of all the failover cluster services on that second node, DTC verification, cluster remote access (for PROD-DB02) and DNS settings (for both PROD-DB01 and PROD-DB02).

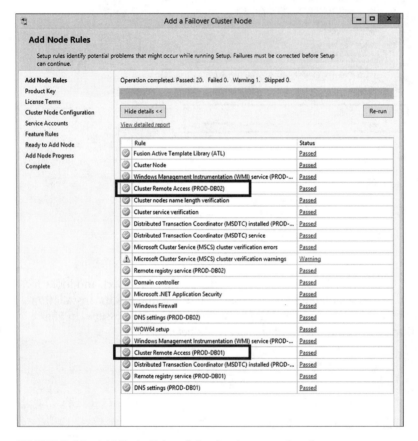

FIGURE 5.14   Add Node Rules dialog for the second node.

Next comes the cluster node configuration, where you identify the SQL Server instance name, verify the name of the node (PROD-DB02 in this example), and verify the cluster network name being used for this cluster node configuration. Figure 5.15 shows this node configuration and that the SQL Server instance (SQL16DXD_DB01) is also already configured with the PROD-DB01 node.

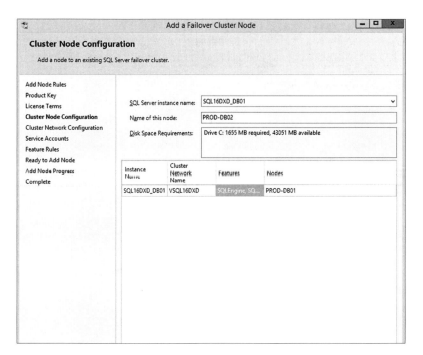

FIGURE 5.15   Cluster Node Configuration dialog for the second node (PROD-DB02).

The cluster network configuration is then identified (verified) next. The current node being added is already associated with the cluster, so you don't have to modify or add an IP address here (unless you are doing multisite configurations). Next comes the specification of the service accounts that are needed by this node for SQL Server. Both the network and the service accounts specifications are shown in Figure 5.16.

Now you have completed the second node's configuration, and you can simply review what is about to be done by the setup process and complete the installation. When it is complete, you may have to restart the server. When all node installations are complete, you should have a fully operational SQL Server clustering configuration.

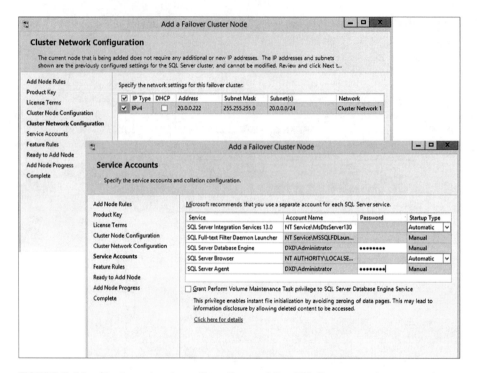

FIGURE 5.16   Cluster network configuration and the SQL Server service accounts.

You should do a quick check to make sure you can get to the database via the virtual SQL Server network cluster name and the old reliable AdventureWorks database that is attached to this SQL Server cluster configuration. You can also test that the nodes fail over properly and allow you to get to your data, regardless of which node is active. You can do this test with a brute-force approach. First, connect to the virtual SQL Server cluster name (VSQL16DXD\SQL16DXD_DB in this example), do a quick SELECT against the Person table, shut down the PROD-DB01 server, and then try to execute the same SELECT against the Person table. When you do this, you get an error saying that the SQL Server cluster name is not connected. After about 4 or 5 seconds, you can issue the same SELECT statement again, and you get success—the result rows from the Person table. This test sequence is shown in Figure 5.17. The left side of the figure shows the connection to the virtual SQL Server cluster name, and just to the right is the failed connection after you have shut down the PROD-DB01 node. Then at the bottom right is the successful SELECT against the Person table, with the expected result rows.

NOTE

Alternatively, you could also do the same SQL Server clustering configuration setup by using the SQL Server setup Advanced option. Either setup process works.

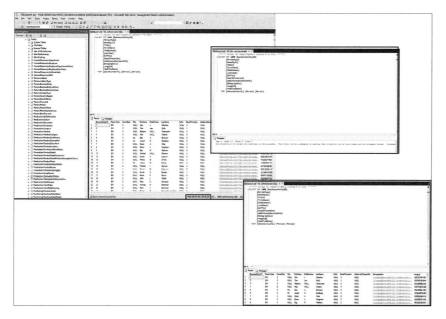

FIGURE 5.17   SQL Server cluster failover test sequence.

Congratulations! You are in high availability mode at the SQL Server instance level!

Potential Problems to Watch Out for with SQL Server Failover Clustering

Many potential problems can arise during setup and configuration of SQL Server clustering. Consider the following:

▶ SQL Server service accounts and passwords should be kept the same on all nodes, or a node will not be able to restart a SQL Server service. You can use `administrator` or a designated account (for example, `Cluster` or `ClusterAdmin`) that has administrator rights within the domain and on each server.

▶ Drive letters for the cluster disks must be the same on all nodes (servers). Otherwise, you might not be able to access a clustered disk.

▶ You might have to create an alternative method to connect to SQL Server if the network name is offline and you cannot connect using TCP/IP. You can use named pipes, specified as `\\.\pipe\$$\SQLA\sql\query`.

▶ When installing SQL failover clustering, you may run into issues related to domain entries needing to be added. If you don't have the correct permissions for this domain entry, the whole process fails. You might have to get your system admin folks involved to correct this issue.

Multisite SQL Server Failover Clustering

Many businesses operate their data centers out of multiple locations or have secondary data centers to provide redundancy, across sites, as a disaster recovery mechanism. A primary reason for doing this is protection from site failure in the event of network, power, infrastructure, or other site disasters. Many solutions have implemented Windows Server and SQL Server failover clustering with this multisite model. A multisite failover cluster includes nodes that are dispersed across multiple physical sites or data centers, with the aim of providing availability across data centers in the case of a disaster at a site. Sometimes multisite failover clusters are referred to as *geographically dispersed failover clusters*, *stretch clusters*, or *multi-subnet clusters*. As you can see in Figure 5.18, a multisite SQL clustering configuration also relies on storage-level replication (typically available via block- or bit-level replication capabilities from SAN or NAS vendors).

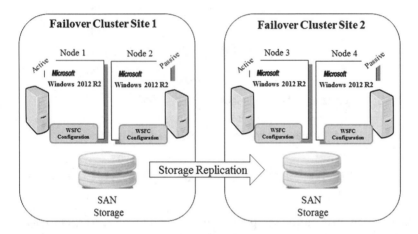

FIGURE 5.18   Multisite SQL clustering configuration from one data center to another.

Scenario 1: Application Service Provider with SQL Server Clustering

Recall from Chapter 3, "Choosing High Availability," that the application service provider (ASP) business scenario (Scenario 1) yielded a high availability selection of hardware redundancy, shared disk RAID arrays, WSFC, and SQL Server clustering. Having these four options together clearly met all the requirements of uptime, tolerance, performance, and costs. The ASP's service level agreement with its customers also allows for brief amounts of downtime to deal with OS upgrades or fixes, hardware upgrades, and application upgrades. The ASP's budget was large enough for extra hardware redundancy to be utilized.

The ASP planned and implemented three separate clusters in order to support its eight major customer applications that are using SQL Server. Each SQL Server cluster was a two-node cluster configured in the active/passive mode. The ASP's customers wanted to make sure that if a failure of a node ever occurred, performance would not be affected. One way to guarantee this is to use the active/passive mode. In other words, an idle node just sits there, waiting to take over in case of failure. When the passive node takes over process-ing, it should be operating at full capacity almost immediately. As illustrated in Figure 5.19, each two-node SQL cluster can support between one and three separate customer applications. The ASP established a guideline of never exceeding three applications per SQL cluster to help mitigate risk overall; all of the ASP's customers agreed to this approach of minimizing risk. The primary customer application shown in Figure 5.19 is an online (Internet) health products order entry (HOE) and distribution system. The HOE database is the main order entry database, with between 50 and 150 concurrent SQL connections. When this ASP someday reaches its tenth major customer application, it will simply create a new two-node cluster. This is proving to be a very scalable, high-performance, risk-miti-gating, and cost-effective architecture for the ASP.

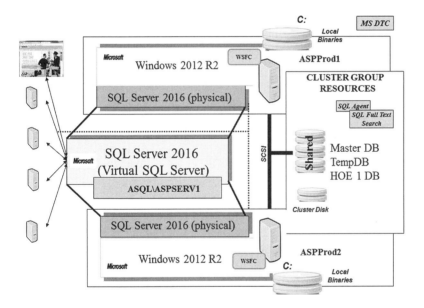

FIGURE 5.19   An ASP's use of SQL Server clustering for HA.

In this case, ROI can be calculated by adding up the incremental costs (or estimates) of the new HA solution and comparing them against the complete cost of downtime for a period of time (1 year in this example).

Previously the total incremental costs were estimated to be in the range **$100k to $250k**, which included the following estimates:

▶ Five new four-way servers (with 64GB RAM, local SCSI disk system RAID 10, two Ethernet NICs, additional SCSI controllers [for shared disk]) at $30k per server

▶ Five Microsoft Windows 2000 Advanced Server licenses ≈ $3k per server (Windows 2003 Enterprise Edition, $4k per server)

▶ Eighteen SCSI disk systems with RAID 10 (minimum of 6 drives per SCSI disk system, 4 shared SCSI disk systems per cluster—72 drives total) ≈ $55k

▶ Five days of additional training costs for system admin personnel ≈ $15k

▶ Two new SQL Server licenses (SQL Server 2016, Enterprise Edition) at $5k per server.

The total incremental costs to upgrade to this SQL clustering high availability solution are approximately $245,000 (approximately $81,666 per two-node cluster).

Let's work through the complete ROI calculation with these incremental costs along with the cost of downtime:

1. Maintenance cost (for a 1-year period):

   ▶ **$15k (estimate)**—Yearly system admin personnel cost (additional time for training of these personnel)

   ▶ **$25k (estimate)**—Recurring software licensing cost (of additional HA components: [5] OS + [2] SQL Server 2016)

2. Hardware cost:

   ▶ **$205k hardware cost**—The cost of additional HW in the new HA solution

3. Deployment/assessment cost:

   ▶ **$20k deployment cost**—The cost of development, testing, QA, and production implementation of the solution

   ▶ **$10k HA assessment cost**

4. Downtime cost (for a 1-year period):

   ▶ If you kept track of last year's downtime record, use that number; otherwise, produce an estimate of planned and unplanned downtime for this calculation. For this scenario, the estimated cost of downtime/hour is **$15k/hour** for this ASP.

   ▶ Planned downtime cost (revenue loss cost) = Planned downtime hours × cost of hourly downtime to the company:

      a. 0.25% (estimate of planned downtime percentage in 1 year) × 8,760 hours in a year = 21.9 hours of planned downtime

      b. 21.9 hours (planned downtime) × $15k/hr (hourly cost of downtime) = $328,500/year cost of planned downtime.

   ▶ Unplanned downtime cost (revenue loss cost) = Unplanned downtime hours × cost of hourly downtime to the company:

      a. .25% (estimate of unplanned downtime percentage in 1 year) × 8,760 hours in a year = 21.9 hours of unplanned downtime

    b. 21.9 hours × $15k/hr (hourly cost of downtime) = $328,500/year cost of unplanned downtime.

ROI totals:

▶ Total costs to get on this HA solution = $285,000 (for the year—slightly higher than the stated immediate incremental costs)

▶ Total of downtime cost = $657,000 (for the year)

The incremental cost is 43% of the downtime cost for 1 year. In other words, the investment of the HA solution will pay for itself in 0.43 year, or approximately 5 months! You can see why this ASP didn't blink an eye and got into this HA solution as rapidly as it could.

Summary

Building out your company's infrastructure with clustering technology at the heart is a huge step toward achieving five 9s reliability. If you do this, every application, system component, and database you deploy on this architecture will have that added element of resilience. WSFC and SQL failover clustering are high availability approaches at the instance level. In many cases, the application or system component changes needed to take advantage of these clustering technologies are completely transparent. Utilizing a combination of NLB and WSFC allows you to not only fail over applications but also scale for increasing network capacity. Many organizations around the globe have used this two-node active/passive SQL Server clustering approach over the past 10 or 15 years.

As you will see with the AlwaysOn features in the next chapter, expanding this resilience to the database tier adds even more high availability and scalability to your implementations if a much higher HA requirement is needed.

5

SQL Server AlwaysOn and Availability Groups

Microsoft continues to push the high availability and performance bar higher and higher. Extensive HA options such as AlwaysOn and availability groups and AlwaysOn failover cluster instances (FCIs), coupled with a variety of other Windows Server family enhancements, provide almost everyone with a chance at achieving the mythical five 9s (that is, 99.999% uptime). Microsoft is investing in this HA approach for most of the next-generation SQL Server HA options. However, you might have noticed that some of the concepts and technical approaches in AlwaysOn availability groups are a bit reminiscent of SQL Server clustering and database mirroring—and that's because they are! Both of these other features paved the way for what we now know as AlwaysOn availability groups. It is also important to remember is that this and other HA options build on top of Windows Server Failover Clustering (WSFC).

AlwaysOn and Availability Groups Use Cases

Typical use cases for using AlwaysOn and availability groups include the following:

▶ You need high availability nearing five 9s (99.999% available). This means your database layer must be super resilient to failure and have nearly no data loss in the case of failure.

▶ For disaster recovery (DR) you need to replicate data to another site (perhaps on the other side of the country or planet), but you can tolerate a little bit of data loss (and data latency).

▶ You have a performance need to offload some operational functions, such as database backups, away from your primary database. These backups must be completely accurate and have the highest integrity for recovery purposes.

▶ You have a performance and availability need to offload read-only processing/access away from your primary transactional database, and you can tolerate a bit of latency. Even when the primary is down, you still provide read-only access to your applications.

All these use cases can be addressed by AlwaysOn availability groups features, and it's easier to do than you think. At the end of this chapter, you will see this approach matched up with the HA application scenarios as well as the full cost justification and factors for you to choose this option if your requirements demand this approach.

Windows Server Failover Clustering

As mentioned earlier in this book, WSFC is considered an essential part of the core HA foundation components. However, it is still possible to build an HA system without it (for example, a system that uses numerous redundant hardware components and disk mirroring or RAID for its disk subsystem). But Microsoft has made WSFC the cornerstone of its clustering capabilities, and WSFC is used by applications that are cluster enabled (or cluster aware). A prime example of a cluster-enabled technology is Microsoft SQL Server 2016 itself (and most of its components). Chapter 4, "Failover Clustering," describes the essence of WSFC, and Chapter 5, "SQL Server Clustering," describes the first SQL Server capability delivered using failover clustering: SQL Server clustering. This chapter discusses another SQL Server capability delivered using failover clustering: AlwaysOn availability groups.

AlwaysOn Failover Clustering Instances

Being "always on" is a pretty powerful statement and commitment. It is now possible to mostly achieve this commitment with infrastructure, instance, database, and client-connectivity-level HA. Built on WSFC, the SQL Server AlwaysOn configuration leverages WSFC to provide a dramatic HA solution that can be built using commodity hardware and/or basic IaaS configurations.

Figure 6.1 shows a fairly basic four-node environment (that is, with four servers) across two network subnets. Each subnet represents an isolated set of processing power (racks) within a larger data center or different subnets within an IaaS provider footprint. Each server is configured with WSFC and has a SQL Server instance installed on it for use with the AlwaysOn availability groups configuration.

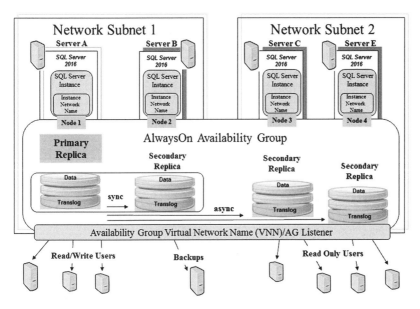

FIGURE 6.1   AlwaysOn availability group four-node configuration.

I explain all the other AlwaysOn availability group configuration options shortly. However, to also emphasize the interoperability of the basic building block of using WSFC, I'd like to draw your attention to Figure 6.2, which shows both a SQL clustering HA instance for Node 1 and an AlwaysOn availability group configuration. This first set of two servers (A and B) form a failover cluster instance node with full SQL Server instance-level resilience. This highly resilient node is also used in an overall availability group configuration to give the primary (the application database that the application uses) the highest level of resilience possible and also to provide additional data resilience to one or more secondary replicas. You don't have to give the primary SQL instance-level availability, but this example shows that you can do more than just simple AlwaysOn configurations. This SQL Server clustered instance shares the database as part of its clustering configuration for the instance. Server A and Server B form the SQL cluster and are configured as an active/passive cluster. The entire SQL cluster is Node 1 in the availability group configuration.

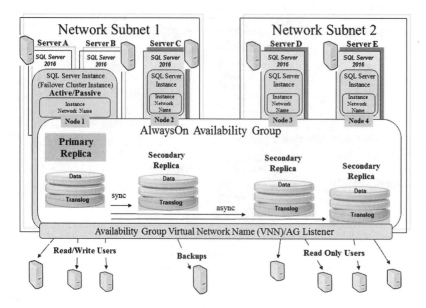

FIGURE 6.2   AlwaysOn availability group components with a SQL clustering primary node configuration.

AlwaysOn and Availability Groups

Remember that availability groups are focused on database-level failover and availability, utilizing a data redundancy approach. Again, borrowing from the database mirroring experience (and underlying technologies), a transactionally consistent secondary replica is made that can be used for both read-only access (active for use at all times) and for failover if the primary database (primary replica) fails for any reason. Looking again at Figure 6.1, you can see a SQL Server AlwaysOn availability group being used for HA and also for distributing the read-only workload off the primary SQL Server instance to the secondary replica. You can have up to eight secondary replicas in an availability group, with the first secondary replica being used for automatic failover (using the synchronous-commit mode) and other secondary replicas available for workload distribution and manual failover use. Remember that this is storing data redundantly, and you can burn up a lot of disk storage fast. When in synchronous-commit mode, that secondary replica can also be used to make database backups because it is completely consistent with the primary replica. Outstanding!

Modes

As with database mirroring, two primary replication modes are used to move data via the transaction log from the primary replica to the secondary replicas: synchronous mode and asynchronous mode.

Synchronous mode means that the data writes of any database change must be done in not only the primary replica but also the secondary replica, as a part of one logical committed transaction.

Figure 6.1 shows a rounded box around both the primary and secondary database that is using the synchronous mode of replication. This can be costly in the sense of doubling the writes, so the connection between the primary and secondary should be fast and nearby (within the same subnet). However, for this same reason, the primary and secondary replicas are in a transactionally consistent state at all times, which makes failover nearly instantaneous. Synchronous mode is used for automatic failover between the primary replica and the secondary replica. You can have up to three nodes in synchronous mode (essentially two secondaries and one primary at once). Figure 6.1 shows that Node 1 and Node 2 are configured to use automatic failover mode (synchronous). And, as previously mentioned, because of this transactional consistency, it is also possible to do database backups against the secondary replica with 100% accuracy and integrity.

Asynchronous mode does not have the commit transaction requirement that synchronous mode has, and it is actually pretty lightweight (from performance and overhead points of view). Even in asynchronous mode, transactions can make it to the secondary replicas pretty quickly (in a few seconds) in most cases. Network traffic and the number of transactions determine the speed. Asynchronous mode can also be used just about anywhere you need it within a stable network (across the country or even to another continent, if you have decent network speeds).

The AlwaysOn availability groups feature also takes advantage of transaction record compression, which compresses all the transaction log records used in database mirroring and AlwaysOn configurations to increase the speed of transmission to the mirror or replicas. This both increases the number of log transactions you can shoot across to the secondary and also makes the size of the transmissions much smaller, so the log records get to their destinations that much faster.

In addition, as with database mirroring, during data replication of the transaction, if data page errors are detected, the data pages on the secondary replica are repaired as part of the transaction writes to the replica and raise the overall database stability even further (if you had not been replicating). This is a nice feature.

Read-Only Replicas
As you can see in Figure 6.1, you can create more secondary replicas (up to eight). However, they must be asynchronous replicas. You can easily add these replicas to the availability group and provide distribution of workload and significant mitigation to your performance. Figures 6.1 and 6.2 show two additional secondary replicas used to handle all the read-only data accesses that would normally be hitting the primary database. These read-only replicas have near-real-time data and can be pretty much anywhere you want (from a stable network point of view).

For Disaster Recovery

Figure 6.3 shows a typical AlwaysOn availability groups configuration for DR. It has a primary replica in Data Center 1, and its secondary replica is in Data Center 2. You would use asynchronous mode here because of the distance and network speeds.

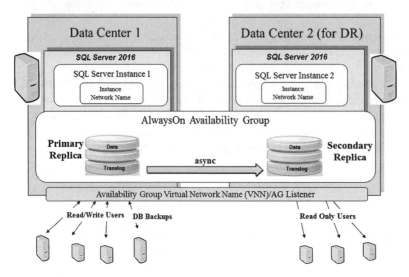

FIGURE 6.3   An AlwaysOn availability group configuration for disaster recovery.

This means that the secondary replica at the DR site is only as good as the most recent transaction that was written asynchronously. Some data loss may happen in this mode, but this easily meets the DR requirements and service levels needed. As a bonus, the DR site (secondary replica) can also be used for read-only data access, as shown in Figure 6.3. You essentially leverage a copy of the primary database that would normally not have been considered available if other DR technologies were used. Most database mirroring or other vendor solutions are in continuous update mode and do not support read-only modes at all.

Availability Group Listeners

If you look back at Figure 6.1, you can see that the virtual network names (VNNs) that are created for the WSFCs are used when an availability group is created. In particular, an availability group must know the VNNs (that reference the individual instances) of all nodes in the availability group. These can be used directly to reference the primary or the secondary replicas. But for more stability (and consistency), you can create an availability group listener as part of the availability group that abstracts these VNNs away from the application that must use the databases. This way, the application sees only one connection name at all times, and the underlying failover state is completely insulated from the application, yielding even higher consistency and availability from an application point of view.

Endpoints

Availability groups also leverage the endpoint concept for all communication (and visibility) from one node to another node in an availability group configuration. These endpoints are the exposed points used by the availability group communication between nodes. This is also the case with database mirroring. Availability group endpoints are created as a part of each availability group node configuration (for each replica).

Combining Failover with Scale-out Options

SQL Server 2016 pushes combinations of options to achieve higher availability levels. Building up an AlwaysOn FCI configuration with AlwaysOn availability groups with two or more replicas launches you into distributed workload scalability and maximum HA.

Building a Multinode AlwaysOn Configuration

This section shows how to build a multinode AlwaysOn configuration, create the clustering configuration, define the availability group, specify the databases roles, replicate the databases, and get the availability group listener up and running. These are the basic steps, which are described in detail in the following sections:

1. Verify that the SQL Server instances are alive and well.

2. Set up WSFC.

3. Prepare the database.

4. Enable AlwaysOn HA.

5. Back up the primary databases.

6. Create the availability group.

7. Select the databases for the availability group.

8. Identify the primary and secondary replicas.

9. Synchronize the data (primary to replica).

10. Set up the listener (availability group listener).

11. Connect using the listener.

12. Fail over to a secondary.

Figure 6.4 shows the basic configuration that you will build in the following sections. There are three nodes to work with, but you will focus on getting the primary and one secondary up and running in this example. The failover cluster will be named DXD_Cluster, the availability group will be named DXD-AG, and the listener will be named DXD-Listener (and use IP address 20.0.0.243). You will use the Microsoft-supplied AdventureWorks database. The third node can be used to create another secondary replica for read-only access if you want or for DR purposes. In this case, you'll pretend it is a DR node (secondary replica).

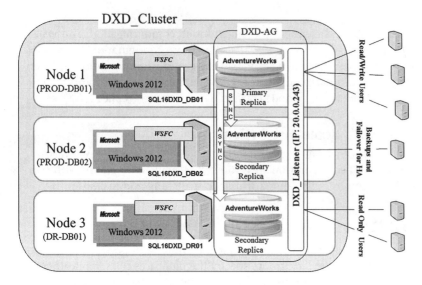

FIGURE 6.4   The DXD AlwaysOn configuration details.

The availability group will be used as follows: primary (Node 1) for both read/write operations and secondary (Node 2) for backup and failover. The other secondary (Node 3, if you add it) can be used for read-only access.

Verifying SQL Server Instances

Assume that you have installed and have running at least two SQL Server instances on separate nodes that can be clustered for this configuration. They don't have to be mirror images of each other, just viable SQL Server instances that can be enabled for AlwaysOn (Enterprise or Developer Editions). Verify that the SQL Server instances are alive and well.

Setting Up Failover Clustering

For each of the servers (nodes), you need to configure WSFC. Chapter 4 shows how to do this via the Server Manager of each node. This chapter does not cover that but does show you what the configured feature should look like before you begin creating your AlwaysOn availability group configuration.

As you can see in Figure 6.5, the Failover Clustering feature must be installed for each node.

FIGURE 6.5   The installed Failover Clustering feature shown from the Server Manager.

You likely need to also run a validation of the cluster configuration.

A number of extensive tests are performed on each node in the cluster that you are configuring. These tests take a bit of time, so go get tea or coffee, and then make sure that you look through the summary report for any true errors. You'll likely see a few warnings that refer to items that were not essential to the configuration (typically some TCP/IP or network-related things). When this is done, you are ready to get into the AlwaysOn business.

Figure 6.6 shows how you create the cluster group access point (named DXD_Cluster) in Failover Cluster Manager. The IP address for this access point is 20.0.0.242.

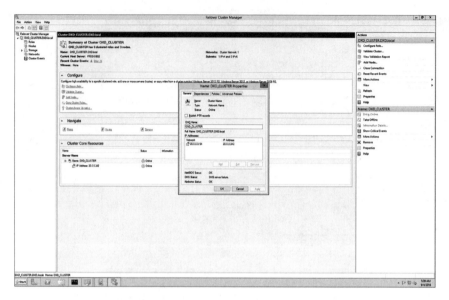

FIGURE 6.6   Using Failover Cluster Manager to create an access point for administering the cluster and cluster name.

This cluster should contain three nodes, `PROD-DB01`, `PROD-DB01`, and `DR-DB01`, as shown in the Failover Cluster Manager in Figure 6.7.

FIGURE 6.7   Failover Cluster Manager with the `DXD_Cluster` cluster and three nodes.

It's now time to start the AlwaysOn configuration on the SQL Server side of the equation.

Preparing the Database

You need to make sure that you have a primary database that can be used for this example. I recommend that you use the AdventureWorks database supplied by Microsoft as the example database that you'll replicate. If you don't already have it on the SQL Server instance you will be using for the primary replica (the PROD-DB01/SQL16DXD_DB01 SQL Server instance in this example), please download it from Microsoft and install it. If you already have another database you want to use, go ahead and use that one. Just make sure Database Recovery Model is set to Full. Availability groups uses transaction logs for replication, and this recovery model must be used.

Enabling AlwaysOn HA

For each of the SQL Server instances that you want to include in the AlwaysOn configuration, you need to enable their instances for AlwaysOn; it is turned off by default. From each node, bring up the SQL Server 2016 Configuration Manager and select the SQL Server Services node in the Services pane. Right-click the SQL Server instance for this node (with instance name SQL16DXD_DB01 in this example) and choose Properties. Figure 6.8 shows the properties of this SQL Server instance. Click the AlwaysOn High Availability tab and check Enable AlwaysOn Availability Groups. (Notice that the cluster name appears in this dialog box because this server was identified already in the cluster configuration step.) Click OK (or Apply), and you see a note about having to restart the service for this option to be used. After you have closed the Properties dialog, go ahead and right-click the SQL Server instance service again, but this time choose the Restart option to enable the AlwaysOn HA feature. For each of the other nodes (SQL16DXD_DB02 and SQL16DXD_DR01 in this example), do the same for the SQL Server configuration and the SQL Server instance that is to be included in the AlwaysOn configuration.

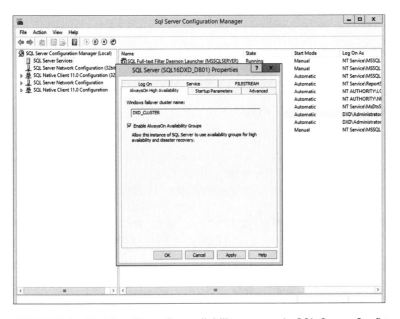

FIGURE 6.8   Enabling AlwaysOn availability groups via SQL Server Configuration Manager.

You could also do this from PowerShell. At the Windows command prompt, just type in SQLPS and press Enter. You then enter the following:

```
Enable -SqlAlwaysOn -ServerInstance SQL16DXD_DB01 -FORCE
```

This command even restarts the SQL Server service for you.

Backing Up the Database

Before you venture on to create the availability group, you should do a full database backup of the primary database (on Node 1: SQL16DXD_DB01). This backup will be used to create the databases on the secondary replicas. From the database node of the primary database (in SQL Server Management Studio [SSMS]), choose to perform a full backup of the database by right-clicking the database, choosing Tasks, and then clicking Back Up. Figure 6.9 shows the Back Up Database dialog that appears. In it, click OK to perform the full backup.

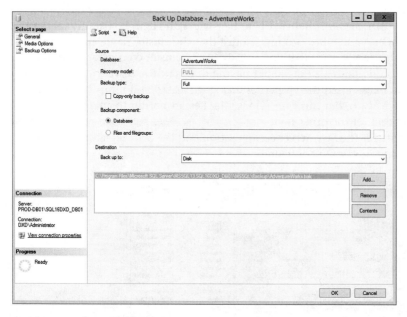

FIGURE 6.9 Doing a full database backup for the primary database (AdventureWorks).

At this point, I usually like to copy this full database backup to each secondary instance and restore it to guarantee that I have exactly the same thing at all nodes before the synchronization begins. When doing these restores, be sure to specify the Restore with No Recovery option. When you finish this, you can move on to creating the availability group.

Creating the Availability Group

From Node 1 (SQL16DXD_DB01 node in this example), expand the AlwaysOn High Availability node for this SQL Server instance (in SSMS). As you can see in Figure 6.10, you can right-click the Availability Group node and choose to create a new availability group (via the wizard). This is where all the action will be in creating the entire availability group.

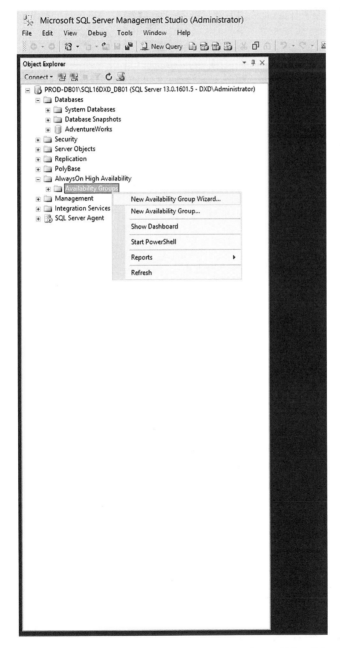

FIGURE 6.10   Invoking the New Availability Group Wizard from SSMS.

In the New Availability Group Wizard, you can specify the availability group name, select the database to replicate, specify the replicas, select the data synchronization, and then do validations. Initially, there is a splash page for the wizard on which you just click Next. This brings you to the Specify Availability Group Name dialog. Figure 6.11 shows this dialog, with the availability group name DXD-AG being specified. Click Next.

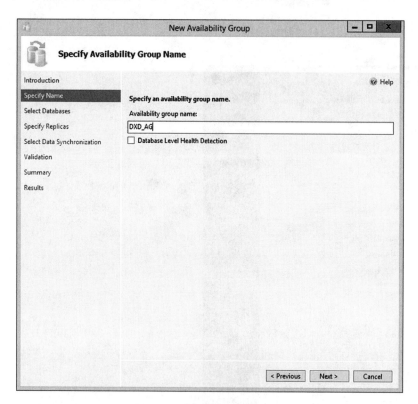

FIGURE 6.11   Specifying the availability group name.

Selecting the Databases for the Availability Group

Next you are asked to identify which application databases you want to include in the availability group. Figure 6.12 shows the list of databases, with AdventureWorks selected. Click Next.

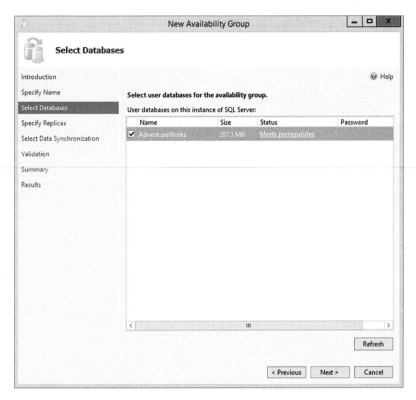

FIGURE 6.12   Specifying the AdventureWorks database for the availability group.

Identifying the Primary and Secondary Replicas

Specifying the replicas and how they will be used is the next step. Initially, there is only one server instance (the primary). Click the Add Replicas button in the lower left (below the Server Instances list) and choose the secondary replication instance you want (SQL16DXD_DB02 in this example—Node 2). Now both the primary and secondary instances should be listed. You also want to specify that each of these should be using automatic failover (up to three secondarys) by checking the check boxes. You also want the synchronous commits (up to three) option for both to get this HA feature.

You should include the third node as well (SQL16DXD_DR01) but do not check the Automatic Failover or Synchronous commit boxes. You want this to be asynchronous replication mode. However, you will allow the third node to be a readable secondary (by selecting Yes). Figure 6.13 shows each failover and commit option specified for each server instance.

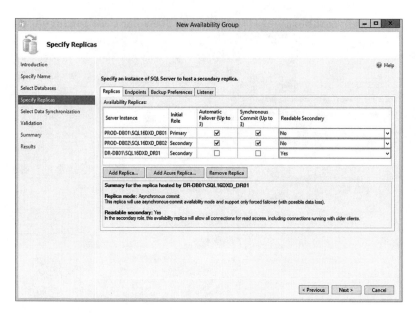

FIGURE 6.13   Specifying the instance of SQL Server to host a secondary replica and the server instance failover options.

Now, if you click on the Endpoints tab, you will see the endpoints that are getting generated for use by the instances to communicate with each other (hadr_endpoint for each SQL Server instance). You don't need to make changes to these, so accept the defaults, as shown in Figure 6.14.

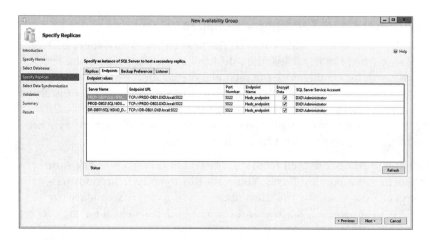

FIGURE 6.14   SQL Server endpoint specifications for the instances.

If you also click the Backup Preferences tab, you can indicate how (and where) you want database backups to be performed once the availability group is formed and the replicas are active. As you can see in Figure 6.15, you can select the Prefer Secondary option for doing database backups, thus relieving the primary from this overhead task. When you select this option, if the secondary isn't available for doing a backup, the primary is used.

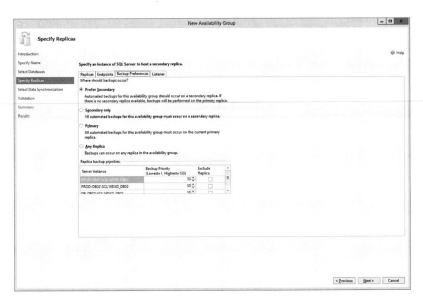

FIGURE 6.15   Prefer Secondary backup preference.

If you click on the Listener tab, you can see that you have two options here: not setting up the availability group listener at this time or creating one now. You'll actually do this a bit later, so skip it for now (by specifying Do Not Create an Availability Group Listener Now) and click Next.

Synchronizing the Data

The last thing you need to do before the validations step is specify your data synchronization preferences. Figure 6.16 shows the various options. If you use the Full option, you get full database and log backups for each selected database. Then these databases get restored to each secondary and joined to the availability group. The Join Only option starts data synchronization when you have already restored a database and log backup (in other words, when you already restored a database at a secondary, and you just want to have that secondary join the availability group). The Skip Initial Data Synchronization option simply means you will do the full backups for the primary databases yourself and restore them when you are ready. Because you already did this part, you can just select the Join Only option here and click Next.

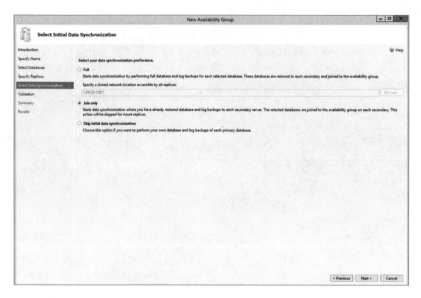

FIGURE 6.16   Specifying the initial data synchronization options for the replicas in the availability group.

NOTE

If you choose the Full option, it is important that the shared network location be fully accessible by the service accounts from all nodes in the availability group (the service account being used by the SQL Server services on each node).

As you can see in Figure 6.17, the validation dialog appears, showing you the success, failure, warnings, or steps skipped in this creation process, based on the options you specified. In Figure 6.17 you can also see the summary dialog of all work to be performed, and you get one last chance to verify the work about to be done before it is executed. Just click Next to finish this process.

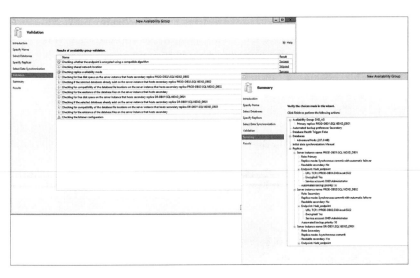

FIGURE 6.17   Validation and summary steps in creating the availability group.

As shown in Figure 6.18, you now see the results of the availability group creation steps. You can see that the secondaries were joined to the availability group (indicated by the arrow in Figure 6.18), and you can see what the availability group node in SSMS will contain for the newly formed availability group. The availability group is functional now. You can see the primary and secondary replicas, the databases within the availability group, and an indication at the database node level about whether the database is synchronized.

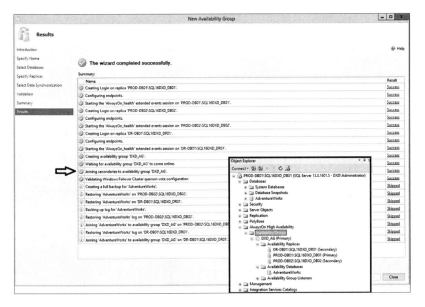

FIGURE 6.18   New Availability Group results dialog along with the SSMS Object Explorer results of the availability group and the joined replicas.

When the status of the databases changes to "synchronized," you are in business. However, to complete the abstraction of instance names away from the applications, you should create the availability group listener to complete this configuration.

Setting Up the Listener

The cluster's VNN gets bound to the availability group listener name in this process. It is also the name exposed to the applications to connect to the availability group. As long as at least one node is functioning in the availability group, the applications never know that any node has failed.

Right-click the availability group you created and choose Add Listener, as shown in Figure 6.19.

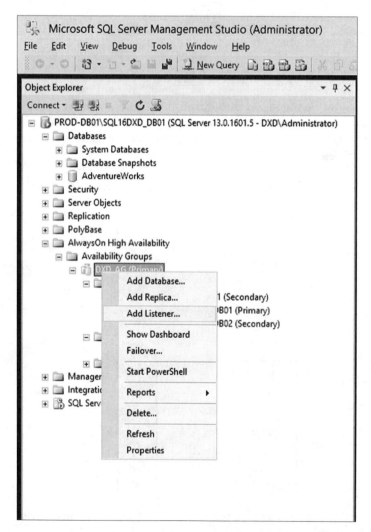

FIGURE 6.19   Specifying the new availability group listener for the new availability group.

You can now specify the listener DNS name (DXD_LISTENER in this example) and the port (use 1433), and you can indicate to use a static IP address for this listener. A small dialog box appears (as shown in Figure 6.20) that indicates the IPv4 address of this listener (20.0.0.243 in this example). Click OK. Figure 6.20 shows the availability group and the new availability group listener you just configured. (By the way, the application can use the listener name or the IP address of the listener to connect to the SQL instance. I'll show you how to do that a bit later.)

FIGURE 6.20   The new availability group listener, ready to use.

That's it. You should be up and running in HA mode and have the listener ready to use by any application.

If the database isn't joining properly or if Object Explorer isn't showing the synchronization state on the secondary, you can right-click the database under the Availability Databases node for that availability group on the secondary and explicitly join the database to the availability group (as shown in Figure 6.21).

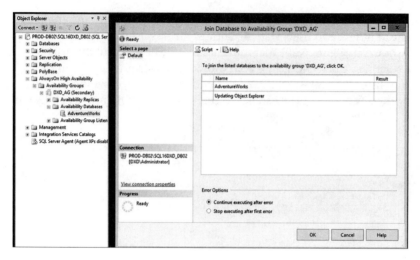

FIGURE 6.21   Explicitly joining the database on the secondary to the availability group.

You have a fully functioning availability group and listener now, and as you can see from the Failover Cluster Manager Roles view (see Figure 6.22), the availability group DXD_AG is running, and the current owner node is PROD-DB01. You can also see in the lower half of this view the status of the availability group resource and the listener resource. All seem to be working and show "Online."

FIGURE 6.22   Reviewing the newly added availability group and listener in Failover Cluster Manager.

Connecting Using the Listener

You can do a quick test with SSMS to connect to the new availability group listener as if it were its own SQL Server instance. As shown in Figure 6.23, you start a new connection dialog that specifies the availability group listener's IP address (20.0.0.243, with port 1433). You could also just specify the listener name (DXD_LISTENER). Go ahead and connect using either method.

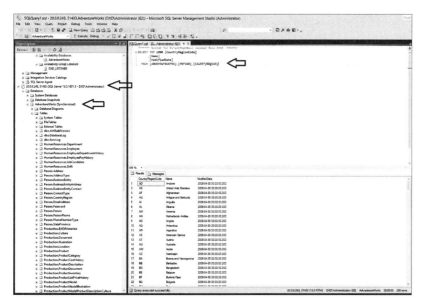

FIGURE 6.23   Connection using the availability group listener (IP address 20.0.0.243, port 1433).

While connected, you can open a new query window (as also shown in Figure 6.23) and select the top 1,000 rows from the CountryRegion table in the Person schema from the AdventureWorks database. You can see that the database is in a synchronized state and is fully functional within the availability group configuration. You are in business! Next you can test the high availability failover from the primary to the secondary.

Failing Over to a Secondary

You can fail over from within SQL Server by right-clicking the primary replica of the Availability Group node and selecting Failover. Or you can do this from the Failover Cluster Manager. Jump back over to the Failover Cluster Manager for node PROD-DB01 and see what things look like from there. Figure 6.24 shows that PROD-DB01 is still the owner node for the availability group, and when you right-click the availability group, you can choose to move the clustered role (as also shown in Figure 6.24). (Moving the clustered role to another node is just another way of saying fail it over to another node.) You can see all other nodes in the availability group, but in this case you want to fail it over to the PROD-DB02 node because this is your secondary for failover. Remember that when you fail over, client connections are broken and then reestablished to the new node, and any in-flight transactions that are not completed during the failover will likely have to be rerun. Also, in Figure 6.24 (at the bottom right), you can see the role status with the owner node changed to PROD-DB02 (the secondary). Now you need to try that SQL query again.

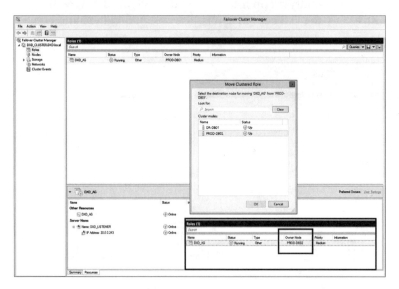

FIGURE 6.24   Moving the cluster role to the PROD-DB02 node.

Figure 6.25 shows the execution of the same query (via the listener) that is satisfying the client connection successfully. This is high availability at work!

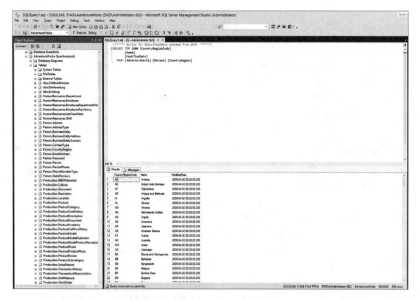

FIGURE 6.25   Successful execution of the SQL query from the listener, showing high availability from an application point of view.

Dashboard and Monitoring

Various system views, a dashboard, and dynamic management views have been added for monitoring (and debugging) the AlwaysOn availability groups feature. You can open the AlwaysOn dashboard by right-clicking the availability group and selecting Show Dashboard. You can use this dashboard to obtain an at-a-glance view of the health of an AlwaysOn availability group, its availability replicas, and databases.

You can use this dashboard to do the following:

▶ Choose a replica for a manual failover.

▶ Estimate data loss if you force failover.

▶ Evaluate data synchronization performance.

▶ Evaluate the performance impact of a synchronous commit secondary replica.

The dashboard also provides key availability group states and performance indicators, including the following:

▶ Replica roll-up state

▶ Synchronization mode and state

▶ Estimated data loss

▶ Estimated recovery time (redo catch-up)

▶ Database replica details

▶ Synchronization mode and state

▶ Time to restore log

SQL Server 2016 has dynamic management views for AlwaysOn availability groups, including the following:

▶ sys.dm_hadr_auto_page_repair

▶ sys.dm_hadr_cluster_networks

▶ sys.dm_hadr_availability_group_states

▶ sys.dm_hadr_database_replica_cluster_states

▶ sys.dm_hadr_availability_replica_cluster_nodes

▶ sys.dm_hadr_database_replica_states

▶ sys.dm_hadr_availability_replica_cluster_states

▶ sys.dm_hadr_instance_node_map

▶ sys.dm_hadr_availability_replica_states

▶ sys.dm_hadr_name_id_map

▶ sys.dm_hadr_cluster

▶ sys.dm_tcp_listener_states

▶ sys.dm_hadr_cluster_members

Finally, catalog views of SQL Server AlwaysOn availability groups make it easy to see key components of the configuration. These include the following:

▶ sys.availability_databases_cluster

▶ sys.availability_groups_cluster

▶ sys.availability_group_listener_ip_addresses

▶ sys.availability_read_only_routing_lists

▶ sys.availability_group_listeners

▶ sys.availability_replicas

▶ sys.availability_groups

NOTE

For availability groups, it is best practice to reduce or remove the quorum voting (weight) of any of your asynchronous secondary's (especially one's you are using for Disaster Recovery). This can be done fairly easily with a Powershell script that looks like the following:

```
-- query the quorum nodes
Import-Module FailoverClusters
$cluster = "PRODICDB_DB"
$nodes = Get-ClusterNode -Cluster $cluster
$nodes | Format-Table -property NodeName, State, NodeWeight

-- change the weight of the secondary replica to 0
Import-Module FailoverClusters
$node = "DRSite-DB01"
(Get-ClusterNode $node).NodeWeight = 0
$cluster = (Get-ClusterNode $node).Cluster
$nodes = Get-ClusterNode -Cluster $cluster
$nodes | Format-Table -property NodeName, State, NodeWeight
```

You might also have to apply a hotfix to WSFC if you are working on an old Windows server version (prior to Windows 2012 R2). You can always take a quick look via a system view SELECT to see what the quorum and voting values are:

```
SELECT  member_name, member_state_desc, number_of_quorum_votes
   FROM   sys.dm_hadr_cluster_members;
```

Scenario 3: Investment Portfolio Management with AlwaysOn and Availability Groups

Recall from Chapter 3, "Choosing High Availability," that the investment portfolio management business scenario (Scenario 3) yielded a high availability selection of storage redundancy, WSFC, and AlwaysOn availability groups. This investment portfolio management application is currently housed in a major server farm in the heart of the world's financial center: New York. Serving North American customers only, this application provides the ability to do full trading of stocks and options in all financial markets (United States and international), along with full portfolio holdings assessment, historical performance, and holdings valuation. Primary users are investment managers for their large customers. Stock purchasing and selling comprise 90% of the daytime activity, and massive assessment, historical performance, and valuation reporting occur after the markets have closed. Three major peaks occur each weekday that are driven by the three major trading markets of the world (United States, Europe, and the Far East). During the weekends, the application is used for the long-range planning reporting and front-loading stock trades for the coming week.

This company opted for the basic hardware/disk redundancy approach on each server, and an AlwaysOn availability group asynchronous secondary replica for failover, offloading of DB backups, and a reporting workload on both the local secondary replica and the Microsoft Azure secondary replica. In fact, most of the reporting was eventually directed to the Microsoft Azure secondary replica; data was only about 10 seconds behind the primary replica, on average. There is now plenty of risk mitigation with this technical architecture, and it is not difficult to maintain (see Figure 6.26).

Once this HA solution was put together, it exceeded the high availability goals on a regular basis. Great performance has also resulted due to the splitting out of the OLTP from the reporting; this is very often a solid design approach.

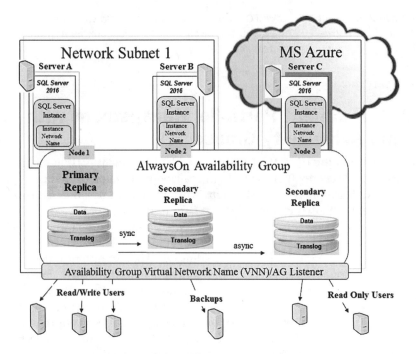

FIGURE 6.26   Portfolio management HA solution technical architecture.

The ROI in this scenario can be calculated by adding up the incremental costs (or estimates) of the new HA solution and comparing them against the complete cost of downtime for a period of time (1 year in this example).

Total incremental costs to upgrade to this AlwaysOn availability groups HA solution is approximately $222,000.

Now, let's work through the complete ROI calculation with these incremental costs along with the cost of downtime:

1. Maintenance cost (for a 1-year period):

    ▶ **$15k (estimate)**—Yearly system admin personnel cost (additional time for training of these personnel)

    ▶ **$50k (estimate)**—Recurring software licensing cost (of additional HA components; [3] OS + [3] SQL Server 2016)

2. Hardware cost:

    ▶ **$100k hardware cost**—The cost of additional HW in the new HA solution

    ▶ **$12k IaaS cost**—That is, 12 × $1,000/month Microsoft Azure IaaS fees

3. Deployment/assessment cost:

   ▶ **$35k deployment cost**—The cost of development, testing, QA, and production implementation of the solution

   ▶ **$10k HA assessment cost**

4. Downtime cost (for a 1-year period):

   ▶ If you kept track of last year's downtime record, use that number; otherwise, produce an estimate of planned and unplanned downtime for this calculation. For this scenario, the estimated cost of downtime/hour is **$150k/hour** for this financial services company. Wow, that is huge!

   ▶ Planned downtime cost (revenue loss cost) = Planned downtime hours × cost of hourly downtime to the company:

   a. 0.25% (estimate of planned downtime percentage in 1 year) × 8,760 hours in a year = 21.9 hours of planned downtime

   b. 21.9 hours (planned downtime) × $150k/hr (hourly cost of downtime) = $3,285,000/year cost of planned downtime. But, because this was planned, there was not to be any financial planning or stock trading during these times, thus pushing this near $0.

   ▶ Unplanned downtime cost (revenue loss cost) = Unplanned downtime hours × cost of hourly downtime to the company:

   a. 0.15% (estimate of unplanned downtime percentage in 1 year) × 8,760 hours in a year = 13.14 hours of unplanned downtime

   b. 13.14 hours × $150k/hr (hourly cost of downtime) = $1,971,000/year cost of unplanned downtime. Ouch!

ROI totals:

▶ Total costs to get on this HA solution = $222,000 (for the year—slightly higher than the stated immediate incremental costs)

▶ Total of downtime cost = $2,000,000 rounded (for the year)

The incremental cost is 13% of the downtime cost for 1 year. In other words, the investment of the HA solution will pay for itself in approximately 1.2 months. From a budget point of view, the company had budgeted $900k for all HA costs. So the implemented HA solution came in way under budget and far exceeded HA goals!

Summary

With SQL Server 2016, it's all about the AlwaysOn features. The adoption of the AlwaysOn and availability groups capabilities has been astonishing. Older, more complex HA solutions are being cast aside left and right in favor of this clean, highly scalable method of achieving five 9s and high performance. It is truly the next generation of HA and scale-out for existing and new database tiers of any kind. Microsoft publicly advises all its customers that have implemented log shipping, database mirroring, and even SQL clustering and advises customers to get to AlwaysOn availability groups at some point. As with Scenario 3, these extreme availability requirements fit very nicely with what availability groups brings to the table: short failover times and very limited data loss. More importantly, transactional performance could be maintained by offloading reporting and backups to secondary replicas.

CHAPTER 7

SQL Server Database Snapshots

Database snapshots have been a feature of competing database products (including Oracle and DB2) for years. Database snapshots are great for fulfilling point-in-time reporting requirements; they directly increase your reporting consistency, availability, and overall performance. They are also great for reverting a database back to a point in time (supporting your recovery time objectives, recovery point objectives, and overall availability) and for potentially reducing the processing impact of querying against primary transactional databases when used with database mirroring. All these factors contribute to the high availability picture in some way. Database snapshots are fairly easy to implement and administer.

However, keep in mind that database snapshots are point-in-time reflections of an entire database and are not bound to the underlying database objects from which they pull their data. A snapshot provides a full, read-only copy of the database at a specific point in time. Because of this point-in-time aspect, data latency must be well understood for all users of this feature: Snapshot data is only as current as when the snapshot was made.

As mentioned previously, database snapshots can be used in conjunction with database mirroring to provide a highly available transactional system and a reporting platform that is created from the database mirror and offloads the reporting away from the primary transactional database, without any data loss impact whatsoever. This is a very powerful reporting and availability configuration. Database mirroring is available in the Standard Edition of SQL Server, whereas database snapshots require the Enterprise Edition of SQL Server.

> **NOTE**
>
> Database mirroring has been earmarked for deprecation for some time. However, it still just keeps being included with each SQL Server release. AlwaysOn availability groups are the recommended new method of creating redundant databases (secondaries) for high availability and offloading of reporting loads to separate SQL instances (see Chapter 6, "SQL Server AlwaysOn and Availability Groups"). However, as you will see in this chapter, database mirroring is extremely effective at creating a single mirrored database and is fairly easy to set up administratively. So, it's okay to use this feature, but just keep in mind that it will likely go away in the next SQL Server version (SQL Server 2018?) or certainly in the one following that (SQL Server 2020?). Or will it?

What Are Database Snapshots?

Microsoft has kept up its commitment of providing a database engine foundation that can be highly available 7 days a week, 365 days a year. Database snapshots contribute to this goal in several ways:

▶ They decrease recovery time of a database because you can restore a troubled database with a database snapshot—referred to as *reverting*.

▶ They create a security blanket (safeguard) before you run mass updates on a critical database. If something goes wrong with the update, the database can be reverted in a very short amount of time.

▶ They quickly provide read-only, point-in-time reporting for ad hoc or canned reporting needs (thus increasing reporting environment availability).

▶ They quickly create read-only, point-in-time reporting and offloaded databases for ad hoc or canned reporting needs from a database mirror (again increasing reporting environment availability and also offloading reporting impact away from your production server/principal database server).

▶ As a bonus, database snapshots can be used to create testing or QA synchronization points to enhance and improve all aspects of critical testing (thus preventing bad code from going into production and directly affecting the stability and availability of that production implementation).

A database snapshot is simply a point-in-time full database view. It's not a copy—at least not a full copy when it is originally created. (I talk about this more in a moment.) Figure 7.1 shows conceptually how a database snapshot can be created from a source database on a single SQL Server instance.

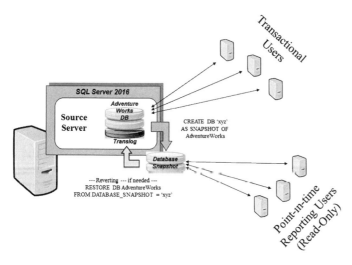

FIGURE 7.1   Basic database snapshot concept: a source database and its database snapshot, all on a single SQL Server instance.

This point-in-time view of a database's data never changes, even though the data (data pages) in the primary database (the source of the database snapshot) may change. It is truly a snapshot at a point in time. For a snapshot, it always simply points to data pages that were present at the time the snapshot was created. If a data page is updated in the source database, a copy of the original source data page is moved to a new page chain, termed the *sparse file* via copy-on-write technology. Figure 7.2 shows the sparse file that is created, alongside the source database itself.

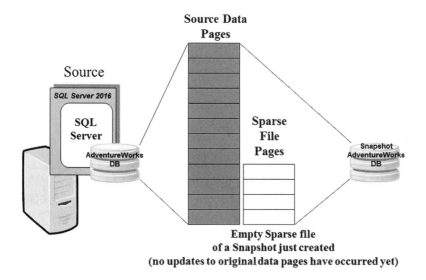

FIGURE 7.2   Source database data pages and the sparse file data pages comprising the database snapshot.

A database snapshot really uses the primary database's data pages up until the point that one of these data pages is updated (that is, changed in any way). As mentioned previously, if a data page is updated in the source database, the original copy of the data page (which is referenced by the database snapshot) is written to the sparse file page chain as part of an update operation, using the copy-on-write technology. It is this new data page in the sparse file that still provides the correct point-in-time data to the database snapshot that it serves. Figure 7.3 illustrates that as more data changes (updates) occur in the source database, the sparse file gets larger and larger with the old original data pages.

Eventually, a sparse file could contain the entire original database if all data pages in the primary database were changed. As you can see in Figure 7.3, which data pages the database snapshot uses from the original (source) database and which data pages it uses from the sparse file are managed by references in the system catalog for the database snapshot. This setup is incredibly efficient and represents a major breakthrough in providing data to others. Because SQL Server is using the copy-on-write technology, a certain amount of overhead is used during write operations. This is one of the critical factors you must sort through if you plan on using database snapshots. Nothing is free. The overhead includes the copying of the original data page, the writing of this copied data page to the sparse file, and the subsequent metadata updating to the system catalog that manages the database snapshot data page list. Because of this sharing of data pages, it should also be clear why database snapshots must be within the same instance of a SQL Server: Both the source database and snapshot start out as the same data pages and then diverge as source data pages are updated. In addition, when a database snapshot is created, SQL Server rolls back any uncommitted transactions for that database snapshot; only the committed transactions are part of a newly created database snapshot. And, as you might expect of something that shares data pages, database snapshots become unavailable if the source database becomes unavailable (for example, if it is damaged or goes offline).

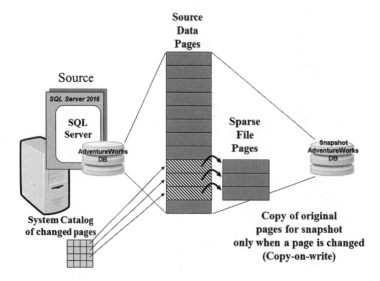

FIGURE 7.3   Data pages being copied to the sparse file for a database snapshot as pages are being updated in the source database.

NOTE

You might plan to do a new snapshot after about 30% of the source database has changed to keep overhead and file sizes in the sparse file at a minimum. The problem that most frequently occurs with database snapshots is related to sparse file sizes and available space. Remember that the sparse file has the potential of being as big as the source database itself (if all data pages in the source database eventually get updated). Plan ahead for this situation!

There are, of course, alternatives to database snapshots, such as data replication, log shipping, and even materialized views, but none are as easy to manage and use as database snapshots.

The following terms are commonly associated with database snapshots:

▶ **Source database**—This is the database on which the database snapshot is based. A database is a collection of data pages. It is the fundamental data storage mechanism that SQL Server uses.

▶ **Snapshot databases**—There can be one or more database snapshots defined against any one source database. All snapshots must reside in the same SQL Server instance.

▶ **Database snapshot sparse file**—This new data page allocation contains the original source database data pages when updates occur to the source database data pages. One sparse file is associated with each database data file. If you have a source database allocated with one or more separate data files, you have corresponding sparse files of each of them.

▶ **Reverting to a database snapshot**—If you restore a source database based on a particular database snapshot that was done at a point in time, you are reverting. You are actually doing a database RESTORE operation with a FROM DATABASE_SNAPSHOT statement.

▶ **Copy-on-write technology**—As part of an update transaction in the source database, a copy of the source database data page is written to a sparse file so that the database snapshot can be served correctly (that is, still see the data page as of the snapshot point in time).

As Figure 7.4 illustrates, any data query using the database snapshot looks at both the source database data pages and the sparse file data pages at the same time. These data pages always reflect the unchanged data pages at the point in time the snapshot was created.

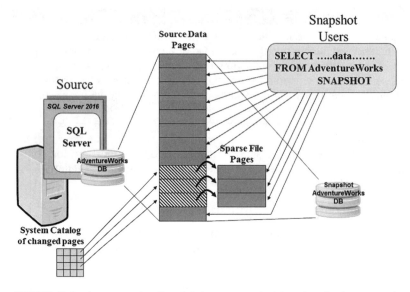

FIGURE 7.4   A query using the database snapshot touches both source database data pages and sparse file data pages to satisfy a query.

Copy-on-Write Technology

The copy-on-write technology that Microsoft first introduced with SQL Server 2005 is at the core of both database mirroring and database snapshot capabilities. This section walks through a typical transactional user's update of data in a source database.

As you can see in Figure 7.5, an update transaction is initiated against the Adventure-Works database (labeled A). As the data is being updated in the source database's data page and the change is written to the transaction log (labeled B), the copy-on-write technology also copies the original source database data page in its unchanged state to the sparse data file (also labeled B) and updates the metadata page references in the system catalog (also labeled B) with this movement.

The original source data page is still available to the database snapshot. This adds extra overhead to any transaction that updates, inserts, or deletes data from the source database. After the copy-on-write technology finishes its write on the sparse file, the original update transaction is properly committed, and acknowledgment is sent back to the transactional user (labeled C).

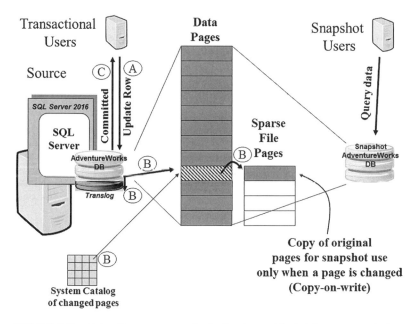

FIGURE 7.5   Using the copy-on-write technology with database snapshots.

Database snapshots cannot be used for any of SQL Server's internal databases—tempdb, master, msdb, or model. Also, database snapshots are supported only in the Enterprise Edition of SQL Server 2016.

When to Use Database Snapshots

As mentioned previously, there are a few basic ways you can use database snapshots effectively. Each use is for a particular purpose, and each has unique benefits. After you have factored in the limitations and restrictions mentioned earlier, you can consider these uses. Let's look at each of them separately.

Reverting to a Snapshot for Recovery Purposes

Probably the most basic usage of database snapshots is to decrease recovery time of a database by restoring a troubled database with a database snapshot—referred to as *reverting*. As Figure 7.6 shows, one or more regularly scheduled snapshots can be generated during a 24-hour period, effectively providing you with data recovery milestones that can be rapidly used. As you can see in this example, four database snapshots are six hours apart (6:00 a.m., 12:00 p.m., 6:00 p.m., and 12:00 a.m.). Each is dropped and re-created once per day, using the same snapshot name. Any one of these snapshots can be used to recover the source database rapidly in the event of a logical data error (such as rows deleted or a table being dropped). This technique is not supposed to take the place of a good maintenance plan that includes full database backups and incremental transaction log dumps. However, it can enable you to get a database back to a particular milestone very quickly.

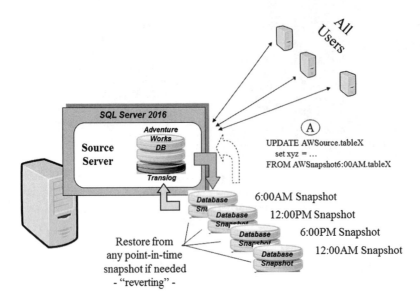

FIGURE 7.6   Basic database snapshot configuration: a source database and one or more database snapshots at different time intervals.

To revert to a particular snapshot interval, you simply use the RESTORE DATABASE command with the FROM DATABASE_SNAPSHOT statement. This is a complete database restore; you cannot limit it to just a single database object. In addition, you must drop all other database snapshots before you can use one of them to restore a database.

As you can see in Figure 7.6, a very specific SQL statement referencing a snapshot could be used if you knew exactly what you wanted to restore at the table and row levels. You could simply use SQL statements (such as an UPDATE SQL statement [labeled A] or an INSERT SQL statement) from one of the snapshots to selectively apply only the fixes you are sure need to be recovered (reverted). In other words, you don't restore the whole database from the snapshot; you use only some of the snapshot's data with SQL statements and bring the messed-up data row values back in line with the original values in the snapshot. This is at the row and column level and usually requires quite a bit of detailed analysis before it can be applied to a production database.

It is also possible to use a snapshot to recover a table that someone accidentally dropped. There is a little data loss since the last snapshot, but it involves a simple INSERT INTO statement from the latest snapshot before the table drop. Be careful here, but consider the value as well.

Safeguarding a Database Prior to Making Mass Changes

You probably plan regular events against your database tables that result in some type of mass update being applied to big portions of the database. If you do a quick database snapshot before any of these types of changes, you are essentially creating a nice safety net for rapid recovery in the event that you are not satisfied with the mass update results. Figure 7.7 illustrates this type of safeguarding technique.

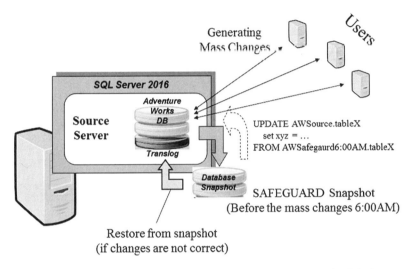

FIGURE 7.7   Creating a before database snapshot prior to scheduled mass updates to a database.

If you are not satisfied with the entire update operation, you can use RESTORE DATABASE from the snapshot and revert it to this point. Or, if you are happy with some updates but not others, you can use the SQL UPDATE statement to selectively update (restore) particular values back to their original values using the snapshot.

Providing a Testing (or Quality Assurance) Starting Point (Baseline)

In testing and the QA phases of your development life cycle, you often need to conduct tests over and over. These are either logic tests or performance tests. To aid testing and QA, you can make database snapshots of a test database prior to full testing (to create a testing baseline database snapshot), and then you can revert the test database back to its original state at a moment's notice by using that baseline snapshot. This procedure can be done any number of times. Figure 7.8 shows how easy it is to simply create a testing reference point (or synchronization point) with a database snapshot.

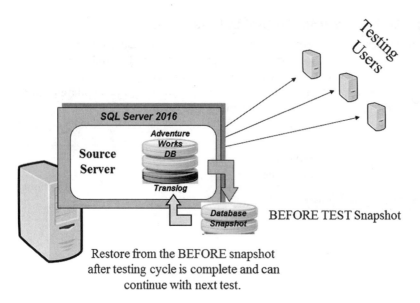

FIGURE 7.8   Establishing a baseline testing database snapshot before running tests and then reverting when finished.

You then just run your test scripts or do any manual testing—as much as you want—and then revert back to this starting point rapidly. Then you run more tests again.

Providing a Point-in-Time Reporting Database

If what you really need is a true point-in-time reporting database from which you can run ad hoc or canned reports, often a database snapshot can serve this purpose much better than log shipping or data replication. Key to determining when you can use this database snapshot technique is whether the reporting load on this database server instance can easily support the reporting workload and whether the update transactions against this database are adversely affected by the database snapshot overhead of each transaction. Figure 7.9 shows the typical database snapshot configuration for one or more database snapshots that are to be used for reporting.

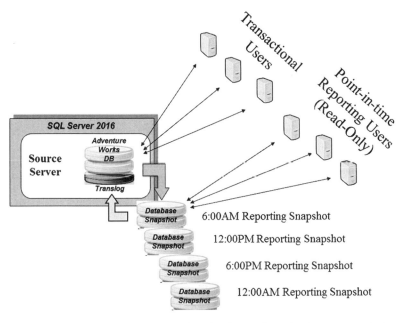

FIGURE 7.9   A point-in-time reporting database via a database snapshot.

Remember that this is a point-in-time snapshot of the source database. How frequently you need to create a new snapshot is dictated by your reporting requirements for data latency (that is, how old the data can be in these reports).

Providing a Highly Available and Offloaded Reporting Database from a Database Mirror

If you are using database mirroring to improve your availability, you can also create a database snapshot against this mirrored database and expose the snapshot to your reporting users. Even though the mirrored database cannot be used for any access whatsoever (it is in constant restore mode), SQL Server allows a snapshot to be created against it (as shown in Figure 7.10). This is a very powerful configuration in that a database snapshot against a mirror does not impact the load of the principal server—guaranteeing high performance against the principal server. Also, when the database snapshot is isolated over to the mirror server, the performance of the reporting users is also more predictable because they are not competing with the transactional users for resources on the principal server. (I explain database mirroring and show you how to configure a database mirror with a database snapshot later in this chapter.) The only real issues arise when the principal server fails over to the mirror database. You then have both transactional and reporting users using the same database server instance, and the performance of them all is affected.

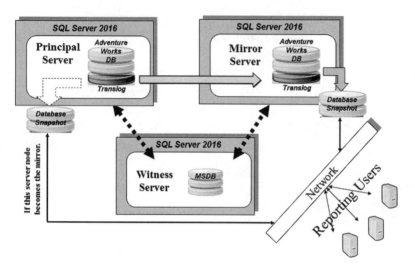

FIGURE 7.10   Creating a database snapshot for reporting against a mirrored database to offload the reporting impact on the principal server.

A possible solution to this situation would be to automatically (or manually) drop the database snapshot on the mirror server if it becomes the principal and create a new snapshot on the old principal server if it is available (it is now the mirror). You then just point all your reporting users to this new database snapshot. This task can be handled fairly easily in an application server layer. This solution is basically a reciprocal principal/mirror reporting configuration approach that always tries to get the database snapshot that is used for reporting to be on the server that is the mirror server. You would never really want to have active database snapshots on both the principal server and mirror server at the same time. That would be way too much overhead for both servers. You want just the database snapshots to be on the mirror server. (I talk quite a bit more about database mirroring later in this chapter.)

Setup and Breakdown of a Database Snapshot

You might actually be surprised to find out how easily you can set up a database snapshot. This simplicity is partly due to the level at which database snapshots are created: at the database level and not at the table level. Setting up a database snapshot only entails running a CREATE DATABASE with the AS SNAPSHOT OF statement. You cannot create database snapshots from SQL Server Management Studio or from any other GUI or wizard for that matter. Everything must be done using SQL scripts. All SQL scripts for this chapter are available to you as a download from the book's companion website for this book (www.informit.com/9780672337765). Further, all examples use the Microsoft AdventureWorks database (converted for SQL Server 2016). The script file, named DBSnapshotSQL2016.sql, also contains a variety of other useful SQL statements to help you better manage a database snapshot environment.

Creating a Database Snapshot

One of the first things you must figure out before you create a database snapshot is whether your source database data portion has more than one physical file in its allocation. All these file references must be accounted for in the snapshot. You execute the system stored procedure sp_helpdb with the source database name as the parameter, as shown here:

```
EXEC SP_HELPDB AdventureWorks
Go
```

The detailed file allocations of this database are as follows:

```
Name                    FileID       File Name
AdventureWorks_Data  1      C:\Server\
            MSSQL13.SQL1016DXD01\DATA\AdventureWorks_Data.mdf
AdventureWorks_Log   2      C:\Server\
            MSSQL13.SQL2016DXD01\MSSQL\DATA\AdventureWorks_Log.ldf
```

You need to worry about only the data portion of the database for the snapshot:

```
CREATE DATABASE SNAP_AdventureWorks_6AM
ON
 ( NAME = AdventureWorks_Data,
   FILENAME= 'C:\Server\ MSSQL13.SQL2016DXD01\MSSQL\DATA\SNAP_AW_data_6AM.snap'
AS SNAPSHOT OF AdventureWorks
go
```

Creating the database snapshot is really that easy. Now let's walk through a simple example that shows how to create a series of four database snapshots against the Adventure-Works source database that represent snapshots six hours apart (as shown in Figure 7.6). Here is the next snapshot to be run at 12:00 p.m.:

```
CREATE DATABASE SNAP_AdventureWorks_12PM
ON
 ( NAME = AdventureWorks_Data,
   FILENAME= 'C:\Server\ MSSQL13.SQL2016DXD01\MSSQL\DATA\SNAP_AW_data_12PM.snap')
AS SNAPSHOT OF AdventureWorks
go
```

These snapshots made at equal time intervals and can be used for reporting or reverting.

NOTE

This book uses a simple naming convention for the database names for snapshots and for the snapshot files themselves. The database snapshot name is the word SNAP, followed by the source database name, followed by a qualifying description of what this snapshot represents, all separated with underscores. For example, a database snapshot that represents a 6:00 a.m. snapshot of the AdventureWorks database would have this name:

```
SNAP_AdventureWorks_6AM
```

The snapshot file-naming convention is similar. The name starts with the word SNAP, followed by the database name that the snapshot is for (AdventureWorks, in this example), followed by the data portion indication (for example, data or data1), a short identification of what this snapshot represents (for example, 6AM), and then the filename extension .snap to distinguish it from .mdf and .ldf files. For example, the snapshot filename for the preceding database snapshot would look like this:

```
SNAP_AdventureWorks_data_6AM.snap
```

This example uses the AdventureWorks database. AdventureWorks currently uses only a single data file allocation for its data portion. Here's how you create the first snapshot, to reflect a 6:00 a.m. snapshot:

1. Create the snapshot on the source database AdventureWorks:

```
Use [master]
go
CREATE DATABASE SNAP_AdventureWorks_6AM
ON ( NAME = AdventureWorks_Data, FILENAME= 'C:\Program Files\
    Microsoft SQL Server\ MSSQL13.SQL2016DXD01\MSSQL\DATA\
    SNAP_AdventureWorks_data_6AM.snap')
AS SNAPSHOT OF AdventureWorks
Go
```

2. Look at this newly created snapshot from the SQL Server instance point of view, using a SQL query against the sys.databases system catalog, as follows:

```
Use [master]
go
SELECT name,
       database_id,
       source_database_id, - source DB of the snapshot
       create_date,
       snapshot_isolation_state_desc
FROM sys.databases
Go
```

This shows the existing source database and the newly created database snapshot:

name	database_id	source_database_id	create_date	snapshot_isolation_state_desc
AdventureWorks	5	NULL	2016-05-21 23:37:02.763	OFF
SNAP_AdventureWorks_6AM	6	5	2016-05-22 06:18:36.597	ON

Note that source_database_id for the newly created database snapshot contains the database ID of the source database.

3. Look at the newly created physical file for the sparse file (for the database snapshot) by querying the `sys.master_files` system catalog:

```
SELECT database_id, file_id, name, physical_name
FROM sys.master_files
WHERE Name = 'AdventureWorks_data'
and is_sparse = 1
go
```

Note that this example focuses on only the sparse files for the newly created database snapshot (that is, the `is_sparse` - 1 qualification). This query results in the following:

```
database_id file_id     name                     physical_name
----------- ----------- ------------------------------------------------------------
6           1           AdventureWorks_Data      C:\Prog...\DATA\
                                                 SNAP_AdventureWorks_data_6AM.snap
```

4. To see the number of bytes that a snapshot sparse file is burning up (growing to), you can issue a series of SQL statements against system catalog views/tables by using `fn_virtualfilestats` and `sys.master_files`. However, the following is a quick-and-dirty stored procedure that makes this task much easier. Just create this stored procedure on your SQL Server instance (in the master database), and you can use it to see the sizes of any database snapshot sparse file on your server (also available in the downloadable SQL script file for this chapter):

```
CREATE PROCEDURE SNAP_SIZE_UNLEASHED2016
      @DBDATA varchar(255) = NULL
AS
if @DBDATA is not null
   BEGIN
      SELECT B.name as 'Sparse files for Database Name',
            A.DbId, A.FileId, BytesOnDisk      FROM fn_virtualfilestats
 (NULL, NULL) A,
            sys.master_files B
      WHERE A.DbID = B.database_id
         and A.FileID = B.file_id
         and B.is_sparse = 1
         and B.name = @DBDATA
   END
ELSE
   BEGIN
      SELECT B.name as 'Sparse files for Database Name',
            A.DbId, A.FileId, BytesOnDisk
      FROM fn_virtualfilestats (NULL, NULL) A,
            sys.master_files B
      WHERE A.DbID = B.database_id
         and A.FileID = B.file_id
```

```
        and B.is_sparse = 1
    END
Go
```

When the `SNAP_SIZE_UNLEASHED2016` stored procedure is created, you run it with or without the name of the data portion of the database for which you have created a snapshot. If you do not supply the data portion name, you see all sparse files and their sizes on the SQL Server instance. The following example shows how to execute this stored procedure to see the sparse file's current size for the `AdventureWorks_data` portion:

```
EXEC SNAP_SIZE_UNLEASHED2016 'AdventureWorks_Data'
Go
```

This results in the detail bytes that the sparse file is using on disk:

```
Sparse files for Database Name  DbId   FileId   BytesOnDisk
-------------------------------------------------------------------------------
AdventureWorks_Data              6      1        3801088
```

Currently, the sparse file is very small (3.8MB) because it was recently created. Little to no source data pages have changed, so it is basically empty right now. It will start growing as data is updated in the source database and data pages are copied to the sparse file (by the copy-on-write mechanism). You can use the `SNAP_SIZE_UNLEASHED2016` stored procedure to keep an eye on the sparse file's size. Believe it or not, the database snapshot is ready for you to use.

5. Use the following SQL statement to select rows from this newly created database snapshot for a typical point-in-time query against the `CreditCard` table:

```
Use [SNAP_AdventureWorks_6AM]
go
SELECT [CreditCardID]
      ,[CardType]
      ,[CardNumber]
      ,[ExpMonth]
      ,[ExpYear]
      ,[ModifiedDate]
  FROM [SNAP_AdventureWorks_6AM].[Sales].[CreditCard]
WHERE CreditCardID = 1
go
```

This statement delivers the correct, point-in-time result rows from the database snapshot:

CreditCardID	CardType	CardNumber	ExpMonth	ExpYear
				ModifiedDate
1	SuperiorCard	33332664695310	11	2006
				2013-12-03 00:00:39.560

You see how this looks by opening SQL Server Management Studio. Figure 7.11 shows the database snapshot database SNAP_AdventureWorks_6AM along with the source database AdventureWorks. It also shows the results of the system queries on these database object properties.

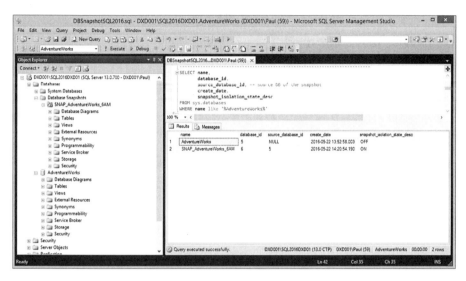

FIGURE 7.11   SSMS snapshot DB branch, system query results, and snapshot isolation state (ON).

You are now in the database snapshot business!

Breaking Down a Database Snapshot

If you want to get rid of a snapshot or overlay a current snapshot with a more up-to-date snapshot, you simply use the DROP DATABASE command and then create it again. The DROP DATABASE command immediately removes the database snapshot entry and all sparse file allocations associated with the snapshot. It's very simple indeed. The following example drops the database snapshot just created:

```
Use [master]
go
DROP DATABASE SNAP_AdventureWorks_6AM
go
```

If you'd like, you can also drop (delete) a database snapshot from SQL Server Management Studio by right-clicking the database snapshot entry and choosing the Delete option. However, it's best to do everything with scripts so that you can accurately reproduce the same action over and over.

Reverting to a Database Snapshot for Recovery

If you have a database snapshot defined for a source database, you can use that snapshot to revert the source database to that snapshot's point-in-time milestone. In other words, you consciously overlay a source database with the point-in-time representation of that database (which you got when you created a snapshot). You must remember that you will lose all data changes that occurred from that point-in-time moment and the current state of the source database. However, this may be exactly what you intend.

Reverting a Source Database from a Database Snapshot

Reverting is just a logical term for using the DATABASE RESTORE command with the FROM DATABASE_SNAPSHOT statement. It effectively causes the point-in-time database snapshot to become the source database. Under the covers, much of this is managed from the system catalog metadata level. However, the result is that the source database will be in exactly the same state as the database snapshot. When you use a database snapshot as the basis of a database restore, all other database snapshots that have the same source database must first be dropped. Again, to see what database snapshots may be defined for a particular database, you can execute the following query:

```
Use [master]
go
SELECT name,
       database_id,
       source_database_id, – source DB of the snapshot
       create_date,
       snapshot_isolation_state_desc
FROM sys.databases
Go
```

This query shows the existing source database and the newly created database snapshot, as follows:

name	database_id	source_database_id	create_date	snapshot_isolation_state_desc
AdventureWorks	5	NULL	2016-02-17 23:37:02.763	OFF
SNAP_AdventureWorks_6AM	9	5	2016-12-05 06:00:36.597	ON
SNAP_AdventureWorks_12PM	10	5	2016-12-05 12:00:36.227	ON

In this example, there are two snapshots against the AdventureWorks database. The one you don't want to use when reverting must be dropped first. Then you can proceed to restore the source database with the remaining snapshot that you want. These are the steps:

1. Drop the unwanted snapshot(s):

```
Use [master]
go
DROP DATABASE SNAP_AdventureWorks_12PM
go
```

2. Issue the RESTORE DATABASE command with the remaining snapshot:

```
USE [master]
go
RESTORE DATABASE AdventureWorks FROM DATABASE_SNAPSHOT =
'SNAP_AdventureWorks_6AM'
go
```

When this process is complete, the source database and snapshot are essentially the same point-in-time database. But remember that the source database quickly diverges as updates begin to flow in again.

Using Database Snapshots with Testing and QA

Reverting to a "golden" copy of a database via a database snapshot is sure to be popular because of the simplicity of creating and reverting. Testing and QA groups will thrive on this feature, and this will directly affect the velocity of testing in an organization. With the increase in the frequency and stability of your testing and QA environments, a direct improvement in the quality of your application should be attainable.

These are the steps:

1. Create the golden database snapshot *before* you run your testing:

```
Use [master]
go
CREATE DATABASE SNAP_AdventureWorks_GOLDEN
ON ( NAME = AdventureWorks_Data, FILENAME= 'C:\Program Files\
    Microsoft SQL Server\ MSSQL13.SQL2016DXD01\MSSQL\DATA\
            SNAP_AdventureWorks_data_GOLDEN.snap')
AS SNAPSHOT OF AdventureWorks
Go
```

2. Run tests or QA to your heart's content.

3. Revert to the golden copy when the testing is completed so that the process can be repeated again, regression testing can be run, stress testing can be done, performance testing can be started, or further application testing can be done:

```
USE [master]
go
RESTORE DATABASE AdventureWorks
FROM DATABASE_SNAPSHOT = 'SNAP_AdventureWorks_GOLDEN'
go
```

Security for Database Snapshots

By default, you get the security roles and definitions that you have created in the source database available to you within the database snapshot *except* for roles or individual permissions that you have in the source database used for updating data or objects. This is referred to as "inherited from the source database." These updating rights are not available to you in a database snapshot. A database snapshot is a read-only database! If you have specialized roles or restrictions you want to be present in the database snapshot, you need to define them in the source database, and you get them instantly. You manage from a single place, and everyone is happy.

Snapshot Sparse File Size Management

Sparse file size is probably the most critical aspect to deal with when managing database snapshots. It is imperative that you keep a close watch on the growing size of any (and all) database snapshot sparse files you create. If a snapshot runs out of space because you didn't manage file size well, it becomes suspect and is not available to use. The only path out of this scenario is to drop the snapshot and re-create it. Following are some issues to consider for sparse files:

▶ Monitor sparse files regularly. Make use of stored procedures such as the SNAP_SIZE_ UNLEASHED2016 stored procedure to help with this situation.

▶ Pay close attention to the volatility of the source database. This rate of change directly translates to the size of the sparse file and how fast it grows. The rule of thumb is to match your drop and re-create of a database snapshot frequency to when the sparse file is at around 30% of the size of the source database. Your data latency user requirements may demand a faster rate of drop/re-create.

▶ Isolate sparse files away from the source database data files. You do not want to compete with disk arm movement in any way. Always work to get disk I/O as parallel as possible.

Number of Database Snapshots per Source Database

In general, you shouldn't have too many database snapshots defined on a database because of the copy-on-write overhead each snapshot requires. However, this depends on the volatility of the source database and a server's capacity. If there is low volatility and the server is not using much CPU, memory, and disk capacity, this database could more readily support many separate database snapshots at once. If the volatility is high and CPU, memory, and perhaps disk capacity are saturated, you should drastically minimize the number of database snapshots.

Adding Database Mirroring for High Availability

Even though database mirroring has been a great addition to SQL Server over the years, it will be deprecated in future releases of SQL Server beyond SQL Server 2016. It is worth noting that the core technology components that comprise database mirroring have all been utilized in AlwaysOn availability groups capability. In the meantime, using database mirroring is still a viable first step in achieving both high availability and distributed workloads and will be around for a few more years at least. Something else to keep in mind is that database mirroring has very few configuration restrictions, whereas AlwaysOn availability groups require minimum OS and SQL Server version levels. This means even the smallest company has a chance at gaining near-real-time database failover without the fancy, expensive hardware required with more complex configurations. With database mirroring, you can set up a near-real-time database failover environment using all conventional, low-cost machines, without any complex hardware compatibility requirements, and database mirroring can fail over in as little as 3 seconds! Database mirroring effectively allows anyone to immediately step up to nearly 99.9% (three 9s) availability at the database layer at a very low cost, and it is easily configured and managed.

> **NOTE**
>
> Database mirroring cannot be implemented on a database that is also configured for filestream storage.

What Is Database Mirroring?

When you mirror a database, you are essentially asking for a complete copy of a database to be created and maintained, with as much up-to-the-second completeness as possible; you are asking for a mirror image. Database mirroring is a database-level feature. This means that there is no support for filtering, subsetting, or any form of partitioning. You mirror a complete database or nothing at all. This limitation actually keeps database mirroring simple and clean to implement. It also certainly provides some drawbacks, such as burning up a lot more disk storage, but what you get in return is well worth the storage cost.

Database mirroring works through the transaction log of the principal database (that is, the database that is to be mirrored). You can mirror only a database that uses the full database recovery model. Otherwise, it would not be possible to forward transaction log entries to another server. Through the use of copy-on-write technology, a change to data in a primary server's database (as reflected in active transaction log entries) is first "copied" to the target server, and then it is "written" (that is, applied or restored) to the target database server (that is, to the mirror server) transaction log. That is why it's called *copy-on-write*.

Database mirroring is very different from data replication. With replication, database changes are at the logical level (INSERT, UPDATE, and DELETE statements; stored procedure executions; and so on), whereas database mirroring uses the actual physical log entries on both the primary database server side and the mirror database server side. Effectively, the physical "active" log records from the transaction log of the principal database are copied and written directly to the transaction log of the mirror database. These physical log record-level transactions can be applied extremely quickly. As these physical log records are being applied to the mirror database, even the data cache reflects the forward application of the log records. This makes the entire database and data cache ready for the principal to take over extremely quickly. In addition, the log records are compressed on the principal side before transmission, which allows more records per transmission to be sent to the mirror server, thus speeding up the whole topology quite a bit. Figure 7.12 shows a typical database mirroring configuration that has three components:

▶ **Principal database server**—This is the source of the mirroring. You can mirror one or more databases on a single SQL Server instance to another SQL Server instance. You cannot mirror a database on one SQL Server instance to itself (that is, the same SQL Server instance). Remember that you mirror a database, not a subset of the database or a single table. It's all or nothing. The principal is the "active" server in the configuration.

▶ **Mirror database server**—The mirror server is the recipient of the mirroring from the principal database server. This mirrored database is kept in hot standby mode and cannot be used directly in any way. It is the "passive" server in the configuration. In fact, after you configure database mirroring, this database shows its status as being in continuous "restore" mode. The reason is that the physical transaction records are continuously applied to this mirror database. This database is essentially a hot standby database and is not available for direct database usage of any kind. It is used in case the principal fails, and it must not be tainted in any way; it must be an exact mirror image of the principal. The one exception to this non-usage scenario is creating database snapshots from the mirror database. (I cover this great capability later in this chapter.)

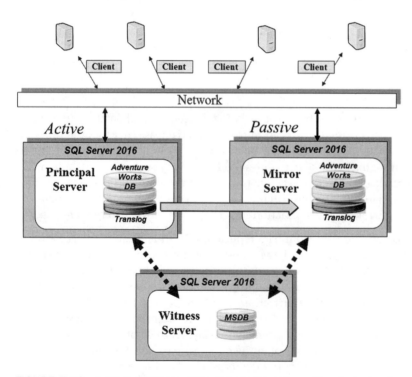

FIGURE 7.12   A basic database mirroring configuration with principal, mirror, and witness servers.

▶ **Witness database server**—You use the witness database server, which is optional, when you want to be continually checking to see if any failures have occurred to the primary database server and to help make the decision to fail over to the mirror database server. Using a witness server is a sound way to configure database mirroring. If you do not identify a witness server, the principal and mirror are left on their own to decide whether to fail over. With the witness server, a quorum is formed (that is, two out of three servers), and it takes the quorum to make a failover decision. A typical scenario is that the principal server fails for some reason, the witness sees this failure, the mirror also sees the failure, and together they agree that the principal is lost and that the mirror must take over the principal role. If the witness still sees that the principal is alive and well, but the communication between the mirror and principal has been broken, the witness does not agree to fail over to the mirror (even though the mirror thinks it must do this because it lost connection to the principal). Witness servers are usually put on separate physical servers.

> **NOTE**
>
> Database mirroring cannot be used for any of SQL Server's internal databases—tempdb, masterdb, msdb, or modeldb. Database mirroring is fully supported in SQL Server Standard Edition, Developer Edition, and Enterprise Edition, but it is not supported in SQL Server Express Edition. However, even machines running SQL Server Express Edition can be used as witness servers.

When to Use Database Mirroring

As mentioned earlier in this chapter, database mirroring elevates the availability level of a SQL Server–based application to a very high level without any special hardware and extra administration staff skills. However, when you should use database mirroring varies depending on your true needs.

Basically, if you need to increase the availability of the database layer, have automatic data protection (that is, redundant storage of data), or decrease the downtime that would normally be required to do upgrades, you can use database mirroring. An ever more popular scenario for database mirroring is when you need to offload reporting that is easily satisfied with periodic database snapshots. This usage provides great relief from heavily burdened transactional servers also used for reporting.

Roles of the Database Mirroring Configuration

As you have seen, a typical database mirroring configuration has a principal server, a mirror server, and a witness server. Each of these servers plays a role at some point. The principal and mirror switch roles, so it is important to understand what these roles are and when a server is playing a particular role.

Playing Roles and Switching Roles

A *role* corresponds to what a server is doing at a particular point in time. There are three possible roles:

▶ **Witness role**—If a server is playing a witness role, it is essentially standing alongside both partners of a database mirror configuration and is used to settle all arguments. It is getting together with any one of the other servers and forming a quorum to come up with decisions. The decision that it will participate in is whether to fail over. That is it. As mentioned before, the witness server can be any edition of a SQL Server (even SQL Server Express, the free version).

▶ **Principal role**—If a server is playing a principal role, it is the server that the application will be connected to and that is generating the transactions. One of the partners in the database mirror must start out as the principal. After a failure, the mirror server takes over the principal role, and the roles reverse.

▶ **Mirror role**—If a server is playing a mirror role, it is the server that is having transactions written to it. It is in a constant recovery state (that is, the database state needed to be able to accept physical log records). One of the partners in the database mirroring configuration must start out in the mirror role. Then, if a failure occurs, the mirror server changes to the principal role.

Database Mirroring Operating Modes

With database mirroring, you have the option of deploying in one of three modes: high safety with automatic failover mode (high availability with a witness server), high safety *without* automatic failover mode (high protection without a witness server), and high-performance mode. Each mode has different failure and protection characteristics and uses the database mirroring configurations slightly differently. As you might expect, the high-performance mode offers the least amount of protection; you must sacrifice levels of protection for performance.

Database mirroring runs with either asynchronous or synchronous operations:

▶ **Synchronous operations**—With synchronous operations, a transaction is committed (that is, written) on both partners of the database mirroring pair. This obviously adds some latency cost to a complete transaction because it is across two servers. High-safety modes use synchronous operations.

▶ **Asynchronous operations**—With asynchronous operations, transactions commit without waiting for the mirror server to write the log to disk. This can speed up performance significantly. High-performance mode uses asynchronous operations.

Whether operations are asynchronous or synchronous depends on the transaction safety setting. You control this setting through the SAFETY option when configuring with Transact-SQL (T-SQL) commands. The default for SAFETY is FULL (which provides synchronous operations). You set it to OFF for asynchronous operations. If you are using the Database Mirroring Wizard, this option is set for you automatically.

Of the three modes, only the high safety with automatic failover mode (high availability mode) requires the witness server. The others can operate fine without this third server in their configuration. Remember that the witness server is looking at both the principal and mirror server and will be utilized (in a quorum) for automatic failover.

Role switching is the act of transferring the principal role to the mirror server. It is the mirror server that acts as the failover partner for the principal server. When a failure occurs, the principal role is switched to the mirror server, and its database is brought online as the principal database.

Failover variations include the following:

▶ **Automatic failover**—Automatic failover is enabled with a three-server configuration involving a principal, a mirror, and a witness server. Synchronous operations are required, and the mirror database must already be synchronized (that is, in sync with the transactions as they are being written to the principal). Role switching is done automatically. This is for high availability mode.

▶ **Manual failover**—Manual failover is needed when there is no witness server and you are using synchronous operations. The principal and mirror are connected to each other, and the mirror database is synchronized. Role switching is done manually. This is for high safety without automatic failover mode (high-protection mode). You are making the decision to start using the mirror server as the principal (no data loss).

▶ **Forced service**—In the case of a mirror server being available but possibly not synchronized, the mirror server can be forced to take over when the principal server has failed. This possibly means data loss because the transactions were not synchronized. This is for either high safety without automatic failover mode (high-protection mode) or high-performance mode.

Setting Up and Configuring Database Mirroring

Microsoft uses a few unique concepts and technologies in database mirroring. You have already learned about the copy-on-write technology. Microsoft also uses *endpoints*, which are assigned to each server in a database mirroring configuration. In addition, establishing connections to each server is much more tightly controlled and requires service accounts or integrated (domain-level) authentication. Within SQL Server, grants must also be given to the accounts that will be executing database mirroring.

You can completely set up database mirroring by using T-SQL scripts, or you can use the Database Mirroring Wizard in SSMS. I advise that you use something that is repeatable, such as SQL scripts, and you can easily generate SQL scripts by using the wizard. It's not fun to have to re-create or manage a database mirroring configuration in the middle of the night. Having this whole process in a script reduces almost all errors.

Getting Ready to Mirror a Database

Before you start setting up and configuring a database mirroring environment, it is best to run through a simple checklist of basic requirements that you need to verify so that you know you are properly mirror a database:

1. Verify that all server instances are at the same service pack level. In addition, the SQL Server edition you have must support database mirroring.

2. Verify that you have as much or more disk space available on the mirror server as on the principal server. You also need the same room for growth on both.

3. Verify that you have connectivity to each server from the others. You can most easily do this by trying to register each SQL Server instance in SSMS. If you can register the server, the server can be used for database mirroring. Do this for the principal, mirror, and witness servers.

4. Verify that the principal server database that is to be mirrored is using the full database recovery model. Because database mirroring is transaction log based, it makes sense to be using the full database recovery model: All transactions are written to the transaction log and are not truncated, as with other database recovery models.

Before you go any further, you must establish the endpoints for each of the servers that will be part of the database mirroring configuration. You can use the Configure Security option of the wizard to do this, but getting into the practice of using SQL scripts is really the best approach. Using SQL scripts is very easy, as you will soon see.

Endpoints utilize TCP/IP addressing and listening ports for all communication between the servers. Within a server, the endpoint is given a specific name (that is, an endpoint name) for easy reference and to establish the partner roles that this server (endpoint) will possibly play. In addition, a connection GRANT is needed for access to be allowed from each server to the other, and a service account should be used for this. This service account is usually a particular login that is known to the domain and is to be used for all connections in the database mirroring topology. Figure 7.13 shows the mirroring database properties of the AdventureWorks database on a SQL Server instance named SQL2016DXD01. As you can see, no server network addresses are set up for database mirroring of any kind, and the mirroring status says "This Database Has Not Been Configured for Mirroring."

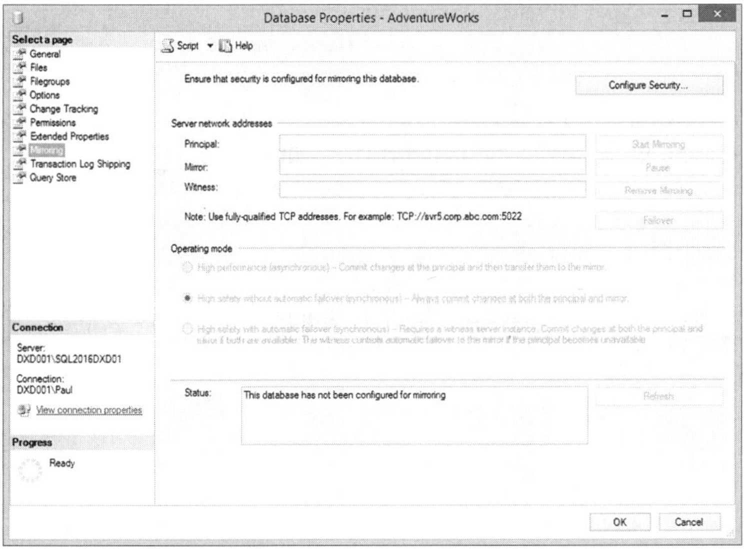

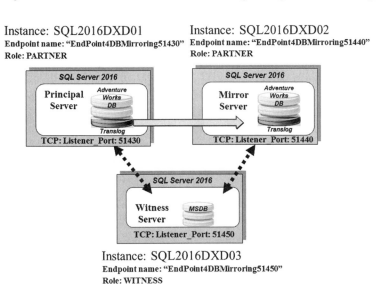

FIGURE 7.13   The Database Properties Mirroring page: mirroring network addressing and mirroring status.

Next, let's look at how to set up high safety with automatic failover mode (high availability mode) database mirroring with principal, mirror, and witness servers. For this, you can mirror the old reliable AdventureWorks database that Microsoft provides with SQL Server (the OLTP version that does not contain filestream files).

Figure 7.14 illustrates the database mirroring configuration to set up.

Instance: SQL2016DXD01   Instance: SQL2016DXD02
Endpoint name: "EndPoint4DBMirroring51430"   Endpoint name: "EndPoint4DBMirroring51440"
Role: PARTNER   Role: PARTNER

SQL Server 2016   SQL Server 2016

Principal   Adventure   Mirror   Adventure
 Server   Works   Server   Works
               DB   DB

        Translog   Translog
TCP: Listener_Port: 51430   TCP: Listener_Port: 51440

        SQL Server 2016

        Witness   MSDB
         Server

        TCP: Listener_Port: 51450

Instance: SQL2016DXD03
Endpoint name: "EndPoint4DBMirroring51450"
Role: WITNESS

FIGURE 7.14   A high availability database mirroring configuration with the AdventureWorks database.

For this example, the initial principal server is the SQL Server instance named SQL2016DXD01, the initial mirror server is the SQL Server instance named SQL2016DXD02, and the witness server is the SQL Server instance named SQL2016DXD03.

You need to establish a local endpoint named EndPoint4DBMirroring9xxx on each of these SQL Server instances and identify the TCP listening port that will be used for all database mirroring communication. I also like to embed the port number as part of the endpoint name, such as EndPoint4DBMirroring51430 for the endpoint that will be listening on port 51430. In this configuration, the principal server will be listening on Port 51430, the mirror server on Port 51440, and the witness server on Port 51450. These port numbers must be unique within a single server machine, and the machine name and port combination must be unique within the network. An example of a fully qualified network address name of a server and the listing port is TCP://DXD001.ADS.DXD.COM:51430, where DXD001.ADS.DXD.COM is the machine name within the domain, and 51430 is the listening port created with the endpoint.

In addition, each server's initial role needs to be specified. For this example, the SQL2016DXD01 instance can play any partner role (that is, a mirror and/or principal), the SQL2016DXD02 instance can play any partner role as well, and the SQL2016DXD03 instance will play the witness role only.

I have included three SQL script templates with this book (available at the companion website for this book title www.informit.com/title/9780672337765) that have working examples of creating the endpoints, granting connection permissions to a login for the endpoints, verifying that the endpoints were created, altering the endpoints, backing up and restoring databases, and backing up and restoring transaction logs.

The first ones to look at are 2016 Create EndPoint Partner1.SQL, 2016 Create EndPoint Partner2.SQL, and 2016 Create EndPoint Witness.SQL. You can leverage these templates to start the setup process if you are not using the Configure Security Wizard.

After you've verified all aspects of the planned mirroring topology, you can configure full database mirroring!

Creating the Endpoints

Each server instance in the database mirroring configuration must have an endpoint defined so that the other servers can communicate with it. This is sort of like a private phone line to your friends. For this example, you can use the scripts provided as opposed to using the Configure Security Wizard. The first endpoint script is in the file 2016 Create EndPoint Partner1.SQL.

From SSMS, you need to open a new query connection to your principal database by selecting File, New and in the New Query dialog, selecting Query with Current Connection. Open the SQL file for the first endpoint.

The following CREATE ENDPOINT T-SQL creates the endpoint named EndPoint4DBMirror-ing1430, with the listener_port value 51430 and the database mirroring role Partner:

```
-- create endpoint for principal server --
CREATE ENDPOINT [EndPoint4DBMirroring51430]
    STATE=STARTED
    AS TCP (LISTENER_PORT = 51430, LISTENER_IP = ALL)
    FOR DATA_MIRRORING (ROLE = PARTNER, AUTHENTICATION = WINDOWS NEGOTIATE
, ENCRYPTION = REQUIRED ALGORITHM RC4)
```

After this T-SQL runs, you should run the following SELECT statements to verify that the endpoint has been correctly created:

```
select name,type_desc,port,ip_address from sys.tcp_endpoints;
select name,role_desc,state_desc from sys.database_mirroring_endpoints;
```

If you also look at the database properties for the AdventureWorks database on the principal server (SQL2016DXD01, in this example), you see the server network address for the principal server automatically appear now when you look at the Database Properties Mirroring page (see Figure 7.15).

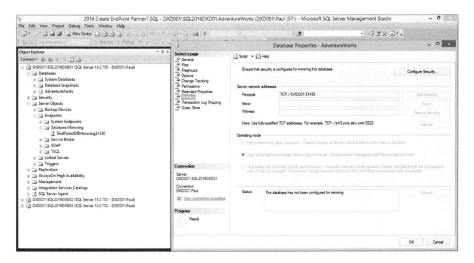

FIGURE 7.15   The Mirroring page of the AdventureWorks database on the principal server with listening port 51430.

Starting with the sample SQL scripts 2016 Create EndPoint Partner2.SQL and 2016 Create EndPoint Witness.SQL, you need to repeat the endpoint creation process for the mirror server (using a listener_port value of 51440) and the witness server (using a listener_port value of 51450) by opening a query connection to each one of these servers and running the following CREATE ENDPOINT commands:

```
-- create endpoint for mirror server --
CREATE ENDPOINT [EndPoint4DBMirroring51440]
    STATE=STARTED
    AS TCP (LISTENER_PORT = 51440, LISTENER_IP = ALL)
    FOR DATA_MIRRORING (ROLE = PARTNER, AUTHENTICATION = WINDOWS NEGOTIATE
, ENCRYPTION = REQUIRED ALGORITHM RC4)
```

For the witness server (notice that the role is now witness), you run the following:

```
-- create endpoint for witness server --
CREATE ENDPOINT [EndPoint4DBMirroring51450]
    STATE=STARTED
    AS TCP (LISTENER_PORT = 51450, LISTENER_IP = ALL)
    FOR DATA_MIRRORING (ROLE = WITNESS, AUTHENTICATION = WINDOWS NEGOTIATE
, ENCRYPTION = REQUIRED ALGORITHM RC4)
```

Granting Permissions

It is possible to have an AUTHORIZATION [login] statement in the CREATE ENDPOINT command that establishes the permissions for a login account to the endpoint being defined. However, separating this out into a GRANT greatly stresses the point of allowing this connection permission. From each SQL query connection, you run a GRANT to allow a specific login account to connect on the ENDPOINT for database mirroring. If you don't have a specific login account to use, default it to [NT AUTHORITY\SYSTEM].

From the principal server instance (SQL2016DXD01), you run the following GRANT (substituting [NT AUTHORITY\SYSTEM] with your specific login account to be used by database mirroring):

```
GRANT CONNECT ON ENDPOINT::EndPoint4DBMirroring51430 TO [NT AUTHORITY\SYSTEM];
```

Then, from the mirror server instance (SQL2016DXD02), you run the following GRANT:

```
GRANT CONNECT ON ENDPOINT:: EndPoint4DBMirroring51440 TO [NT AUTHORITY\SYSTEM];
```

Then, from the witness server instance (SQL2016DXD03), you run the following GRANT:

```
GRANT CONNECT ON ENDPOINT:: EndPoint4DBMirroring51450 TO [NT AUTHORITY\SYSTEM];
```

Creating the Database on the Mirror Server

When the endpoints are configured and roles are established, you can create the database on the mirror server and get it to the point of being able to mirror. You must first make a backup copy of the principal database (AdventureWorks, in this example). This backup will be used to create the database on the mirror server. You can use SSMS tasks or SQL scripts to do this. The SQL scripts (DBBackupAW2016.sql), which are easily repeatable, are used here.

On the principal server, you make a complete backup as follows:

```
BACKUP DATABASE [AdventureWorks]
    TO DISK = N'C:\Program Files\Microsoft SQL
Server\MSSQL13.SQL2016DXD01\MSSQL\Backup\AdventureWorks4Mirror.bak'
    WITH FORMAT
GO
```

Next, you copy this backup file to a place where the mirror server can reach it on the network. When that is complete, you can issue the following database RESTORE command to create the AdventureWorks database on the mirror server (using the WITH NORECOVERY option):

```
-- use this restore database(with NoRecovery option)
to create the mirrored version of this DB --
RESTORE FILELISTONLY
   FROM DISK = 'C:\Program Files\Microsoft SQL
Server\MSSQL13.SQL2016DXD01\MSSQL\Backup\AdventureWorks4Mirror.bak'
go
RESTORE DATABASE AdventureWorks
   FROM DISK = 'C:\Program Files\Microsoft SQL
              Server\MSSQL13.SQL2016DXD01\MSSQL\Backup\AdventureWorks4Mirror.bak'
  WITH NORECOVERY,
       MOVE 'AdventureWorks_Data' TO 'C:\Program Files\Microsoft SQL
              Server\MSSQL13.SQL2016DXD02\MSSQL\Data\AdventureWorks_Data.mdf',
       MOVE 'AdventureWorks_Log'  TO 'C:\Program Files\Microsoft SQL
              Server\MSSQL13.SQL2016DXD02\MSSQL\Data\AdventureWorks_Log.ldf'
GO
```

Because you don't necessarily have the same directory structure on the mirror server, you use the MOVE option as part of this restore to place the database files in the location you desire.

The restore process should yield something that looks like the following result set:

```
Processed 24216 pages for database 'AdventureWorks', file 'AdventureWorks_Data' on
file 1.
Processed 3 pages for database 'AdventureWorks', file 'AdventureWorks_Log' on file
1.
RESTORE DATABASE successfully processed 24219 pages in 5.677 seconds (33.328 MB/sec).
```

You must now apply at least one transaction log dump to the mirror database. This brings the mirror database to a point of synchronization with the principal and leaves the mirror database in the restoring state. At this database recovery point, you can run through the Database Mirroring Wizard and start mirroring for high availability.

From the principal server, you dump (that is, back up) a transaction log as follows:

```
BACKUP LOG [AdventureWorks] TO
DISK = N'C:\Program Files\Microsoft SQL
Server\MSSQL13.SQL2016DXD01\MSSQL\Backup\AdventureWorks4MirrorLog.bak'
WITH FORMAT
Go
Processed 4 pages for database 'AdventureWorks', file 'AdventureWorks_Log'
on file 1.
BACKUP LOG successfully processed 4 pages in 0.063 seconds (0.496 MB/sec).
```

Then you move this backup to a place where it can be reached by the mirror server. When that is done, you restore the log to the mirror database. From the mirror server, you restore the transaction log as follows:

```
RESTORE LOG [AdventureWorks]
    FROM  DISK = N'C:\Program Files\Microsoft SQL
          Server\MSSQL13.SQL2016DXD02\MSSQL\Backup\AdventureWorks4MirrorLog.bak'
    WITH  FILE = 1, NORECOVERY
GO
```

> **NOTE**
>
> In the `WITH FILE =` statement, the file number must match the value in the backup log results (see the on `file 1` reference in the previous code).

The restore log process should yield something that looks like the following result set:

```
Processed 0 pages for database 'AdventureWorks', file 'AdventureWorks_Data' on file 1.
Processed 4 pages for database 'AdventureWorks', file 'AdventureWorks_Log' on file 1.
RESTORE LOG successfully processed 4 pages in 0.007 seconds (4.464 MB/sec).
```

> **NOTE**
>
> You might need to update the `FILE = x` entry in the `RESTORE LOG` command to correspond to the on `file` value given during the log backup.

You are now ready to mirror the database in high availability mode.

Identifying the Other Endpoints for Database Mirroring

To get the nodes in the topology to see each other, you have to identify the endpoints and listener port values to the databases involved in the database mirroring configuration (the principal and mirror). This also activates database mirroring. This process requires altering the database by using either the SET PARTNER or SET WITNESS statements within the ALTER DATABASE command. The Database Mirroring Wizard can also do this step for you, but doing it manually is easy.

You identify the unique endpoint listening port values for each endpoint that are unique within the server. They are port values 51430, 51440, and 51450 in this example.

Remember that you will be doing this *after* you create the AdventureWorks database on the mirror server side (using database and log restores). After creating that database, you can run the following ALTER DATABASE command on the mirror server (SQL2016DXD02 in this example) to identify the principal for the mirror to partner with:

```
-- From the Mirror Server Database: identify the principal server endpoint --
ALTER DATABASE AdventureWorks
    SET PARTNER = ' TCP://DXD001:51430'
GO
```

Now, you are ready for the final step: From the principal server, you identify the mirror and witness. After you complete this step, the database mirroring topology tries to synchronize itself and begin database mirroring. The following statements identify the mirror server endpoint and witness server endpoint to the principal server's database:

```
-- From the Principal Server Database: identify the mirror server endpoint --
ALTER DATABASE AdventureWorks
    SET PARTNER = 'TCP://DXD001:51440'
GO
-- From the Principal Server Database: identify the witness server endpoint --
ALTER DATABASE AdventureWorks
  SET WITNESS = 'TCP://DXD001:51450'
GO
```

You do not have to alter any database from the witness server.

When this process completes successfully, you are mirroring! In fact, with this configuration, you are in automatic failover mode.

If you have issues or just want to start over, you can drop an endpoint or alter an endpoint quite easily. To drop and existing endpoint, you use the DROP ENDPOINT command. In this example, the following command would drop the endpoint you just created:

```
-- To DROP an existing endpoint --
DROP ENDPOINT EndPoint4DBMirroring51430;
```

Altering an endpoint (for example, to change the listener_port value) is just as easy as dropping one. The following example shows how to alter the currently defined endpoint to a new listener_port value of 51435 because of a conflict at the network level:

```
-- To ALTER an existing endpoint --
ALTER ENDPOINT EndPoint4DBMirroring51430
   STATE = STARTED
   AS TCP( LISTENER_PORT = 51435 )
   FOR DATABASE_MIRRORING (ROLE = PARTNER)
```

7

However, because you use the port in the endpoint name, it might be best to just drop and create a new endpoint to fit the naming convention. Either way, you can easily manipulate these endpoints to fit your networking needs.

As you can see in Figure 7.16, the databases are fully synchronizing for mirroring, and you are now in full-safety high availability mode.

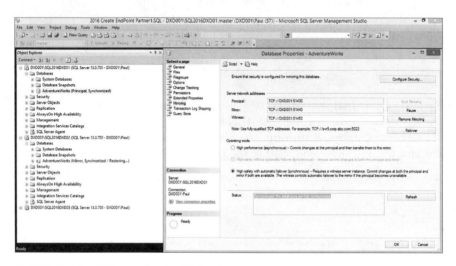

FIGURE 7.16   Fully synchronized DB mirroring.

If you look at the SQL Server log file (that is, the current log), you can see SQL server log entries indicating that database mirroring is active:

```
05/16/2016 23:42:06,spid31s,Unknown,Database mirroring is active
          with database 'AdventureWorks' as the principal copy.
05/16/2016 23:41:01,spid54,Unknown,Database mirroring has been enabled on
          this instance of SQL Server.
05/16/2016 23:03:01,spid54,Unknown,The Database Mirroring endpoint is now
          listening for connections.
05/16/2016 23:03:01,spid54,Unknown,Server is
          listening on [ 'any' <ipv4> 51430].
```

Monitoring a Mirrored Database Environment

After active mirroring has started, you can monitor the complete mirrored topology in a few ways. You should start by registering the database being mirrored in the feature in SSMS called Database Mirroring Monitor. Database Mirroring Monitor allows you to monitor roles of the mirroring partnership (that is, principal, mirror, and witness), see the history of transactions flowing to the mirror server, see the status and speed of this transaction flow, and set thresholds to alert you if failures or other issues occur. In addition, you can administer the logins/service accounts being used in the mirrored database topology.

Figure 7.17 shows how you launch the Database Mirroring Monitor from SSMS: You right-click the principal database being mirrored, choose Tasks, and then choose Launch Database Mirroring Monitor.

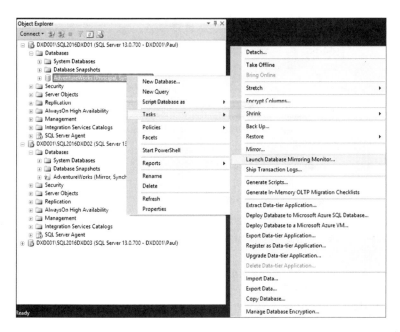

FIGURE 7.17   Launching Database Mirroring Monitor from SSMS.

You must register the database being mirrored. To do so, you select the principal or mirror server instance and set the Register check box for the database. Database Mirroring Monitor registers the database and both partner server instances, as shown in Figure 7.18.

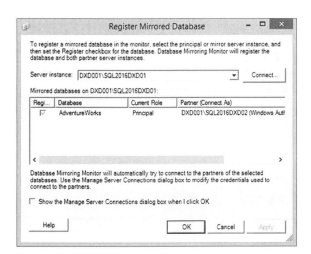

FIGURE 7.18   Registering the mirrored database in Database Mirroring Monitor.

After the database is registered, all partners and the witness server instances show up in the Database Mirroring Monitor, as shown in Figure 7.19.

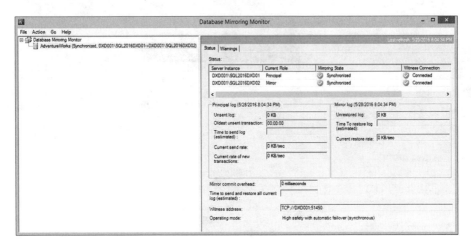

FIGURE 7.19   The registered database and status of each mirroring partner.

At a glance, you can see which server is playing what role (principal or mirror) and whether each partner has defined and is connecting to a witness server. In addition, you can see the unsent log (in size), the unrestored log (in size), when the oldest unsent transaction occurred, the amount of time it took to send the transaction to the mirror server instance, the send rate (KB/second), the current rate at which the transactions get restored (KB/second), the mirror commit overhead (in milliseconds), the listener port of the witness server instance, and the operating mode of the mirroring (in this case, high safety with automatic failover—synchronous).

Figure 7.20 shows the detailed transaction history for a particular part of the mirroring flow (either the send-out of the principal part or the restore to the mirror part). You can click the appropriate partner to see all transaction history details of the mirrored copy and restore process. I've included a stored procedure named TRAFFIC_GENERATOR2016 in the file called TRAFFIC_GENERATOR2016.sql on the companion website for this book. This procedure will generate a good amount of sales order transactions against the AdventureWorks database so that you can monitor how transactions are mirrored. Go ahead, give it a try.

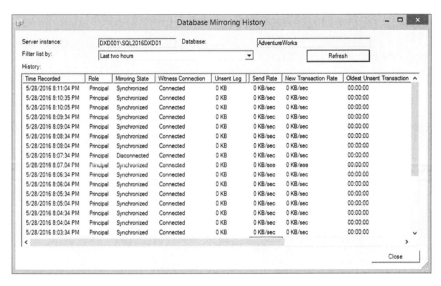

FIGURE 7.20   Transaction history of mirroring partners.

From the Database Properties Mirroring page, you can easily pause (and resume) database mirroring if you suspect that there are issues related to the mirroring operation. In addition, you can see what role each server instance is playing.

Removing Mirroring

Very likely, you will have to remove all traces of database mirroring from each server instance of a database mirroring configuration at some point. Doing so is actually pretty easy. Basically, you have to disable mirroring of the principal, drop the mirror server's database, and remove all endpoints from each server instance. You can simply start from the Database Properties page and the Mirroring option and do the whole thing. Alternatively, you can do this through SQL scripts. Let's first use the Mirroring options. Looking at the options in Figure 7.21, you simply choose to remove mirroring (from the principal server instance). This is just a bit too easy to do—almost dangerous!

FIGURE 7.21   Removing database mirroring.

The mirroring process is immediately disabled. When mirroring is disabled, you can drop the database on the mirror server instance, remove the endpoints on each server instance (that is, principal, mirror, and witness instances), and be done—all through SSMS. This approach is straightforward.

If you're removing mirroring with SQL scripts, however, you need to break the mirroring from the principal, remove the principal's endpoint, drop the mirror database and remove the mirror's endpoint, and then drop the witness server's endpoint. At this point, all mirroring is removed. The following example shows how to remove the database mirroring configuration you just set up.

The ALTER DATABASE and DROP ENDPOINT SQL commands break mirroring on the principal and remove the endpoint:

```
ALTER DATABASE AdventureWorks set partner off
go
DROP ENDPOINT EndPoint4DBMirroring51430
go
```

From the mirror server instance (not the principal!), you run the DROP DATABASE and DROP ENDPOINT SQL commands, as follows:

```
DROP DATABASE AdventureWorks
go
DROP ENDPOINT EndPoint4DBMirroring51440
go
```

From the witness server instance, you remove the endpoint as follows:

```
DROP ENDPOINT EndPoint4DBMirroring51450
go
```

To verify that you have removed these endpoints from each server instance, you simply run the following SELECT statements:

```
select name,type_desc,port,ip_address from sys.tcp_endpoints
select name,role_desc,state_desc from sys.database_mirroring_endpoints
```

All references to the endpoints and roles are removed.

You can also take a peek at the SQL Server log entries being made as you remove database mirroring:

```
06/17/2016 00:26:21,spid57,Unknown,The Database Mirroring
        endpoint has stopped listening for connections.
06/17/2016 00:25:18,spid9s,Unknown,Database mirroring connection error 4
        'The connection was closed by the remote end<c/> or an error
        occurred while receiving data: '64(The specified network
        name is no longer available.)'' for 'TCP://DXD001:51450'.
06/17/2016 00:25:00,spid9s,Unknown,Database mirroring connection error 4
        'The connection was closed by the remote end<c/> or an error
        occurred while receiving data: '64(The specified network
        name is no longer available.)'' for 'TCP://DXD001:51440'.
06/17/2016 00:23:59,spid24s,Unknown,Database mirroring has
        been terminated for database 'AdventureWorks'.
```

These are all informational messages only. No user action is required. As you can see from these messages, you are now in a state of no database mirroring. You have to completely build up database mirroring again if you want to mirror the database again.

Testing Failover from the Principal to the Mirror

From the SSMS, you can easily fail over from the principal to the mirror server instance (and back again) by clicking the Failover button on the Database Properties Mirroring page, as shown in Figure 7.22.

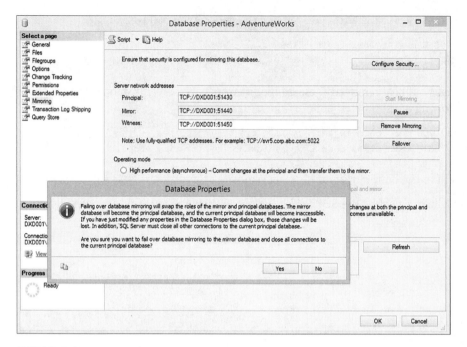

FIGURE 7.22   Testing failover of a mirrored database.

You must test failover at some point to guarantee that it works. When you click the Failover button for this database mirroring configuration, you are prompted to continue with the failover by clicking Yes or No. Remember that clicking Yes closes all connections to the principal server instance that are currently connected to this database. (Later in this chapter, I show you how to make your clients aware of both the principal and mirror server instances so that they can just pick up and run against either server instance, by design.)

Now, if you look at the Database Properties Mirroring page (see Figure 7.23), you see that the principal and mirror listener port values have switched: The principal instance is now port value 51440, and the mirror instance is port value 51430. The server instances have completely switched their roles. You must now go to the server instance playing the principal role to fail over back to the original operating mode. If you try to open the current mirror server instance database, you get an error stating that you cannot access this database because it is in restore mode.

You can also manually run an ALTER DATABASE command to force failover to the mirrored server, as follows:

```
ALTER DATABASE AdventureWorks set partner FAILOVER;
```

This command has the same effect as using SSMS or even shutting down the principal SQL Server instance service.

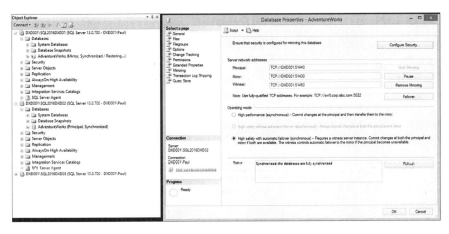

FIGURE 7.23   Server instances switch roles following a failover.

NOTE

You cannot bring the principal offline as you can do in an unmirrored configuration.

Client Setup and Configuration for Database Mirroring

Any client application is able to connect to either partner in a mirrored configuration.
The client would, of course, be connecting only to the server instance that is the current
principal. With the help of an extension to the client connection configuration file, all
.NET applications can easily add both partners to their connection string information, and
when a principal fails, they can automatically establish a connection to the new principal
(in a mirrored configuration). The expanded connection string information that you provide in the configuration file (`app.config`) for your application is illustrated below. This
enhancement uses the `Failover Partner=` addition that identifies the proper failover
server instance for this mirrored configuration:

```xml
<?xml version="1.0" encoding="utf-8" ?>
<configuration>
    <configSections>
    </configSections>
    <connectionStrings>
        <add name="WindowsApplication4.Properties.Settings.
                AdventureWorksConnectionString"
        connectionString="Data Source=DXD001\SQL2012DXD01;
                    Failover Partner=DXD001\SQL2012DXD02;
                    Initial Catalog=AdventureWorks;
                    Integrated Security=True"
        providerName="System.Data.SqlClient" />
    </connectionStrings>
</configuration>
```

Setting Up DB Snapshots Against a Database Mirror

As I suggested earlier in this chapter, you can use database mirroring to improve availability; you can also create a database snapshot against this mirrored database and expose the snapshot to your reporting users. Doing so further enhances the overall database availability to all end users (transactional and reporting users). In addition, it serves to isolate the reporting users from the transactional users. The reporting users are connected to the mirror server's version of the database (via a database snapshot of the mirrored database), and their reporting queries do not impact the principal server in any way. Remember that the mirrored database is not usable for any access whatsoever (it is in constant restore mode). SQL Server allows a snapshot to be created against it (refer to Figure 7.10). As mentioned previously, the only real issues arise when the principal server fails over to the mirror database. When the mirror server takes over for the principal, the database snapshot terminates its reporting user connections. The reporting users only need to reconnect to pick up where they left off. However, you now have both transactional and reporting users using the same database server instance, and performance of all is affected.

A possible solution to this situation would be to automatically (or manually) drop the database snapshot on the mirror server if it becomes the principal and create a new snapshot on the old principal server if it is available (that is, is now the mirror). You then just point all your reporting users to this new database snapshot. This process can be handled fairly easily in an application server layer. This is basically a reciprocal principal/mirror reporting configuration approach that always tries to get the database snapshot that is used for reporting to be on the server that is the mirror server. You would never really want to have active database snapshots on both the principal server and mirror server at the same time.

Reciprocal Principal/Mirror Reporting Configuration

The following steps outline the method to create the snapshot on the mirror, drop it when the mirror becomes the principal, and create a new snapshot against the old principal (now the mirror):

1. Create the database snapshot on a mirrored database server for reporting on the mirror server (DXD001\SQL2016DXD02):

```
Use [master]
go
CREATE DATABASE SNAP_AdventureWorks_REPORTING
ON ( NAME = AdventureWorks_Data, FILENAME= 'C:\Program Files\
    Microsoft SQL Server\MSSQL13.SQL2016DXD02\MSSQL\DATA\
        SNAP_AdventureWorks_data_REPORTING.snap')
AS SNAPSHOT OF AdventureWorks
Go
```

As you can see in Figure 7.24, this would be the live configuration of the principal server (DXD001\SQL2016DXD01), the mirror server (DXD001\SQL2016DXD02), and the reporting database snapshot (SNAP_AdventureWorks_REPORTING), as shown from SQL Server Management Studio.

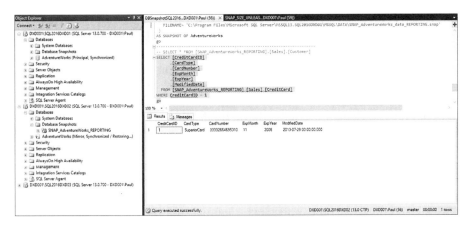

FIGURE 7.24   SQL Server Management Studio, showing database mirroring with a database snapshot for reporting configuration.

If the principal fails over to the mirror, you drop the database snapshot that is currently created off that database and create a new one on the old principal (now the mirror), as shown in the following steps.

2. Drop the reporting database snapshot on the new principal server (the principal is now DXD001\SQL2016DXD02):

```
Use [master]
go
DROP DATABASE SNAP_AdventureWorks_REPORTING
go
```

3. Create the new reporting database snapshot on the new mirrored database server (the mirror is now DXD001\SQL2016DXD01):

```
Use [master]
go
CREATE DATABASE SNAP_AdventureWorks_REPORTING
ON ( NAME = AdventureWorks_Data, FILENAME= 'C:\Program Files\
    Microsoft SQL Server\ MSSQL13.SQL2016DXD01\MSSQL\DATA\
        SNAP_AdventureWorks_data_REPORTING.snap')
AS SNAPSHOT OF AdventureWorks
Go
```

That's it. You now have your reporting users completely isolated from your principal server (and the transactional users) again. Life can return to normal very quickly.

Scenario 3: Investment Portfolio Management with DB Snapshots and DB Mirroring

As defined in Chapter 1, "Understanding High Availability," this business scenario is about an investment portfolio management application housed in a major server farm in the heart of the world's financial center: New York City. Serving North American customers only, this application provides the ability to do full trading of stocks and options in all financial markets (United States and international), along with full portfolio holdings assessment, historical performance, and holdings valuation. Primary users are investment managers for their large customers. Stock purchasing/selling comprise 90% of the daytime activity, with massive assessment, historical performance, and valuation reporting done after the markets have closed. Three major peaks occur each weekday, driven by the three major trading markets of the world (United States, Europe, and the Far East). During the weekends, the application is used for the long-range planning reporting and front-loading stock trades for the coming week.

Availability:

▶ 20 hours per day

▶ 7 days per week

▶ 365 days per year

   Planned downtime: 4%

   Unplanned downtime: 1% will be tolerable

   Availability possible category: High availability

The stock updates and the weekend reporting needs are the most significant things to support, with medium reporting needs during the day, but only as of a point in time. Performance of the OLTP portion of this application must not be sacrificed in any way.

Based on these priorities, costs and desire to be fairly simple to manage and maintain, the company initially opted to use database mirroring (for availability of the principal) and database snapshots (for point-in-time reporting). The company couldn't take on an Azure IaaS option right away. This is under reevaluation now for next year's possible upgrades of the solution. "Crawl before you walk" was the mantra the company kept bringing up over and over.

The company had previously estimated the total incremental costs to be between **$100k and $250k**, which include the following estimates:

▶ Two new multi-core servers with 64GB RAM at $50k per server

▶ Two Microsoft Windows 2012 Server licenses

▶ Two SQL Server Enterprise Edition licenses

▶ Twelve days of additional training costs for personnel

There are no special hardware or SCSI controllers needed to implement database mirroring or database snapshots. The total incremental cost to build this high availability solution is approximately $163,000 (total costs—as follows).

Now, let's work through the complete ROI calculation for these incremental costs, along with the cost of downtime:

1. Maintenance cost (for a 1-year period):

   ▶ **$7.7k (estimate)**—Yearly system admin personnel cost (additional time for training of these personnel)

   ▶ **$25.5k (estimate)**—Recurring software licensing cost

2. Hardware cost:

   ▶ **$100k hardware cost**—The cost of the additional HW in the new HA solution

3. Deployment/assessment cost:

   ▶ **$25k deployment cost**—The cost of development, testing, QA, and production implementation of the solution

   ▶ **$5k HA assessment cost**

4. Downtime cost (for a 1-year period):

   ▶ If you kept track of last year's downtime record, use that number; otherwise, produce an estimate of planned and unplanned downtime for this calculation. For this scenario, the estimated cost of downtime/hour is $150k/hour—which is massive!

   ▶ Planned downtime cost (revenue loss cost) = Planned downtime hours in this business don't cost anything really. This is a brick-and-mortar company that advertises normal hours of operation and prohibits data changes outside these advertised windows. It operates on the stock market time window.

   ▶ Unplanned downtime cost (revenue loss cost) = Unplanned downtime hours × cost of hourly downtime to the company:

      a. 1% (estimate of unplanned downtime percentage in one year) × 8,760 hours in a year = 87.6 hours of unplanned downtime

      b. 87.6 hours × $150k/hr (hourly cost of downtime) = $13,140,000/year cost of unplanned downtime. Total revenue is $4.6 billion/year.

ROI totals:

▶ Total costs to get on this HA solution = $163,000 (for the initial year and roughly $32.5k/year for subsequent years)

▶ Total of downtime cost = $13,140,000 (for the year)

The incremental cost is about 1.24% of the downtime cost for 1 year. In other words, the investment of this particular HA solution will pay for itself in 1.1 hours! This is a huge ROI in an extremely short amount of time.

After building this HA solution, the uptime goal was achieved easily. Occasionally, there were some delays in resyncing the mirror when one would fail over to the other. Over the past year, this choice has yielded 99.9% availability of the principal DB (for the OLTP activity), easy management, and point-in-time offloaded reporting to the mirror. It has been remarkable in meeting the point-in-time needs of this company. Overall, the users are extremely happy with performance and availability. They are now looking at the next possible upgrade scenarios to reduce downtime to 0.05% (that is, 99.95% uptime) for next year.

Summary

This chapter covers two fairly complex and complimentary solutions that can potentially be leveraged for high availability needs. Both are fairly easy to implement and manage. Both are also time tested and have provided many years of success to many companies around the globe. A database snapshot can be thought of as an enabling capability with many purposes. It can be great for fulfilling point-in-time reporting requirements easily, reverting a database to a point in time (recoverability and availability), insulating a database from issues that may arise during mass updates, and potentially reducing the processing impact of querying against the primary transactional databases (via database mirroring and database snapshots). You must remember that database snapshots are point in time and read-only. The only way to update a snapshot is to drop it and re-create it. Data latency of this point-in-time snapshot capability must always be made very clear to any of its users.

A database snapshot is a snapshot of an entire database, not a subset. This clearly makes data snapshots very different from alternative data access capabilities, such as data replication and materialized views. This feature has been made possible via a major breakthrough from Microsoft called copy-on-write technology. This is certainly an exciting extension to SQL Server but is not to be used as a substitute for good old database backups and restores. Database snapshots is one capability that I recommend you consider using as soon as possible.

Database mirroring provides a way for users to get to a minimum level of high availability for their databases and applications without having to use complex hardware and software configurations (as are needed with Cluster Services, SQL Server clustering, and higher OS and SQL editions that support AlwaysOn configurations). Even though database mirroring has been a great addition to SQL Server, it will be deprecated in the not-too-distant future, so use some caution here. As mentioned earlier in this chapter, the core technology components that comprise database mirroring have been utilized in the AlwaysOn availability groups capability. In fact, it is at the core of availability groups (which is explained in Chapter 6). Both of these technologies will play nicely into some organizations' needs for high availability and, as your confidence with these technologies increases, they will provide a basis for graduating to more robust solutions as your needs change.

CHAPTER 8

SQL Server Data Replication

Yes, you can use data replication as a high availability solution! It depends on your HA requirements, of course. Originally, the Microsoft SQL Server implementation of data replication was created to distribute data to another location for location-specific use. Replication can also be used to "offload" processing from a very busy server, such as an online transaction processing (OLTP) application server to a second server for use for things like reporting or local referencing. In this way, you can use replication to isolate reporting or reference-only data processing away from the primary OLTP server without having to sacrifice performance of that OLTP server. Data replication also is well suited to support naturally distributed data that has very distinct users (such as a geographically oriented order entry system). As data replication has become more stable and reliable, it has been used to create "warm," almost "hot," standby SQL Servers. If failures ever occur with the primary server in certain replication topologies, the secondary (replicate) server can still be able to be used for work. When the failed server is brought back up, the replication of data that changed will catch up, and all the data will be resynchronized.

Data Replication for High Availability

A few basic types of data replication methods are available with SQL Server 2016: snapshot replication, transactional replication, and merge replication. Each is used for different user scenarios, and there are variations of each for specific purposes. (We don't get into all the variations in this chapter because they are not all for high availability.)

After we look at the replication types, we'll look at a publisher, distributor, and subscriber metaphor.

Snapshot Replication

Snapshot replication involves making an image of all the tables in a publication at a single moment in time and then moving that entire image to the subscribers. Little overhead on the server is incurred because snapshot replication does not track data modifications, as the other forms of replication do. It is possible, however, for snapshot replication to require large amounts of network bandwidth, especially if the articles being replicated are large. Snapshot replication is the easiest form of replication to set up, and it is used primarily with smaller tables for which subscribers do not have to perform updates. An example of this might be a phone list that is to be replicated to many subscribers. This phone list is not considered to be critical data, and the frequency with which it is refreshed is more than enough to satisfy all its users.

Transactional Replication

Transactional replication is the process of capturing transactions from the transaction log of the published database and applying them to the subscription databases. With SQL Server transactional replication, you can publish all or part of a table, views, or one or more stored procedures as an article. All data updates are then stored in a distribution database and sent, and subsequently applied to, any number of subscribing servers. Obtaining these updates from the publishing database's transaction log is extremely efficient. No direct reading of tables is required except during initialization process, and only the minimal amount of traffic is generated over the network. This has made transactional replication the most often used method.

As data changes are made, they are propagated to the other sites in near real time; you determine the frequency of this propagation. Because changes are usually made only at the publishing server, data conflicts are avoided for the most part. For example, subscribers of the published data usually receive these updates in a few seconds, depending on the speed and availability of the network.

Merge Replication

Merge replication involves getting the publisher and all subscribers initialized and then allowing data to be changed at all sites involved in the merge replication at the publisher and at all subscribers. All these changes to the data are subsequently merged at certain intervals so that, again, all copies of the database have identical data. Occasionally, data conflicts have to be resolved. The publisher does not always win in a conflict resolution. Instead, the winner is determined by whatever criteria you establish.

With transactional replication in the instantaneous replication mode, data changes on the primary server (publisher) are replicated to one or more secondary servers (subscribers) extremely quickly. This type of replication can essentially create a "warm standby" SQL Server that is as fresh as the last transaction log entries that made it through the distribution server mechanism to the subscriber. In many cases, it can actually be considered a hot standby because of increasingly faster network speeds between locations. And, along the way, there are numerous side benefits, such as achieving higher degrees of scalability and mitigating failure risk. Figure 8.1 shows a typical SQL Server data replication configuration that can serve as a basis for high availability and that also, at the same time, fulfills a reporting server requirement.

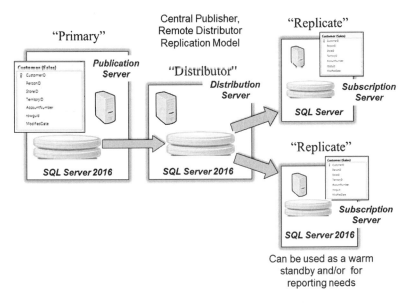

FIGURE 8.1   Basic data replication configuration for HA.

This particular data replication configuration is a central publisher/remote distributor replication model. It maximizes performance by isolating processing away from the primary server (publisher), including the data distribution mechanism (the distribution server) part of the replication model.

There are a few things to deal with if ever the replicate needs to become the primary server (that is, take over the work from the primary server). Essentially, it takes a bit of administration that is *not* transparent to the end user. Connection strings have to be changed, ODBC data sources need to be updated, and so on. But this administration may take minutes as opposed to hours of potential database recovery time, and it may well be tolerable to the end users. There is also a risk of not having all the transactions from the primary server make it over to the replicate (subscriber). Remember that the replicated database will only be as fresh as the last updates distributed to it. With today's fast network speeds, this risk is typically very minor. Most companies would be willing to live with this small risk for the sake of availability. For databases that are primarily read-only, with low-to-medium data and schema volatility, this is a great way to distribute the load and mitigate risk of failure, thus achieving high availability.

What Is Data Replication?

In its classic definition, data replication is based on a *store-and-forward* data distribution model, as shown in Figure 8.2. Data that is stored (and created) in one location can be automatically "forwarded" to one or more distributed locations.

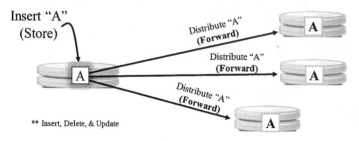

FIGURE 8.2   Store-and-forward data distribution model.

A comprehensive data distribution model would address updates, deletions, data latency, and autonomy for data and schemas. It is this data distribution model that Microsoft's data replication facility implements. There are four primary scenarios for using data replication:

▶ **Reporting/ODS**—As shown in Figure 8.3, you may want to offload the processing from the primary server to a separate reporting server for reporting purposes. This server is typically in read-only mode, and it contains all the data that is needed to satisfy reporting requirements. The classic scenario that this provides is to create an operational data store (that is, a replica of the primary database with some transformation or exclusions of data or tables—only the data that is needed for reporting).

▶ **Enabling/partitioning**—You might need to provide vertical or horizontal subsets of the primary server's data to other servers so that they are working (updating) only their own data. The primary server should contain everyone's data, though. This scenario can directly support high availability. An example is when you need to have your European and Asian users using their own data but you need their changes to be continuously fed to corporate headquarters.

▶ **Regionalization**—The regionalization scenario is for when a region is managing (inserting, updating, and deleting) its own data but another region only needs to have visibility to the other region's data (in read-only mode). This is often the case with global sales organizations and their sales order activity (for example, North American orders versus European orders).

▶ **Failover**—Finally, you could be replicating all data on a server to another server so that if the primary server crashes, users can switch to this failover server quickly and continue to work with little downtime or data loss.

Each of these scenarios supports parts or all of a high availability solution.

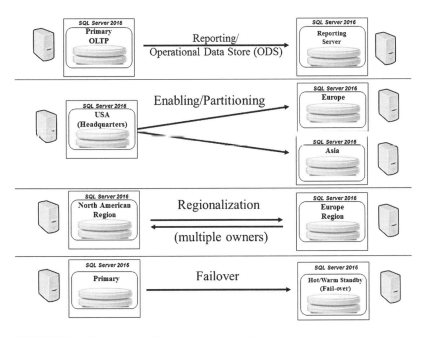

FIGURE 8.3   Data replication primary scenarios.

The Publisher, Distributor, and Subscriber Metaphor

Any SQL Server can play up to three distinct roles in a data replication environment:

▶ Publication server (the publisher of data)

▶ Distribution server (the distributor of data)

▶ Subscription server (the subscriber to the data being published)

The *publication server* (publisher) contains the database or databases to be published. This is the source of the data that is to be replicated to other servers. In Figure 8.4, the Customers table in the AdventureWorks database is the data to be published. To publish data, the database that contains the data must first be enabled for publishing.

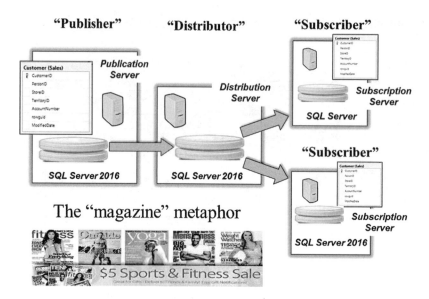

FIGURE 8.4   The publisher, distributor, and subscriber "magazine" metaphor.

The *distribution server* (distributor) can either be on the same server as the publication server or on a different server—for example, a remote distribution server. This server contains the distribution database, also called the store-and-forward database, which holds all the data changes that are to be forwarded from the published database to any subscription servers that subscribe to the data. A single distribution server can support several publication servers. The distribution server is the workhorse of data replication.

The *subscription server* (subscriber) contains a copy of the database or portions of the database that are being published. The distribution server sends any changes made to a table in a published database to the subscription server's copy of that table. There can be one or more subscribers. SQL Server 2016 also supports heterogeneous subscribers. Nearly any ODBC- or OLE-compliant database (such as Oracle) can be a subscriber to data replication.

Publications and Articles

Along with these distinct server roles, Microsoft utilizes a few more metaphors. These are publications and articles. A *publication* is a group of one or more articles and is the basic unit of data replication. An *article* is a pointer to a single table, or a subset of rows or columns of a table, that will be made available for replication.

A single database can contain more than one publication. You can publish data from tables, database objects, the execution of stored procedures, and even schema objects, such as referential integrity constraints, clustered indexes, nonclustered indexes, user triggers, extended properties, and collation. Regardless of what you plan to replicate, all articles in a publication are synchronized at the same time. Figure 8.5 shows a typical publication with three articles. You can choose to replicate whole tables or just parts of tables via filtering.

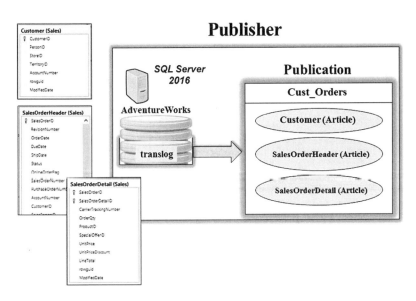

FIGURE 8.5   Cust_Orders publication (AdventureWorks DB).

Filtering Articles

You can create articles on SQL Server in several different ways. The basic way to create an article is to publish all the columns and rows that are contained in a table. Although this is the easiest way to create articles, your business needs might require that you publish only certain columns or rows from a table. This is referred to as *filtering*, and it can be done both vertically and horizontally. *Vertical filtering* filters only specific columns, whereas *horizontal filtering* filters only specific rows. In addition, SQL Server 2016 provides the added functionality of join filters and dynamic filters. (We discuss filtering here because, depending on what type of high availability requirements you have, you may need to employ one or more of these techniques within data replication.)

As you can see in Figure 8.6, you might only need to replicate a customer's customer ID, `TerritoryID`, and the associated customer account numbers to various subscribing servers around your company (vertical filtering). Or, as shown in Figure 8.7, you might need to publish only the Customers table data that is in a specific region, in which case you would need to geographically partition the data (horizontal filtering).

It is also possible to combine both horizontal and vertical filtering, as shown in Figure 8.8. This allows you to pare out unneeded columns and rows that aren't required for replication. For example, you might only need the "west" (`TerritoryID=1`) region data and need to publish only the `CustomerID`, `TerritoryID`, and `AccountNumber` data.

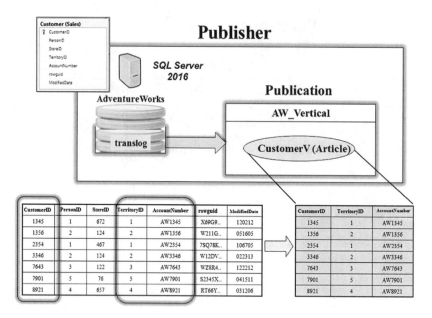

FIGURE 8.6   Vertical filtering is the process of creating a subset of columns from a table to be replicated to subscribers.

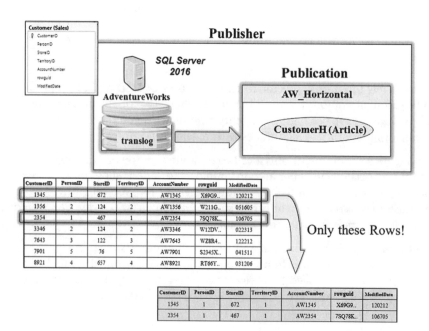

FIGURE 8.7   Horizontal filtering is the process of creating a subset of rows from a table to be replicated to subscribers.

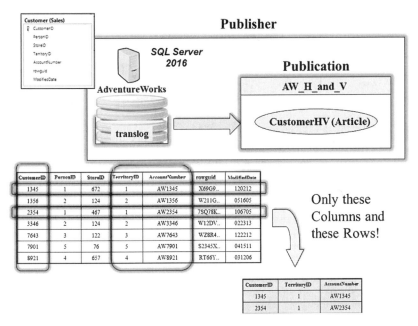

FIGURE 8.8   Combining horizontal and vertical filtering allows you to pare down the information in an article to only the important information.

As mentioned earlier, it is now possible to use join filters. *Join filters* enable you to go one step further for a particular filter created on a table to another. For example, if you are publishing the Customers table data based on the region (west), you can extend filtering to the Orders and Order Details tables for the west region customers' orders only, as shown in Figure 8.9. This way, you will only be replicating orders for customers in the west to a location that only needs to see that specific data. This can be very efficient if it is done well.

You also can publish stored procedure executions as articles, along with their parameters. This can be either a standard procedure execution article or a serializable procedure execution article. The difference is that the latter is executed as a serializable transaction, and the other is not. A serializable transaction is a transaction that is being executed with the serializable isolation level, which places a range lock on the affected data set, preventing other users from updating or inserting rows into the data set until the transaction is complete.

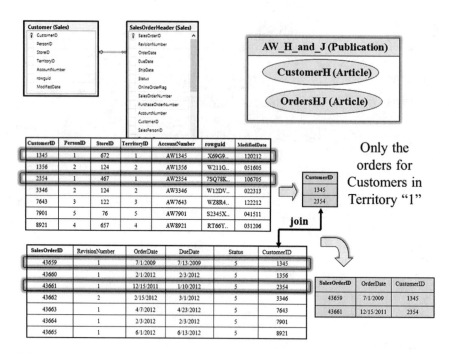

FIGURE 8.9   Horizontal and join publication.

What publishing stored procedure executions as articles gets you is a major reduction of mass SQL statements being replicated across your network. For instance, if you wanted to update the Customers table for every customer between customerID 1 and customerID 5000, the Customers table updates would be replicated as a large multistep transaction involving 5,000 separate update statements. This would significantly bog down your network. However, with stored procedure execution articles, only the execution of the stored procedure is replicated to the subscription server, and the stored procedure is executed on that subscription server. Figure 8.10 illustrates the difference in execution described earlier. Some subtleties when using this type of data replication processing can't be overlooked, such as making sure the published stored procedure behaves the same on the subscribing server side. Just to be safe, you should have abbreviated testing scripts that can be run on the subscriber, whose results will be verified with the same results on the publisher.

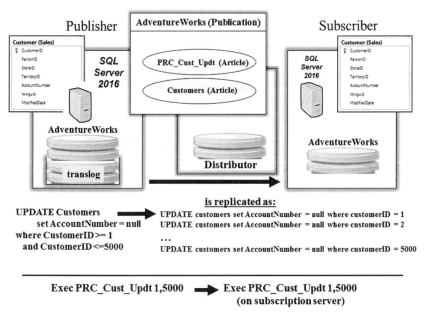

FIGURE 8.10   Stored procedure execution comparison.

Now, it is essential to learn about the different types of replication scenarios that can be built and the reasons any one of them would be desired over the others. It is worth noting that Microsoft SQL Server 2016 supports replication to and from many different hetero-geneous data sources. For example, OLE DB or ODBC data sources (including Microsoft Exchange, Microsoft Access, Oracle, and DB2) can subscribe to SQL Server publications, as well as publish data.

Replication Scenarios

In general, depending on your business requirements, you can implement one of several different data replication scenarios, including the following:

▶ Central publisher

▶ Central publisher with a remote distributor

▶ Publishing subscriber

▶ Central subscriber

▶ Multiple publishers or multiple subscribers

▶ Merge replication

▶ Peer-to-peer replication

▶ Updating subscribers

For high availability, the two central publisher topologies are the most appropriate. These two are, by far, the best to use for a near-real-time and simple-to-set-up hot/warm spare HA solution.

> **NOTE**
>
> To learn more about other uses of data replication, refer to Sams Publishing's *SQL Server Unleashed*, which expands on this subject for all processing use case scenarios.

Central Publisher

The central publisher replication model, as shown in Figure 8.11, is Microsoft's default scenario. In this scenario, one SQL Server performs the functions of both publisher and distributor. The publisher/distributor can have any number of subscribers, which can come in many different varieties, such as most SQL Server versions, MySQL, and Oracle.

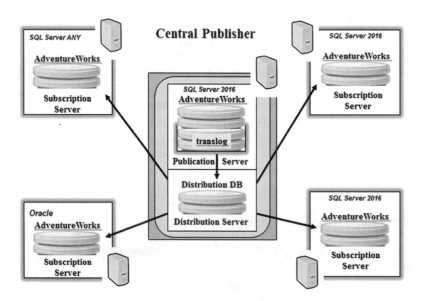

FIGURE 8.11   The central publisher scenario is a simple and frequently used scenario.

The central publisher scenario can be used in the following situations:

▶ To create a copy of a database for ad hoc queries and report generation (classic use)

▶ To publish master lists to remote locations, such as master customer lists or master price lists

▶ To maintain a remote copy of an OLTP database that can be used by the remote sites during communication outages

▶ To maintain a spare copy of an OLTP database that can be used as a hot spare in case of server failure

However, it's important to consider the following for this scenario:

▶ If your OLTP server's activity is substantial and affects greater than 10% of your total data per day, then this central publisher scenario is not for you. Other replication configuration scenarios will better fit yours need or, if you're trying to achieve HA, another HA option may serve you better.

▶ If your OLTP server is maxed out on CPU, memory, and disk utilization, you should consider using another data replication scenario. Again, the central publisher scenario is not for you. There would be no bandwidth on this server to support the replication overhead.

Central Publisher with a Remote Distributor

The central publisher with remote distributor scenario, as shown in Figure 8.12, is similar to the central publisher scenario and can be used in the same general situations. The major difference between the two is that a second server is used to perform the role of distributor. This is highly desirable when you need to free the publishing server from having to perform the distribution task from a CPU, disk, and memory point of view.

This is also the best scenario for expanding the number of publishers and subscribers. Also remember that a single distribution server can distribute changes for several publishers. The publisher and distributor must be connected to each other via a reliable, high-speed data link. This remote distributor scenario is proving to be one of the best data replication approaches due to its minimal impact on the publication server and maximum distribution capability to any number of subscribers.

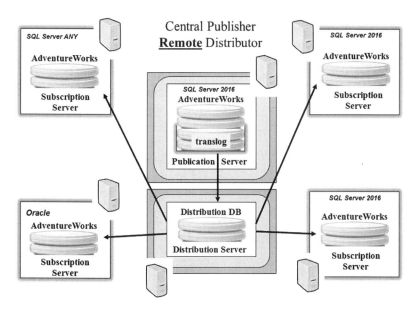

FIGURE 8.12   The central publisher with remote distributor topology is used when the role of distributor is removed from the publishing server.

As mentioned previously, the central publisher remote distributor approach can be used for all the same purposes as the central publisher scenario, and it also provides the added benefit of having minimal resource impact on your publication servers. If your OLTP server's activity affects more than 10% of your total data per day, this scenario can usually handle it without much issue. If your OLTP server has overburdened its CPU, memory, and disk utilization, this topology easily solves this issue as well.

In terms of high availability, this data replication model is the best, hands down! It not only reduces the workload on the publication server (helping performance and scalability) but also keeps the distribution mechanism isolated from the publisher, which is desirable in the event of publisher failures. The distribution server can still be pumping updates to a subscriber even though the publisher has failed (until the distribution queue is empty). You can then easily switch your client applications over to use a subscriber for as long as your publisher remains down (which could be a long time, depending on the failure). Your overall availability increases.

Subscriptions

A subscription is essentially a formal request and registration of that request for data that is being published. By default, you subscribe to all articles of a publication.

When a subscription is being set up, you have the option of either having the data pushed to the subscriber server or pulling the data to the subscription server when it is needed. This is referred to as either a *push subscription* or a *pull subscription*.

Pull Subscriptions

As shown in Figure 8.13, a pull subscription is set up and managed by the subscription server. The biggest advantage here is that pull subscriptions allow the system administrators of the subscription servers to choose what publications they will receive and when they will be received. With pull subscriptions, publishing and subscribing are separate acts and are not necessarily performed by the same user. In general, pull subscriptions are best when the publication does not require high security or when subscribing is done intermittently, as the subscriber's data needs to be periodically brought up to date.

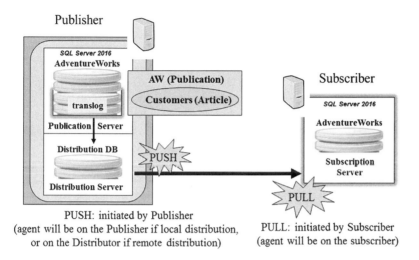

FIGURE 8.13   Push subscription initiated by publisher and pull subscription initiated by subscriber.

Push Subscriptions

A push subscription is created and managed by the publication server. In effect, the publication server is pushing the publication to the subscription server. The advantage of using push subscriptions is that all the administration takes place in a central location. In addition, publishing and subscribing happen at the same time, and many subscribers can be set up at once. A push subscription is recommended when dealing with heterogeneous subscribers because of the lack of pull capability on the subscription server side. You may want to use the push subscription approach for a high availability configuration that will be used in a failover scenario.

The Distribution Database

The distribution database is a special type of database installed on the distribution server. This database, known as a store-and-forward database, holds all the transactions that are waiting to be distributed to any subscribers. This database receives transactions from any published databases that have designated it as their distributor. The transactions are held here until they are sent to the subscribers successfully. After a period of time, these transactions are purged from the distribution database.

The distribution database is the "heart" of the data replication capability. As you can see in Figure 8.14, the distribution database has several MS tables, such as MSrepl_transactions. These tables contain all the necessary information for the distribution server to fulfill the distribution role. These tables include the following:

▶ All the different publishers that will use it, such as MSpublisher_databases and MSpublication_access

▶ The publications and articles that it will distribute, such as MSpublications and MSarticles

▶ The complete information for all the agents to perform their tasks, such as `MSdistribution_agents`

▶ The complete information of the executions of these agents, such as `MSdistribution_history`

▶ The subscribers, such as `MSsubscriber_info`, `MSsubscriptions`, and so on

▶ Any errors that occur during replication and synchronization states, such as `MSrepl_errors`, `MSsync_state`, and so on

▶ The commands and transactions that are to be replicated, such as `MSrepl_commands` and `MSrepl_transactions`

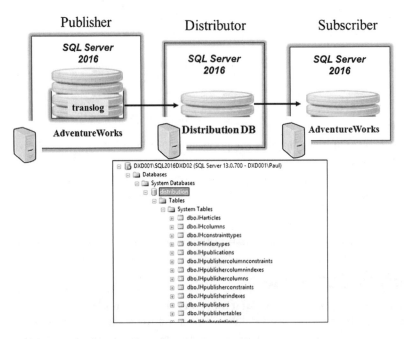

FIGURE 8.14   Tables of the distribution database.

Replication Agents

SQL Server utilizes replication agents to do different tasks during the replication process. These agents are constantly waking up at some frequency and fulfilling specific jobs. Let's look at the main ones.

The Snapshot Agent

The snapshot agent is responsible for preparing the schema and initial data files of published tables and stored procedures, storing the snapshot on the distribution server, and recording information about the synchronization status in the distribution database. Each publication has its own snapshot agent that runs on the distribution server.

When you set up a subscription, it is possible to manually load the initial snapshot onto the server. This is known as manual synchronization. For extremely large databases, it is frequently easier to dump the database to tape and then reload the database on the subscription server. If you load the snapshot this way, SQL Server assumes that the databases are already synchronized and automatically begins sending data modifications.

The snapshot agent carries out the following series of tasks:

1. The snapshot agent is initialized. This initialization can be immediate or at a designated time in your company's nightly processing window.

2. The agent connects to the publisher.

3. The agent generates schema files with the .sch file extension for each article in the publication. These schema files are written to a temporary working directory on the distribution server. These are the `Create Table` statements that will be used to create all objects needed on the subscription server side. They will exist only for the duration of the snapshot processing!

4. All the tables in the publication are locked (held). The locking is required to ensure that no data modifications are made during the snapshot process.

5. The agent extracts a copy of the data in the publication and writes it into the temporary working directory on the distribution server. If all the subscribers are SQL Servers, then the data will be written using a SQL Server native format, with the .bcp file extension. If you are replicating to databases other than SQL Server, the data will be stored in standard text files, with the .txt file extension. The .sch file and the .txt files/.bcp files are known as a *synchronization set*. Every table or article has a synchronization set.

6. The agent executes the object creations and bulk copy processing at the subscription server side in the order in which they were generated (or it skips the object creation part if the objects have already been created on the subscription server side and you have indicated this during setup). This takes a while, so it is best to do this during an off time to avoid affecting the normal processing day. Network connectivity is critical here, and snapshots often fail at this point.

7. The snapshot agent posts the fact that a snapshot has occurred and what articles/publications were part of the snapshot to the distribution database. This is the only thing that is sent to the distribution database.

8. When all the synchronization sets have finished being executed, the agent releases the locks on all the tables of this publication. The snapshot is now considered finished.

CAUTION

Make sure you have enough disk space on the drive that contains the temporary working directory (the snapshot folder). The snapshot data files may be huge, and that is a primary reason for the high rate of snapshot failure. The amount of disk space also directly affects high availability. Filling up a disk will translate to some additional unplanned downtime. You've been warned!

The Log Reader Agent

The log reader agent is responsible for moving transactions marked for replication from the transaction log of the published database to the distribution database. Each database published using transactional replication has its own log reader agent that runs on the distribution server.

After initial synchronization has taken place, the log reader agent begins to move transactions from the publication server to the distribution server. All actions that modify data in a database are logged in the transaction log in that database. Not only is this log used in the automatic recovery process, it is also used in the replication process. When an article is created for publication and the subscription is activated, all entries about that article are marked in the transaction log. For each publication in a database, a log reader agent reads the transaction log and looks for any marked transactions. When the log reader agent finds a change in the log, it reads the change and converts it to a SQL statement that corresponds to the action that was taken in the article. These SQL statements are then stored in a table on the distribution server, waiting to be distributed to subscribers.

Because replication is based on the transaction log, several changes are made in the way the transaction log works. During normal processing, any transaction that has either been successfully completed or rolled back is marked inactive. When you are performing replication, completed transactions are not marked inactive until the log reader process has read them and sent them to the distribution server.

NOTE

Truncating and fast bulk-copying into a table are non-logged processes. In tables marked for publication, you cannot perform non-logged operations unless you temporarily turn off replication on that table. Then you need to re-sync the table on the subscriber before you reenable replication.

The Distribution Agent

A distribution agent moves transactions and snapshots held in the distribution database out to the subscribers. This agent isn't created until a push subscription is defined.

Subscribers not set up for immediate synchronization share a distribution agent that runs on the distribution server. Pull subscriptions, to either snapshot or transactional publications, have a distribution agent that runs on the subscriber.

In transactional replication, the transactions have been moved into the distribution database, and the distribution agent either pushes out the changes to the subscribers or pulls them from the distributor, depending on how the servers are set up. All actions that change data on the publishing server are applied to the subscribing servers in the same order in which they were incurred.

The Miscellaneous Agents

Several miscellaneous agents have been set up to do house cleaning around the replication configuration. These agents include the following:

▶ **Agent History Clean Up: distribution**—This agent clears out the agent history from the distribution database every 10 minutes (by default). Depending on the size of the distribution, you might want to vary the frequency of this agent.

▶ **Distribution Clean Up: distribution**—This agent clears out replicated transactions from the distribution database every 72 hours (by default). This agent is used for snapshot and transactional publications only. If the volume of transactions is high, the frequency of this agent's execution should be adjusted upward so the distribution database isn't too large. You also need to adjust the frequency of synchronization with the subscribers.

▶ **Expired Subscription Clean Up**—This agent detects and removes expired subscriptions from the published databases. As part of the subscription setup, an expiration date is set. This agent usually runs once per day by default, and you don't need to change this.

▶ **Reinitialize Subscriptions Having Data Validation Failures**—This agent is manually invoked. It is not on a schedule, but it could be. It automatically detects the subscriptions that failed data validation and marks them for re-initialization. This can then potentially lead to a new snapshot being applied to a subscriber that had data validation failures.

▶ **Replication Agents Checkup**—This agent detects replication agents that are not actively logging history. This is critical because debugging replication errors often depends on an agent's history that has been logged.

User Requirements Driving the Replication Design

As mentioned before, the business requirements drive your replication configuration and method. The Phase 0 high availability assessment results will help you pick the right type of replication to use. The answers you gave and the path that was followed through the HA decision tree got you to this point to begin with. However, adding more thoroughness in requirements gathering is highly recommended to get a prototype up and running as quickly as possible. Doing so will allow you to measure the effectiveness of one replication approach over the other.

> **NOTE**
>
> If you have triggers on your tables and want them to be replicated along with your table, you might want to revisit them and add a line of code that reads NOT FOR REPLICATION so that the trigger code isn't executed redundantly on the subscriber side. So, for a trigger (an insert, update, or delete trigger) on the subscriber, you would use the NOT FOR REPLICATION statement for the whole trigger (placed before the AS statement of the trigger). If you want to be selective on a part of the trigger code (for example, FOR INSERT, FOR UPDATE, FOR DELETE), you put NOT FOR REPLICATION immediately following the statements you don't want to execute and put nothing on the ones you do want to execute.

Setting Up Replication

In general, SQL Server 2016 data replication is exceptionally easy to set up via SQL Server Management Studio. Be sure to generate SQL scripts for every phase of your replication configuration. In a production environment, you most likely will rely heavily on scripts and will not have the luxury of having much time to set up and break down production replication configurations via manual configuration steps.

You have to define any data replication configuration in the following order:

1. Create or enable a distributor to enable publishing.

2. Enable/configure publishing (with a distributor designated for a publisher).

3. Create a publication and define articles within the publication.

4. Define subscribers and subscribe to a publication.

Next you will set up a transactional replication configuration (as shown in Figure 8.15) with three servers and publish the AdventureWorks database to a secondary server (subscriber) to fulfill the high availability hot/warm spare use case.

In this example you will use the SQL2016DXD01 instance as the publisher, the SQL2016DXD02 server as the remote distributor, and SQL2016DXD03 as the subscriber. As you know, you start the whole configuration process by enabling the distribution server first. One thing you will notice with the replication configuration capabilities in SQL Server Management Studio is the extensive use of wizards.

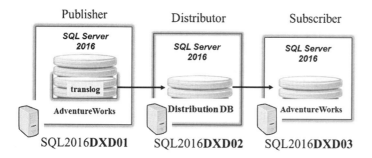

FIGURE 8.15   A central publisher with remote distributor configuration for HA.

Enabling a Distributor

The first thing you need to do is to designate a distribution server to be used by the publisher. As discussed earlier, you can either configure the local server as the distribution server or choose a remote server as the distributor. For this HA configuration, you want a remote distribution server that is separate from the publisher. You'll also have to be a member of the SYSADMIN server role to use these configuration wizards. From the intended distribution server (SQL2016DXD02 in this example), you right-click on the replication node to invoke the distribution configuration wizard (see Figure 8.16).

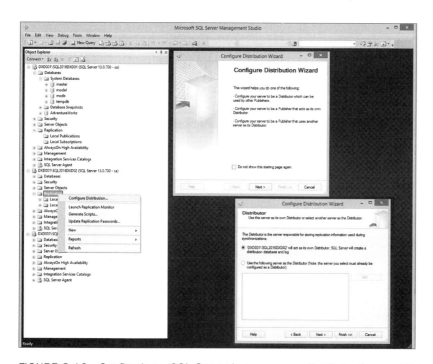

FIGURE 8.16   Configuring a SQL Server instance as a distributor for a publisher.

Figure 8.16 shows the first option selected, designating the SQL2016DXD02 server to act as its own distributor, which will result in the distribution database being created on this server.

Next, as shown in the upper left of Figure 8.17, you are asked to specify a snapshot folder. Give it the proper network pathname. Remember that tons of data will be moving through this snapshot folder, so it should be on a drive that can support the snapshot without filling up the drive. Next comes the distribution database name and location on the distribution server. It's best to just accept the defaults here, as shown in the upper right of Figure 8.17. Next, you specify what publisher this distribution server will distribute for. As shown in the lower left of Figure 8.17, add (and check) the SQL2016DXD01 server to the publishers list. Finally, the wizard finishes the distribution processing (as shown in the lower right of Figure 8.17) by creating the distribution database and setting up the distribution agents needed, along with the access to the publication server for any database that is to be published later.

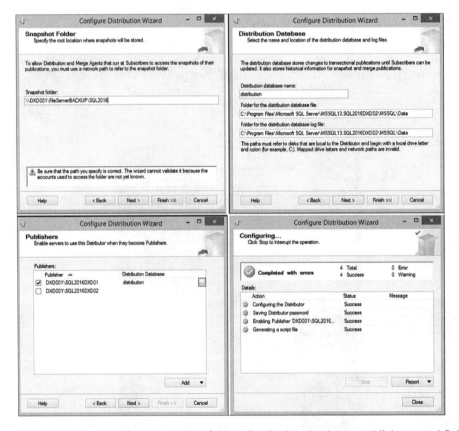

FIGURE 8.17   Specify the snapshot folder, distribution database, publishers, and finish processing.

Now you can get to the business of creating a publisher and a publication for the HA configuration.

Publishing

Because you have created a remote distributor, you only need to "configure" a publisher to use the remote distributor and then create the publications that are to be published.

As you can see in Figure 8.18, in SQL Server Management Studio, you can navigate to the Replication node in the Object Explorer on the publication server and right-click the Local Publication node to choose to create new publications, launch replication monitor, generate scripts, or configure distribution (if you need to do this locally). In this example, you want the DXD001\SQL2016DXD01 SQL Server. Choose New Publication to invoke the New Publication Wizard.

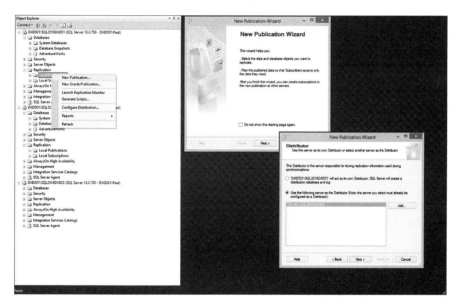

FIGURE 8.18   New Publication Wizard and specifying the distributor.

The next dialog in this wizard prompts you for the distributor. In this case, select the second option to specify the SQL2016DXD02 server as the distributor (thus a remote distributor). Because you already enabled this server as a distributor and identified the SQL2016DX01 server as a publisher, the option appears by default. Click Next to create this remote distributor. Now you are ready to create a publication.

Creating a Publication

You are now prompted to select the database for which you are going to set up a publication (as shown in the upper left of Figure 8.19). For this example, you'll be publishing the AdventureWorks database.

You are now asked to specify the type of replication method for this publication (as you can see in the upper right of Figure 8.19). This will be either a snapshot publication, transactional publication, peer-to-peer publication, or merge publication. Select a transactional publication in this case.

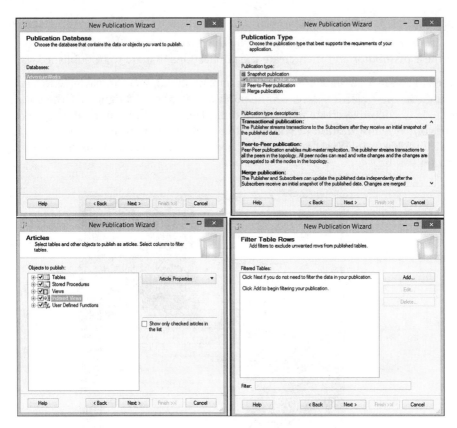

FIGURE 8.19   Choosing the publication database, publication type, and articles to publish.

In the Articles dialog, you are prompted to identify articles in your publication (see the bottom left of Figure 8.19). You must include at least one article in your publication. For this example, select all the objects to publish: Tables, Views, Indexed Views, User Defined Functions, and Stored Procedures. Remember that you are trying to create an exact image of the publisher to use as a warm standby, and it must have all objects included. If your table has triggers, you may elect to leave this item unchecked and then run a script on the subscription side with the trigger code that contains the NOT FOR REPLICATION option. You will not be doing any table filtering for this HA publication, so just click Next in that dialog.

For transactional replication, you must determine how the snapshot portion of the replication will occur. The snapshot agent will create a snapshot immediately and keep that snapshot available to initialize subscriptions. This will include a snapshot of the schema and the data. You can choose to have the snapshot agent run immediately as opposed to setting a scheduled time for it to begin its processing, as shown in the upper left of Figure 8.20. You also need to provide access credentials to the snapshot agent for it to connect to the publisher for all the publication creation activity and the log reader agent processing (which will feed the transactions to the subscriber via the distributor), as shown in the upper right of Figure 8.20. In the next dialog box, indicate what you want done at the end of the wizard processing.

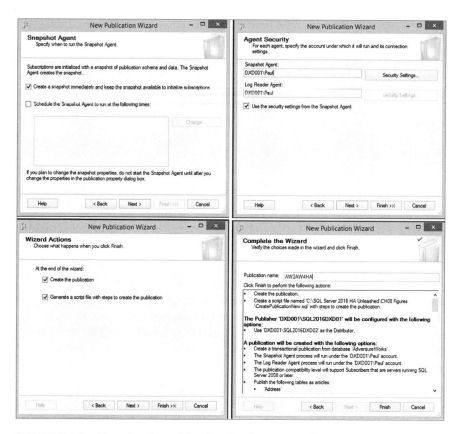

FIGURE 8.20   Choosing the publication database, specifying the publication type, and identifying what server type the subscribers will be.

The last dialog box in Figure 8.20 shows a summary of the tasks that will be processed and the place where you will name the publication. Name it AW2AW4HA (for AdventureWorks to AdventureWorks for high availability).

Figure 8.21 shows the creation processing steps for this new publication. All action statuses should read Success. Now that you have installed and configured the remote distributor, enabled publishing, and created a publication, you need to create a subscription.

FIGURE 8.21   Enterprise Manager with a new snapshot and log reader agents.

Creating a Subscription

Remember that you can create two types of subscriptions: push and pull. Pull subscriptions allow remote sites to subscribe to publications and initiate their processing from the subscriber side. Push subscription processes are performed and administered from the distributor side. Because you are creating this subscriber to be a failover server, you should choose to use the push subscription approach because you don't want additional agents on that subscriber, and you want to administer all processing from one place (the distributor).

Figure 8.22 shows the creation of a new subscription on the subscription server. In this example, it is the SQL2016DXD03 server. You simply right-click the Local Subscriptions replication node option and select New Subscriptions.

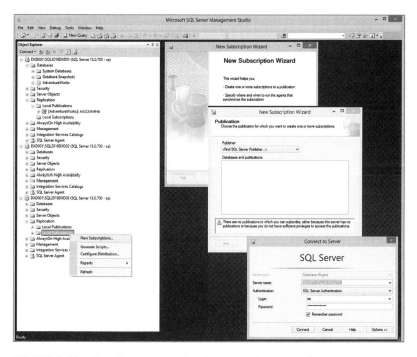

FIGURE 8.22   Creating a new subscription on the subscriber.

In particular, you will be creating a push subscription (pushed from the distributor), so you need to identify the publisher that you'll be subscribing to. As shown on the right in Figure 8.22, you select <Find SQL Server Publisher>, which allows you to connect to the desired SQL Server instance (SQL2016DXD01 in this case) and establish access to the publications on that publisher. Once you're connected, the publications available on that publisher are listed for you to choose from (as shown in the upper left of Figure 8.23).

8

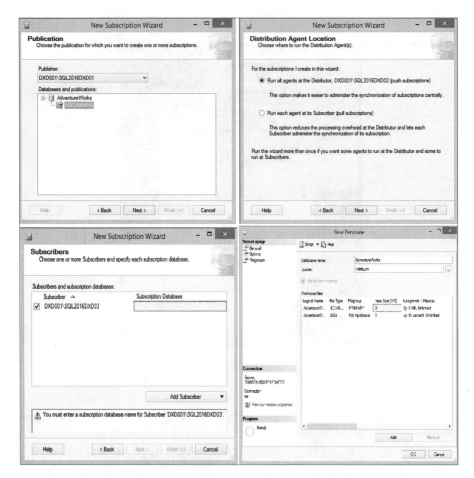

FIGURE 8.23   Choosing the publication to subscribe to.

Once you've selected the publication you are interested in subscribing to, you need to decide whether this will be a push-or-pull subscription. As mentioned earlier, you want to make this a push subscription that will run all agents on the distribution server, so select the first option, as shown in the upper right of Figure 8.23.

Next, you need to identify the database location for the subscriber (SQL2016DXD03 in this example) and specify the name of the database that will be the target of the subscription. In this case, give the database the same name as the original database because you will potentially use this database for failover for your applications. As shown in Figure 8.23, choose to create a new database with the same name (AdventureWorks), which will receive the publication from the publisher.

You've now identified the database to hold the publication. Next, you specify the access credentials (accounts) that the distribution agents use for the subscriber. Figure 8.24 shows the selected subscriber database (AdventureWorks) and the distribution agent security specification. Once access is specified, the synchronization schedule must be established for the transactions to be pushed to the subscriber. You want the latency to be as short as possible to guarantee that data is being pushed to the subscriber as quickly as possible. As shown in the lower left of Figure 8.24, choose the Run Continuously mode for synchronization. This means that as transactions arrive at the distributor, they will be continuously pushed to the subscriber as fast as possible. This should limit unapplied transactions at the subscriber significantly.

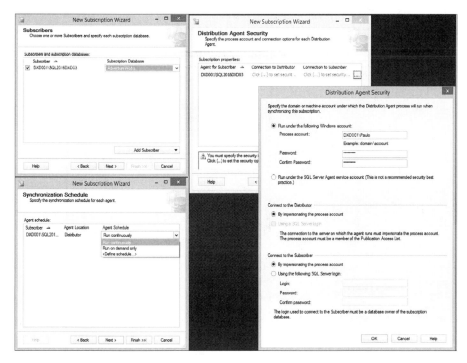

FIGURE 8.24   Setting distribution agent access and the synchronization schedule.

As you can see in Figure 8.25, you have to specify how the subscription will be initialized and when that should take place. You have an option to create the schema and data at the subscriber (and also to do it immediately) or to skip this initialization altogether because you have already created the schema and loaded the data manually. Choose to have the initialization create the schema and initialize the data immediately by checking the Initialize box and selecting Immediately. This is all you have to do at this point. The next dialog shows the summary of what is about to be initiated. Once you kick this off, the Creating Subscription(s) dialog shows you the progress of the subscription creation. By now you have probably noticed that you are always asking for the wizard to generate the script for what it is executing, so you can do this later without having to wade through the wizard. This is a solid management procedure. This book includes all the scripts you need for setting up the replication topology you've just walked through.

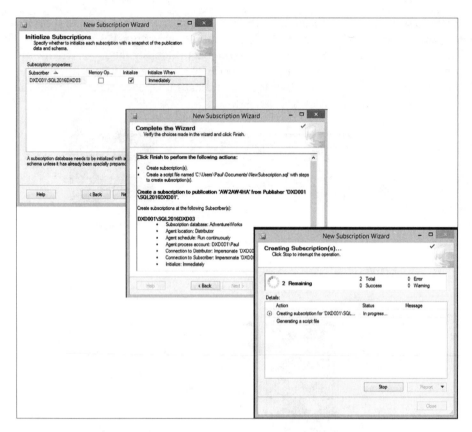

FIGURE 8.25   Initializing the subscription, reviewing all tasks to be completed, and creating the subscription immediately.

Now you must wait for the agents to kick in and do their jobs of snapshotting, creating schemas, loading data, and synchronizing continuously.

Figure 8.26 shows the agents that are created for publications and the push from the distributor to the subscriber. There are a few other agent jobs listed for housecleaning, re-initialization, and checkups.

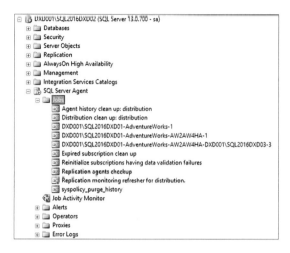

FIGURE 8.26   SQL Server agents on the distributor for the publication and the push subscription.

Now replication is all set up, and the only thing left to do is wait. If you have specified that the schema and data are to be created immediately, things start happening quickly.

You see the snapshot agent start up and begin creating schema files (.sch files) extracting the data into .bcp files, and putting everything in the snapshot folder on the distribution server. Figure 8.27 shows a list of the data files being created as part of the snapshot processing that will be used to initialize the subscription.

Name	Date modified	Type	Size
AccountNumber_126	8/21/2016 12:46 AM	SQL Server Replica...	1 KB
AdditionalCont1d18c1a7_118	8/21/2016 12:46 AM	SQL Server Replica...	8 KB
Address_2#1	8/21/2016 12:45 AM	SQL Server Replica...	155 KB
Address_2#2	8/21/2016 12:45 AM	SQL Server Replica...	158 KB
Address_2#3	8/21/2016 12:45 AM	SQL Server Replica...	158 KB
Address_2#4	8/21/2016 12:45 AM	SQL Server Replica...	158 KB
Address_2#5	8/21/2016 12:45 AM	SQL Server Replica...	158 KB
Address_2#6	8/21/2016 12:45 AM	SQL Server Replica...	159 KB
Address_2#7	8/21/2016 12:45 AM	SQL Server Replica...	158 KB
Address_2#8	8/21/2016 12:45 AM	SQL Server Replica...	159 KB
Address_2#9	8/21/2016 12:45 AM	SQL Server Replica...	158 KB
Address_2#10	8/21/2016 12:45 AM	SQL Server Replica...	158 KB
Address_2#11	8/21/2016 12:45 AM	SQL Server Replica...	158 KB
Address_2#12	8/21/2016 12:45 AM	SQL Server Replica...	159 KB
Address_2#13	8/21/2016 12:45 AM	SQL Server Replica...	159 KB
Address_2#14	8/21/2016 12:45 AM	SQL Server Replica...	159 KB
Address_2#15	8/21/2016 12:45 AM	SQL Server Replica...	158 KB
Address_2#16	8/21/2016 12:45 AM	SQL Server Replica...	119 KB
Address_2	8/21/2016 12:46 AM	SQL Server Replica...	1 KB
Address_2	8/21/2016 12:46 AM	SQL Server Replica...	1 KB
Address_2	8/21/2016 12:46 AM	SQL Server Replica...	14 KB
AddressType_3	8/21/2016 12:45 AM	SQL Server Replica...	1 KB
AddressType_3	8/21/2016 12:46 AM	SQL Server Replica...	1 KB
AddressType_3	8/21/2016 12:46 AM	SQL Server Replica...	1 KB
AddressType_3	8/21/2016 12:46 AM	SQL Server Replica...	11 KB
AWBuildVersion_4	8/21/2016 12:45 AM	SQL Server Replica...	1 KB
AWBuildVersion_4	8/21/2016 12:46 AM	SQL Server Replica...	1 KB

FIGURE 8.27   Schema and data files created in the snapshot folder that are used to initialize the subscription.

The distribution agent applies the schemas to the subscriber. The bulk copying of the data into the tables on the subscriber side follows accordingly. After this bulk copying is done, the initialization step is complete, and active replication begins.

That's it! You are now in active replication. As any change is made to the publisher, it is continuously replicated to the subscriber—in most cases within a few seconds.

If the publisher fails for any reason and cannot be recovered normally, the subscriber server can be put into service by pointing all the client applications to this new server.

Switching Over to a Warm Standby (Subscriber)

If it is done properly, failing over to a warm standby (subscriber) in a replication configuration can be done in less than 2 minutes if the failure is detected early. There are a few main areas to consider:

▶ You need to determine what has failed. Has the publisher failed only? Have the most recent transactions been replicated to the subscriber?

▶ You need to define the process that must be run to make the subscriber the primary server.

▶ You need to define the process that must be followed to point the client to the new primary server (the standby).

▶ You need to define the process for switching this all back to the way it was before the failure occurred (if desired).

You can also use your warm standby (subscriber) as a temporary place to switch your read-only client activity to while you do upgrades on the publisher. When the upgrades are complete, you can switch back to the publisher (that has been upgraded) and then repeat the upgrade for the subscriber (warm standby server), thus increasing the overall availability of your system.

Scenarios That Dictate Switching to the Warm Standby

The main reason you are building a warm standby configuration with replication is so you can fail over to it when the primary server fails. In other words, it does not come back up after automatic SQL Server recovery has attempted to bring it back online. Your database is basically completely unavailable and unusable for any number of reasons (failed disk, failed memory, and so on). When using replication configurations, these are the basic failure scenarios you must deal with:

▶ **Publisher fails, distributor alive, subscriber alive**—You can use the subscriber for your client connections after the distributor has distributed all published transactions to the subscriber.

▶ **Publisher fails, distributor fails, subscriber alive**—You can use the subscriber for your client connections after you have renamed the SQL Server instance to the publisher's name. Some data loss may have occurred.

Switching Over to a Warm Standby (the Subscriber)

Assuming that the primary server (publisher) is not available for any number of reasons and won't be available for the foreseeable future, you must now make your warm standby the primary server. Follow these steps:

1. Verify that the last set of transactions that made it to the distributor have been replicated to the subscriber by reviewing the history of the distribution agent. This should be up to the minute (if not to the second).

2. Remove replication from the subscriber by executing the system stored procedure `sp_removedbreplication` at the subscriber. You can also use the `delete` option for the local subscriber node in the replication options on the subscriber.

3. Disable all replication agents (log reader agent, distribution agent, and so on). Don't delete them; just disable them. (You will clean up later.)

Before the standby database is made available to the clients for use, be sure you have set the recovery mode to `full` if it was previously set to `simple` or `bulkcopy`. Then run your backup/recovery scripts to initiate database backups and transaction log backups immediately.

Turning the Subscriber into a Publisher (if Needed)

If you have to use a subscriber as your failover SQL Server instance, you need to be prepared to turn this subscriber into a publisher (if needed). You would need to do this, for example, if the subscriber were taking over the publisher's job permanently (until it failed and a switchback needed to occur). You should keep all replication configurations in script form. This includes a version of replication scripts that can enable the subscriber as a publisher and start publishing.

> **TIP**
>
> Make sure you have kept your SQL logins/users synchronized and up to date in both the publisher and the subscriber SQL Server instances.

Monitoring Replication

When replication is up and running, you need to monitor the replication and see how things are running. You can do this in several ways, including using SQL statements, SQL Server Management Studio's Replication Monitor, and Windows Performance Monitor (PerfMon counters).

Basically, you are interested in the agent's successes and failures, the speed at which replication is done, and the synchronization state of tables involved in replication (that is, all data rows present on both the publisher and the subscriber). Other things to watch for are the sizes of the distribution database, the growth of the subscriber databases, and the available space on the distribution server's snapshot working directory.

SQL Statements

You need to validate that the data is in both the publisher and the subscriber. You can use the publication validation stored procedure (sp_publication_validation) to do this fairly quickly. This will give you actual row count validation. The following command checks the row counts of the publication and subscribers:

```
exec sp_publication_validation @publication = N'AW2AW4HA'
go
```

This is what the command yields:

```
Generated expected rowcount value of 19614 for Address.
Generated expected rowcount value of 6 for AddressType.
Generated expected rowcount value of 1 for AWBuildVersion.
Generated expected rowcount value of 2679 for BillOfMaterials.
Generated expected rowcount value of 20777 for BusinessEntity.
Generated expected rowcount value of 19614 for BusinessEntityAddress.
Generated expected rowcount value of 909 for BusinessEntityContact.
Generated expected rowcount value of 20 for ContactType.
Generated expected rowcount value of 238 for CountryRegion.
Generated expected rowcount value of 109 for CountryRegionCurrency.
Generated expected rowcount value of 19118 for CreditCard.
Generated expected rowcount value of 8 for Culture.
Generated expected rowcount value of 105 for Currency.
Generated expected rowcount value of 13532 for CurrencyRate.
Generated expected rowcount value of 20420 for Customer.
Generated expected rowcount value of 1597 for DatabaseLog.
Generated expected rowcount value of 16 for Department.
Generated expected rowcount value of 13 for Document.
Generated expected rowcount value of 19972 for EmailAddress.
Generated expected rowcount value of 290 for Employee.
Generated expected rowcount value of 296 for EmployeeDepartmentHistory.
Generated expected rowcount value of 316 for EmployeePayHistory.
```

SQL Server Management Studio

SSMS has a couple great ways to monitor both the synchronization status of replication and the overall health of what you are replicating. Figure 8.28 shows the View Synchronization Status option for a publication. This example shows the most recent activity that was just executed. It is also possible to stop and start synchronization from here. (Please be careful!)

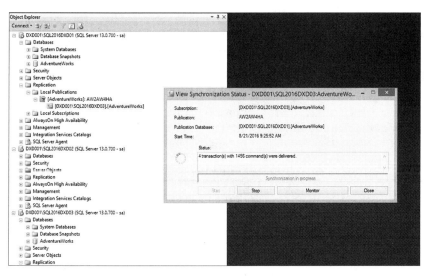

FIGURE 8.28   View Synchronization Status option for the publication to the subscriber.

You can also get an in-depth view of the replication topology via the Replication Monitor. Just right-click the replication node (or any of the replication branch item) in SSMS. Choose to launch the Replication Monitor, and you see the publishers and subscribers for your replication topology (as shown in Figure 8.29).

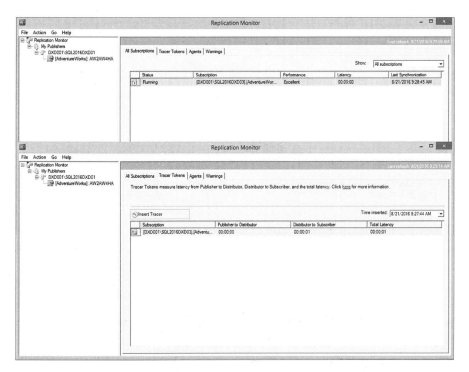

FIGURE 8.29   Replication Monitor and all subscriptions and tracer tokens.

In Replication Monitor, you can see the activity for publishers and agents, and you can use the Warnings tab to configure alerts when certain values start to be exceeded (such as latency). The All Subscriptions tab shows you the overall status (Running in the example shown in Figure 8.29). It shows the subscriber, the overall performance (Excellent in this case), the latency, and the last synchronization that was run. In addition, you can drill down into any of the agents via the Agents tab to see the full execution history. Finally, you can generate a synthetic transaction (tracer token) that is sent through the replication topology (starting from the publisher to the distributor and out to the subscriber). The bottom half of Figure 8.29 shows a well-performing replication topology with 1-second latency. Awesome!

Through SSMS, you can invoke the validate subscriptions processing to see whether replication is in sync. Under the Publishers branch of the Replication node, simply right-click the publication you wish to validate and select Validate Subscriptions. You can validate all subscriptions or just a particular one, as shown in Figure 8.30. You can then view the validation results via the distribution agent history.

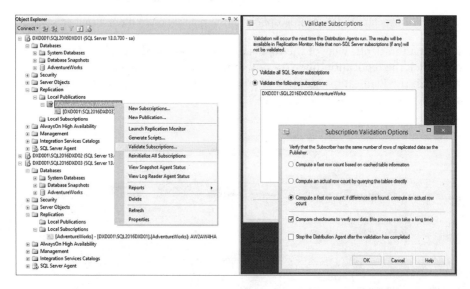

FIGURE 8.30   Validating subscriptions to ensure that the publisher and subscriber are in sync.

The Windows Performance Monitor and Replication

You can use Windows Performance Monitor to monitor the health of your replication scenario. Installing SQL Server adds several new objects and counters to Performance Monitor:

► `SQLServer:Replication Agents`—This object contains counters used to monitor the status of all replication agents, including the total number running.

► `SQLServer:Replication Dist`—This object contains counters used to monitor the status of the distribution agents, including the latency and the number of transactions transferred per second.

▶ SQLServer:Replication Logreader—This object contains counters used to monitor the status of the log reader agent, including the latency and the number of transactions transferred per second.

▶ SQLServer:Replication Merge—This object contains counters used to monitor the status of the merge agents, including the number of transactions and the number of conflicts per second.

▶ SQLServer:Replication Snapshot—This object contains counters used to monitor the status of the snapshot agents, including the number of transactions per second.

Backup and Recovery in a Replication Configuration

Something that will reap major benefits for you after you have implemented a data replication configuration is a replication-oriented backup strategy. You must realize that the scope of data and what you must back up together has changed. In addition, you must be aware of what the recovery timeframe is and plan your backup/recovery strategy for this. You might not have multiple hours available to recover an entire replication topology. When you have databases that are conceptually joined, you might need to back them up together, as one synchronized backup.

When backing up environments, back up the following at each site:

▶ Publisher (published database, MSDB, and master)

▶ Distributor (distribution database, MSDB, and master)

▶ Subscribers (optional subscriber database)

Maintaining a regular backup of the publisher databases and leveraging the SQL Server Replication Monitor's built-in ability to reinitialize one or more subscriptions on demand provides a simple recovery strategy.

You could further limit regular backups to your publication databases and rely on SQL Server replication scripting to provide a method for reestablishing replication if you need to restore the entire replication environment.

Another strategy involves backing up only the publisher and the distributor, as long as the publisher and distributor are synchronized. This strategy allows you to restore a replication environment completely. Backing up a subscriber is optional but can reduce the time it takes to recover from a subscriber failure.

Always make copies of your replication scripts and keep them handy. At a very minimum, keep copies at the publisher and distributor and one more location, such as at one of your subscribers. You will end up using these for recovery someday.

Don't forget to back up the master database and MSDB when any new replication object is created, updated, or deleted.

Back up the publication database after doing any of the following:

8

- ▶ Creating new publications
- ▶ Altering any publication property, including filtering
- ▶ Adding articles to an existing publication
- ▶ Performing a publicationwide re-initialization of subscriptions
- ▶ Altering any published table with a replication schema change
- ▶ Performing on-demand script replication
- ▶ Cleaning up merge metadata (that is, running `sp_mergecleanupmetadata`)
- ▶ Changing any article property, including changing the selected article resolver
- ▶ Dropping any publications
- ▶ Dropping any articles
- ▶ Disabling replication

Back up the distribution database after doing any of the following:

- ▶ Creating or modifying replication agent profiles
- ▶ Modifying replication agent profile parameters
- ▶ Changing the replication agent properties (including schedules) for any push subscriptions

Back up the subscription database after doing any of the following:

- ▶ Changing any subscription property
- ▶ Changing the priority for a subscription at the publisher
- ▶ Dropping any subscriptions
- ▶ Disabling replication

Back up the MSDB system database after doing any of the following:

- ▶ Enabling or disabling replication
- ▶ Adding or dropping a distribution database (at the distributor)
- ▶ Enabling or disabling a database for publishing (at the publisher)
- ▶ Creating or modifying replication agent profiles (at the distributor)
- ▶ Modifying any replication agent profile parameters (at the distributor)
- ▶ Changing the replication agent properties (including schedules) for any push subscriptions (at the distributor)
- ▶ Changing the replication agent properties (including schedules) for any pull subscriptions (at the subscriber)

Back up the master database after doing any of the following:

▶ Enabling or disabling replication

▶ Adding or dropping a distribution database (at the distributor)

▶ Enabling or disabling a database for publishing (at the publisher)

▶ Adding the first or dropping the last publication in any database (at the publisher)

▶ Adding the first or dropping the last subscription in any database (at the subscriber)

▶ Enabling or disabling a publisher at a distribution publisher (at the publisher and distributor)

▶ Enabling or disabling a subscriber at a distribution publisher (at the subscriber and distributor)

In general, even when you walk up and pull the plug on a distribution server, publication server, or any subscribers, automatic recovery works well to get you back online and replicating quickly without human intervention.

Scenario 2: Worldwide Sales and Marketing with Data Replication

As defined in Chapter 1, "Understanding High Availability," this common business scenario is about a major chip manufacturer that has created a highly successful promotion and branding program, which results in billions of dollars in advertising dollars being rebated back to its worldwide sales channel partners. These sales channel partners must enter their complete advertisements (newspaper, radio, TV, other) and are measured in terms of ad compliance and logo usage and placements. If a sales channel partner is in compliance, it receives up to 50% of the cost of its advertisement back from this chip manufacturer. There are three major advertising regions: Far East, Europe, and North America. Each region produces a huge daily influx of new advertisement information that is processed on the primary server in North America. Then for the rest of each day, the regions review compliance results and run other types of major sales reports for their region only. As you might also recall, application mix is approximately 75% online entry of advertisement events and 25% regional management and compliance reporting.

Availability:

▶ 24 hours per day

▶ 7 days a week

▶ 365 days a year

   Planned downtime: **3%**

   Unplanned downtime: **2%** will be tolerable

It turns out that the regional reporting and query processing is the most important (most critical) part of this application. Each region must be able to query the compliance and

advertisement information in this database as it interacts with its regional channel partners and provides compliance status and rebate information rapidly (including dollar figures). This often requires specialized reports that span numerous advertisement events and
impact very large amounts of money. The online data entry of the advertisement information is done around the clock by third-party data entry companies; it must be done
directly on the central database (behind extensive firewalls and security). Performance of
the OLTP portion of this application must not be sacrificed in any way.

Each separate server has basic hardware/disk redundancy and one SQL Server instance,
and it is configured with SQL Server's robust transactional data replication implementation. This replication implementation creates three regional reporting images of the primary marketing database (MktgDB). These distributed copies alleviate the major reporting
burden against the OLTP (primary) database, and any one of them can serve as a warm
standby copy of the database in the event of a major database problem at headquarters.
Overall, this distributed architecture is easy to maintain and keep in sync, and it is highly
scalable. To date, there has not been a major failure that has required a complete switcho-
ver to one of the subscribers. However, the subscribers are in position to handle this if
ever required. In addition, the performance of each reporting server has been so outstanding that each region has brought in business objects and built its own unique reporting
front end to this data.

The company had previously estimated the total incremental costs to be between **$10k
and $100k,** which included the following estimates:

▶ Three new two-way servers (with 4GB RAM and local SCSI disk system RAID 10—15
  new drives total) at $10k per server (one for the North American reporting/spare
  server, one for Europe, and one for the Far East)

▶ Three Microsoft Windows 2000 Server licenses at ~ $1.5k per server

▶ Two days of additional training costs for system admin personnel at ~ $5k

▶ Four new SQL Server licenses (SQL Server 2016—the remote distributor and three
  new subscribers) at $5k per server

There are no special hardware or SCSI controllers needed to implement data replication.
The total incremental cost to build this high availability solution is approximately $89,500
(total costs—as follows).

Now, let's work through the complete ROI calculation for these incremental costs, along
with the cost of downtime:

1. Maintenance cost (for a 1-year period):

    ▶ **$5k (estimate)**—Yearly system admin personnel cost (additional time for train-
    ing of these personnel)

    ▶ **$24.5k (estimate)**—Recurring software licensing cost (of additional HA compo-
    nents; 3 OS + 4 SQL Server 2016)

2. Hardware cost:

  ▶ **$30k hardware cost**—The cost of the additional hardware in the new HA solution

3. Deployment/assessment cost:

  ▶ **$20k deployment cost**—The cost of development, testing, QA, and production implementation of the solution

  ▶ **$10k HA assessment cost**

4. Downtime cost (for a 1-year period):

  ▶ If you kept track of last year's downtime record, use that number; otherwise, produce an estimate of planned and unplanned downtime for this calculation. For this scenario, the estimated cost of downtime/hour is $5h/hour.

  ▶ Planned downtime cost (revenue loss cost) = Planned downtime hours × cost of hourly downtime to the company:

  a. 3% (estimate of planned downtime percentage in 1 year) × 8,760 hours in a year = 262.8 hours of planned downtime

  b. 262.8 hours × $5k/hr (hourly cost of downtime) = $1,314,000/year cost of planned downtime

  ▶ Unplanned downtime cost (revenue loss cost) = Unplanned downtime hours × cost of hourly downtime to the company:

  a. 2% (estimate of unplanned downtime percentage in 1 year) × 8,760 hours in a year = 175.2 hours of unplanned downtime

  b. 175.2 hours × $5k/hr (hourly cost of downtime) = $876,000/year cost of unplanned downtime

ROI totals:

▶ Total costs to get on this HA solution = $89,500 (for the initial year and roughly $24.5k/year for subsequent years)

▶ Total of downtime cost = $2,190,000 (for the year)

The incremental cost is about 4% of the downtime cost for 1 year. In other words, the investment of this particular HA solution will pay for itself in 18.9 hours! This is a huge ROI in a very short amount of time. And it provides a great scalable and flexible platform to grow on.

After building this HA solution, the uptime goal was achieved easily. Occasionally, there were some delays in resyncing the data at each regional site (subscribers). But, overall, the users were extremely happy with performance and availability. This is a great example of knowing what your HA options are and how to minimize hardware, software, and maintenance costs.

Summary

Data replication is a powerful feature of SQL Server that can be used in many business situations. Companies can use replication for anything from roll-up reporting to relieving the main server from ad hoc queries and reporting. However, applying it as a high availability solution can be very effective if your requirements match well to its capability. Determining the right replication option and configuration to use is somewhat difficult, but actually setting it up is pretty easy. Microsoft has come a long way in this regard. As with Scenario 2, if your requirements are not extreme availability, you may use data replication for high availability. It is more than production-worthy, and the flexibility it offers and the overall performance are just short of incredible, incredible, incredible (replication humor for you).

CHAPTER 9

SQL Server Log Shipping

A direct method of creating a completely redundant database image for higher availability is to use log shipping. Microsoft certifies log shipping as a method of creating an "almost" hot spare. Some folks use log shipping as an alternative to data replication. Log shipping used to be referred to as "poor man's replication" when replication was an add-on product. Now that log shipping and replication are both included in the box, neither one is really any more expensive to implement than the other. However, they differ in terms of *how* they replicate. Log shipping uses the transaction log entries, whereas replication uses SQL statements. This is hugely different. The log shipping method has three components:

▶ Making a full backup of a database (database dump) on a "source" server (which you want to be the origin of all transactions to other servers)

▶ Creating a copy of that database on one or more other servers from that dump (called *destinations*)

▶ Continuously applying transaction log dumps from that "source" database to the "destination" databases

This is the dump, copy, restore sequence. In other words, log shipping effectively replicates the data of one server (the source) to one or more other servers (the destinations) via transaction log dumps. Destination servers are read-only.

Poor Man's High Availability

Figure 9.1 shows a typical log shipping configuration with two destination pairs. A destination pair is any unique source server/destination server combination. You can have any number of source/destination pairs. This means you can have from 1 to *N* replicated images of a database using log shipping—for example, at different data centers. Then, if the source server ever fails, you can easily use one of the destination servers to take over for the source server, thus achieving some level of high availability (only losing the availability time it takes to switch over to one of the destination servers). However, you need to understand that each destination server will only be as up to date with its data as the last transaction log restore applied to it.

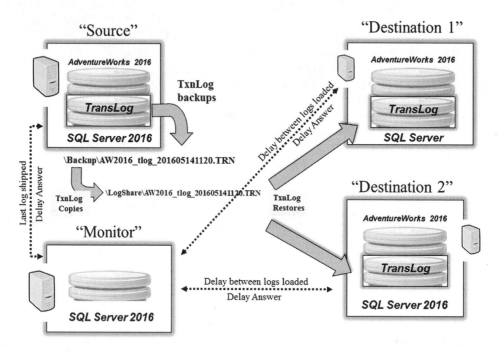

FIGURE 9.1   Log shipping with two read-only destination servers and a separate monitor server.

As you can also see in Figure 9.1, log shipping uses a monitor server to help keep track of the current state of the log shipping. The monitor server is another SQL Server instance. A couple jobs are created within SQL Server Agent on the monitor server. In addition, several tables in the MSDB database are used exclusively for keeping the log shipping information; these tables all begin with `log_shipping_`. In a nutshell, the monitor server keeps track of when the last transaction log backup was shipped from the source database to the destinations, keeps track of the delays between the logs that get loaded on the destinations, and indicates whether delay times are being exceeded.

Data Latency and Log Shipping

Determining the right delays to specify depends on the data latency you can tolerate and how quickly you need to be notified when log shipping breaks down. Your high availability service level agreement will dictate this to you. If there is a breakdown in log shipping, such as the loads on the destination are not being done or are taking longer than what has been set up, the monitor server will generate alerts. It is a good general practice to isolate the monitor server to a separate server by itself so that this critical monitoring of log shipping is not affected if the source server or any destination servers fail (refer to Figure 9.1).

(refer to Figure 9.1)

> **NOTE**
>
> You can actually set up log shipping to work entirely within a single SQL Server instance if you wish. This may be useful if you're doing extensive testing or in other situations that can benefit from a separate copy of the "source" database or if you want to isolate reporting to a separate SQL Server instance. Log shipping is typically done from one SQL Server instance to another, regardless of the location of the destination server (as in another data center). You are only limited by the communication stability and consistency between SQL instances.

The amount of data latency that exists between the source and destination database images is the main determining factor in understanding the state of your recoverability and failover capabilities. You need to set up these data latency (delay) values as part of the log shipping configuration.

These are the primary factors in using log shipping as the method of creating and maintaining a redundant database image:

▶ Data latency is an issue. This is the time between the transaction log dumps on the source database and when these dumps get applied to the destination databases.

▶ Sources and destinations must be the same SQL Server version.

▶ Data is read-only on the destination SQL Server until the log shipping pairing is broken (as it should be to guarantee that the translogs can be applied to the destination SQL Server).

The data latency restrictions might quickly disqualify log shipping as a foolproof high availability solution, though. However, log shipping might be adequate for certain HA situations. If a failure ever occurs on the primary SQL Server, a destination SQL Server that was created and maintained via log shipping can be swapped into use at a moment's notice. It would contain exactly what was on the source SQL Server (right down to every user ID, table, index, and file allocation map, except for any changes to the source database that occurred after the last log dump was applied). This directly achieves a level of high availability. It is still not quite completely transparent, though, because the SQL Server instance names are different, and the end user may be required to log in again to the new SQL Server instance. But unavailability is usually minimal.

Design and Administration Implications of Log Shipping

From a design and administration point of view, you need to consider some important aspects associated with log shipping:

▶ User IDs and their associated permissions are copied as part of log shipping. They are the same at all servers, which might or might not be what you want.

▶ Log shipping has no filtering. You cannot vertically or horizontally limit the data that will be log shipped.

▶ Log shipping has no ability to do data transformation. No summarizations, format changes, or things like this are possible as part of the log shipping mechanism.

▶ Data latency is a factor. The amount of latency is dependent upon the frequency of transaction log dumps being performed at the source and when they can be applied to the destination copies.

▶ Sources and destinations must be the same SQL Server version.

▶ All tables, views, stored procedures, functions, and so on are copied.

▶ Indexes cannot be tuned in the copies to support any read-only reporting requirements.

▶ Data is read-only (until log shipping is turned off).

If these restrictions are not going to cause you any trouble and your high availability requirements dictate a log shipping solution, then you can proceed with confidence in leveraging this Microsoft capability.

> **NOTE**
>
> Log shipping in MS SQL Server 2016 is extremely stable, but it will eventually be deprecated (that is, dropped from SQL Server in future releases). Many organizations are using availability groups instead, but log shipping may be all that you really need, depending on your basic needs, and doesn't require things like failover clustering services.

Setting Up Log Shipping

In order to use log shipping for a high availability solution, you should plan on having at least three separate servers available. One server is the "source" SQL Server, from which you will identify a database to log ship. This is your primary SQL Server instance and database. Another server will be the "destination" SQL Server that is the target of the log shipping and will be your secondary server for failover. The third server is the "monitor" SQL Server that keeps track of the log shipping tasks and timeliness. You can configure log shipping without a monitor server, but experience shows that a separate monitor server to alert you when issues arise is the most prudent configuration, especially for achieving high availability.

This chapter assumes that you are using the Full recovery model (or bulk-logged) for database backup, since this creates transactions in the transaction log that will be the source of log shipping. If you chose the Simple recovery model, there would be nothing to log ship, since the transaction log would be truncated on a regular basis. In fact, the log shipping option would not even be available for any database that has this recovery model chosen.

Before Creating Log Shipping

As part of setting up log shipping from Microsoft SQL Server Management Studio (SSMS), you should quickly register all SQL Server instances that will be used in the log shipping model. You do this by right-clicking each SQL Server instance and choosing Register.

> **NOTE**
>
> When you configure log shipping, a series of recurring SQL Server Agent jobs are created on the SQL Server instances being used in your configuration:
>
> ▶ A job for database backup (if you have specified one on the source server)
>
> ▶ A job for transaction log backups (on the source server)
>
> ▶ A job for log shipping alerts (on the monitor server)
>
> ▶ Two jobs on the destination server for copying and loading (restoring) the transaction log

Remember that you should make sure that each SQL Server instance in your log shipping configuration has its corresponding SQL Server Agent running, since tasks will be created on each SQL Server instance and won't get executed unless SQL Server Agent is functioning and has permissions to access what they will need. The login that you use to start the SQL Server and SQL Server Agent services must have administrative access to the log shipping plan jobs, the source server, and the destination server. The user who sets up log shipping must be a member of the SYSADMIN server role, which gives the user permission to modify the database to do log shipping.

Next, you need to create a network share on the primary server where the transaction log backups will be stored. You do this so that the transaction log backups can be accessed by the log shipping jobs (tasks). This is especially important if you use a directory that is different from the default backup location. Here is how it looks:

`\\SourceServerXX\NetworkSharename`

In this chapter you will create log shipping for the AdventureWorks database that is shipped with SQL Server 2016 (and is available at www.msdn.com). If you don't already have this database downloaded, please get it now and install it on the source SQL Server instance. Figure 9.2 shows the log shipping configuration you will set up. The SQL2016DXD01 server instance will be the source, the SQL2016DXD02 server instance will be the destination, and the SQL2016DXD03 server instance will be the monitor. Be sure to set the AdventureWorks database recovery model to be Full so that the Ship Transaction Logs task is available for this database.

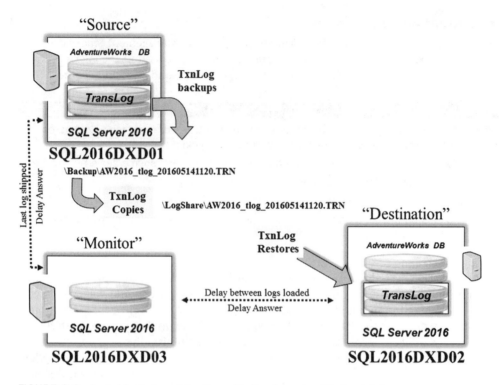

FIGURE 9.2   Log shipping configuration with the AdventureWorks database.

Using the Database Log Shipping Task

Now you are ready to begin the log shipping setup process. Microsoft has placed this capability within the database tasks. As you can see in Figure 9.3, you start the Ship Transaction Logs task for the source database to begin the setup (on the SQL2016DXD01 server instance in this example). This brings you to the Transaction Log Shipping database properties page for this database, where you can set up, configure, and initiate log shipping.

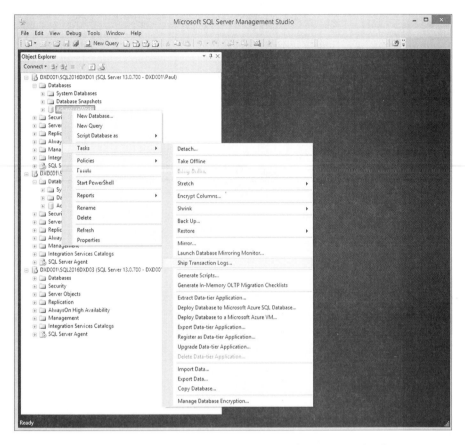

FIGURE 9.3   Starting the Ship Transaction Logs task for a source database.

As you can see in Figure 9.4, you have to enable this database as the primary database in the log shipping configuration by clicking the check box at the top. As you define all the other properties to this log shipping configuration, they will be visible from this database properties Transaction Log Shipping page. Once you check the Enable check box, the Backup Settings option becomes available so you can specify all that you need.

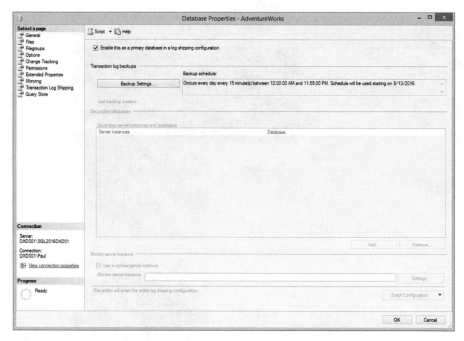

FIGURE 9.4   Database Properties page for log shipping settings.

Now, click on the Backup Settings button and, as you can see in Figure 9.5, you can specify all backup and file server settings. You need to specify the full network path to the backup folder that will be used to store the transaction log backups to be shipped. It is important to grant read and write permissions on this folder to allow the service account to use this (on the source server). It is also important to grand read permissions to the account that will be executing the copy jobs; the transaction log copies/moves to the destination servers. Specify the network path \\DXD001\FileServerBACKUP.

FIGURE 9.5   Transaction Log Backup Settings page.

Accept LSBackup_AdventureWorks (the default name) as the backup job name for the SQL Server agent job that does the transaction log backups at some frequency. For this example, set up the backups to run every 5 minutes (the default is 15 minutes) because you need more current data (more frequent pushes of transactions to the destination server). If you click the Schedule button to the right of the Job Name field, you can set the schedule frequency (as shown in Figure 9.6).

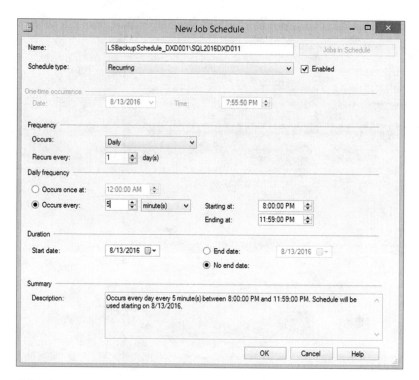

FIGURE 9.6   New Job Schedule page.

Once you have specified the transaction log settings and schedule, you can continue to specify the destination servers (secondary server instances and databases) along with the monitor server instance that will be keeping track of the log shipping timing.

To set up the monitor server instance, click the Use a Monitor Server Instance check box at the bottom of the Database Properties page and click the Settings button to connect to the SQL Server instance that will serve as the monitor for log shipping. This also generates a local SQL Server Agent job for alerting when issues such as timing problems arise. As shown in Figure 9.7, you want to connect to the SQL2016DXD03 server instance as your monitor server.

Now you can add the destination server instance and database you are targeting for log shipping. On the Database Properties page, click the Add button for adding secondary server instances and databases (in the middle portion of this page). As you can see in Figure 9.8, you need to connect to the destination (secondary) server instance with the appropriate login credentials. You can then finish specifying how you want to initiate log shipping on that server (SQL2016DXD02 in this example), including creating the destination database if it doesn't exist yet or restoring a full backup to that destination database if it exists already.

FIGURE 9.7   Database Properties page with the monitor server instance configured.

FIGURE 9.8   Transaction log backup schedule frequency settings.

For the destination (secondary) server, you need to specify the copy files schedule to hold the transaction logs copied from the source server, as shown in Figure 9.9. In addition, you specify the restore transaction log schedule, which applies the transaction logs to the destination server (secondary) database, as also shown in Figure 9.9. For this example, set all schedule frequencies to be at 5-minute intervals to achieve more data.

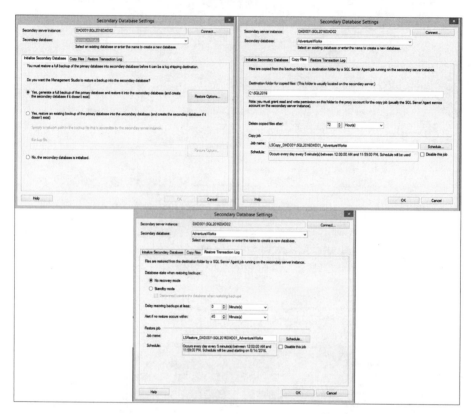

FIGURE 9.9   Destination (secondary) server and database initialization settings.

When the destination (secondary) server settings are all configured, the backup, copy, and restore process begins. Figure 9.10 shows the final configuration all set up and the process of restoring the backup to the destination (secondary) database beginning. By clicking the Script Configuration button, you can specify to generate the entire log shipping configuration in script form. (It is included in this chapter's SQL script downloads.)

Figure 9.11 shows the SQL Server Agent jobs executing away and the destination server database in Restoring mode. This means the transaction logs are being applied to this secondary database, and the database can be used for failover if needed.

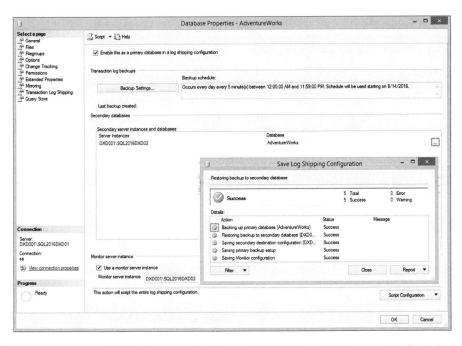

FIGURE 9.10   Transaction log shipping database properties completely configured and beginning processing.

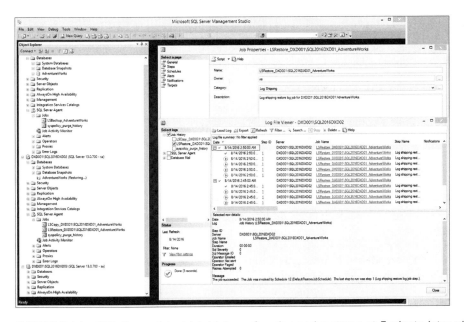

FIGURE 9.11   SQL Server Agent job history of copies and restores at 5-minute intervals.

In Restoring mode, no access to the destination database is allowed. You can use the Standby mode to allow the destination database to be used for query processing. However, the transaction log restore jobs may get held up (that is, queued up) until any existing connections are terminated. (You'll learn more about this in a bit.) This isn't necessarily the end of the world. You will still be able to apply those transaction logs when the read-only activity is finished. Remember that the data in this destination database is only as current as the last transaction log restore. Figure 9.12 shows the same overall log shipping configuration but with the destination database in Standby mode. You can also see in Figure 9.12 the results of a read-only query against the destination database Person table.

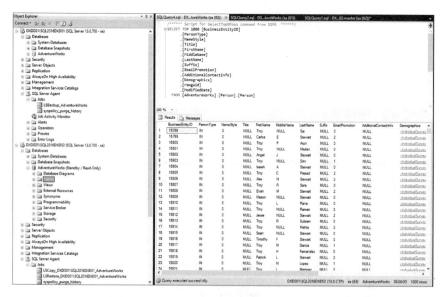

FIGURE 9.12   Log shipping in Standby mode and querying destination database data.

NOTE

Log shipping and disk space may affect high availability. The directory location you specify for your transaction log dumps should be large enough to accommodate a very long period of dump activity. You may want to consider using the Remove Files Older Than option to delete backup files from the source server's transaction log directory after a specified amount of time has elapsed. But remember that disk space is not endless. It will fill up eventually unless you specify something for this option.

The database load state identifies how a destination database (the target of the log shipping process) is to be managed during data loads:

▶ No Recovery mode indicates that this destination database is not available for use. The destination database will be in No Recovery mode as a result of either the RESTORE LOG or RESTORE WITH NORECOVERY operations. When and if the source server fails, the mode for this destination database will be changed so that it can be used.

▶ Standby mode indicates that this destination database is available for use but in
read-only mode. The destination database will be placed in Standby mode as a result
of either the `RESTORE LOG` or `RESTORE DATABASE WITH STANDBY` operation.

This example allows for read-only access to this destination database if you specify the
Standby mode option. You should also specify the Terminate Users in Database option
since any restore operation (of transaction logs) will fail if any users are connected to the
destination database. This might seem a bit abrupt, but it is critical to keeping the database
intact and ensuring an exact image of the source database. The users can reestablish the
connection to this destination database after the restore process is complete (which is usually very quickly). As you specify the frequency of these restores, you need to consider the
usage of this destination database as a secondary data access point (such as for reporting).

NOTE

If you are going to use the destination database for reporting, you might want to decrease
the frequency of these backups and copies/loads since the reporting requirements may
well tolerate something less frequent. However, if the destination server is to be a hot
spare for failover, you might even want to increase the frequency to a few minutes apart
for both the backups and the copies/loads.

A quick look at the monitor server instance and the job history of the LSAlert SQL Server
Agent task shows a clean and healthy log shipping monitoring sequence. You would want to
use this SQL Server Agent task to send out alerts (for example, emails, SMS messages) when
log shipping is failing. Figure 9.13 shows the last successful task executions from the monitor
server instance. You can also execute a few simple `SELECT` statements on the monitor server
instance (against the MSDB database tables for log shipping). You can usually look at the
`msdb..log_shippping_monitor_history_detail` table to get a good idea of what is going on:

```
SELECT * FROM msdb..log_shipping_monitor_history_detail
WHERE [database_name] = 'AdventureWorks'
```

FIGURE 9.13   The monitor server instance Log Shipping Alerts task.

6

Each of the SQL Server instances in your topology has a series of log shipping tables in the MSDB database:

```
log_shipping_primary_databases
log_shipping_secondary_databases
log_shipping_monitor_alert
log_shipping_monitor_error_detail
log_shipping_monitor_history_detail
log_shipping_monitor_primary
log_shipping_monitor_secondary
log_shipping_plan_databases
log_shipping_plan_history
log_shipping_plans
log_shipping_primaries
log_shipping_secondary
log_shipping_secondaries
```

Each appropriate table will be used, depending on the role the server plays in the topology (source, destination, or monitor).

> **NOTE**
>
> You will *not* find entries in all tables in all SQL Servers in your topology. Only the tables that are needed by each server's functions will have rows. So don't be alarmed.

When the Source Server Fails

When the source server fails, you can quickly enable the destination server database to take over the work for your application (in full transactional mode). From the destination server (since the source server is dead in the water), you run the sp_delete_log_shipping_secondary_database stored procedure for the database. This removes all the log shipping tasks that were in place for copy and restore processing. Then you simply run the RESTORE DATABASE 'dbname' WITH RECOVERY command. You can then connect your application to this fully functioning database and be on your merry way. This should take more than a few minutes in total and should achieve high availability recovery well within your business needs.

Scenario 4: Call Before Digging with Log Shipping

As you saw in Chapter 3, "Choosing High Availability," the call before digging business scenario (Scenario 4) combined hardware redundancy, shared disk RAID arrays, SQL clustering, and log shipping. This is a very critical system during its planned hours of operation, but it has low-performance goals and low cost of downtime (when it is down). Regardless, it is highly desirable for this system to be up and running as much as possible. Having that warm standby with log shipping provides just enough of an insurance policy in case the whole SQL cluster configuration fails.

Thanks to this HA solution, the company easily achieved its uptime goal was achieved easily. In fact, after 3 months, the log shipping configuration was disabled. Two days after the log shipping was disabled, the whole SQL clustering configuration failed (Murphy's law). The log shipping was rebuilt, and this configuration has remained in place since then. Performance has been exceptional, and this application continuously achieves its availability goals. Figure 9.14 shows the current HA solution with log shipping.

▶ Availability:

    ▶ 15 hours per day (5:00 a.m.–8:00 p.m.)

    ▶ 6 days per week (closed on Sunday)

    ▶ 312 days per year

▶ Planned downtime: 0%

▶ Unplanned downtime: 0.5% (less than 1%) will be tolerable

The company had previously estimated the total incremental costs to be between **$10k and $100k**, which included the following estimates:

▶ Three new four-way servers (with 4GB RAM, local SCSI disk system RAID 10, two Ethernet NICs, and an additional SCSI controller [for shared disk]) at $25k per server

▶ Two Microsoft Windows 2000 Advanced Server licenses at ~$3k per server (Windows 2003 Enterprise Edition, $4k per server)

▶ One shared SCSI disk system with RAID 5 (minimum of 10 drives per SCSI disk system) at ~$5k

▶ Four to five days of additional training costs for system admin personnel t ~$12k

▶ Two new SQL Server licenses (SQL Server 2000, Enterprise Edition) at $5k per server

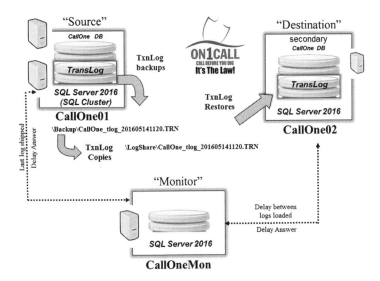

FIGURE 9.14   Call before digging high availability "live solution" with log shipping.

The total incremental costs to upgrade to this SQL clustering with log shipping high availability solution was approximately $108,000—just slightly over the earlier estimates.

Now, let's work through the complete ROI calculation with these incremental costs, along with the cost of downtime:

1. Maintenance cost (for a 1-year period):

   ▶ **$12k (estimate)**—Yearly system admin personnel cost (additional time for training of these personnel)

   ▶ **$16k (estimate)**—Recurring software licensing cost (of additional HA components; 2 OS + 2 SQL Server 2000)

2. Hardware cost:

   ▶ **$80k hardware cost**—The cost of additional hardware in the new HA solution)

3. Deployment/assessment cost:

   ▶ **$20k deployment cost**—The cost of development, testing, QA, and production implementation of the solution

   ▶ **$10k HA assessment cost**

4. Downtime cost (for a 1-year period):

   ▶ If you kept track of last year's downtime record, use that number; otherwise, produce an estimate of planned and unplanned downtime for this calculation. For this scenario, the estimated cost of downtime/hour is $2k/hour.

   ▶ Planned downtime cost (revenue loss cost) = Planned downtime hours × Cost of hourly downtime to the company (should be $0).

   ▶ Unplanned downtime cost (revenue loss cost) = Unplanned downtime hours × Cost of hourly downtime to the company:

      a. 0.5% (estimate of unplanned downtime percentage in 1 year) × 8,760 hours in a year = 43.8 hours of unplanned downtime

      b. 43.8 hours × $2k/hr (hourly cost of downtime) = $87,600/year cost of unplanned downtime

ROI totals:

▶ Total costs to get on this HA solution = $128,000 (for the year—slightly higher than the immediate incremental costs stated above)

▶ Total of downtime cost = $87,600 (for the year)

The incremental cost is about 123% of the downtime cost for 1 year. In other words, the investment of the HA solution will pay for itself in 1 year and 3 months! This is well within the ROI payback the company was looking for, and it will provide a solid HA solution for years to come.

Summary

In contrast to data replication and SQL clustering, log shipping is fairly easy to configure. It also doesn't have many hardware or operating system restrictions. Log shipping is a good option because it not only provides high availability but also ensures your data against hardware failures. In other words, if one of the disks on the source (primary) server stops responding, you can still restore the saved transaction logs on the destination (secondary) server and upgrade it to a primary server, with little or no loss of work. In addition, log shipping does not require that the servers be in close proximity. And, as added benefits, log shipping supports sending transaction logs to more than one secondary server and enables you to offload some of the query processing and reporting needs to these secondary servers.

As indicated earlier, log shipping is not as transparent as failover clustering or availability groups because the end user will not be able to connect to the database for a period of time, and users must update the connection information to the new server when it becomes available. Remember that, from a data synchronization point of view, you are only able to recover the database up to the last valid transaction log backup, which means your users may have to redo some of the work that was already performed on the primary server. It is possible to combine log shipping with replication and/or failover clustering to overcome some of these disadvantages. Your particular HA requirements may be very well supported with a log shipping model.

6

CHAPTER 10

High Availability Options in the Cloud

Most organizations have started to do parts of their workload on any number of cloud platforms. Some organizations are already completely cloud based. Application options on software as a service (SaaS) cloud-based platforms (such as Salesforce, Box, NetSuite, and others) are rapidly growing in popularity. There are also many cloud computing options to choose from these days, such as Microsoft Azure, Amazon, Rackspace, IBM, Oracle, and so on. An organization must weigh many factors in deciding whether to use cloud computing. Cost is usually not what drives a company to use or not use cloud computing; rather, things like performance and very often security are the deciding factors. Equally as important is the legacy systems involves; some of them simply are not good candidates for 100% cloud-based deployment. However, if your organization is already using or is about to use cloud computing, the SQL Server family of products and Windows Server editions have positioned you well to either take baby steps to the cloud or go all in as fast as you want. Some of the Microsoft options available to you are cloud hosting (infrastructure as a service [IaaS]), Azure SQL Database (which is really a database platform as a service [PaaS] offering), and several hybrid options that combine your existing on-premises deployment with Azure options to get you started on cloud computing capabilities that will quickly enhance your high availability position.

This chapter introduces high availability options that you can leverage in two ways: as a way to extend your current on-premises deployment (a hybrid approach to HA in the cloud) and as a 100% cloud-based approach to achieving

HA for your applications (or just your database tiers). This chapter also describes a little about the big data HA story, which is further detailed in Chapter 11, "High Availability and Big Data Options."

A High Availability Cloud Nightmare

On October 21, 2016, a major distributed denial-of-service (DDoS) attack occurred across many major Internet/cloud-based companies, including Amazon, Box, Twitter, Netflix, Spotify, PayPal, GitHub, and Reddit (to name a few). Basically, all of these companies were unable to provide their services for a period of time (they were *not available*). As you already know, this is a factor to consider in HA assessment and should be a part of determining what HA solution you choose and how it should be configured. Figure 10.1 shows the extent of this DDoS attack across the United States. It was truly a nightmare for each of these providers, whose underlying deployments simply couldn't react fast enough to this type of failure (attack).

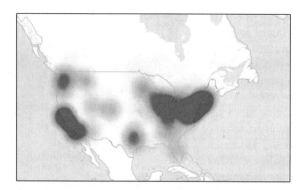

DDoS Attack (October 21, 2016)

FIGURE 10.1   A recent DDoS attack that made numerous organizations unavailable across the United States.

Even though some parts of these companies' tiers were unaffected, the combined stack they use was simply overwhelmed and unavailable. There are options to combat this type of HA risk—things like geographic partitioning and multisite failover options, for example. There are also some huge disaster recovery and business continuity implications at hand (as discussed in Chapter 13, "Disaster Recovery and Business Continuity").

This chapter describes several HA options you can start with to leverage the cloud alone or in conjunction with your on-premises deployments to mitigate your risk of nightmares like this one. It is imperative to understand that your company's exposure to failure includes everything you deploy *and* everything you use as a service from another provider (for example, Amazon, Box, Microsoft). The trick is to get something resilient configured to lower your overall risk so you can sleep better at night.

HA Hybrid Approaches to Leveraging the Cloud

For those who have extensive on-premises deployments and are anxious to get to the cloud somehow to better support high availability needs, this section hits on a few of the low-hanging-fruit options that can radically increase your overall availability and get you partially in the cloud. We categorize these HA options—with some parts on your on-premises platforms and some parts on a cloud-based solution such as Microsoft Azure—as hybrid approaches.

NOTE

Most of the big players—like Microsoft, Amazon, and Rackspace—provide numerous solutions and options in cloud-based computing. This chapter focuses on the options that best serve a mostly Microsoft stack. However, to be fair, although we describe a Microsoft Azure option, there might very well be a similar option on Amazon or another service.

The following sections look at a few natural extensions to the cloud for the following legacy on-premises HA or partial HA solutions you might already have in place, including the following:

▶ Extending data replication topologies to the cloud

▶ Creating a Stretch Database on Microsoft Azure from your on-premises database

▶ Creating an AlwaysOn availability group on the cloud

▶ Adding a new destination node in the cloud for your existing log shipping configuration

Figure 10.2 shows each of these options with portions of the corresponding topologies on MS Azure (in the cloud). Microsoft has made it very clear that it wants to protect all the existing investment you have already put into place and, at the same time, provide you with expansion options to meet your future needs. The following sections describe a number of ways to fairly easily to get into the cloud to fulfill your high availability needs.

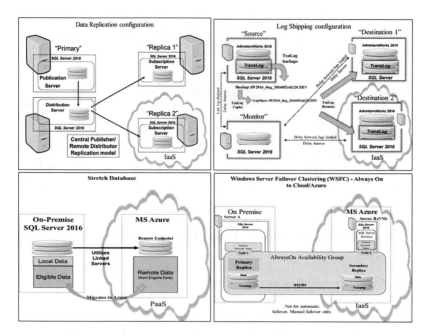

FIGURE 10.2   Extending your current technology to the cloud to enhance HA.

Extending Your Replication Topology to the Cloud

Some of the factors you must consider when extending a data replication topology to the cloud are connectivity, stability, and bandwidth. If your current infrastructure is on a slow network backbone, and it is already saturated with internal network traffic, you might want to consider upgrading it *before* you extend a part of your topology across it. When you are in a position to extend an existing replication topology, you must decide exactly what you want to have in the cloud replica. If your first foray to the cloud is to be a warm standby in case of failure, then the entire database should be the scope for this replication extension. You might also consider taking advantage of this cloud-based replication node for other purposes as well, such as offloaded regional reporting. Figure 10.3 shows an existing on-premises replication topology that may be similar to a topology that has served you well over the years. It uses the classic central publisher/remote distributor replication model.

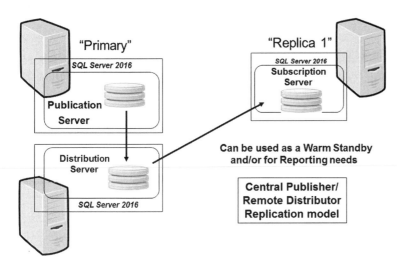

FIGURE 10.3   On-premises publisher, distributor, and single-subscriber replication topology.

To extend to the cloud, you would have to set up complete network connectivity to the Azure-based IaaS environment, install SQL Server 2016 (including allowing for replication), and set up a continuous subscription to the primary's publication. Figure 10.4 illustrates a new cloud IaaS environment that extends the existing central publisher/ remote distributor replication model.

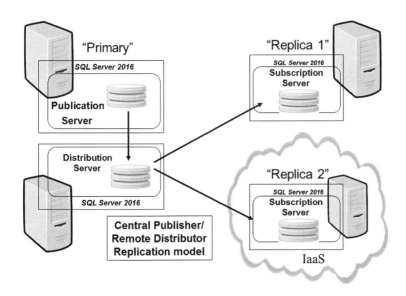

FIGURE 10.4   Extending a replication topology to Azure (IaaS).

There is really nothing different to do from a database setup point of view to get this replication node up and running. Having Azure utilize your Active Directory domain, roles, and permissions is very straightforward as well. And you can easily make this a push subscription.

In the event of a complete failure of your primary server (the publisher), you can choose to use the new cloud-based replica to either continue to provide reporting to the enterprise or make it (manually) be the primary database for your applications. You, of course, have the same option with any existing subscribers internally, but now you have an additional cloud-based option in your HA configuration. This further mitigates your company's risk of complete failures. It is also a fairly easy option to provide to your organization—with no new technology and no new overhead but further risk mitigation achieved. This hybrid cloud approach is likely to raise your overall HA uptime percentage into the high 9s for your database tier.

Extending Log Shipping to the Cloud for Additional HA

Log shipping, as described in Chapter 9, "SQL Server Log Shipping," is really the poor man's data replication. Extending log shipping to the cloud isn't much different from extending your replication topology, as just described. Once again, the primary things you must consider when extending a log shipping topology to the cloud are connectivity, stability, and bandwidth. You will be "shipping" transaction log backup files (potentially not small files) at a certain frequency. You must consider this traffic and load on your network *before* you extend a part of your topology across it. When you are in a position to extend an existing log shipping topology, you will have to initialize the destination database in the Azure IaaS environment just as you would do for an on-premises installation. Again, you will be able to use this newly extended database in the cloud for failover. You might also consider taking advantage of the cloud-based copy for other purposes, such as offloaded regional reporting.

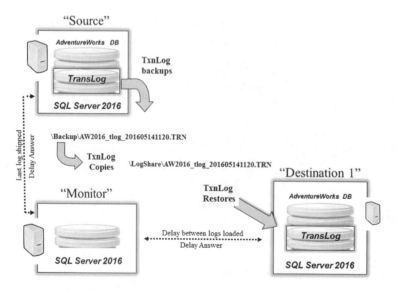

FIGURE 10.5   On-premises log shipping topology.

Figure 10.5 illustrates an existing on-premises log shipping topology that may be similar to a topology that has served you well over the years. To extend to the cloud, Figure 10.6 illustrates a new cloud IaaS environment that extends the existing log shipping topology. You would have to set up complete network connectivity to the Azure-based IaaS environment, install SQL Server 2016, make sure log shipping tasks can get to the log share folders, and set up a log shipping frequency that you feel comfortable with. It should be fairly frequent to reduce the burden on your network at any one time (that is, so you do not have bursts of large file movement but rather trickles of smaller log files more frequently).

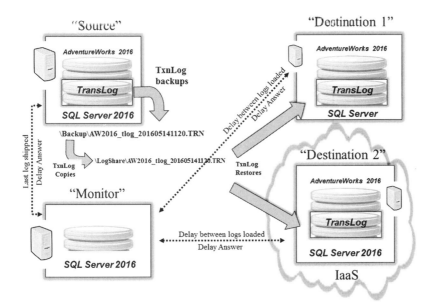

FIGURE 10.6   Extending a log shipping topology to Azure (IaaS).

There is really nothing different to do from a database setup point of view to get this second, cloud-based log shipping replica up and running. As mentioned previously, having Azure utilize your Active Directory domain, roles, and permissions is very straightforward as well.

As you also saw with the replication topology, in the event of a complete failure of your primary server (the source), you can choose to use the new cloud-based version to continue to provide reporting to the enterprise or make it (manually) be the database for your application. You, of course, have the same option with any existing destination replica internally, but now you have an additional cloud-based option in your HA configuration. Once again, this further mitigates your company's risk of complete failures. It is also a fairly easy option to provide to your organization—with no new technology and no new overhead but further risk mitigation achieved. This hybrid cloud approach is likely to raise your overall HA uptime into the high 9s for your database tier.

10

Creating a Stretch Database to the Cloud for Higher HA

From a complete data redundancy point of view, a Stretch Database provides only a partial solution for high availability. Figure 10.7 shows the breakdown of current versus historical data in a typical OLTP database that might be a good candidate for the Stretch Database feature.

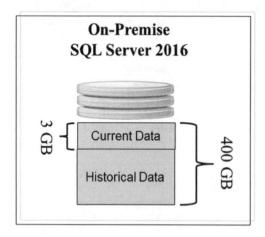

FIGURE 10.7   Typical OLTP database breakdown of current versus historical data for a large database.

The Stretch Database capability takes infrequently accessed data that meets certain criteria and pushes this data to the cloud via the linked server mechanism (see Figure 10.8). The net effect is a significantly smaller primary database, increased performance for current data, and significantly decreased times to back up and restore your local database, which, in turn, directly affects your RTO and RPO numbers. This can have a huge impact on your overall HA experience. Put simply, backing up and restoring a 400GB database is very different from backing up and restoring a 3GB database. Using the Stretch Database capability allows you the luxury of smaller database backups/restores without the loss of any of that 397GB of data and without the loss of access to that 397GB of data.

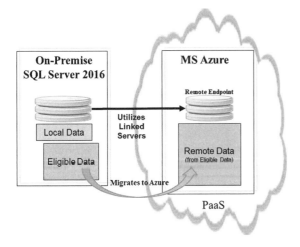

FIGURE 10.8 How Stretch Database reduces the local database size and migrates this data to the cloud.

Using AlwaysOn and Availability Groups to the Cloud

If you have a current HA configuration (such as SQL clustering) that is *not* using AlwaysOn availability groups, you can massively raise your HA capabilities to the cloud without having to disrupt your current configuration. Figure 10.9 shows an existing SQL clustering configuration that is configured into an active/passive failover configuration. Such a configuration may have served you well, but it can be easily extended to the cloud to replicate the primary database using AlwaysOn availability groups for further HA and the offloading of processing.

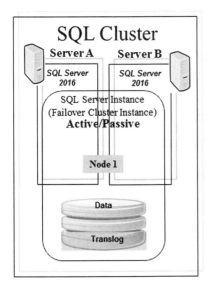

FIGURE 10.9 Standard SQL clustering failover configuration on-premises.

Remember that SQL clustering is built on WSFC. The AlwaysOn availability group also utilizes WSFC for cross-server HA configurations. Figure 10.10 shows how an existing on-premises SQL clustering HA configuration can be further extended to an Azure IaaS cloud-based AlwaysOn availability group configuration. You should implement this by using asynchronous mode (not synchronous) to get an almost real-time fully replicated database in the cloud for failover (manual failover) and offloading of processing for things like reporting.

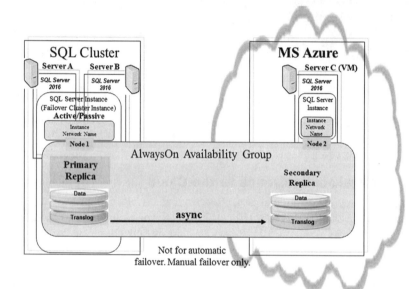

FIGURE 10.10   Extending a SQL clustering failover configuration onto the cloud with AlwaysOn availability groups.

As you can see in Figure 10.11, you could just as easily extend a standard SQL Server configuration (which is not a SQL clustering configuration) to the cloud for HA. You would just need to make sure WSFC is enabled both on-premises and on the cloud IaaS secondary. Again, because you are replicating to the cloud, you would do this by using asynchronous mode and utilize manual failover in the event of an on-premises failure. This is a very significant and easy way to decrease your company's failure risk.

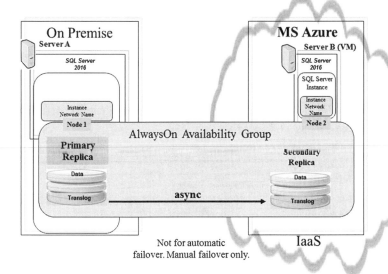

FIGURE 10.11   Extending a standard SQL Server configuration onto the cloud with AlwaysOn and Availability Groups for HA.

Using AlwaysOn and Availability Groups in the Cloud

If you are ready to fully move to the cloud in at least an IaaS deployment (but are not ready for PaaS yet), you can do so with a full HA configuration for your primary database's failover protection and for disaster recovery. You essentially need to build out a series of IaaS environments, install SQL Server on each environment, and configure an AlwaysOn availability group to achieve high availability at the SQL Server instance level and at the database level (as illustrated in Figure 10.12). This is basically the same thing you would do on-premises, but it's completely in the cloud (on IaaS).

When you have all your SQL Servers on the cloud, you can use the synchronous mode for replication between the primary and the secondary, and you get instantaneous failover if one server becomes unavailable. In addition, you might want to have a geographically distant cloud IaaS environment (perhaps even on a different IaaS vendor's platform) that you replicate to for disaster recover. (More on this strategy in Chapter 13, "Disaster Recovery and Business Continuity.") And, one last option you can take advantage of on Azure is to utilize the Azure Blog storage to store database backups. The HA architecture and infrastructure behind Microsoft's blog storage are exceptional and have some of the best SLAs in the industry.

10

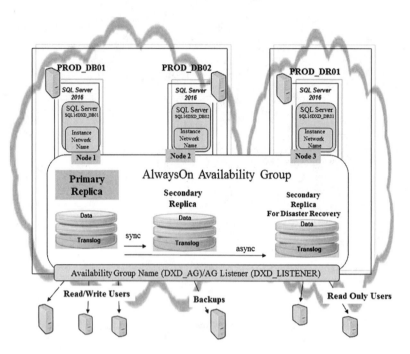

FIGURE 10.12   IaaS-based AlwaysOn availability group HA configuration with DR.

Using Azure SQL Database for HA in the Cloud

More and more organizations are taking advantage of Microsoft's Azure SQL Database PaaS offering for all their database needs *and* for high availability and disaster recovery. Azure SQL Database is essentially a complete SQL Server database on the cloud as a service. You don't need to install SQL Server or configure a Windows Server. Everything you can do in your current SQL Server database you can do with Azure SQL Database.

As you can see in Figure 10.13, a SQL database exists in an Azure regional data center (Region 1), from which you access it and use it for your application's database. However, from an HA point of view, you also have your database redundantly stored in three other locations in that region for your data's safety, thanks to Geo Redundant Storage (GRS).

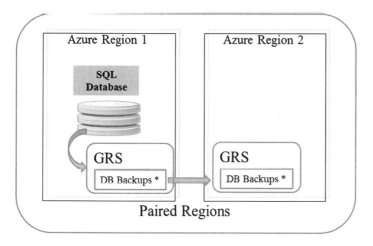

FIGURE 10.13   Azure SQL Database and HA.

In addition, database backups of your Region 1 database are sent to another Azure regional data center (Region 2) for further data protection. Once stored on the GRS of the second, "paired," region's GRS, this too is redundantly stored in three other locations in that region. As of this writing, the paired regions are illustrated in Figure 10.14. For example, if you are using a SQL database in the North American geography, you might be put on a North Central US data center that is paired with the South Central US data center.

Paired Regions

Geography	Paired regions	
North America	North Central US	South Central US
North America	East US	West US
North America	US East 2	US Central
North America	West US 2	West Central US
Europe	North Europe	West Europe
Asia	South East Asia	East Asia
China	East China	North China
Japan	Japan East	Japan West
Brazil	Brazil South (1)	South Central US
Australia	Australia East	Australia Southeast
US Government	US Gov Iowa	US Gov Virginia
India	Central India	South India
Canada	Canada Central	Canada East
UK	UK West	UK South

FIGURE 10.14   Azure SQL Database paired regions.

For every SQL database, automatic database backups of various types are done at various frequencies:

▶ Weekly full database backups

▶ Hourly differential database backups

▶ Transaction log backups every 5 minutes

These full and differential backups are also replicated to the "paired" data centers, and they can be used to restore within a regional data center or to another data center. If restoring from another region's backups, you can expect one hour's data loss. If you are restoring from within the same region, data loss is typically extremely small (minutes at worst).

Using Active Geo Replication

Active Geo Replication (AGR) is essentially the AlwaysOn availability group capability implemented as a built-in service for Azure SQL Database. In the same way you identify a primary replica and secondary replicas in a normal Windows availability group configuration, you can do the same for an Azure SQL Database AGR configuration. However, the replication mode you can use is only asynchronous: Only one of the secondaries can be used for failover, and you can't replicate to more than four readable secondaries, as shown in Figure 10.15.

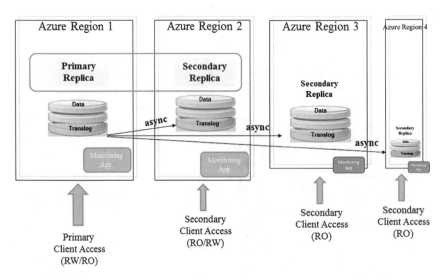

FIGURE 10.15   Typical OLTP database breakdown of current versus historical data for a large database.

With AGR, you can operate in an active/passive scenario (as in availability groups), active/active full load–balancing mode, and active/passive failover, where you promote a secondary to be the primary in the event of a failure on the primary. All other secondaries are only ever in read-only mode.

So, with AGR, you can have up to four readable secondaries, you can choose the regions where you want your secondaries, and you can use asynchronous mode (which means there is potentially some data loss). AGR is best for critical applications and can provide 99.99% (four 9s) availability for your applications.

HA When Using Azure Big Data Options in the Cloud

High availability for big data options is a bit complicated but on the other hand pretty easy to deal with because HA is designed into the Hadoop Distributed File System (HDFS) architecture from the ground up. (Chapter 11 explains much more about all the big data options with HDInsight offerings from Microsoft Azure.) As you can see in Figure 10.16, there are several components to the HDInsight and Data Lake analytics offerings in Azure. The storage-level mechanisms that are a part of HDFS form the core HA capability by design.

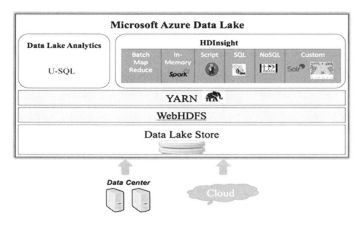

FIGURE 10.16   Azure big data options and components.

Basically, this setup distributes data across multiple nodes so that any data or node can be re-created from the other or a node can take over for another. This gives the next generation of big data processing a remarkable level of high availability that is built in.

Summary

Whether you are trying to expand into the cloud in a hybrid (partial) approach or go 100% into the cloud, you must consider how high availability will be provided for any configuration you use. This chapter has shown how to extend your current SQL Server deployment into the cloud by using hybrid approaches for each of the major types of HA configurations. Select the one that you have experience with first and then move to others that have more resilience as your business requirements warrant. This chapter

10

demonstrates was how easy it is to extend your environments into the cloud without much disruption to your current implementations. However, if you make that first big step, the HA improvements (and advantages) are huge. If you are choosing to go 100% into the cloud with Azure IaaS options, you can readily build out everything you currently have on-premises already. As you grow, you simply dynamically expand that footprint. One step further is to utilize Azure SQL Database for a PaaS solution with high availability. This offering is taking over the PaaS market like wildfire.

CHAPTER 11

High Availability and Big Data Options

With the exponential growth of data generated by individuals and corporations, big data applications have garnered a lot of attention. It all started with the publication of a monumental white paper by Google on using GFS (Google File System) for storage and MapReduce for processing back in 2003. A year later, Doug Cutting and Michael Cafarella created Apache Hadoop. Since then, Hadoop and several other open source Apache projects have created an entire ecosystem to address diverse scenarios and create amazing applications. These big data ecosystems can be deployed in the cloud or on-premises. In the cloud, the two most prominent offerings are AWS (Amazon Web Services) from Amazon and Azure from Microsoft. The Azure offering has come a long way and now provides a rich set of enterprise-caliber big data implementation options. Over a period of time, Microsoft has developed a full stack for this big data ecosystem, ranging from Azure storage, Hadoop cluster implementation, and recently advanced analytics, including machine learning.

This chapter introduces various Microsoft big data offerings and a few third-party offerings. It also describes the high availability features that are part of the big data solutions. Finally, this chapter provides some real-life use cases for highly available big data solutions in the cloud. Because Microsoft has decided to embrace the Hadoop architecture in its Azure deployment for big data, all Azure big data deployments naturally inherit the resilience and failover features at their lowest levels. (More on this HA architecture later.)

Big Data Options for Azure

Azure is a Microsoft cloud offering that provides a wide range of services, such as computing, storage, analytics, database, web, mobile, and networking services.

Microsoft has implemented Hadoop-based big data solutions using the Hortonworks Data Platform (HDP), which is built on open source components in conjunction with Hortonworks. The HDP is 100% compatible with Apache Hadoop and the open source community distributions. All the components are tested in typical scenarios to ensure that they work together correctly and that there are no versioning or compatibility issues.

Microsoft and Hortonworks offer three solution options:

▶ **HDInsight**—This cloud-hosted service available to Azure subscribers uses Azure clusters to run HDP and integrates with Azure storage. HDInsight is discussed in detail later in this chapter.

▶ **HDP for Windows**—This is a complete package that you can install on a Windows Server to build your own fully configurable big data clusters based on Apache Hadoop. It can be installed on physical on-premises hardware or on virtual machines in the cloud (on Azure).

▶ **Microsoft Analytics Platform System**—This is a combination of the massively parallel processing (MPP) engine in Microsoft Parallel Data Warehouse (PDW) with Hadoop-based big data technologies. It uses HDP to provide an on-premises solution that contains a region for Hadoop-based processing, together with PolyBase—a connectivity mechanism that integrates the MPP engine with HDP, Cloudera, and remote Hadoop-based services such as HDInsight. It allows data in Hadoop to be queried and combined with on-premises relational data and data to be moved into and out of Hadoop.

The intelligence and analytics category of services from Azure is a growing collection of big data and analytics capabilities, as illustrated in Figure 11.1.

The following sections introduce the various Azure offerings in big data and analytics.

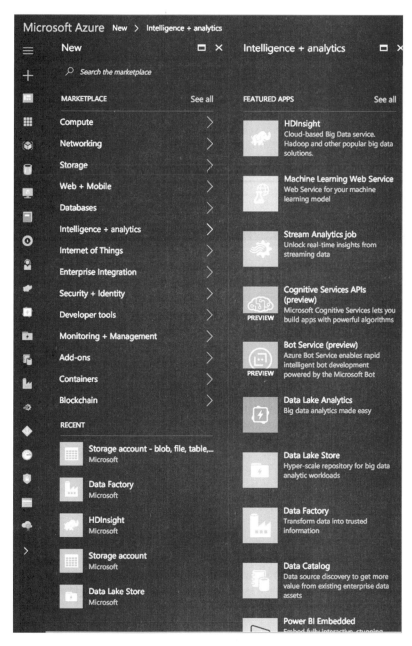

FIGURE 11.1   Azure offerings in the intelligence and analytics category.

HDInsight

HDInsight is the Azure managed cloud service, which provides the capability to deploy Apache Hadoop, Spark, R, HBase, and several other big data components. HDInsight is discussed in detail later in this chapter.

Machine Learning Web Service

Machine Learning Web Service is a collection of easy-to-use wizard-based analytics services that make it possible to quickly create and deploy a wide range of predictive models. Microsoft also offers Machine Learning Studio, which provides a drag-and-drop interface that allows you to create complex models using several built-in machine learning algorithms, as shown in Figure 11.2.

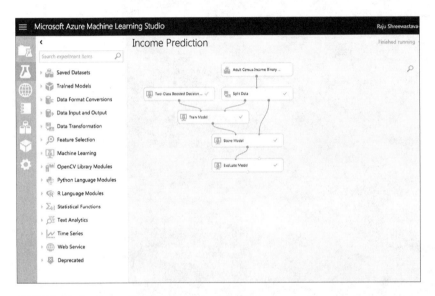

FIGURE 11.2   Azure Machine Learning Studio.

Stream Analytics

Stream Analytics is a fully managed, cost-effective, real-time event processing engine that can handle a wide range of streaming sources, such as sensors, websites, social media, applications, and infrastructure systems.

Cognitive Services

Cognitive Services is a rich set of smart APIs that enable natural and contextual interactions for language, speech, search, vision, knowledge, and so on.

Data Lake Analytics

Data Lake Analytics makes big data analytics much easier. This service takes care of the infrastructure deployment and configuration for your data lakes. This, in turn, frees up big data users to focus on the actual data access and usage needed to fulfill business requirements.

Data Lake Store

Data Lake Store is a managed cloud storage offering that is compatible with Hadoop Distributed File System (HDFS). It is integrated with Azure Data Lake Analytics and HDInsight.

Figure 11.3 shows some of the other Data Lake offerings on Azure:

FIGURE 11.3   Azure big data core services offering.

▶ Cloudera was one of the very early companies to identify the market need to support customers for big data software. Cloudera has contributed to several projects in Apache's open source community, including Hue and Impala. For more details, see www.cloudera.com.

▶ Hortonworks has taken a more open source route and contributed directly to the open source projects, such as the cluster management tool Ambari. The Azure HDInsight offering from Microsoft is based on the Hortonworks distribution. For more details, see http://hortonworks.com.

▶ Revolution Analytics is a statistical software company focused on developing open source and open-core versions of the free and open source software R for enterprise, academic, and analytics customers. Microsoft acquired Revolution Analytics in 2015 and has since then integrated R offerings in the Azure platform.

Companies like Cloudera and Hortonworks are referred as distributors of Apache Hadoop and other open source big data software. The main service of these companies is to provide support for big data–related open source software. They also provide packaging and training services, as illustrated in Figure 11.4.

FIGURE 11.4   Common services of big data distributors.

Data Factory

Azure Data Factory allows you to compose and orchestrate data services for data movement and transformation. It supports a wide range of data stores, including Azure data stores, SQL and NoSQL databases, flat files and several other data containers as sources and includes an array of transformation activities that can range from simple high-level APIs like Hive and Pig to advanced analytics using machine learning.

Power BI Embedded

Power BI Embedded brings the capability of interactive reports in Power BI to the Azure platform. Power BI Desktop users, OEM vendors, and developers can create custom data visualizations in their own applications.

Microsoft Azure Data Lake Services

The list of big data services keeps growing. Of the offerings just presented, HDInsight, Data Lake Analytics, and Data Lake Store work together to enable the big data capabilities on the Azure platform. The next section does a deep dive into these primary big data services on Azure. Figure 11.5 shows that the overall Microsoft Azure data lake services are Data Lake Analytics, HDInsight, YARN, WebHDFS, and the Data Lake Store.

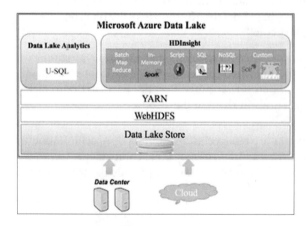

FIGURE 11.5   Azure data lake services.

HDInsight Features

As you can also see in Figure 11.5, Azure HDInsight is the primary big data product. It is from Apache Hadoop and powered by the Microsoft Cloud, which means it follows the Hadoop architecture and can process petabytes of data. As you probably already know, big data can be structured, unstructured, or semi-structured.

HDInsight allows you to develop in your favorite languages. HDInsight supports programming extensions of many languages and frameworks, such as C#, .NET, Java, and JSE/J2EE.

With the use of HDInsight, there is no need to worry about the purchase and maintenance of hardware. There is also no time-consuming installation or setup.

For data analysis you can use Excel or your favorite business intelligence (BI) tools, including the following:

▶ Tableau

▶ Qlik

▶ Power BI

▶ SAP

You can also customize a cluster to run other Hadoop projects, such as the following:

▶ Pig

▶ Hive

▶ HBase

▶ Solr

▶ MLlib

Using NoSQL Capabilities

Traditional relational databases have been used for decades for transactional and data warehousing applications. As the volume of data has increased and much more unstructured data has been created, the need for NoSQL databases has emerged. There are currently hundreds of NoSQL databases on the market, providing various storage capabilities for specific use cases and faster analytical processing.

Database options can be broadly classified into six categories, as illustrated in Figure 11.6:

▶ Relational/OLTP (online transaction processing)

▶ OLAP (online analytical processing)

▶ Column-family

▶ Key/value

▶ Document

▶ Graph

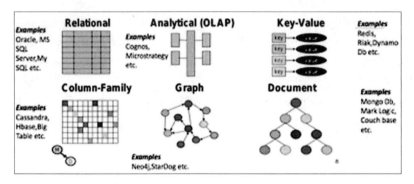

FIGURE 11.6   NoSQL data storage options.

A great NoSQL database option is HBase. It is a NoSQL columnar data store built on top of HDFS. It is modeled after Google BigQuery, which is the highly compressed data storage system on GFS. You can use Apache HBase when you need random, real-time read/write access to your big data. This project's goal is to host very large tables—billions of rows times and millions of columns—utilizing clusters of commodity hardware. HBase can be coupled with Hive, HBase, Pig, Sqoop, Flume, Solr, and other products. For more details, see http://hbase.apache.org.

Real-Time Processing

HDInsight is equipped with Apache Storm, which is an open source real-time event-processing system. It enables users to analyze the real-time data from the Internet of Things (IoT), social networks, and sensors.

Spark for Interactive Analysis

HDInsight is equipped with Apache Spark, an open source project that can be run on large-scale data for interactive analytic purposes. Spark can execute queries more than 100 times faster than traditional big data queries. This includes executing queries for real-time streaming and graph processing.

R for Predictive Analysis and Machine Learning

HDInsight is also equipped with the R server for Hadoop. With R, you can handle 100 times more data than was previously possible, and you can achieve query speeds up to 50 times faster (when equipped with Hadoop and Spark).

HDInsight provides the following additional features (see Figure 11.7):

▶ Automatic provisioning of clusters

▶ High availability and reliability of clusters (as discussed later in this chapter)

▶ Efficient and economic data storage and blob storage that is all Hadoop compatible and comes with Data Factory, where you can store some data free of cost

▶ Cluster-scaling features for easy scaling within a cluster

▶ Virtual network support to keep clusters safe and secure

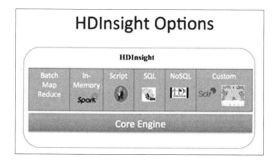

FIGURE 11.7   HDInsight options.

Azure Data Lake Analytics

Big data analytics involves processing large data sets to discover hidden patterns, unknown correlations, market trends, customer preferences, and other useful business information.

In the Azure ecosystem, Microsoft offers Data Lake Analytics to enable users to focus on business logic. This service takes care of the deployment and configuration of infrastructure components. Data Lake Analytics is a highly scalable service that is capable of handling jobs of any size.

Data Lake Analytics provides the following additional features:

▶ **Security**—Data Lake Analytics is compatible with Azure Active Directory, providing capability for controlling authentication and authorization based on roles.

▶ **Cost-effectiveness**—Data Lake Analytics can handle workloads of any size with ease. For a user, it is just like adjusting the dial of processing capability while still paying for only compute used. Upon completion of a job, the service automatically releases the resources, reducing the overall cost.

▶ **U-SQL compatibility**—It is compatible with U-SQL query language, which is a known skill among SQL and .NET developers.

▶ **Data set diversity**—Data Lake Analytics makes it possible to analyze a diverse set of Azure data sources, such as SQL Server on Azure, Azure SQL Database, Azure SQL Data Warehouse, Azure Blob storage, and Azure Data Lake Store.

As you can see in Figure 11.8, Data Lake Analytics uses HDFS to support compatibility within HDFS.

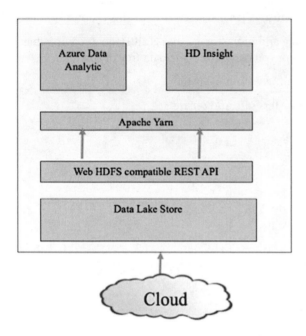

FIGURE 11.8   Azure Data Lake Analytics and Storage.

Azure Data Lake Store

A *data lake* is a storage repository that holds a huge amount of raw data in its original format until it is needed for processing. Whereas a hierarchical data warehouse stores data in files or folders, a data lake uses a flat architecture to store data.

Microsoft has created Azure Data Lake Store to enable the data lake concept in the cloud. It acts as a hyperscale repository for big data analytics workloads. It enables you to store any type, size, and ingestion speed from social media, transactional system, databases, log events, sensors, and so on in a centralized repository. It supports HDFS and Azure Data Lake Store Filesystem (adl://). Systems like HDInsight that are compatible with Azure Data Lake File system provide better performance on Data Lake Store.

Data Lake Store provides the following additional features:

▶ **Security**—Data Lake Store is compatible with Azure Active Directory, providing capability for controlling authentication and authorization based on roles. Authentication can be achieved through Azure Active Directory (AAD) and authorization of data using access control lists (ACLs)

▶ **Freedom from storage limits**—In Azure Data Lake Store, a single file can be petabytes in size, as no limits are placed on the sizes of single files or overall storage.

▶ **High availability**—To ensure fault tolerance, redundant copies of files are stored based on the replication principles of HDFS. The default replication factor is three—that is, data is stored redundantly three times to ensure recoverability and availability—but this factor can be adjusted if required.

High Availability of Azure Big Data

High availability of Azure big data needs to be considered at both the data and services levels. Let's first look at data and, in particular, data redundancy.

Data Redundancy

For data redundancy, Hadoop enables fault tolerance capabilities by storing redundant copies of data. This is very similar to RAID storage but is actually built into the architecture and implemented with software. The default replication level for any data field stored in Hadoop is three. This can be adjusted in the hdfs-site.xml configuration file if needed.

Data in Microsoft Azure storage is always replicated, and you have the option of selecting the replicated data copy to be within the same data center (region) or to different data centers (regions).

During the creation of your storage account, four replication options are available (see Figure 11.9):

FIGURE 11.9 Azure storage replication options.

▶ **Read-access geo-redundant storage (RA-GRS)**—This is the default storage account
option, which maximizes availability and is commonly used for high availability. It
provides read-only access to your data at a secondary location, along with the replication across two regions provided by GRS.

▶ **Zone-redundant storage (ZRS)**—ZRS provides three copies of data replicated across
data centers within one or two regions. This, unto itself, provides an additional layer
of fault tolerance in the event that the primary data center is unavailable. ZRS has
some limitations, as is it available for blob storage only.

▶ **Locally redundant storage (LRS)**—This is the simplest and lowest-cost option for
replication, involving making three copies of data within the data center spread to
three difference storage nodes. Rack-level awareness is achieved by storing the copies

over different fault domains (FDs) and upgrade domain (UDs) to provide fault tolerance in case a failure impacts a single rack.

▶ **Geo-redundant storage (GRS)**—GRS replicates the three copies made with LRS to
another region hundreds of miles away from the primary region. So, if the primary
region becomes unavailable, your data is still available in another region.

High Availability Services

An HDInsight cluster provides two head nodes to increase availability and reliability (see
Figure 11.10). It also can have from 1 to *N* data nodes (and must have at least 1 data node).

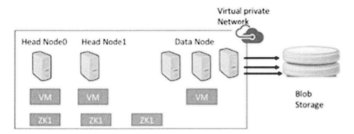

FIGURE 11.10   The architecture of head nodes and data nodes of a Hadoop cluster.

How to Create a Highly Available HDInsight Cluster

There are two different tools you can use to create a Hadoop cluster:

▶ You can create an HDInsight cluster through the Azure Management Portal.

▶ You can create an HDInsight cluster through Windows Azure PowerShell (a set
of modules that provide cmdlets to manage Azure). For more details on Azure
PowerShell, visit https://docs.microsoft.com/en-us/azure/powershell-install-configure.

To follow along with the examples in this chapter, you need to have an active Azure subscription and create a simple Hadoop cluster. Before you can create an HDInsight cluster,
you also need to have an Azure storage account, which will be used by the Azure HDInsight cluster. The storage account will be used to store files and data files for the default
containers. Here's all you have to do:

1. Navigate to the Azure portal, at https://portal.azure.com.

2. Log in, and you see the default dashboard, shown in Figure 11.11, with the services
available in the Azure portal.

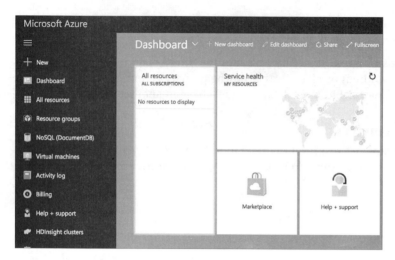

FIGURE 11.11   Microsoft Azure portal.

3. Select the Storage Accounts option from the menu on the left (see Figure 11.12).

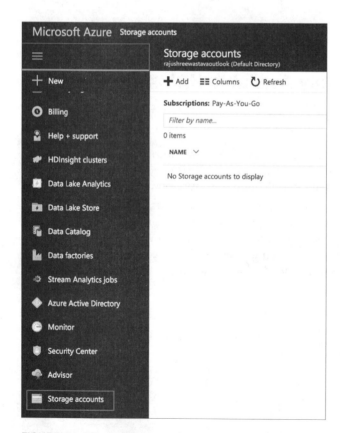

FIGURE 11.12   Setting up a storage account.

4. Click Add to add a new storage account (see Figure 11.13).

FIGURE 11.13   Adding a storage account.

5. Provide the necessary details, including a unique name, replication, and the resource group. Figure 11.14 shows the default replication option, Read-access geo-redundant storage (RA-GRS), selected. You can select a different option if needed.

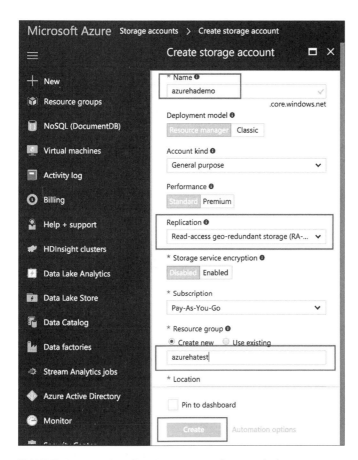

FIGURE 11.14   Creating the storage characteristics.

6. Click Create. After a few minutes, the new storage account is available (see Figure 11.15).

7. To create an HDInsight cluster, select the HDInsight Cluster Resource option in the menu on the left for all resources and click Add (see Figure 11.16).

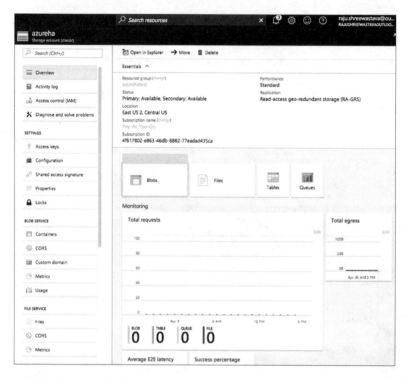

FIGURE 11.15   Creating a storage and resource group.

FIGURE 11.16   Adding a Hadoop HDInsight cluster.

8. Provide a unique cluster name (see Figure 11.17) and select the cluster type (see Figure 11.18).

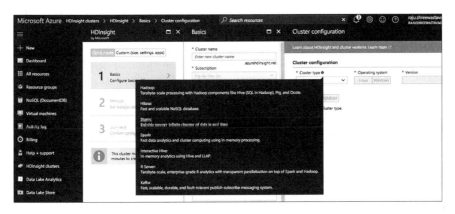

FIGURE 11.17   Creating a Hadoop cluster type.

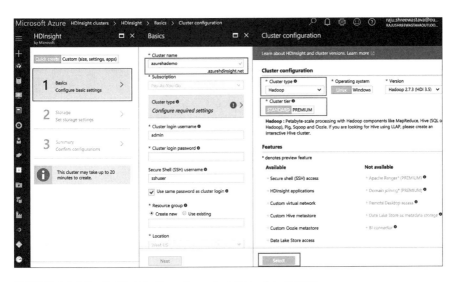

FIGURE 11.18   Setting further characteristics of a cluster.

9. Select the operating system. As you can see in Figure 11.18, you have an option to select the Linux or Windows operating system and can choose among a few recent Linux versions supported by Azure. Microsoft continues to support a few older versions as it moves to new versions. You can also select between the Standard and Premium cluster tiers:

▶ **Standard**—A standard tier contains all the basic, yet necessary, functionalities needed to successfully run an HDInsight cluster in the cloud.

▶ **Premium**—The premium tier has all the functionality in the standard tier, plus enterprise-grade features such as multiuser authentication, authorization, and auditing.

Click the Select button to continue the cluster creation process.

As you can see in Figure 11.19, additional third-party applications such as Datameer can be added to the cluster. For the HA demo cluster, you should not select any additional applications.

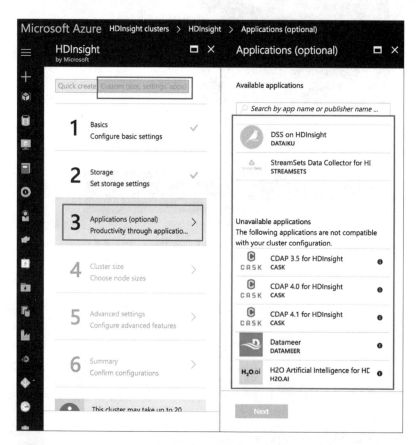

FIGURE 11.19   Other third-party applications that can be added to a cluster.

10. As shown in Figure 11.20, provide credentials for the cluster by creating a cluster username login and an SSH username login. Click Next to store the entered information.

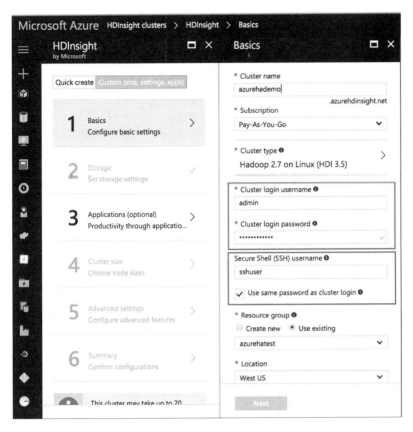

FIGURE 11.20   Setting up credentials for a Hadoop cluster.

11. Provide the data source configuration, as shown in Figure 11.21, by selecting the storage account that was created before. The data source will be the Azure storage account. The location of the cluster will be the same as the location of the primary data source. In this case, you're using the storage account you created in steps 3–6.

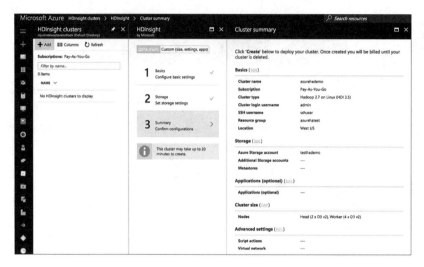

FIGURE 11.21   Specifying data sources.

12. In the pricing section, select the number and types of worker nodes and head nodes. For the high availability HDInsight default, provide two head nodes, as shown in Figure 11.22.

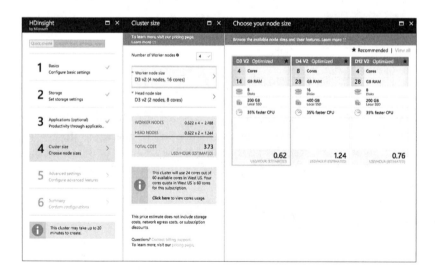

FIGURE 11.22   Choosing the configuration and price level of an Azure Hadoop cluster.

13. When you are done providing information, click the Create button to begin the cluster creation process (as shown in Figure 11.23). You can use the automation option hyperlink to get the script for this cluster creation, which you can then use to create the cluster by using automation instead of the wizard.

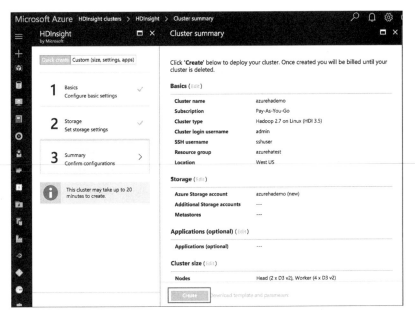

FIGURE 11.23   Creating a Hadoop cluster.

The deployment takes a few minutes, but when it finishes, you will have created your first highly available HDInsight cluster (see Figure 11.24).

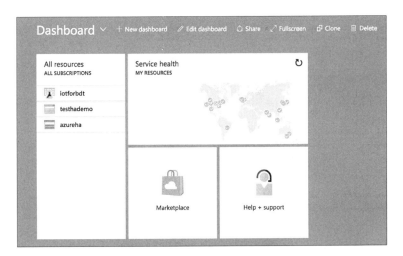

FIGURE 11.24   Successful creation of an Azure Hadoop cluster.

As you can see in Figure 11.25, the All Resources view shows all the items you have created (the resource group, the storage account, and the cluster).

FIGURE 11.25   The All Resources view of a Hadoop cluster.

The HDInsight cluster overview dashboard (see Figure 11.26) provides a good overview of all the major things associated with this cluster, including the status (Running), the URL, subscription information, and access to other things relevant to the cluster, such as activity logs, access control, and so on.

FIGURE 11.26   The Hadoop cluster overview dashboard.

Accessing Your Big Data

As you can see in Figure 11.27, you can check the activity log on the cluster by using the Activity Log option.

FIGURE 11.27   Checking the activity log of a Hadoop cluster.

You can log in to the cluster by using the SSH hostname and login that you created earlier, as shown in the following example:

```
$ ssh demo_user@azurehademo ssh.azurehdinsight.net
The authenticity of host 'azurehademo-ssh.azurehdinsight.net' can't be established.
RSA key fingerprint is xx.
Are you sure you want to continue connecting (yes/no)? yes
Warning: Permanently added 'azurehademo-ssh.azurehdinsight.net,40.84.55.141' (RSA)
to the list of known hosts.
Authorized uses only. All activity may be monitored and reported.
demo_user@azurehademo-ssh.azurehdinsight.net 's password:
Welcome to Ubuntu 14.04.5 LTS (GNU/Linux 4.4.0-47-generic x86_64)
    * Documentation: https://hetp.ubuntu.com/
Get cloud support with Ubuntu Advantage Cloud Guest:
    http://www.ubuntu.com/business/services/cloud
Your Hardware Enablement Stack (HWE) is supported until April 2019.
The programs included with the Ubuntu system are free software;
the exact distribution teris for each program are described in the individual files
in /usr/share/doc/./copyright.
Ubuntu comes with ABSOLUTELY NO WARRANTY, to the extent permitted by applicable law.
demo user@hn0-azureh:~$
```

You can also run some simple Hadoop commands, such as to get a list of HDFS files, invoke Hive, and check available hive tables, as shown here:

```
demo user@hn0-azureh:~$hadoop fs -ls /
Found 12 items
drwxr-xr-x        - root   supergroup        0 2016-11-25 04:16 /HdiSarnples
drwxr-xr-x        - hdfs   supergroup        0 2016-11-25 04:01 /amns
drwxr-xr-x        - hdfs   supergroup        0 2016-11-25 04:01 /amnshbase
```

```
drwxrwxrwx        - yarn   hadoop        0 2016-11-25 04:01 /app-logs
drwxr-xr-x        - yarn   hadoop        0 2016-11-25 04:01 /atshistory
drwxr-xr-x        - root   supergroup    0 2016-11-25 04:01 /example
drwxr-xr-x        - hdfs   supergroup    0 2016-11-25 04:01 /hdp
drwxr-xr-x        - hdfs   supergroup    0 2016-11-25 04:01 /hive
drwxr-xr-x        -mapred supergroup    0 2016-11-25 04:01 /mapred
drwxrwxrwx        -mapred hadoop        0 2016-11-25 04:01 /mr-history
drwxrwxrwx        -hdfs   supergroup    0 2016-11-25 04:01 /tmp
drwxr-xr-x        -hdfs   supergroup    0 2016-11-25 04:01 /user
demo_user@hn0-azureh:~$
```

You can invoke Hive in the newly created cluster as shown here:

```
demo_user@hn0-azureh:$ hive
WARNING: Use "yarn jar" to Launch YA!1 applications.
Logging initialized using configuration in file:/etc/hive/2.4.4.0-10/0/hive-log4j.
properties
hive> show databases;
OK
default
Tinie taken: 1.272 seconds. Fetched: 1 row(s)
hive> show tables;
hivesampletable
Tinie taken: 0.133 seconds, Fetched: 1 row(s)
```

If this is an experimental cluster, you'll likely want it to go away after you are done playing with it so that you don't incur any charges. As you can see in Figures 11.28 and 11.29, it is easy to delete a cluster and a storage account.

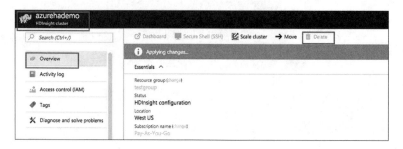

FIGURE 11.28   Removing/deleting a Hadoop cluster.

FIGURE 11.29   Removing/deleting a storage account.

In this section you have learned how to create a highly available HDInsight cluster and storage account.

The Seven-Step Big Data Journey from Inception to Enterprise Scale

For organizations and companies already using Microsoft Azure as their cloud service provider, the choice of HDInsight for a big data Hadoop implementation is a natural next step to take. But before you go off and start creating big data clusters, you should read this section, which steps through a process to help you be successful in this big data endeavor.

This section provides some basic guidelines for you to consider as part of seven-step big data journey from inception to enterprise scale. These steps (illustrated in Figure 11.30) are designed to get you where you are going reasonably safely (without major blunders):

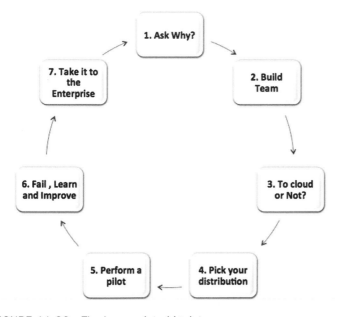

FIGURE 11.30   The journey into big data.

1. **Ask "Why?"**—Before embarking on the big data journey, it is important to assess whether your organization really needs a big data solution. As you can see in Figure 11.31, the five *Vs* of big data—volume, variety, velocity, veracity, and value—can be a guiding compass when you're deciding on the need for big data as part of your business solutions. Even if you do not have a huge volume of data, you may need other *Vs*, like variety, due to semi-structured or unstructured data processing needs.

   In real estate, it is all about location, location, location. In the big data world, it is all about use case, use case, use case.

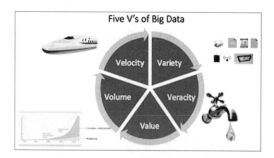

FIGURE 11.31   The five **Vs** of big data.

2. **Build a solid team**—Identifying skilled and experienced resources can be a challenging task in the big data domain. But having a great team or not can be a deal breaker in a big data implementation. It is very important to build a well-rounded team with experience using technologies and business domain knowledge. In addition to including solid big data engineers, it is equally important to have other skills, such as analysis, design, architecture, testing, and product management, included as part of this team.

3. **Cloud or not?**—One of the key determinations in the early planning stages is whether to build in the cloud or not. Certain conditions, such as compliance or regulatory and security needs, may require an organization to keep things on-premise. For implementing in the cloud, the offerings from Microsoft (Azure) or Amazon (AWS) are good choices.

   A cloud implementation can provide the following key benefits:

   ▶ Agility

   ▶ Cost-effectiveness

   ▶ Scalability

   ▶ Easier maintenance

   A cloud implementation also poses some challenges:

   ▶ Security

   ▶ Industry compliance needs

   ▶ Privacy concerns

4. **Pick a distribution**—Several big data software distribution companies, including Cloudera, Hortonworks, MapR, Amazon EMR, and Microsoft HDInsight, provide Hadoop offerings on top of the Apache Hadoop stack. Apache's open source offering is free but typically involves more complex setup and maintenance. Picking the flavor to use can come down to several factors, such as what services come with the offering. Most offerings provide the following common services:

   ▶ **Packaging**—The various Hadoop ecosystem components may be packaged or bundled together and tested for compatibility. This can make deployments much easier and faster.

   ▶ **Support**—The primary revenue source for some of these distribution companies, support can range from consulting to online help to troubleshooting. You really need to look at the depth of a company's knowledge on core concepts such as designs, technology, and production deployments.

   ▶ **Training**—Most companies provide training and certification on their offerings. Look for the ones that offer training for each of the team member roles. You'll want to have everyone trained.

   Along with these common services, each distribution provides some unique offerings or approaches to differentiate itself. For example, Hortonworks has taken a complete open source route, and MapR has created proprietary offerings like MapR-FS.

5. **Perform a proof of concept or a pilot project**—Most companies start with a proof of concept (POC) or a fairly simple pilot project. The challenge with POCs is that if they're not done exhaustively, they don't always provide real-life results. For this reason, it is often advisable to perform a pilot project with a real big data use case. This would also help get some immediate value to the business as you size up your next steps.

6. **Fail, learn, and improve**—After the pilot implementation, learning and tuning the solution will be an ongoing journey. Different departments, such as marketing, finance, and so on, need to be brought on slowly as you extend your big data solution.

7. **Take it to the enterprise**—After two or three big data projects, it is time to think of taking big data to the enterprise level. During this phase, you need to create the big data foundation, build on smaller successes, and scale out to the rest of the enterprise.

Other Things to Consider for Your Big Data Solution

Of course, organizations must consider the many other things that should be put into place and will change over time as they build up their big data solutions and provide these solutions to the users in the organization. Especially important are making sure the data is available, is managed, and evolves. Here are a few key areas to focus on:

▶ **High availability and disaster recovery**—As the critically of the big data projects in an organization increases, it is natural to consider them tier 1 (business-required) applications needing high availability and disaster recovery capabilities. Add your big data applications to your DR and HA planning.

▶ **Governance**—Data governance is crucial in the big data world.

▶ **Monitoring**—Failures are commonplace events for many big data solutions. Proactive monitoring systems help keep a system running and highly available.

▶ **Usage analysis**—After several projects have been implemented, expanding to a larger user base and to different departments of the organization can happen fairly quickly. With that in mind, make sure you fully understand who and how these expanding big data platforms are being used and adjust, optimize, and scale accordingly.

▶ **Automation**—Be sure to have as much automation built out as possible for any (and all) repetitive tasks. It will help lower costs, increase stability, and reduce errors across the board.

Several other nonfunctional requirements, such as security, adoption strategy, cost, and performance optimizations, are also crucial for your success.

Azure Big Data Use Cases

As mentioned earlier in this chapter, reality-based use cases for big data implementations are an essential requirement for any organization getting into the big data business. The following sections outline some of the broad categories in which big data solutions are typically implemented.

Use Case 1: Iterative Exploration

A very common big data pattern is for iterative exploration of the mass volumes of data (structured, unstructured, or semi-structured). Iterative exploration is typically used for experimenting with data sources to discover whether they can provide useful information or for handling data that you cannot process using traditional database systems. For example, you might collect feedback from customers through website clicks (click streams), email, blogs, other web pages, or external sources such as social media sites. You can then analyze this massive data set to get a picture of user sentiment for your products or user behavior. You might be able to combine this information with other data, such as demographic data that indicates population density and characteristics in each city where your products are sold.

Use Case 2: Data Warehouse on Demand

Big data solutions can also allow you to store both the source data and the results of queries executed over this data for analysis. You can store schemas (or, to be precise, metadata) for tables that are populated by the queries you execute. In this way, you essentially create analytic views into large amounts of data for analysis that were never possible before. It is very effective to create data warehouses that are robust and reasonably low cost to maintain (which is especially useful if you need to store and manage huge volumes of data).

Use Case 3: ETL Automation

You can use big data platforms to extract and transform data before you load it into your existing databases or data visualization tools. Often this automation is well suited to performing categorization, segmentation, and contextual adjustment of data, and also for extracting summary results to remove duplication and redundancy. The industry refers to this as extract, transform, and load (ETL) processing.

Use Case 4: BI Integration

Data warehouse/business intelligence platforms have many advantages and capabilities that differentiate them from OLTP database systems. There are unique and special processing considerations for integrations. For example, you can integrate at different levels of a dimension or provide data enrichment for further BI analysis, depending on the way you intend to use the data obtained from your big data solution.

Use Case 5: Predictive Analysis

As big data solutions are getting more mature, more advanced use cases such as predictive modeling and predictive analysis using machine learning emerge. It becomes possible to provide options, optimizations, or recommendations based on massively more data points that may evolve over time (machine learning aspects). Several vendors are providing machine learning offerings, as shown in Figure 11.32.

FIGURE 11.32   Big data machine learning options.

Summary

This chapter introduces some of the main products, approaches, and use cases for big data surrounding the Microsoft Azure offerings. It is important to look at the high availability capabilities as big data solutions become more like traditional tier 1 (business-required) applications. This chapter talks about how high availability is "designed into" the processing architecture of Hadoop platforms. Big data is here to stay and is rapidly becoming a part of any company's data foundation, and for this reason you should not treat it any differently from your other traditional data platforms. Big data is an integrated part of your entire data platform. Later chapters show how this all comes together into a complete data picture with high availability across all components. In some companies, big data analysis is determining the companies' future existence. Big data systems are critical systems for a company, and they should be highly available to some degree. Microsoft has answered the call for supporting big data on-premises and in the cloud with Azure, and building your big data solutions has never been easier. However, do not forgo high availability. Big data won't be useful to anyone if the big data containers are down.

CHAPTER 12

Hardware and OS Options for High Availability

As you put together high availability solutions that meet your business needs, you will have many different hardware and operating system options to consider. As first described in Chapter 1, "Understanding High Availability," your high availability is only as good as your weakest link in your full system stack. It is essential that you look at every layer in your system and understand what options you need to consider in order to achieve your desired HA result. However, you may be dealing with limited hardware resources, various and sometimes restrictive storage options, certain operating system editions and their limitations, hybrid systems that span both on-premises servers and cloud-based servers (infrastructure as a service [IaaS]), 100% virtualized servers (on-premises), or 100% cloud-based compute power variations (for example, on Azure or Amazon). All these must be considered, regardless of where your footprint is. You must also be aware of what is available for things like server backup images, database-level backups, varying virtualization options, and live migrations (from one server to another in case of failure or increases in workloads). People used to think that a database will run more slowly on a virtual machine (VM). If you are actually experiencing such a thing, though, it is usually a result of a poorly configured VM, not the database engine.

Organizations around the world are pushing to get much of their stacks in the cloud, one way or another. Welcome to the new world of infinite computing. The world has crossed the threshold of accepting the cloud as a production-worthy solutions, especially if HA and disaster recovery options are present. If your organization has decided that having a backup site available on AWS or Azure is acceptable, then why wouldn't you just start there to begin with? This is a good question to ask management. However, if you just aren't ready to go 100% cloud-based yet, you need to get your on-premises and hybrid acts together.

Generally speaking, it is best to architect for the "shared nothing" approach for data and servers. In other words, you should always have secondary resources available for failover at both the compute and storage levels. Many organizations are already virtualized, both on-premises and in the cloud. Figure 12.1 illustrates the multiple VMs within a Windows 2012 hypervisor server architecture.

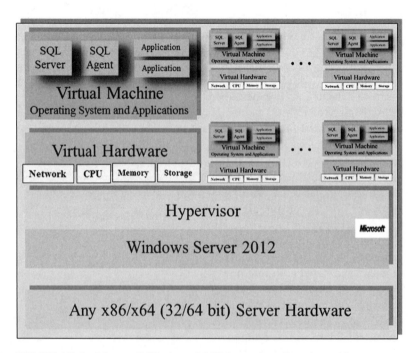

FIGURE 12.1   Microsoft Windows 2012 hypervisor virtual machines.

Server HA Considerations

Still at the heart of many on-premises and virtualized systems is failover clustering for both physical servers and VMs.

Failover Clustering

In Windows Server 2012 and later, you can create a cluster with up to 64 nodes and 8,000 VMs. Failover clustering requires some type of shared storage so the data can be accessed by all nodes and will work with most SANs (storage area networks), using a supported protocol. Failover clustering includes a built-in validation tool (Cluster Validation) which can verify that the storage, network, and other cluster components will work correctly. Figure 12.2 shows SAN storage shared across multiple virtual machine nodes.

SAN storage can be categorized into three main types:

▶ **SAN using a host bus adapter (HBA)**—This is the most traditional type of SAN. Supported types include Fibre Channel and Serial Attached SCSI (SAS). Fibre Channel tends to be more expensive but offers faster performance than SAS.

▶ **SAN using Ethernet**—In recent years, network bandwidth has become significantly faster, matching speeds that were previously possible only with HBA-based storage fabric. This has enabled Ethernet-based solutions to be offered at much lower costs, although they still require dedicated NICs and networks. The two protocols supported by failover clustering are iSCSI and Fibre Channel over Ethernet (FCoE).

▶ **SMB3 file server**—Server Message Block (SMB) protocol is a Microsoft-centric, application-layer network protocol used for file sharing on a file server. A traditional file share is a location for storing data that's accessible by multiple servers. With the introduction of Windows Server 2012, it has become possible to store the virtual hard disk for a VM on this file share, which allows it to function as a very affordable shared storage type that allows all cluster nodes to access it at once. This has proven to be very reliable and helps simplify failover cluster configurations.

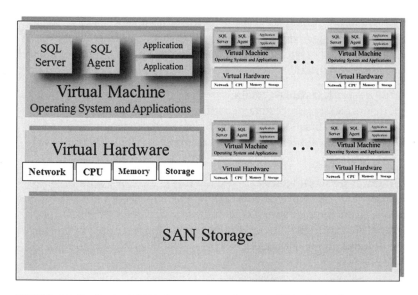

FIGURE 12.2   Typical SAN storage shared across VMs (nodes).

With Windows Server 2008 R2, failover clustering introduced a software-defined disk virtualization layer known as Cluster Shared Volumes (CSV), which enables a single LUN to store multiple VMs that may run on different cluster nodes. When deploying failover clustering for VMs with a SAN, it is strongly recommended that you turn on CSV for all your shared disks so you can simplify storage management by consolidating many VMs onto a single disk. Traditional cluster disks do not permit multiple nodes to access the same disk at the same time; this adds a bit of complexity to storage management.

Networking Configuration

Optimizing a cluster's networks is critical for high availability because networks are used for administration, VM access, health checking, live migration, and, often, storage in the case of an Ethernet-based solution or Hyper-V over SMB. The cluster nodes can be on the same subnet or different subnets, and the cluster will automatically configure the networks when the cluster is created or a new network is added.

You must use Hyper-V Manager to create identical virtual networks and switches on every cluster node so that your VMs can connect to other services. These virtual networks must be named the same on every node in the cluster so that the VM will always be able to connect to the same network, using its name, regardless of which host the VM is running on.

Every cluster requires at least two networks for redundancy. If one network becomes unavailable, the traffic is rerouted through the redundant network. The best practice is to have a dedicated network of at least 1Gbps for each network traffic type:

▶ **Live migration network traffic**—In a live migration—which means moving a running VM from one host to another—the memory of the VM is copied between the hosts through a network connection. This data movement causes a large spike in network traffic as several gigabytes of data are sent through the network as fast as possible. A dedicated network is strongly recommended so the live migration doesn't interfere with other network traffic.

▶ **Host management network traffic**—Certain types of administration tasks require large amounts of data to be sent through a network, such as performing a backup with third-party products such as Veeam Backup & Replication, deploying a VM on a host from a library, or replicating a VM. Ideally, this type of traffic should have a dedicated network.

▶ **Storage using Ethernet network traffic**—If you are using iSCSI, FCoE, or an SMB3 file server for storage, you must have a dedicated network connection for this storage type. It is important to ensure that your network has enough bandwidth to support the needs of all VMs on that host. The performance of all the VMs on a host will slow down if they cannot access data fast enough.

When a cluster is created, it assigns a different value to each of the networks based on the order in which it discovers different network adapters. NICs, which have access to a default gateway, are designated for use with client and application traffic because the cluster assumes that this network has an external connection. This value is known as the *network priority*. Windows Server failover clustering does not require identical hardware

for each host (node), as long as the entire solution does not fail any of the cluster validation tests. Because some hosts may be more powerful than others or have different access
speeds to the storage, you may want certain VMs to run on specific hosts.

Clustered Virtual Machine Replication

Windows Server 2012 introduced a new feature for Hyper-V that provides Hyper-V VM
disaster recovery by replicating virtual hard disks to a different site (or data center) or
even to Microsoft Azure. The Hyper-V Replica feature needs to be enabled for any server
or cluster node that's hosting or receiving a replicated VM. Each VM can be individually
configured and tested for replication and then send a copy of its data asynchronously
every 30 seconds, 5 minutes, or 15 minutes.

On a failover cluster, you configure a Hyper-V Replica differently by creating a new
clustered workload using the Hyper-V Replica Broker role. This is a highly available
replication-service version, which means the replication engine itself fails over between
cluster nodes to ensure that replication always occurs.

Virtualization Wars

At one time, VM's were unstable, slow, and hard to manage. With big providers such
as VMware and Microsoft, the server virtualization world is now massively successful,
completely reliable, and extremely dynamic to manage.

Live migration, as mentioned earlier in this chapter, entails moving active VMs between
physical hosts with no service interruption or downtime. A VM live migration allows
administrators to perform maintenance and resolve a problem on a host without affecting
users. It is also possible to optimize network throughput by running VMs on the same
hypervisor, automating Distributed Resource Scheduler (DRS), and doing automatic load
balancing of disks—moving the disks of a VM from one location to another while the VM
continues to run on the same physical host. This all adds up to higher availability.

As you might already know, Microsoft introduced the ability to move VMs across Hyper-V
hosts with Windows Server 2008 R2. This required VMs to reside on shared storage as
part of a cluster. With Windows Server 2012 and Server 2012 R2, Microsoft continued to
gain ground on VMware, introducing additional migration capabilities that put Microsoft
more or less on par with VMware. Now, since Windows Server 2012 R2, Hyper-V can store
VMs on SMB file shares and allows live migrations on running VMs stored on a central
SMB between nonclustered and clustered servers, so users can benefit from live migration
capabilities without investing in a fully clustered infrastructure (see Figure 12.3).

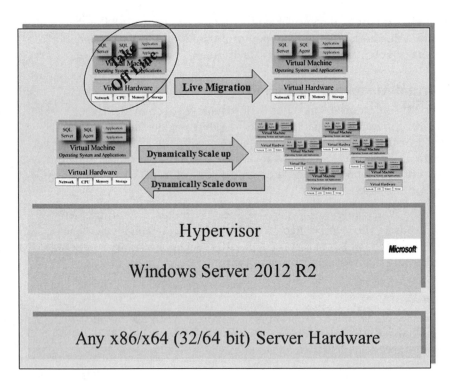

FIGURE 12.3   Doing live migrations with zero downtime on Windows 2012 R2.

Windows Server 2012 R2's live migration capability also leverages compression, which reduces the time needed to perform live migration by 50% or more. Live migration in Windows Server 2012 R2 utilizes improvements in the SMB3 protocol as well. If you are using network interfaces that support remote direct memory access (RDMA), the flow of live migration traffic is faster and has less impact on the CPUs of the nodes involved. Storage live migration was introduced to the Hyper-V feature set with Windows Server 2012. Windows Server 2008 R2 allowed users to move a running VM using traditional live migration, but it required a shutdown of the VM to move its storage.

Backup Considerations

Contemporary storage backup technology uses techniques such as changed block tracking to back up virtual machines. VMs are well suited to storing backup data on disk as they require access to the initial backup plus all data changes to perform restores. However, disk-based backup isn't necessarily scalable and doesn't always offer easy portability when you need to take data offsite for full disaster recovery. Options such as creating synthetic backups based on the original backup plus all subsequent incremental block changes can often meet a recovery need. But remember that when failure happens, it is not just data that needs to be restored but the full working environment. Further, disaster recovery is not possible without a backup in the first place.

Figure 12.4 illustrates the possible backup and recovery scope across on-premises, infrastructure as a service (IaaS), platform as a service (PaaS), and any number of software as a service (SaaS) applications that are a part of a business.

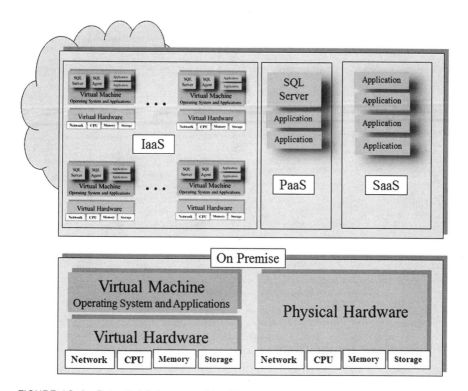

FIGURE 12.4   Potential full scope of backing up a business.

Virtualization changes everything and increases the number of options. First, data can be easily backed up as part of an image of a given VM, including application software, local data, settings, and memory. Second, there is no need for a physical server rebuild; the VM can be re-created in any other compatible virtual environment. This may be spare in-house capacity or acquired from a third-party cloud service provider. This means most of the costs of redundant systems disappear. However, PaaS and SaaS components that are a part of your business scope must now be coordinated with your conventional backup methods, which presents numerous challenges. Disaster recovery is cheaper, quicker, easier, and more complete in a virtual world. In general, much faster recovery time objectives (RTOs) are easier to achieve now.

Providers are popping up left and right, claiming that they can provide you with disaster recovery as a service (DRaaS). Such a service would include having your most critical systems fully restored and running as quickly as possible, including the associated data on a DRaaS site, as illustrated in Figure 12.5.

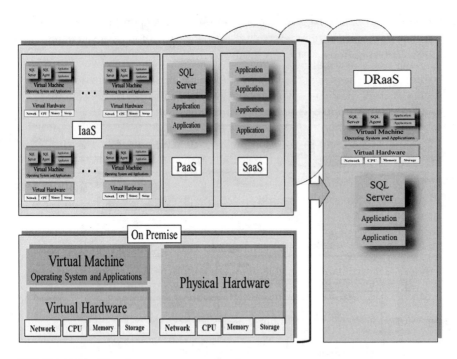

FIGURE 12.5   Disaster recovery as a service.

Integrated Hypervisor Replication

Virtualization platform providers such as VMware, Microsoft Hyper-V, and Citrix Xen offer varying levels of VM replication services embedded in their products. These services are tightly integrated into the hypervisor itself, which gives them the potential to achieve the performance needed for continuous data protection (CDP) using shadow VMs as virtual hot standbys. This, in turn, can drastically reduce both RPOs and RTOs across the board.

VM Snapshots

Many VM tools take incremental snapshots of a VM at given frequencies. This usually involves a short pause in the VM that lasts long enough to copy its data, its memory, and other relevant elements very quickly. These VM snapshots can then be used to re-create the VM anywhere that is specified in a relatively short amount of time. The RPO depends on how often snapshots are taken. The RTO depends on how quickly the entire VM becomes available in an alternate location. This approach started to show up in the VM world from companies such as Veeam, VMware, Microsoft Hyper-V, and others.

Other, more traditional backup suppliers have adapted their products to compete directly with VM snapshot capabilities. Backup Exec (from Symantec) mostly matches the capability and performance of VM snapshotting. Other vendors, such as Dell, claim that their solutions avoid the pausing of VMs altogether and have zero effect on the VMs. One advantage these traditional providers have is that they support both the new VM world and all of your legacy world. And, of course, many IaaS providers, such as Azure, Amazon, and Rackspace, provide VM replication, enabling users to put their own failover in place without too much hassle (for an additional cost, of course).

Disaster Recovery as a Service (DRaaS)

As previously mentioned, there is plenty of growth in the industry around cloud platform services designed for nothing but disaster recovery. Such DRaaS offerings claim to be able to reasonably recover a company's primary workload in a fairly short amount of time. The RPOs and RTOs vary, of course, based on which snapshot technique, backup technique, replication, or method is used. Three big names in these services are SunGard, IBM, and now Microsoft (via their Site Recovery service on Azure).

An important question for your organization to examine is "If you are using the cloud as a DR site option, then why wouldn't you consider using the cloud for your normal processing needs in the first place?"

Summary

This chapter gives a bit of a perspective on HA considerations related to the hardware and operating systems that much of the industry is using today. The vast majority of organizations—perhaps 80% of them—are now fairly far along in utilizing virtualized environments for both ease of management and HA reasons. As mentioned in this chapter, there are several things to be aware of in a virtualized environment, such as the network and how many NICs you must have for HA, storage considerations such as whether to use SANs, and different methods of taking VM snapshots and creating data backups that might be available in your emerging environments (perhaps even using DRaaS as these options become more mainstream). Taking a hard look at each of these hardware and OS factors is a basic foundational part of creating high availability and disaster recovery. When you have a good grasp of the hardware and OS factors, you can layer on the more conventional HA configurations that most optimally meet your company's overall HA requirements.

CHAPTER 13

Disaster Recovery and Business Continuity

What? You think disasters never happen? Your SQL Servers and applications have been running fine for months on end? What could possibly happen to your data center in Kansas? If you think it can't happen to you, you are dreaming. Disasters happen in all sorts of sizes, shapes, and forms. Whether a disaster is human-caused (terrorism, hacking, viruses, fires, human errors, and so on), natural (weather, earthquakes, fires, and so on), or just a plain failure of some kind (server failure), it can be catastrophic to your company's very existence.

Some estimate that companies spend up to 25% of their budget on disaster recovery plans in order to avoid bigger losses. Of companies that have had a major loss of computerized records, 43% never reopen, 51% close within 2 years, and only 6% survive in the long term Institute (see www.datacenterknowledge.com/archives/2013/12/03/study-cost-data-center-downtime-rising). Which way would you go on this subject? I'm sure you are really thinking about getting serious about devising some type of disaster recovery (DR) plan that supports your company's business continuity (BC) requirements. It must be able to protect the primary (typically revenue-generating) applications that your business relies on. Many applications are secondary when it comes to DR and BC. Once you have identified what systems need to be protected, you can go about planning and testing a true disaster plan, using all the best disaster recovery capabilities you have at your disposal.

Microsoft doesn't have something it calls "disaster recovery for SQL Server," but it does have many of the pieces of the puzzle that can be leveraged in your specialized plans for your own disaster recovery effort. Microsoft's newest solutions for disaster recovery include the AlwaysOn features and some Azure options (to use the cloud as a viable recovery site and as an architecture itself). In addition, Microsoft continues to release enhancements to existing features that are highly leveraged for various approaches to disaster recovery in many SQL Server environments. In particular, log shipping is still being used to create redundant systems for DR purposes; a few types of data replication topologies are available, such as peer-to-peer replication; and change data capture (CDC) is a poor-man's approach to DR. Database mirroring (even though it will be deprecated someday) is another viable feature that can be used to support both active/active and active/passive disaster recovery needs. With Windows 2012 and newer, multisite clustering allows you to fail over to a completely different data center location. As mentioned earlier, the AlwaysOn availability group feature can be used to provide a multisite DR option for both onsite and cloud-based options to DR. Finally, the cloud-based solutions continue to expand, with Azure, Amazon, and others allowing for built-in DR options to geographically remote sites and as extensions to your current on-premises solutions. These offerings, and other more traditional offerings, round out the arsenal from Microsoft on giving you the comfortable feeling of attaining business continuity.

How to Approach Disaster Recovery

Often, disaster recovery specialists refer to a seven-tiered disaster recovery paradigm. These tiers of DR capability levels start at the bottom of the disaster recovery capability food chain—Tier 0, no offsite data and possibly no recovery—and progress up to the highest level of disaster recovery capability possible—Tier 7, with zero to near-zero data loss and highly automated recovery. This chapter presents a simplified and more generalized five-level (Tier 0 through Tier 4) representation that should aide you in understanding DR and how you can approach it more readily. Let's start with where most small to midsize companies find themselves—with little to nothing in the way disaster recovery plans and operating at a fairly high-risk exposure level. These folks are at the very bottom of the upside-down pyramid in Figure 13.1, at Level 1—or perhaps they're not even in the DR pyramid at all (below the line, at Level 0, with no data backup offsite at all).

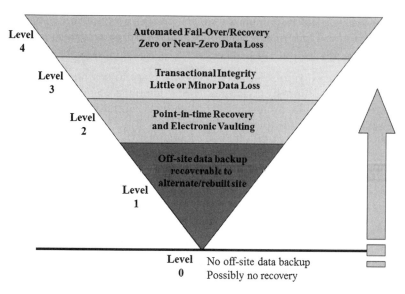

FIGURE 13.1   Disaster recovery pyramid.

Very likely, many of these companies are running a huge risk that they may not really want to face. The good news is that getting to a more protected level with your SQL Server–based applications isn't really very hard to do. But nothing is free; once you establish some type of DR plan and create the technical process and mechanisms for your DR, you still have to implement it and test it.

Read more about the disaster recovery levels in this model so you can get an idea of where your company is now and where you want it to go:

▶ **Level 0**—At Level 0, you basically have to pick up the pieces (after a fire or something) and see what is salvageable from your site. Even the best onsite backup plans are rendered meaningless in regard to disaster recovery if the backups were not stored somewhere safe (offsite). But, let's be realistic: Being at Level 0 is a major risk.

▶ **Level 1**—If you are even remotely serious about disaster recovery, you must get to Level 1 as soon as possible. We are talking about some very basic capability of creating a recoverable image (database backups, system configuration backups, user ID, permissions, role backups, and so on) that can effectively allow you to rebuild your critical applications and databases that are running on SQL Server at an alternate location. There will probably be data loss involved, but it may not be enough to cause your company to completely go out of business. If you are not doing this right now, do it today!

▶ **Level 2**—Level 2 adds a very much more real-time recovery timeframe into the mix and is getting to more of a point-in-time recovery capability. Capabilities such as electronic vaulting aid greatly in being able to rapidly restore systems (databases) and get back online within a very short amount of time. There is still a certain level of data loss at this level. That cannot be avoided.

▶ **Level 3**—Level 3 moves you to the complexities of recovering transactional integrity in your applications and minimizing your data losses. This requires much more effort, resources, and sophistication but is very doable.

▶ **Level 4**—Finally, many larger companies have Level 4 in place to completely protect themselves from single-site failures or disasters without missing a single order transaction. This chapter identifies the different SQL Server–based options that allow you to achieve from Level 1 through Level 4 DR.

Best practice is to devise a highly efficient disaster recovery plan in support of your business continuity needs and then test it completely. Make sure it considers all aspects of completely being able to come up onto an alternate location as smoothly and quickly as possible and with minimal data loss. Defining a disaster recovery plan can be a tedious job because of the potential complexities of the configuration. You also need to understand that to survive a disaster only means that you have to recover the most critical applications that are core to your business's existence. Everything else can be rebuilt or put back together in due time. But, keep in mind, a disaster recovery plan is essential to your company's very existence and should be treated as such. Your objective should be to move up the pyramid (to Level 4 or near it) to match your company's needs for business continuity. You don't want to take weeks to recover from a failed data center disaster and eventually go out of business; industry statistics are against you if you haven't prepared.

Disaster Recovery Patterns

In general, you should consider three main DR patterns when trying to achieve Level 1 through Level 4 DR:

▶ Active/passive DR sites pattern

▶ Active/active DR sites pattern

▶ Active multisite DR sites pattern

The following sections describe these patterns in detail.

Active/Passive DR Sites Pattern

Figure 13.2 illustrates the active/passive disaster recovery configuration, which is probably the most common DR in the world. It involves a primary site (the normal environments in which you do business day in and day out) and a passive DR site. This passive DR (alternative) site can be anything and anywhere. It could be a hot alternate site that is ready for you to apply a current database backup to (and application image, too), or it could be a cold alternate site that you have to either go out and lease, co-locate with, or build completely from scratch. Microsoft also offers Azure in the cloud (infrastructure as a service) as a potential location for your DR site. The available resources, money, and business needs determine what method you will decide on. Obviously, the colder your DR site, the longer it will take for you to recover using it. A small to midsized company typically takes between 23 and 31 days to completely rebuild the essential systems on an alternate site (DR site). This may or may not be acceptable to your organization. A thorough understanding of what your company's needs are will dictate your choices.

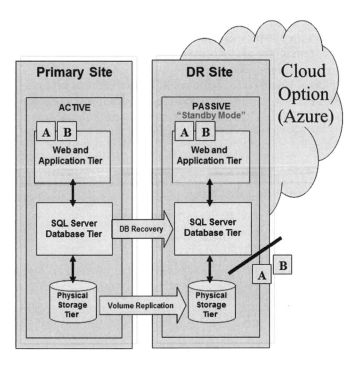

Active/Passive DR

FIGURE 13.2   Active/passive DR sites pattern.

The basic Microsoft products to help you achieve this DR pattern are database backups taken offsite and readily recallable to recover (restore) your database tier and, for those who have a hot DR site available, using data replication to the DR site, log shipping, asynchronous database mirroring, and AlwaysOn availability groups asynchronous replicas. There are also some third-party products, such as Symantec's Veritas Volume Replicator, to push physical byte-level changes to the passive (hot) DR site physical tier level. In most of these options, the DR site is passive, literally sitting there idle until it is needed. As you can see in Figure 13.2, application A and application B are in both sites, but only one site is active. The exception to this rule is when you are using Microsoft data replication, database snapshots with database mirroring, or an AlwaysOn configuration for DR. In such a case, application A and application B reporting users (under the line, to the right of the passive SQL Server database tier) might be able to take advantage of read-only database snapshots or a readable secondary replica. Even in those cases, the DR site will not be available for transactional changes (updates, deletes, inserts); it offers read access only.

NOTE

Remember that log shipping and database mirroring are both on the way out in future Microsoft releases, so don't plan too much new usage of these features.

Active/Active DR Sites Pattern

The active/active DR sites pattern faces a few issues, such as the need to make sure that no application keeps "state" from one transaction to the other (referred to as "stateless"). In addition, the application and/or the web tier needs to be able to route user connections (the load) to either site in some type of balanced or round-robin method. This is often done with things like big IP routers that use round-robin routing algorithms to determine which site to direct connections to. In Figure 13.3, application A is available equally on either site.

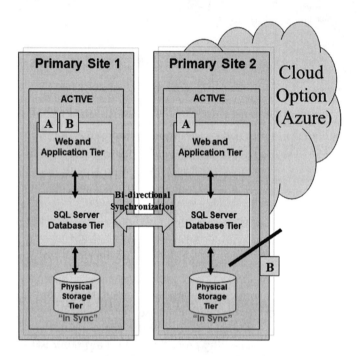

Active/Active DR

FIGURE 13.3   Active/active DR sites pattern.

Active/active configurations can be created using peer-to-peer continuous data replication as well as other multi-updating subscriber replication topologies. A slight twist to having two primary sites is to have one primary site and a secondary site that isn't processing transactions but is being actively used for reporting and other things (just no processing that is changing anything). This type of capability is easily created with AlwaysOn availability group configurations (primary and any number of secondary replicas). Application B's transactional processing is available only on Primary Site 1 (for all of its features) but uses Primary Site 2 to offload its reporting (again, below the line, to the right of the SQL Server database tier). In the event of a primary failure, the secondary site can take over full primary site responsibilities quickly (in seconds). This is sort of active/passive, with active "secondary usage" on the passive site (following the active/passive DR pattern just described). This type of configuration can also be provided using database mirroring and database snapshots (for the reporting). Azure can also easily support hosting the alternative site (Site 2) without much additional modification to your on-premises site configuration and system. There are plenty of advantages to these variations, and they greatly distribute workload and allow you to move up the DR pyramid.

Active Multisite DR Pattern

The use of an active multisite DR pattern is gaining in popularity for larger global organizations that also want to distribute their processing more regionally. An active multisite DR configuration contains three or more active sites, with the intention of using any one of them as the DR site for the other (as shown in Figure 13.4). This pattern allows you to distribute your applications redundantly between any pair of sites—but usually not to all three (or more). For instance, you could have half of Primary Site 1's applications redundantly on Primary Site 2 and the other half redundantly on Primary Site 3. You could thereby further spread out the risk at any one site and greatly increase your odds of uninterrupted processing.

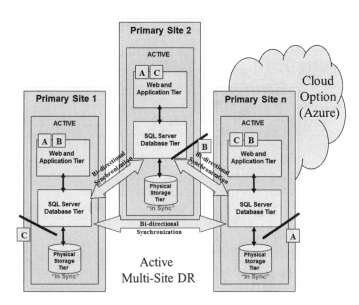

FIGURE 13.4   Active multisite DR pattern.

Again, having "stateless" applications is critical here, as is smart routing of all connections to the appropriate sites. Using continuous data replication, AlwaysOn availability groups, database mirroring, or even CDC options allows you to easily create such a DR topology. And, again, you also have the secondary usage variation available to you if one or more alternative sites are passive (with secondary usage supporting reporting) and any of these multiple sites can be cloud based (on Azure or using other cloud provider options).

Choosing a Disaster Recovery Pattern

The preceding sections reduce all the possible DR patterns to three simple ones that, at a foundational level, represent what you need to do to support the level of business continuity your company demands. Various companies can tolerate various levels of loss because of the nature of their business. At the highest levels, it is fairly easy to match these patterns to what your business requires. In this chapter, we look at the SQL Server capabilities that are available to help you implement these patterns.

A global company may devise a DR configuration that reserves each major data center site in a region as the active or passive DR site for another region. Figure 13.5 shows one large high-tech company's global data center locations. Its Alexandria, Virginia, site is also the passive DR site for its Phoenix, Arizona, site. Its Paris, France, regional site is also the DR site for its Alexandria, Virginia, site, and so on. More and more, we are seeing the use of a single cloud site (utilizing Azure or Amazon EC2) as the default DR site for even multi-data center global topologies.

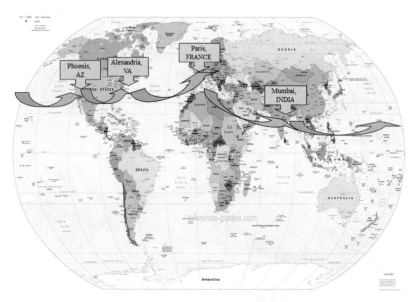

FIGURE 13.5   Using active regional sites for passive DR.

For companies that have multiple data center sites but only need to support the active/ passive DR pattern, a very popular variation, called *reciprocal DR*, can be used. As shown in Figure 13.6, there are two sites (Site 1 and Site 2). Each is active for some applications (Applications 1, 3, and 5 on site 1 and Applications 2, 4, and 6 on site 2). Site 1's applications are passively supported on Site 2, and Site 2's applications are passively supported on Site 1. Rolling out the configuration this way eliminates the "stateless" application issue completely and is fairly easy to implement. It is also possible to provide the passive applications' data via database snapshots at the other reciprocal site (for free!), further leveraging distributing workload geographically.

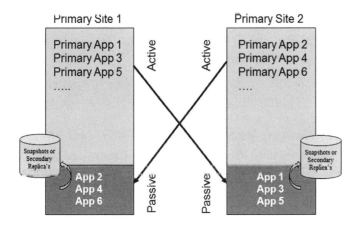

Reciprocal DR

FIGURE 13.6   Reciprocal DR.

This configuration also spreads out the risk of losing all applications if one site ever happens to be lost (as in a disaster). The Microsoft products that can help you achieve this DR pattern variation are data replication to the DR site, log shipping, AlwaysOn availability groups, CDC (to the passive application), and even asynchronous database mirroring with database snapshots available to help with some distributed reporting. As noted previously, third-party products such as Symantec's Veritas Volume Replicator can be used to push physical byte-level changes to the passive (hot) DR site physical tier level.

Recovery Objectives

You need to understand two main recovery objectives: the point in time to which data must be restored to be able to successfully resume processing (called the *recovery point objective* [RPO]) and the acceptable amount of downtime that is tolerable (called the *recovery time objective* [RTO]). The RPO is often thought of as the time between the last backup and the point when the outage occurred. It indicates the amount of data that will be lost. The RTO is determined based on the acceptable downtime in case of a disruption of operations. It indicates the latest point in time at which the business operations must resume after disaster (that is, how much time can elapse).

The RPO and RTO form the basis on which a data protection strategy is developed. They help provide a picture of the total time that a business may lose due to a disaster. The two metrics together are very important requirements when designing a solution. Let's put these terms in the form of algorithms:

> **RTO** = Difference between the *time* of the disaster and the *time* the system is operational – *Time* operational (up) – *Time* disaster occurred (down)

> **RPO** = *Time* since the last backup of complete transactions representing data that must be re-acquired or entered – *Time* disaster occurred – *Time* of last usable data backup

Therefore:

Total lost business time = *Time* operational (up) − *Time* disaster occurred (down) − *Time* of the last usable data backup

Knowing your RPO and RTO requirements is essential in determining what DR pattern to use and what Microsoft options to utilize.

A Data-centric Approach to Disaster Recovery

Disaster recovery is a complex undertaking unto itself. However, it isn't really necessary to recover every system or application in the event of a disaster. Priorities must be set on exactly which systems or applications must be recovered. These are typically the revenue-generating applications (such as order entry, order fulfillment, and invoicing) that your business relies on to do basic business with its customers. You set the highest priorities for DR with those revenue-generating systems. Then the next level of recovery is for the second-priority applications (such as a human resources system).

After you prioritize which applications should be part of your DR plans, you need to fully understand what must be included in recovery to ensure that these priority applications are fully functional. The best way is to take a data-centric approach, which focuses on what data is needed to bring up the application. Data comes in many flavors, as Figure 13.7 shows:

▶ **Metadata**—The data that describes structures, files, XSDs, and so on that the applications, middleware, or back end needs

▶ **Configuration data**—The data that the application needs to define what it must do, that the middleware needs to execute with, and so on

▶ **Application data values**—The data within your database files that represents the transactional data in your systems

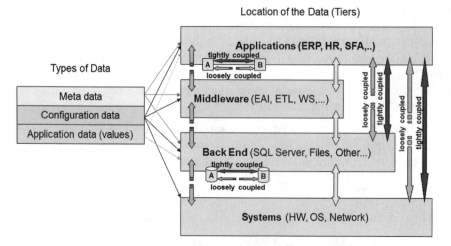

FIGURE 13.7   Types of data and where the data resides.

After you identify which applications you must include in your DR plans, you must make sure you back up and are able to recover the data from each of those application (metadata, configuration data, and application data). As part of this exercise, you must determine how tightly or loosely coupled the data is to other applications. In other words (as you can also see in Figure 13.7), if on the back-end tier, database A has the customer order transactions data and database B has the invoicing data, both must be included in the DR plans because they are tightly coupled in a business sense. In addition, you must know how tightly or loosely coupled the application stack components are with each layer. In other words (again looking at Figure 13.7), if the enterprise resource planning (ERP) application (in the application tier) requires some type of middleware to be present to handle all its messaging, that middleware tier component is tightly coupled (in a technology sense) with the ERP application.

Microsoft Options for Disaster Recovery

Now that you know the fundamental DR patterns and also recognize how to identify the highest-priority applications and their tightly coupled components for DR, let's look again at the specific Microsoft options available to implement various DR solutions. These options include data replication, log shipping, database mirroring, database snapshots, AlwaysOn availability groups, and various Azure (cloud) options.

Data Replication

A solid and stable Microsoft option that can be leveraged for disaster recovery is data replication. Not all variations of data replication fit this bill, though. However, the central publisher replication model using either continuous or very frequently scheduled distribution is very good for creating a hot spare of a SQL Server database across almost any geographic distance, as shown in Figure 13.8. The primary site is the only one actively processing transactions (updates, inserts, deletes) in this configuration, with all transactions being replicated to the subscriber, usually in a continuous replication mode.

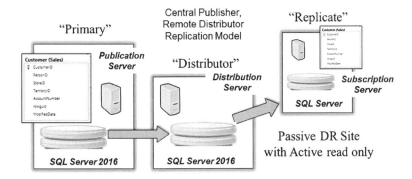

FIGURE 13.8   Central publisher data replication configuration for active/passive DR.

The subscriber at the DR site is as up-to-date as the last distributed (replicated) transaction from the publisher—usually near real-time. The subscriber can be used for a read-only type of processing if controlled properly if and that read-only access does not hinder the replication processing and put your DR pattern at risk.

The peer-to-peer replication option provides a viable active/active capability that keeps both primaries in sync as transactions flow into each server's database, as shown in Figure 13.9. Both sites contain a full copy of the database, and transactions are consumed and then replicated simultaneously between them.

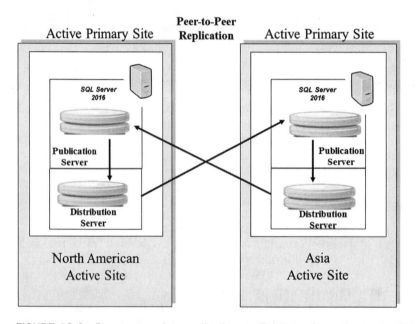

FIGURE 13.9   Peer-to-peer data replication configuration for active/active DR.

These days, it is also easy to set up a subscriber in the cloud (like on Azure) and use it as a DR site. The central publisher data replication configuration is fairly easy to set up to replication to the cloud (see Figure 13.10). In fact, it is so easy to do that it will likely be the first way to get into the DR business for many organizations.

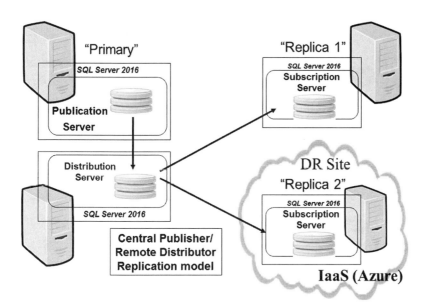

FIGURE 13.10   Central publisher data replication configuration to the cloud for DR.

Log Shipping

As you can see in Figure 13.11, log shipping is readily usable for the active/passive DR pattern. However, log shipping is only as good as the last successful transaction log shipment. The frequency of these log ships is critical in the RTO and RPO aspects of DR. Log shipping is really not a real-time solution. Even if you are using continuous log shipping mode, there is a lag of some duration due to the file movement and log application on the destination.

Remember that Microsoft is deprecating log shipping, and it is perhaps not a good idea to start planning a future DR implementation that will go away.

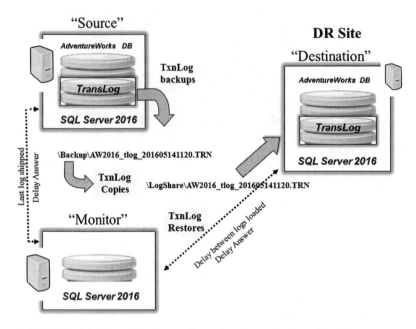

FIGURE 13.11   Log shipping configuration for active/passive DR pattern.

Database Mirroring and Snapshots

Database mirroring has seen a very big uptake in usage by companies around the globe, thanks to its ease of configuration and its great high availability benefits. Despite its popularity, Microsoft has announced that it is deprecating database mirroring. It might take many years for this to happen, so it is a very good DR option now for those who need to get this done fast, but it may not be a good idea to plan on database mirroring long term.

In either a high availability mode (synchronous) or performance mode (asynchronous), database mirroring can help minimize data loss and time to recover (RPO and RTO). As shown in Figure 13.12, database mirroring can be used across any reasonable network connection that may exist from one site to another. It effectively creates a mirror image that is completely intact for failover purposes if a site is lost. It is viable in both an active/passive pattern and in an active/active pattern (where a database snapshot is created from the unavailable mirror database and is used for active reporting).

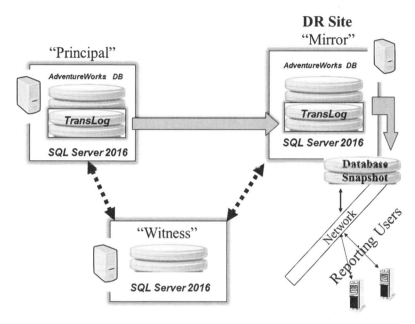

FIGURE 13.12   Database mirroring with database snapshots for an active/passive (active) DR pattern.

Change Data Capture

We haven't talked much about change data capture (CDC) in this book because there are typically far better and less complicated methods for creating replicas of your data. However, if you are among the companies that are already using CDC, you can also consider using it for both DR and for high availability (failover). CDC is a method of getting updates, deletes, and inserts from one database to another via the log reader. It utilizes a set of stored procedures and tables (change tables) on the source database side and quickly pumps those data changes over to a target database with 100% data integrity. CDC as a DR option makes sense for those that can afford this type of data lag and don't mind having a spare DR site that is only as up to date as the last set of pushed changes (which is pretty darn good). CDC requires significant change table setup and additional stored procedures. It is not guaranteed to be real-time, and sometimes resynchronizations need to be done to get the tables back in line. As you can see in Figure 13.13, CDC can be used across any reasonable network connection that may exist from one site to another and can even target a cloud SQL Server instance (hosted by Azure).

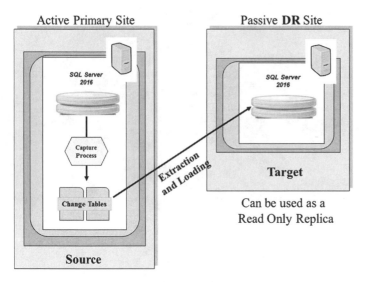

FIGURE 13.13   Change data capture for an active/passive DR option.

AlwaysOn and Availability Groups

AlwaysOn and availability groups has been around since SQL Server 2012. For disaster recovery, the use of the AlwaysOn availability groups to replicate data to other locations for DR is becoming the preferred path. AlwaysOn has actually taken the best from database mirroring and SQL clustering to give a wide array of configuration options for both high availability and disaster recovery. As you can see in Figure 13.14, one active site (a primary replica and a secondary replica configured for synchronous replication and automatic failover) can replicate its data to another secondary site (a secondary replica for DR). This secondary site (secondary replica) can also be used as a read-only database. If the primary site fails (due to a disaster of some kind), the secondary site can still be operational for read-only processing and can easily be enabled for all transactional activity. This capability can help minimize data loss and significantly reduce the time to recover (RPO and RTO).

Configuring an asynchronous secondary site across major networks (one network to another) can now be done fairly easily. However, this remote secondary will only be as current as the last asynchronous replication transaction that was replicated to it. This is typically only a few seconds these days, though. In addition, the secondary site for DR can be on a cloud provider such as Azure or Amazon because the replication mode is asynchronous (see Figure 13.15).

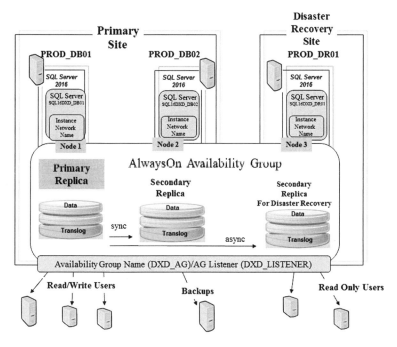

FIGURE 13.14   AlwaysOn availability groups for an active/active DR across sites.

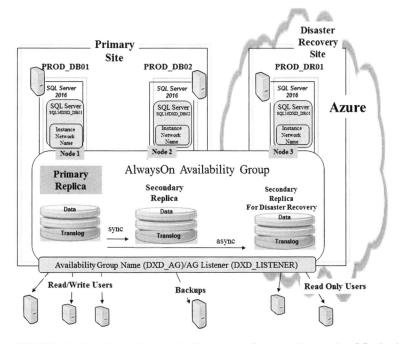

FIGURE 13.15   AlwaysOn availability groups for an active/active DR site in the cloud.

Azure and Active Geo Replication

If you are deploying 100% of your applications and databases on a cloud provider such as Microsoft's Azure, you have some built-in options for availability and disaster recovery. If you use SQL Azure, you have the standard database redundancy on the same region site, redundancy onto a second region site (to a secondary replica), and now a third region site for a secondary replica of your data in an asynchronous replication mode. This third region, as shown in Figure 13.16, can be a disaster recovery site in and active/passive pattern. It could also be used for reporting users if needed, but at the very least, it provides a fall backup (DR) site that is guaranteed to be in a third processing region (site) very different from the first two regions. This provides very solid risk mitigation for most companies.

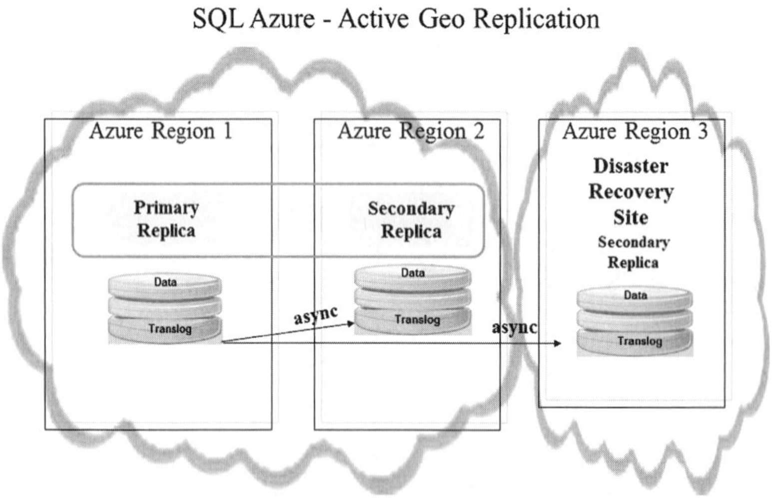

FIGURE 13.16   SQL Azure active geo replication configuration for and active/passive DR pattern.

The Overall Disaster Recovery Process

To complete the DR planning for your SQL Server platform, you must do much more homework and preparation. This section explains a great overall disaster approach that includes pulling all the right information together, executing a DR plan, and testing it thoroughly.

In general, you need to defined and executed a number of things as the basis for an overall disaster recovery process or plan. The following list clearly identifies what you need to do:

1. Create a disaster recovery execution tasks/run book. It should include all the steps to take to recover from a disaster and cover all system components that need to be recovered.

2. Arrange for or procure a server/site to recover to. This should be a configuration that can house what is needed to get you back online.

3. Guarantee that a complete database backup/recovery mechanism is in place (including offsite/alternate site archive and retrieval of databases).

4. Guarantee that an application backup/recovery mechanism is in place (for example, COM+ applications, .NET applications, web services, other application components, and so on).

5. Make sure you can completely re-create and resynchronize your security (Microsoft Active Directory, domain accounts, SQL Server logins/passwords, and so on). This is called "security resynchronization readiness."

6. Make sure you can completely configure and open up network/communication lines. This also includes ensuring that routers are configured properly, IP addresses are made available, and so on.

7. Train your support personnel on all elements of recovery. You can never know enough ways to recover a system. And it seems that a system never recovers the same way twice.

8. Plan and execute an annual or biannual disaster recovery simulation. The 1 or 2 days that you spend on this will pay you back a hundred times over if a disaster actually occurs. And, remember, disasters come in many flavors.

NOTE

Many organizations have gone to the concept of having hot alternate sites available via stretch clustering or log shipping techniques. Costs can be high for some of these advanced and highly redundant solutions.

The Focus of Disaster Recovery

If you create some very solid, time-tested mechanisms for re-creating your SQL Server environment, they will serve you well when you need them most. This section discusses the things to focus on for disaster recovery.

Always generate scripts for as much of your work as possible (anything created using a wizard, SMSS, and so on). These scripts will save your hide. They should include the following:

▶ Complete replication buildup/breakdown scripts

▶ Complete database creation scripts (DB, tables, indexes, views, and so on)

▶ Complete SQL login, database user IDs, and password scripts (including roles and other grants)

▶ Linked/remote server setup (linked servers, remote logins)

▶ Log shipping setup (source, target, and monitor servers)

▶ Any custom SQL Agent tasks

▶ Backup/restore scripts

▶ Potentially other scripts, depending on what you have built on SQL Server

Make sure to document all aspects of SQL database maintenance plans being used. This includes frequencies, alerts, email addresses being notified when errors occur, backup file/device locations, and so on.

Document all hardware/software configurations used:

▶ Leverage `sqldiag.exe` for this (as described in the next section).

▶ Record what accounts were used to start up the SQL Agent service for an instance and to start up the MS Distributed Transaction Coordinator (MS DTC) service. This step is especially important if you're using distributed transactions and data replication.

▶ Script and record the following SQL Server implementation characteristics for a SQL Server instance are:

  ▶ `select @@SERVERNAME`—Provides the full network name of the SQL Server and instance.

  ▶ `select @@SERVICENAME`—Provides the Registry key under which Microsoft SQL Server is running.

  ▶ `select @@VERSION`—Provides the date, version, and processor type for the current installation of Microsoft SQL Server.

  ▶ `exec sp_helpserver`—Provides the server name; the server's network name; the server's replication status; and the server's identification number, collation name, and time-out values for connecting to, or queries against, linked servers. Here is an example of its use:

    ```
    exec sp_helpserver;
    ```

  ▶ `exec sp_helplogins`—Provides information about logins and the associated users in each database.

  ▶ `exec sp_linkedservers`—Returns the list of linked servers defined in the local server.

  ▶ `exec sp_helplinkedsrvlogin`—Provides information about login mappings defined against a specific linked server used for distributed queries and remote stored procedures.

  ▶ `exec sp_server_info`—Returns a list of attribute names and matching values for Microsoft SQL Server. Here is an example of its use:

    ```
    use master;
    exec sp_server_info;
    ```

▶ exec `sp_helpdb dbnameXYZ`—Provides information about a specified database or all databases. This includes the database allocation names, sizes, and locations. Here is an example of its use:

```
exec sp_helpdb dbnameXYZ;
```

▶ exec `sp_spaceused`—Provides the actual database usage information of both data and indexes for the specified database name (`dbnameXYZ`). Here is an example of its use:

```
use dbnameXYZ;
exec sp_spaceused;
```

▶ exec `sp_configure`—Gets the current SQL Server configuration values by running `sp_configure` (with show advanced option), as shown in the following example:

```
USE master;

EXEC sp_configure 'show advanced option', '1';
RECONFIGURE;
EXEC sp_configure;
```

name	minimum	maximum	config_value	run_value
access check cache bucket count	0	65536	0	0
access check cache quota	0	2147483647	0	0
Ad Hoc Distributed Queries	0	1	0	0
affinity I/O mask	-2147483648	2147483647	0	0
affinity mask	-2147483648	2147483647	0	0
affinity64 I/O mask	-2147483648	2147483647	0	0
affinity64 mask	-2147483648	2147483647	0	0
Agent XPs	0	1	1	1
allow updates	0	1	0	0
awe enabled	0	1	0	0
backup compression default	0	1	0	0
blocked process threshold (s)	0	86400	0	0
c2 audit mode	0	1	0	0
clr enabled	0	1	0	0
common criteria compliance enabled	0	1	0	0
cost threshold for parallelism	0	32767	5	5
cross db ownership chaining	0	1	0	0
cursor threshold	-1	2147483647	-1	-1
Database Mail XPs	0	1	0	0
default full-text language	0	2147483647	1033	1033
default language	0	9999	0	0
default trace enabled	0	1	1	1
disallow results from triggers	0	1	0	0

EKM provider enabled	0	1	0	0
filestream access level	0	2	2	2
fill factor (%)	0	100	0	0
ft crawl bandwidth (max)	0	32767	100	100
ft crawl bandwidth (min)	0	32767	0	0
ft notify bandwidth (max)	0	32767	100	100
ft notify bandwidth (min)	0	32767	0	0
index create memory (KB)	704	2147483647	0	0
in-doubt xact resolution	0	2	0	0
lightweight pooling	0	1	0	0
locks	5000	2147483647	0	0
max degree of parallelism	0	64	0	0
max full-text crawl range	0	256	4	4
max server memory (MB)	16	2147483647	2147483647	2147483647
max text repl size (B)	-1	2147483647	65536	65536
max worker threads	128	32767	0	0
media retention	0	365	0	0
min memory per query (KB)	512	2147483647	1024	1024
min server memory (MB)	0	2147483647	0	0
nested triggers	0	1	1	1
network packet size (B)	512	32767	4096	4096
Ole Automation Procedures	0	1	0	0
open objects	0	2147483647	0	0
optimize for ad hoc workloads	0	1	0	0
PH timeout (s)	1	3600	60	60
precompute rank	0	1	0	0
priority boost	0	1	0	0
query governor cost limit	0	2147483647	0	0
query wait (s)	-1	2147483647	-1	-1
recovery interval (min)	0	32767	0	0
remote access	0	1	1	1
remote admin connections	0	1	0	0
remote login timeout (s)	0	2147483647	20	20
remote proc trans	0	1	0	0
remote query timeout (s)	0	2147483647	600	600
Replication XPs	0	1	0	0
scan for startup procs	0	1	0	0
server trigger recursion	0	1	1	1
set working set size	0	1	0	0
show advanced options	0	1	1	1
SMO and DMO XPs	0	1	1	1
SQL Mail XPs	0	1	0	0
transform noise words	0	1	0	0

two digit year cutoff	1753	9999	2049	2049
user connections	0	32767	0	0
user options	0	32767	0	0
xp_cmdshell	0	1	0	0

▶ List disk configurations, sizes, and current size availability (using standard OS directory listing commands on all disk volumes being used).

▶ Capture the sa login password and OS administrator password so that anything can be accessed and anything can be installed (or re-installed).

▶ Document all contact information for your vendors, including the following:

▶ Microsoft support services contacts (do you use "Premier Product Support Services"?)

▶ Storage vendor contact info

▶ Hardware vendor contact info

▶ Offsite storage contact info (to get your archived copy fast)

▶ Network/telecom contact info

▶ Your CTO, CIO, and other senior management contact info

▶ CD-ROMs/DVDs available for everything (SQL Server, service packs, operating system, utilities, and so on)

Using sqldiag.exe

One good way to get a complete environmental picture is to run the sqldiag.exe program provided with SQL Server 2016 on your production box (which you would have to re-create on an alternate site if a disaster occurred). It is located in the Binn directory, where all SQL Server executables reside (C:\Program Files\Microsoft SQL Server\130\ Tools\Binn). This program shows how the server is configured, all hardware and software components (and their versions), memory sizes, CPU types, operating system version and build information, paging file information, environment variables, and so on. If you run this program on your production server periodically, it provides good environment documentation to supplement your disaster recovery plan. This utility is also used to capture and diagnose SQL Server–wide issues and has a prompt that you must respond to when re-creating issues on which you want to collect diagnosis information. Figure 13.17 shows the expected execution command and system information dialog window.

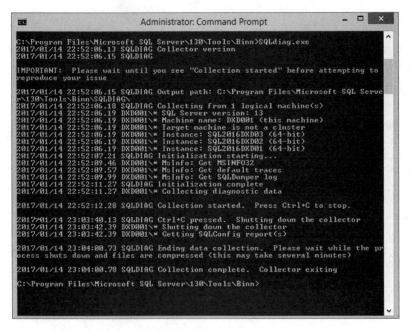

FIGURE 13.17   sqldiag.exe execution.

NOTE

For the purposes of this chapter, when prompted for the SQLDIAG collection, you can just terminate that portion by pressing Ctrl+C.

To run this utility, you open a command prompt and change directory to the SQL Server Binn directory. Then, at the command prompt, you run sqldiag.exe:

```
C:\Program Files\Microsoft SQL Server\130\Tools\Binn> sqldiag.exe
```

The results are written into several text files within the SQLDIAG subdirectory. Each file contains different types of data about the physical machine (server) that SQL Server is running on and information about each SQL Server instance. The machine (server) information is stored in a file named *XYX_MSINFO32.TXT*, where *XYX* is the machine name. It contains a verbose snapshot of everything that relates to SQL Server (in one way or another) and all the hardware configuration, drivers, and so on. It is the tightly coupled metadata and configuration information directly related to the SQL Server instance. The following is an example of part of what it contains:

```
System Information report written at: 12/08/16 21:18:01
System Name: DXD001
[System Summary]


Item                   Value
OS Name                Microsoft Windows Vista Premium
```

```
Version                  6.1.7601 Service Pack 1 Build 7601
Other OS Description     Not Available
OS Manufacturer          Microsoft Corporation
System Name              DATAXDESIGN-PC
System Manufacturer      TOSHIBA
System Model             Satellite P745
System Type              x64-based PC
Processor Intel(R) Core(TM) i3-2350M CPU @ 2.30GHz, 2300 Mhz, 2 Core(s), 4 Logical
Processor(s)
BIOS Version/Date        TOSHIBA 2.20, 10/30/2015
SMBIOS Version           2.6
Windows Directory        C:\windows
System Directory         C:\windows\system32
Boot Device              \Device\HarddiskVolume1
Locale                   United States
Hardware Abstraction Layer   Version = "6.1.7601.17514"
User Name                DXD001\DATAXDESIGN
Time Zone                Pacific Daylight Time
Installed Physical Memory (RAM)   Not Available
Total Physical Memory    11.91 GB
Available Physical Memory   8.83 GB
Total Virtual Memory     19.8 GB
Available Virtual Memory   8.54 GB
Page File Space          5.91 GB
Page File                C:\pagefile.sys
```

A separate file is generated for each SQL Server instance you have installed on a server. These files are named *XYZ_ABC*_sp_sqldiag_Shutdown.OUT, where *XYZ* is the machine name and *ABC* is the SQL Server instance name. This file contains most of the internal SQL Server information regarding how it is configured, including a snapshot of the SQL Server log as this server is operating on this machine. The following example shows this critical information from the DXD001_SQL2016DXD01_sp_sqldiag_Shutdown.OUT file:

```
2016-12-08 20:53:27.810 Server    Microsoft SQL Server 2016 - 13.0.700.242 (X64)
    Dec 8 2016 20:23:12
    Copyright (c) Microsoft Corporation
    Developer Edition (64-bit) on Windows 8.1 Pro <X64> (Build 9600: Hypervisor)
2016-12-08 20:53:27.840 Server     (c) Microsoft Corporation.
2016-12-08 20:53:27.840 Server     All rights reserved.
2016-12-08 20:53:27.840 Server     process ID is 4204.
2016-12-08 20:53:27.840 Server     System Manufacturer: 'TOSHIBA', System Model:
'Satellite P745'.
2016-12-08 20:53:27.840 Server     Authentication mode is MIXED.
2016-12-08 20:53:27.840 Server     Logging SQL Server messages in file 'C:\Program
    Files\Microsoft SQL Server\MSSQL13.SQL2016DXD01\MSSQL\Log\ERRORLOG'.
2016-12-08 20:53:27.840 Server     The service account is 'DXD001\Paul'. This is an
    informational message; no user action is required.
```

```
2016-12-08 20:53:27.850 Server        Registry startup parameters:
        -d C:\Program Files\Microsoft SQL Server\MSSQL13.SQL2016DXD01\MSSQL\DATA\
master.mdf
        -e C:\Program Files\Microsoft SQL Server\MSSQL13.SQL2016DXD01\MSSQL\Log\
ERRORLOG
        -l C:\Program Files\Microsoft SQL Server\MSSQL13.SQL2016DXD01\MSSQL\DATA\
mastlog.ldf
2016-12-08 20:53:27.850 Server        Command Line Startup Parameters:
        -s "SQL2016DXD01"
2016-12-08 20:53:28.770 Server        SQL Server detected 1 sockets with 2 cores per
socket and 4 logical processors per socket, 4 total logical processors; using 4 log-
ical processors based on SQL Server licensing. This is an informational message; no
user action is required.
2016-12-08 20:53:28.770 Server        SQL Server is starting at normal priority base
(=7). This is an informational message only. No user action is required.
2016-12-08 20:53:28.770 Server        Detected 6051 MB of RAM. This is an informa-
tional message; no user action is required.
2016-12-08 20:53:28.790 Server        Using conventional memory in the memory
manager.
2016-12-08 20:53:29.980 Server        This instance of SQL Server last reported using
a process ID of 6960 at 12/4/2016 12:28:56 AM (local) 12/4/2016 7:28:56 AM (UTC).
This is an informational message only; no user action is required.
```

From this output, you can ascertain the complete SQL Server instance information as it was running on the primary site. It is excellent documentation for your SQL Server implementation. You should run this utility regularly and compare the output with prior executions' output to guarantee that you know exactly what you have to have in place in case of disaster.

Planning and Executing Disaster Recovery

The process of planning and executing complete disaster recovery is serious business, and many companies around the globe set aside a few days a year to perform this exact task. It involves the following steps:

1. Simulate a disaster.

2. Record all actions taken.

3. Time all events from start to finish. Sometimes this means someone is standing around with a stopwatch.

4. Hold a postmortem following the DR simulation.

Many companies tie the results of a DR simulation to the IT group's salaries (their raise percentage). This is more than enough motivation for IT to get this drill right and to perform well.

Correcting any failures or issues that occur is critical. The next time might not be a simulation.

Have You Detached a Database Recently?

You should consider all methods of backup and recovery when dealing with DR. A crude but extremely powerful method for creating a snapshot of a database (for any purpose, even for backup and recovery) is to simply detach a database and attach it in another location—pretty much anywhere. There will be some downtime while the database is detached, while the database files (.mdf and .ldf) are compressed, during the data transfer of these files (or a single zipped file) from one location to another, while the files are uncompressed, and while the database is being attached. This approach is crude, but it's fairly fast and extremely safe. All in all, it is a very reliable way to move an entire database from one place to another.

To give you an example of what it takes, a database that is about 30GB can be detached, compressed, moved to another server across a network (with a 10GB backbone), uncompressed, and attached in about 10 minutes. You should make sure your administrators know that this is a possibility in a pinch.

Third-Party Disaster Recovery Alternatives

Third-party alternatives for replication, mirroring, and synchronization that support disaster recovery are fairly prevalent. Symantec and a handful of other companies lead the way with very viable, but often expensive, solutions. Many of these solutions are bundled with their disk subsystems (which makes them easy to use and manage out-of-the-box). Following are some very strong options:

▶ **Symantec**—The Symantec replication solutions, including Veritas Storage Replicator and Veritas Volume Replicator, can create duplicate copies of data across any distance for data protection. These are certified with SQL Server. See www.symantec.com.

▶ **SIOS**—The SteelEye DataKeeper family of data replication, high availability clustering, and disaster recovery products are for Linux and Windows environments. They are all certified solutions (on a variety of other vendor products) across a wide range of applications and databases running on Windows and Linux, including mySAP, Exchange, Oracle, DB2, and SQL Server. See www.steeleye.com.

▶ **EMC**—EMC Corporation provides cost-effective, continuous remote replication and continuous data protection via tools such as AutoStart, MirrowView, Open Migrator/ LM, Replication Manager, and RepliStor. The Legato AA family of products includes capabilities required to manage system performance and to automate recovery from failures. Legato AA also automates data mirroring and replication, to enable data consolidation, migration, distribution, and preservation through failures and disasters. See www.emc.com.

If you are already a customer of one of these vendors, you should look closely at these options.

Disaster Recovery as a Service (DRaaS)

As described in Chapter 12, "Hardware and OS Options for High Availability," an emerging DR option is cloud-based services designed specifically for disaster recovery. These DRaaS offerings claim to be able to reasonably recover a company's primary workload in a fairly short amount of time. As an example, Microsoft's Azure Site Recovery can protect Microsoft Hyper-V, VMware, and physical servers, and you can use Azure or your secondary datacenter as your recovery site. Site Recovery coordinates and manages the ongoing replication of data by integrating with existing technologies, including System Center and Microsoft SQL Server AlwaysOn. The RPOs and RTOs will vary, of course, based on which snapshot, backup, and other methods are used.

Summary

You must deal with perhaps thousands of considerations when you are building a viable production implementation—let alone one that needs to have disaster recovery built in. You would be well advised to make the extra effort of first properly determining which disaster recovery solution matches your company's needs and then switching focus to what is the most effective way to implement that chosen solution. If, for example, you choose data replication to support your DR needs, you must determine the right type of replication model to use (for example, central publisher, peer-to-peer), what the limitations might be, the failover process that needs to be devised, and so on. Understanding other characteristics of your DR needs, such as what applications or databases are tightly coupled to your most important revenue-generation applications, is paramount. Disaster recovery planning is important, and testing a DR solution to make sure it works is even more important. You don't want to test your DR solution for the first time when your primary site has actually failed.

If you haven't yet implemented disaster recovery, you need to set some short-term attainable goals of getting to DR Level 1, which gives you a basic level of protection and mitigates some of the risk from a disaster. Then you can start pushing upward to Level 2 and beyond to create the highest DR capability possible within your budget and capabilities. And keep in mind that DR may be available with a product you are already using.

CHAPTER 14

Bringing HA Together

As you have no doubt surmised by now, evaluating, selecting, designing, and implementing the right high availability solution should not be left to the weak at heart or the inexperienced. There is too much at stake for your company to end up with mistakes in this process. For this reason, I again stress that you should use your best technologists for any HA assessment you do *or* get some outside help from someone who specializes in HA assessments—and get it fast.

The good news is that achieving the mythical five 9s (a sustained 99.999% availability of your application) can be done, if you follow the steps that outlined in this book. In addition, you have now had a chance to thoroughly dig into the primary HA solutions from Microsoft (failover clustering, SQL clustering, replication, database mirroring/snapshots, log shipping, availability groups, virtual machine snapshots, and backup and replication approaches) and should be getting a feel for what these tools can do for you. This chapter combines this exposure and capability information together into a coherent step-by-step methodology for getting your applications onto the correct high availability solution. But first, a few words about the hardware and software foundation you put into place.

Foundation First

Whereas in real estate the mantra is "location, location, location," in HA solutions, it is "foundation, foundation, foundation." Laying in the proper hardware and software components will allow you to build most HA solutions in a solid and resilient way. As you can see in Figure 14.1, these foundation elements relate directly to different parts of your system stack. And in most cases, it really doesn't matter where the environments are (on-premises, in the cloud, virtualized, or raw iron).

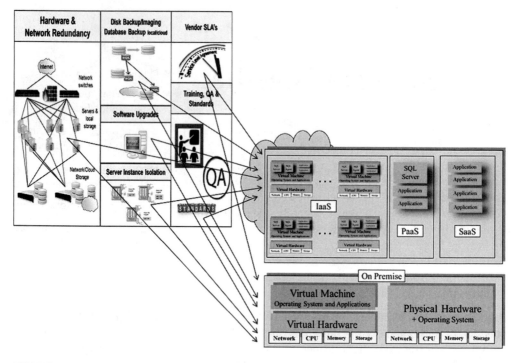

FIGURE 14.1 Foundational elements and their effects on different system stack components.

Specifically, these are the foundational elements:

▶ Putting hardware/network redundancies into place shores up your network access and the long-term stability of your servers.

▶ Making sure all network, OS, application, middleware, and database software upgrades are always kept at the highest release levels possible (including antivirus software) affects most components in the system stack.

▶ Deploying comprehensive and well-designed disk backups and DB backups directly impacts your applications, middleware, and databases, as well as the stability of your operating systems. This might also take the form of virtual machine snapshots or other options you might have available to you in your foundation.

▶ Establishing the necessary vendor service level agreements/contracts affects all components of the system stack (hardware and software), especially if you're using IaaS, SaaS, PaaS, and DRaaS.

▶ Comprehensive end-user, administrator, and developer training including extensive QA testing has a great impact on the stability of your applications, databases, and the OS itself.

Without making any further specialized HA changes, this basic foundation offers a huge degree of availability (and stability) in itself—but not necessarily five 9s. Adding specialized high availability solutions to this foundation allows you to push toward higher HA goals.

In order to select the "right" high availability solution, you must gather the specialized high availability detail requirements of your application. Very often, characteristics related to high availability are not considered or are neglected during the normal requirements gathering process. As discussed in Chapter 3, "Choosing High Availability," gathering these requirements is best done by initiating a full-blown Phase 0 HA assessment project that runs through all the HA assessment areas (which are designed to flesh out HA requirements specifically). Then, based on the software available, the hardware available, and these high availability requirements, you can match and build the appropriate HA solution on top of your solid foundation.

If your application is already implemented (or is about to be implemented), then you will really be doing a high availability "retrofit." Coming in at such a late stage in the process may or may not limit the HA options you can select. It of course depends on what you have built. It is possible, however, to match up HA solutions that meet HA needs and don't result in major rewrites of applications.

Assembling Your HA Assessment Team

If you haven't done this before, then here's what you need to do to assemble the right folks for doing an HA assessment. Three players have to be the core members of any HA assessment effort: the project coordinator/manager, who will drive the whole thing; the lead technologist/architect, who thoroughly understands HA and the technology stack at your company; and the lead business architect, who understands the application inside and out and also can calculate the exact business value of all applications. In addition, several other groups or representatives who cover all areas of hardware, software, security, and end users will be tapped during the HA assessment process.

The team should include the following members:

▶ **HA project lead/champion**—The project lead will drive all meetings, schedule all participants, and manage the day-to-day tasks.

▶ **System architect/data architect (SA/DA)**—Someone with both extensive system design and data design experience will be able to understand the hardware, software, and database aspects of high availability.

▶ **Senior business analyst (SBA)**—This person must be completely versed in development methodologies and the business requirements that are being targeted by the application (and by the assessment).

▶ **Part-time senior technical lead (STL)**—A software engineer type with good overall system development skills can help in assessing the coding standards that are being followed, the completeness of the system testing tasks, and the general software configuration that has been (or will be) implemented.

14

The following roles should also participate, as needed:

▶ End users/business management

▶ Corporate business continuity group (if one exists)

▶ IT system software/administration group

▶ IT data/database administration group

▶ IT security/access control group

▶ IT application development group

▶ IT production support group

Setting the HA Assessment Project Schedule/Timeline

After you have a team assembled, you need to get this project on the calendars of all the as-needed participants and HA project members. You should aim for a fast timeline for an HA assessment and selection process (within a 2-week time window). Here are the major events to schedule over a 2-week time frame:

1. Gather HA requirements (all)

   ▶ HA assessment kickoff/introduction to process (3 hours)

   ▶ HA assessment information gathering sessions—five to seven JAD-style assessment meetings (2 to 3 hours each) over the course of 5 days

   ▶ HA primary variables gauge (2 hours)

2. Review HA assessment requirements (team/management) (2 hours)

   ▶ Sign off on these requirements (management) (1 hour)

3. Selection of HA solution (team leads) (8 hours)

4. Review of HA solution selection and ROI (team leads/management) (2 hours)

   ▶ Sign off on HA solution selection (1 hour)

5. Commitment of resources/project for implementation (management) (3–8 hours of planning/scheduling/resourcing time)

All time in between meetings is spent assembling the information and following up on requirements not covered in these formal JAD sessions or meeting individually with people who are not present or on follow-ups to garner information that was not provided during the formal JAD meetings. The review sessions are critical to help drive this type of assessment project to completion quickly and to get full buy-in and visibility of the findings and decisions. The formal sign-off process following the requirements and selection events gives the assessment the proper teeth.

Faster timelines can be achieved, depending on the complexity and state of the application being considered for high availability.

Doing a Phase 0 High Availability Assessment

Now that you have your team together and have scheduled the major events and meetings for the HA assessment and selection, you need to introduce all members to what an HA assessment is and the key things you are trying to identify. You should present the main HA assessment ideas listed below during your kickoff session and explain them thoroughly, providing examples where possible. It's a good idea to provide this high-level list to all members before you meet for the first time to help set the stage.

> **NOTE**
>
> As a bonus to our readers, a sample Phase 0 HA assessment template (a Word document named HA0AssessmentSample.doc) is available on the book's companion website for download at www.informit.com/title/9780672337765.

You are seeking the following high-level information:

- What are the current and future characteristics of your application?
- What are the requirements related to your service level agreements (SLAs)?
- What RTOs and RPOs do you need for each application?
- What is the impact (cost) of downtime?
- What are your vulnerabilities (hardware, software, human errors, and so on)?
- What is your timeline for implementing a high availability solution?
- What is your budget for a high availability solution?

In addition, you will want to drill down into as much detail as possible in the following areas:

- Analysis of the current state/future state of the application
- Hardware configuration/options available
- Software configuration/options available
- Backup/recovery procedures used
- Standards/guidelines used
- Testing/QA process employed
- Business continuity desired (for the most critical applications)

▶ Personnel administering the systems assessed

▶ Personnel developing the systems assessed

A Phase 0 HA assessment can be tackled in two major steps:

1. Explore the detailed landscape of your application and environment. This step is broken down into six discreet tasks that you should address in as much detail as possible.

2. Complete the primary variable gauge and use it to communicate the assessment findings to management and the development team.

After these first two steps are completed, the selection of the right HA solution can be done fairly easily.

Step 1: Conducting the HA Assessment

Each task of the HA assessment is designed to identify different characteristics of your environment, your personnel, your policies, and your goals that directly relate to high availability. This step involves the following tasks:

▶ **Task 1**—Describe the current state of the application. This involves the following points:

   ▶ Data (data usage and physical implementation)

   ▶ Process (business processes being supported)

   ▶ Technology (hardware/software platform/configuration)

   ▶ Backup/recovery procedures

   ▶ Standards/guidelines used

   ▶ Testing/QA process employed

   ▶ Service level agreement (SLA) currently defined

   ▶ Level of expertise of personnel administering system

   ▶ Level of expertise of personnel developing/testing system

▶ **Task 2**—Describe the future state of the application. This involves the following points:

   ▶ Data (data usage and physical implementation, data volume growth, data resilience)

   ▶ Process (business processes being supported, expanded functionality anticipated, and application resilience)

▶ Technology (Hardware/software platform/configuration, new technology being acquired)

▶ Backup/recovery procedures being planned

▶ Standards/guidelines used or being enhanced

▶ Testing/QA process being changed or enhanced

▶ SLA desired—Examples of real-world SLAs can be difficult to find because they are considered confidential business information, much like other contract terms. However, there are a few places you can look. First, you can check the agreements you have with your own vendors. Many times, the SLAs you will be able to offer are bounded by the SLAs offered by vendors on which you rely. For example, if your Internet service provider guarantees only 99% uptime, it would be impractical for you to commit to delivering 99.5% uptime. You can also check the contracts of companies similar to yours that were filed with the SEC during the initial public offering process. These contracts tend to represent the largest and most important deals, and they often contain SLA terms that you can use as a benchmark.

▶ Level of expertise of personnel administering system (planned training and hiring)

▶ Level of expertise of personnel developing/testing system (planned training and hiring)

▶ **Task 3**—Describe the unplanned downtime reasons at different intervals (past 7 days, past month, past quarter, past 6 months, past year).

If this is a new application, Task 3 is to create an estimate of the future month, quarter, 6-month, and 1-year intervals.

▶ **Task 4**—Describe the planned downtime reasons at different intervals (past 7 days, past month, past quarter, past 6 months, past year).

If this is a new application, Task 4 is to create an estimate of the future month, quarter, 6-month, and 1-year intervals.

▶ **Task 5**—Calculate the availability percentage across different time intervals (past 7 days, past month, past quarter, past 6 months, past year). Refer to Chapter 1, "Understanding High Availability," for this complete calculation.

If this is a new application, Task 5 is to create an estimate of the future monthly, quarter, 6-month, and 1-year intervals.

▶ **Task 6**—Calculate the loss of downtime. This involves the following points:

▶ **Revenue loss (per hour of unavailability)**—For example, in an online order entry system, look at any peak order entry hour and calculate the total order amounts for that peak hour. This will be your revenue loss per hour value.

▶ **Productivity dollar loss (per hour of unavailability)**—For example, in an internal financial data warehouse that is used for executive decision support, calculate the length of time that this data mart/warehouse was not available within the past month or two and multiply this by the number of executives/managers who were supposed to be querying it during that period. This is the "productivity effect." Multiply this by the average salary of these execs/managers to get a rough estimate of productivity dollar loss. This does not consider the bad business decisions they might have made without having their data mart/warehouse available and the dollar loss of those bad business decisions. Calculating a productivity dollar loss might be a bit aggressive for this assessment, but there needs to be something to measure against and to help justify the return on investment. For applications that are not productivity applications, this value will not be calculated.

▶ **Goodwill dollar loss (in terms of customers lost per hour of unavailability)**—It's extremely important to include this component. Goodwill loss can be measured by taking the average number of customers for a period of time (such as last month's online order customer average) and comparing it with a period of processing following a system failure (where there was a significant amount of downtime). Chances are that there was a drop-off of the same amount that can be rationalized as goodwill loss (that is, the online customer didn't come back to you but went to the competition). You must then take that percentage drop-off (for example, 2%) and multiply it by the peak order amount averages for the defined period. This period loss number is like a repeating loss overhead value that should be included in the ROI calculation for every month.

If this is a new application, Task 6 is to create an estimate of the losses.

After you have completed these tasks, you are ready to move on to step 2: gauging the HA primary variables.

Step 2: Gauging HA Primary Variables

You should be able to specify the following primary variables:

▶ **Uptime requirement**—This is the goal (from 0% to 100%) of what you require from your application for this application's planned hours of operation.

▶ **Time to recover**—This is a general indication (from long to short) of the amount of time required to recover an application and put it back online. This could be stated in minutes, hours, or just in terms of long, medium, or short amount of time to recover. This is the RTO.

▶ **Tolerance of recovery time**—You should describe what the impact might be (from high to low tolerance) of extended recovery times needed to resynchronize data, restore transactions, and so on. This is mostly tied to the time to recover variable but can vary widely, depending on who the end users of the system are.

▶ **Data resiliency**—You should describe how much data you are willing to lose and whether it needs to be kept intact (that is, have complete data integrity, even in failure). Often described in terms of low- to high-data resiliency. This is the RPO.

▶ **Application resiliency**—You need an application-oriented description of the behavior you are seeking (from low- to high-application resiliency). In other words, should your applications (programs) be able to be restarted, switched to other machines without the end user having to reconnect, and so on?

▶ **Degree of distributed access/synchronization**—For systems that are geographically distributed or partitioned (as are many global applications), it is critical to understand how distributed and tightly coupled they must be at all times (indicated by the degree of distributed access and synchronization required). A low specification of this variable indicates that the application and data are very loosely coupled and can stand on their own for periods of time and can then be resynchronized at a later date.

▶ **Scheduled maintenance frequency**—You need to determine the anticipated (or current) rate of scheduled maintenance required for the box, OS, network, application software, and other components in the system stack (from often to never).

▶ **Performance/scalability**—This is a firm requirement of the overall system performance and scalability needed for the application (from low- to high-performance need). This variable drives many high availability solutions because high performance systems often sacrifice many of the other variables mentioned here (for example, data resilience).

▶ **Cost of downtime ($ lost/hour)**—You need to estimate or calculate the dollar (or euro, yen, and so forth) cost for every minute of downtime (from low to high cost). You will usually find that the cost is not a single number, like an average cost per minute. In reality, short downtimes have lower costs, and the costs (losses) grow exponentially for longer downtimes. You should also try to factor in a goodwill cost (or loss).

▶ **Cost to build and maintain the high availability solution ($)**—This last variable may not be known initially. However, as you near the design and implementation of a high availability system, the costs come barreling in rapidly and often make certain decisions for you.

As you can see in Figure 14.2, you can think of each of these variables as an oil gauge or temperature gauge. You simply place an arrow along the gauge of each variable to estimate the approximate temperature or level of a particular variable.

NOTE

We provide a sample template of the primary variables gauge and other HA representations for download. Look for the PowerPoint document named HAOAssessmentSample.ppt on the Sams Publishing website at www.informit.com/title/9780672337765.

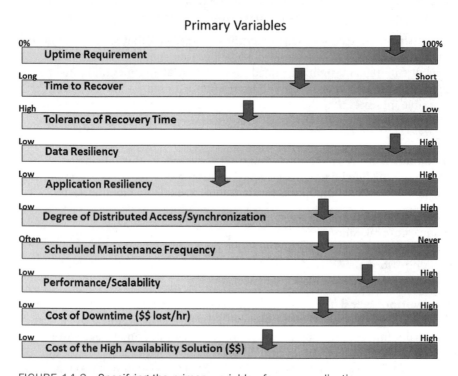

FIGURE 14.2   Specifying the primary variables for your applications.

High Availability Tasks Integrated into Your Development Life Cycle

As you can well imagine, if you had been considering the high availability needs and characteristics since the very beginning of all development projects, you would be in a much better position to "design in" and "design for" an optimal HA solution. Let's quickly revisit how you might have integrated your high availability elements into a traditional development life cycle so that you can better understand the assessment process.

Enhancing your current development life cycle deliverables with the tailored HA deliverables depicted in Figure 14.3 is fairly easy.

Development Methodology

"With High Availability built in"

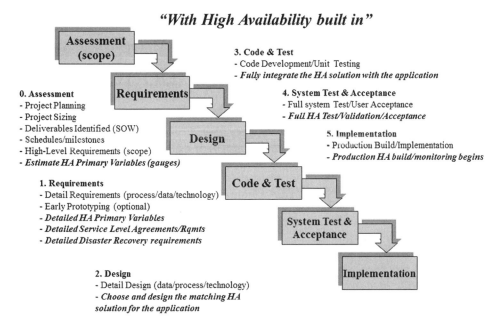

Assessment (scope)

0. Assessment
- Project Planning
- Project Sizing
- Deliverables Identified (SOW)
- Schedules/milestones
- High-Level Requirements (scope)
- *Estimate HA Primary Variables (gauges)*

Requirements

1. Requirements
- Detail Requirements (process/data/technology)
- Early Prototyping (optional)
- *Detailed HA Primary Variables*
- *Detailed Service Level Agreements/Rqmts*
- *Detailed Disaster Recovery requirements*

Design

2. Design
- Detail Design (data/process/technology)
- *Choose and design the matching HA solution for the application*

3. Code & Test
- Code Development/Unit Testing
- *Fully integrate the HA solution with the application*

4. System Test & Acceptance
- Full system Test/User Acceptance
- *Full HA Test/Validation/Acceptance*

5. Implementation
- Production Build/Implementation
- *Production HA build/monitoring begins*

Code & Test

System Test & Acceptance

Implementation

FIGURE 14.3   Traditional development life cycle with high availability tasks built in.

As you can see in this traditional "waterfall" methodology, every phase of the life cycle has a new task or two that specifically calls out high availability issues, needs, or characteristics (see the **bold italic text**):

▶ Phase 0: Assessment (scope)

　▶ *Estimate the high availability primary variables (gauges)*

Using the HA primary variables gauge to do estimations is extremely valuable at this early stage in the life cycle.

▶ Phase 1: Requirements

　▶ *Detailed high availability primary variables*

　▶ *Detailed service level agreements/requirements*

　▶ *Detailed disaster recovery requirements*

Fully detailing the HA primary variables, defining the SLAs, and putting together the early disaster recovery requirements will position you to make well-founded design decisions and HA solution decisions in later phases.

▶ Phase 2: Design

　▶ *Choose and design the matching high availability solution for the application*

In Phase 2 you select the HA solution that best meets your high availability requirements.

▶ Phase 3: Coding and Testing

  ▶ *Fully integrate the high availability solution with the application*

Each step in coding and testing should include an understanding of the high availability solution that has been chosen. Unit testing may also be required on certain high availability options.

▶ Phase 4: System Testing and Acceptance

  ▶ *Full high availability testing/validation/acceptance*

Full-scale system and acceptance testing of the high availability capabilities must be completed without any issues whatsoever. During this phase, a determination of whether the high availability option truly meets the availability levels must be strictly measured. If it doesn't, you may have to iterate back to earlier phases and modify your HA solution design.

▶ Phase 5: Implementation

  ▶ *Production high availability build/monitoring begins*

Finally, you will be ready to move your application and your thoroughly tested high availability solution into production mode confidently. From this point, your system will be live, and monitoring of the high availability application begins.

Selecting an HA Solution

The HA selection process consists of evaluating your HA assessment findings (requirements) using the hybrid decision-tree evaluation technique (with the Nassi-Shneiderman charts) presented in Chapter 3. Recall that this decision tree technique evaluates the assessment findings against the following questions:

1. What percentage of time must the application remain up during its scheduled time of operation? (The goal!)

2. How much tolerance does the end user have when the system is not available (planned or unplanned unavailability)?

3. What is the per-hour cost of downtime for this application?

4. How long does it take to get the application back online following a failure (of any kind)? (Worst case!)

5. How much of the application is distributed and will require some type of synchronization with other nodes before all nodes are considered to be 100% available?

6. How much data inconsistency can be tolerated in favor of having the application available?

7. How often is scheduled maintenance required for this application (and environment)?

8. How important are high performance and scalability?

9. How important is it for the application to keep its current connection alive with the end user?

10. What is the estimated cost of a possible high availability solution? What is the budget?

By systematically moving through the decision tree and answering the case constructs for each question, you can work through a definitive path to a particular HA solution. This process is not foolproof, but it is very good at helping you hone in on an HA solution that matches the requirements being evaluated. Figure 14.4 shows an example of the Scenario 1 (application service provider [ASP]) results from using this process. Remember that the questions are cumulative. Each new question carries along the responses of the preceding questions. The responses, taken together, determine the HA solution that best fits.

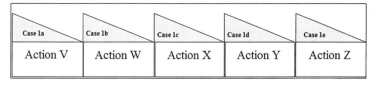

Case 1a	Case 1b	Case 1c	Case 1d	Case 1e
Action V	Action W	Action X	Action Y	Action Z

1. 1e → Extreme Availability goal (99.95% or higher)
2. 1e+2d → Very low tolerance of downtime
3. 1e+2d+3e → $15k/hr cost of downtime (High Cost)
4. 1e+2d+3e+4c → Average recovery time
5. 1e+2d+3e+4c+5a → No distributed components or synchronization
6. 1e+2d+3e+4c+5a+6b → A little data inconsistency can be tolerated
7. 1e+2d+3e+4c+5a+6b+7c → Average amount of scheduled downtime
8. 1e+2d+3e+4c+5a+6b+7c+8d → Performance is very much important
9. 1e+2d+3e+4c+5a+6b+7c+8d+9b → Connection can be re-established
10. 1e+2d+3e+4c+5a+6b+7c+8d+9b+10c → Moderate HA Cost/Good budget

Best fitting HA Solution (together)

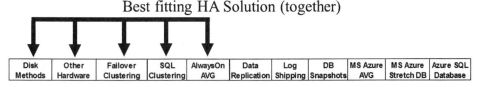

Disk Methods	Other Hardware	Failover Clustering	SQL Clustering	AlwaysOn AVG	Data Replication	Log Shipping	DB Snapshots	MS Azure AVG	MS Azure Stretch DB	Azure SQL Database

FIGURE 14.4   Scenario 1: ASP, Nassi-Shneiderman HA questions results with the resulting HA selection.

As you can see, this analysis for Scenario 1, featuring an ASP, yielded a high availability selection of hardware redundancy, shared disk RAID arrays, failover clustering, SQL clustering, and AlwaysOn availability groups. Having these options together clearly met all of the ASP's requirements of uptime, tolerance, performance, distributing workload, and costs. The ASP's service level agreement with its customers also allows for brief amounts of downtime to deal with OS upgrades or fixes, hardware upgrades, and application upgrades. The ASP's budget was enough for a large amount of hardware redundancy.

Figure 14.5 shows the production implementation of the ASP's HA solutions. It is a two-node SQL cluster (in an active/passive configuration) along with an availability group primary and three secondary replicas. The first secondary is the synchronous failover node, and the other two are asynchronous read-only secondaries used for possible reporting offloading and even disaster recovery. (Servers D and E are on a separate network subnet and located in another data center.) This implementation is proving to be a very scalable, high-performance, risk mitigating, and cost-effective architecture for the ASP.

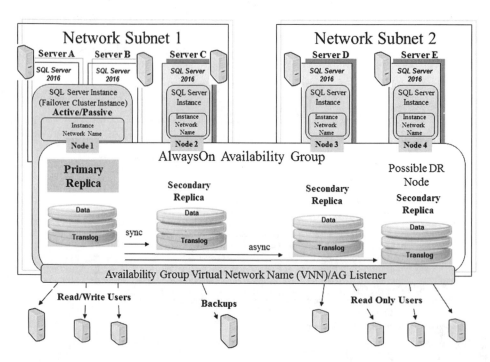

FIGURE 14.5   ASP high availability "live solution" with SQL clustering and AlwaysOn availability groups.

Determining Whether an HA Solution Is Cost-Effective

Perhaps one of the most important calculations you will do as part of the HA assessment is determining the return on your investment (ROI). In other words, will the HA solution you pick be cost-effective, and how quickly will it pay for itself? The ROI for an HA solution can be estimated during the assessment process and then finalized during the HA selection process. Coming up with the downtime cost is essential to being able to measure the ROI of an HA solution. So, spend some extra time researching the cost that downtime really has for your company. If this is for a new system, you can use a similar application's downtime costs adjusted by what you think the new application's financial impact would be. Recall that an HA solution's ROI can be calculated by adding up the incremental costs (or estimates) of the new HA solution and comparing them against the complete cost of downtime for a period of time (such as 1 year).

Using the Scenario 1 example, this section shows how to estimate the total costs (incremental + deployment + assessment) to get to the selected SQL clustering high and AlwaysOn and availability groups high availability solution.

We had to determine the downtime costs (unplanned and planned) at an hourly dollar value (for the planned hours of operation), and finally we were able to determine the percentage of these HA implementation costs compared to the cost of downtime. This revealed that the total implementation cost of this HA solution is 41.86% of the downtime cost for 1 year. In other words, the investment of the HA solution will pay for itself in 0.41 year, or approximately 5 months! Figure 14.6 shows this entire ROI calculation done in Excel. The last line of the spreadsheet shows the length of time to recover the investment (your costs). This spreadsheet (HAAssessmentOROI.xls) is available on the book's companion website at www.informit.com/title/9780672337765.

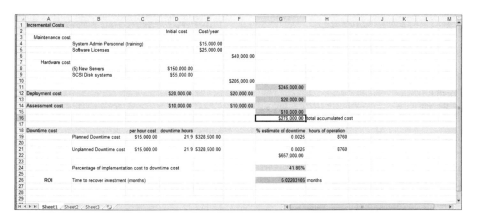

FIGURE 14.6   ROI calculation Excel spreadsheet for Scenario 1.

The full ROI calculation contains these cost enumerations:

1. Maintenance cost (for a 1-year period):

   ▶ **$15k (estimate)**—Yearly system admin personnel cost (additional time for training of these personnel)

   ▶ **$25k (estimate)**—Recurring software licensing cost (of additional HA components; 5 OS + 5 SQL Server 2016)

2. Hardware cost:

▶ **$205k hardware cost**—The cost of additional HW in the new HA solution

3. Deployment/assessment cost:

▶ **$20k deployment cost**—The cost of development, testing, QA, and production implementation of the solution

▶ **$10k HA assessment cost**

4. Downtime cost (for a 1-year period):

▶ If you kept track of last year's downtime record, use that number; otherwise, produce an estimate of planned and unplanned downtime for this calculation. For this scenario, the estimated cost of downtime/hour is **$15k/hour** for this ASP.

▶ Planned downtime cost (revenue loss cost) = Planned downtime hours × cost of hourly downtime to the company:

a. 0.25% (estimate of planned downtime percentage in 1 year) × 8,760 hours in a year = 21.9 hours of planned downtime

b. 21.9 hours (planned downtime) × $15k/hr (hourly cost of downtime) = $328,500/year cost of planned downtime

▶ Unplanned downtime cost (revenue loss cost) = Unplanned downtime hours × cost of hourly downtime to the company:

a. 0.25% (estimate of unplanned downtime percentage in 1 year) × 8,760 hours in a year = 21.9 hours of unplanned downtime

b. 21.9 hours × $15k/hr (hourly cost of downtime) = $328,500/year cost of unplanned downtime

ROI totals:

▶ Total costs to get on this HA solution = $275,000 (for the year)

▶ Total of downtime cost = $657,000 (for the year)

As you can see, these numbers are compelling. You can imagine that presenting such numbers can help push decisions through a bit faster with the bean counters and the controller who must be involved with this type of investment decision. Just the process of determining a downtime cost can yield startling revelations. This cost can be shocking, and when folks figure out how much money they really are losing when systems aren't available, your whole implementation timeline may be accelerated.

Summary

Pushing through a formal HA assessment for your application, making an HA selection, and planning its implementation put you just shy of the actual production implementation of the HA solution. To implement the selected HA solution, you can follow the detailed steps in the appropriate HA options chapters that correspond to your particular selection results .You will be building up a test environment first, then a formal QA environment, and finally a production deployment. You will find that knowing how to implement any one of these HA options beforehand takes the risk and guessing out of the whole process. If you have completely thrashed through your HA requirements for your applications to an excruciating level of detail, proceeding all the way to your production implementation will hopefully be mostly anticlimactic. And, to top that off, you will also know how much money it will take to achieve this HA solution and what the payback will be in terms of ROI if downtime should occur (and how quickly you will achieve this ROI). You can safely say you have considered all the essential factors in determining a high available solution and that you are fairly ready to get that HA solution into place.

14

Upgrading Your Current Deployment to HA

Hopefully you are upgrading your current SQL Server deployment to high availability as a sane and measured course of business and not because you have just had a major disaster or an extended amount of unavailability. Either way, though, you must actually have a lot of information and analysis available to get from where you are now to where you need to be.

It all begins with understanding why you need HA and a full assessment of exactly what type of HA you should have in place that meets your company's needs. From your HA assessment, you will be able to determine what HA configuration you should have in place (your target HA deployment). You also need to understand exactly what your current deployment is composed of so that you can create a GAP analysis of that shows the details of what you currently have and what you need to put into place for HA. As a part of this GAP analysis, you should also factor in what disaster recovery solution you may need and add it to your planning exercise. As mentioned in earlier chapters, it is much easier to include a DR solution now than it used to be; you will have no regrets if you make DR part of your plans. Once you have a full GAP analysis done, you can list the hardware, software, and cloud components that you'll need to acquire to become fully operational in your planned HA target. Due to the rapidly dropping prices of all these components, you will likely be pleased with the price tag associated with this type of upgrade.

Other planning will be needed for things like operational tasks and education needed by the dev ops team, storage and capacity planning, data migration or SQL license upgrade (for example, from Standard to Enterprise if using the AlwaysOn features), and a target date for doing the upgrade. It is a very good idea to plan on applying HA to two environments: your staging or system test environment and, of course, your production environment. You can fully test your HA capabilities in the staging/system test environment and then switch to your production environment when you know everything works. (You do not need to have HA in your dev or test environments.)

> **NOTE**
>
> Some organizations don't think they need their staging/system test environments to be HA. It is ultimately up to you. I don't like testing HA in my production environments until I'm confident that I'm ready to deploy it there.

Finally, you will be entering into a whole new world of HA performance monitoring that will keep you informed about the constant health of your HA deployment. This health monitoring is likely very different from what you have done in the past, in the non-HA world. This chapter uses Scenario 1, featuring the application service provider (ASP),as an example of planning and deploying a new HA solution. You will see that this is a whole lot easier to do than you might think, and you'll probably kick yourself for not moving to a HA solution sooner.

Quantifying Your Current Deployment

As mentioned earlier, you do not need to have HA for your dev or test environments. However, you do need to be on the same SQL Server version and edition that your production SQL Server environment will have. As part of the initial planning for an upgrade to a new HA deployment, you should make a robust list of all software and hardware components, their characteristics (sizes, number of CPUs, number of NICs, and so on), network configurations and IP addresses, software and operating system versions, patches, and application versions and editions you are running.

As you can see in Figure 15.1, the original server configuration in Scenario 1 was pretty good and served the ASP well for very large application loads, but it was simply not highly available, and it had no disaster recovery whatsoever. The dev and test servers were half as big as the production server but on the same SQL Server and OS versions. The staging/system test server was a mirror image of the production server.

> **NOTE**
>
> For clarity, this chapter looks only at the database server(s), not the web or application servers. However, this chapter does show the file server that is the container of all database backups.

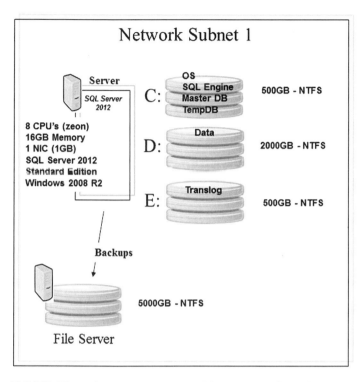

FIGURE 15.1   Scenario 1's original DB server configuration.

Scenario 1 Original Environment List

The following is the production hardware/software configuration for Scenario 1:

▶ Database server:

  ▶ **CPU**—8 Intel Zeon processors

  ▶ **Memory**—16GB

  ▶ **Network interface cards**—1 NIC (1GB)

  ▶ **Storage and volume configuration:**

    C: Drive (500GB) SATA drive 10,000 rpm, local binaries/OS

    D: Drive (2,000GB) SATA drive 10,000 rpm

    E: Drive (500GB) SATA drive 10,000 rpm

▶ **Operating system**—Windows Server 2008 R2

  ▶ **SQL Server edition**—SQL Server 2012, Service Pack 1, Standard Edition

15

▶ File server:

  ▶ **Storage configuration:**

  ▶ C: Drive (5,000GB) SATA drive 10,000 rpm

The following is the staging/system test hardware/software configuration for Scenario 1:

▶ Database server:

  ▶ **CPU**—8 Intel Zeon processors

  ▶ **Memory**—16 GB

  ▶ **Network interface cards**—1 NIC (1GB)

  ▶ **Storage and volume configuration:**

    C: Drive (500GB) SATA drive 10,000 rpm, local binaries/OS

    D: Drive (2,000GB) SATA drive 10,000 rpm

    E: Drive (500GB) SATA drive 10,000 rpm

  ▶ **Operating system**—Windows Server 2008 R2

  ▶ **SQL Server edition**—SQL Server 2012, Service Pack 1, Standard Edition

The following is the development hardware/software configuration for Scenario 1:

▶ Database server:

  ▶ **CPU**—4 Intel Zeon processors

  ▶ **Memory**—8 GB

  ▶ **Network interface cards**—1 NIC (1GB)

  ▶ **Storage and volume configuration:**

    C: Drive (500 GB) SATA drive 10,000 rpm, local binaries/OS

    D: Drive (500 GB) SATA drive 10,000 rpm

    E: Drive (500 GB) SATA drive 10,000 rpm

  ▶ **Operating system**—Windows Server 2008 R2

  ▶ **SQL Server edition**—SQL Server 2012, Service Pack 1, Developer Edition

The following is the test hardware/software configuration for Scenario 1:

▶ Database server:

  ▶ **CPU**—4 Intel Zeon processors

  ▶ **Memory**—8 GB

  ▶ **Network interface cards**—1 NIC (1GB)

  ▶ **Storage and volume configuration:**

    C: Drive (500GB) SATA drive 10,000 rpm, local binaries/OS

    D: Drive (500GB) SATA drive 10,000 rpm

    E: Drive (500GB) SATA drive 10,000 rpm

  ▶ **Operating system**—Windows Server 2008 R2

  ▶ **SQL Server edition**—SQL Server 2012, Service Pack 1, Developer Edition

As you can see in Figure 15.1, the DBAs have correctly isolated the SQL Server engine and TempDB storage away from the application database data portion storage and also isolated the application database's transaction log storage away from the application database data portion storage. This industry best practice leads to minimal disk drive contention.

From this point on, this chapter excludes the file server, dev, test, and staging/system test servers from the discussion. However, at the very least, you will likely need to upgrade your OS and your SQL Server versions on those servers to be consistent with your new target HA versions.

Deciding What HA Solution You Will Upgrade To

Chapter 14, "Bringing HA Together," took you through a formal HA assessment process, using the Scenario 1 ASP as an example. The results of that process for the ASP yielded a target HA and DR solution including both server-level redundancy (with SQL clustering) and database redundancy via AlwaysOn availability groups with three secondary replicas. Secondary Replica 1 will be in synchronous replication mode with the primary replica for automatic failover. Secondary Replicas 2 and 3 will be in asynchronous mode with the primary replica and will be used for reporting and other noncritical user access. In addition, Secondary Replica 3 will also be the disaster recovery node and will be put in Azure (that is, in the cloud). Figure 15.2 shows this planned HA configuration.

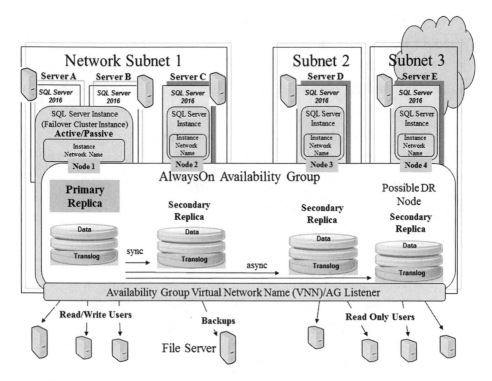

FIGURE 15.2   Planned HA configuration for Scenario 1 (database tier only).

It is now time to list what the characteristics for these new target servers will need to be to support the intended HA solution. At a very minimum, Scenario 1 has the following characteristics:

▶ Upgrading the OS from Windows Server 2008 R2 to Windows Server 2012

▶ Adding some NAS storage for the shared storage for the SQL cluster (Server A and Server B in Figure 15.2)

▶ Adding one additional NIC per server for network redundancy

▶ Increasing the memory from 16GB to 32GB per server

▶ Upgrading the SQL Server version and editions from 2008 R2 Standard Edition to 2016 Enterprise Edition to take advantage of all the latest SQL Server improvements and the AlwaysOn availability group features

The next step is to compare the original processing, storage, and transactional volume needs to what is needed to build out that target HA configuration as well as a DR solution. Luckily, SQL Server 2016 makes it easy to add DR. In this scenario, DR can be achieved by just replicating asynchronously to a third secondary in the cloud (on Azure).

Scenario 1 Target HA Environment List

The following is the production (Server A) hardware/software configuration for Scenario 1:

- ▶ Database server:

    - ▶ **CPU**—16 Intel Zeon processors

    - ▶ **Memory**—32GB

    - ▶ **Network interface cards**—2 NICs (10GB)

    - ▶ **Storage and volume configuration:**

        C: Drive (500GB) SATA drive 15,000 rpm, local binaries/OS

        D: Shared NAS with cache 5,000GB (5TB)

        E: Shared NAS with cache 5,000GB (5TB)

        F: Quorum drive (shared with Server B via failover clustering)

    - ▶ **Operating system**—Windows Server 2012

    - ▶ **SQL Server edition**—SQL Server 2016, Enterprise Edition

The following is the production (Server B) hardware/software configuration for Scenario 1:

- ▶ Database server:

    - ▶ **CPU**—16 Intel Zeon processors

    - ▶ **Memory**—32GB

    - ▶ **Network interface cards**—2 NICs (10GB)

    - ▶ **Storage and volume configuration:**

        C: Drive (500GB) SATA drive 15,000 rpm, local binaries/OS

        D: Shared NAS with cache 5,000GB (5TB)

        E: Shared NAS with cache 5,000GB (5TB)

        F: Quorum drive (shared with Server A via failover clustering)

    - ▶ **Operating system**—

        Windows Server 2012

    - ▶ **SQL Server edition**—SQL Server 2016, enterprise edition

The following is the production (Server C) hardware/software configuration for Scenario 1:

- ▶ Database server:

    - ▶ **CPU**—16 Intel Zeon processors

    - ▶ **Memory**—32GB

    - ▶ **Network interface cards**—2 NIC (10GB)

15

▶ **Storage and volume configuration:**

C: Drive (500GB) SATA drive 15,000 rpm - local binaries/OS

D: Drive (2,000GB) SATA drive 15,000 rpm

E: Drive (500GB) SATA drive 15,000 rpm

▶ **Operating system**—Windows Server 2012

▶ **SQL Server edition**—SQL Server 2016, enterprise edition

The following is the production (Server D) hardware/software configuration for Scenario 1:

▶ Database server:

    ▶ **CPU**—8 Intel Zeon processors

    ▶ **Memory**—16 GB

    ▶ **Network interface cards**—2 NICs (10GB)

    ▶ **Storage and volume configuration:**

    C: Drive (500GB) SATA drive 15,000 rpm, local binaries/OS

    D: Drive (2,000GB) SATA drive 15,000 rpm

    E: Drive (500GB) SATA drive 15,000 rpm

    ▶ **Operating system**—Windows Server 2012

▶ **SQL Server edition**—SQL Server 2016, Enterprise Edition

The following is the production disaster recovery server (Server E) hardware/software configuration for Scenario 1:

▶ Database server:

    ▶ **CPU**—8 processors

    ▶ **Memory**—16 GB

    ▶ **Network interface cards**—2 NICs

    ▶ **Storage and volume configuration:**

    C: Drive (500GB)

    D: Drive (2,000GB)

    E: Drive (500GB)

    ▶ **Operating system**—Windows Server 2012

    ▶ **SQL Server edition**—SQL Server 2016, Enterprise Edition

    ▶ **Location**—Azure IaaS (in the cloud)

Servers D and E, which are secondary replicas, don't need to be as beefed up as the others because they are used for offloading of reporting user accesses and for DR purposes. On the other hand, Server A, Server B, and Server C should be nearly the same in terms of processing power and memory. Server A and Server B are also sharing storage; Server C is not. This configuration will feature SQL clustering with Server A and Server B for server redundancy and then Server C for database redundancy in automatic failover mode, and, finally, with Server D and Server E for additional database redundancy for offloading of reporting load accesses and a disaster recovery site in the cloud (Azure).

It's time to order this equipment and get the OSs upgraded and SQL Server installed across the board. A way to cut costs in this scenario would be to repurpose the original server into one of the secondary replicas (for example, Server D in Figure 15.2). Lots of options exist for retiring hardware, reusing it, or for using IaaS in the cloud.

Planning Your Upgrade

After you have received all the new hardware and software and set it up in your data centers, you can continue with your detailed planning for your HA upgrade. The following is a list of items you would likely have to deal with for a successful HA upgrade in Scenario 1:

▶ Having the network IP addresses for failover clustering and AlwaysOn availability group configurations

▶ Installing SQL Server 2016 Enterprise Edition on five production servers

▶ Ensuring that storage allocations/drives are ready on each server

▶ Enabling failover clustering on all servers

▶ Making database backups and beginning the upgrade

▶ Upgrading the SQL Server 2012 application databases to SQL Server 2016

▶ Configuring Server A and Server B to be a SQL cluster (see Chapters 4, "Failover Clustering," and 5, "SQL Server Clustering")

▶ Configuring AlwaysOn availability groups for your SQL Server cluster (primary replica), Server C (secondary replica), and Server D and Server E (secondary replicas) (see Chapter 6, "SQL Server AlwaysOn and Availability Groups")

▶ Verifying that your applications can access the newly created SQL Server instances, which means you must have migrated all the needed logins (for SQL or Active Directory) to the new server environments

▶ Verifying that your application test suites run successfully

▶ Verifying that the HA configuration functions properly (both automatic failover and manual failover)

▶ Verifying that your DR configuration can be used successfully

Doing Your Upgrade

In general, you should upgrade all your dev, test, and staging/system testing environments first. This includes the OS (for example, upgrading Windows Server 2008 R2 to Windows Server 2012), upgrading from SQL Server 2008 R2 to SQL Server 2016, and so on. You should also have your SQL cluster fully configured and running in the new production environment, all your secondary replica servers up and running (each joined to the availability group), and basically nothing left to do other than to restore and enable each secondary replica with a copy of the primary replica.

When the application team gives you the greenlight, you can enable the HA configuration in production. This involves the following steps:

1. Do a transaction log backup of each primary database.

2. Do a full database backup of each primary database.

3. Do another transaction log backup of each primary database.

4. Copy these backups to each secondary replica in the topology.

5. Restore the transaction log and databases backups (with the No Recovery option) onto each secondary replica, one at a time.

6. Join the primary database to the availability group.

7. Join the secondary databases to the availability group, one at a time.

When you are done with these steps, you will be up and running in your high availability configuration. It would be wise to enable a database backup maintenance plan on your secondary replica that is synchronously replicated from your primary. You should also add some logic to your maintenance plans to test who owns the primary role in a primary/secondary replica model. The following code snippet can detect who is the primary very easily and initiate a database backup from whichever SQL Server instance is the secondary. If the secondary is not available, it takes the backup of the primary (that is, it makes a contingency backup):

```
IF sys.fn_hadr_backup_is_preferred_replica( 'YourDBnameHere' ) = 1
BEGIN
    PRINT 'This instance is the preferred replica'
    EXEC msdb.dbo.sp_start_job N'YourDBnameHere Backup.Subplan_1';
END
ELSE
BEGIN
    PRINT 'This instance is not the preferred replica'
END
```

Next, you will have to fully test your application and make sure it functions properly under failover and disaster recovery conditions.

Testing Your HA Configuration

You are now ready to thrash your HA configuration as much as possible to simulate all possible failure scenarios. Before you get started with failure testing for an AlwaysOn availability group configuration (as in Scenario 1), you should verify that your replication is working to all secondary replicas. You can do this easily by just inserting a row into a table of your application on the primary replica and verifying that it is replicated to all the secondary replicas. Then you can delete this row from the primary and verify that it is deleted in all the secondary replicas. After that you have validated that your HA configuration is doing what it is supposed to be doing (that is, replicating data), you can proceed to the testing of failure and failover scenarios.

The most common failure scenario is an AlwaysOn availability group configuration failing over the primary server to the secondary. Figure 15.3 shows the Failover Cluster Manager and the different views (Node, Roles, Storage, Networks, and Cluster events).

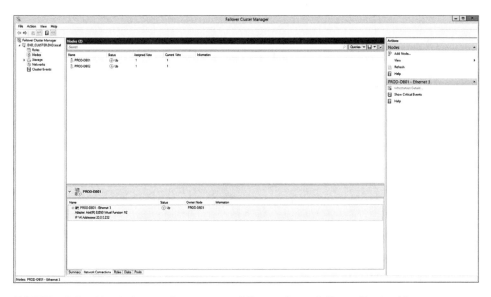

FIGURE 15.3   Simulating a primary server failure using a Failover Cluster Manager move.

To simulate a failure, you can fail over (move) the role of primary to the secondary replica. You could also just stop the primary SQL Server instance or pull the plug on that server. Using Failover Cluster Manager is a bit less messy and fully simulates a failure event. To see this in action, right-click the Roles option (node) and select Move. When you are prompted to select a node to become the primary node in the cluster, select the secondary server from the list. You should see that the primary role is now owned by the old secondary replica, which is now the primary replica. You can repeat this move as many times as you wish.

When you're satisfied that the primary and secondary replicas are failing over properly, repeat the same test by connecting to the listener and running SELECT queries. Run through the failover sequences and verify that the test query returns rows, regardless of which SQL Server is the primary or secondary. You should also repeat this type of testing with INSERTS, UPDATES, and DELETES.

You will also want to test manual failover to a secondary replica and also manual failover to your disaster recovery secondary replica. To do this, you must bring down (or remove) the primary and synchronous secondary replicas and then manually enable the other secondary replica for full transactional activity. The same goes for the disaster recovery secondary replica.

Finally, you need to validate a series of SQL Server Agent jobs (maintenance plans for backups and monitoring) to make sure they are functioning properly on each server instance. These are likely candidates:

▶ The database full backup maintenance plan

▶ The transaction log incremental backups maintenance plan (if you're doing incrementals)

▶ The contingency database full backup maintenance plan (if you're using one)

▶ The contingency transaction log incremental backups maintenance plan (if you're using one)

▶ The PerfMon data collection jobs for collecting monitoring of each server

Monitoring Your HA Health

For the AlwaysOn availability group HA configuration, you can set up PerfMon counters that specifically address the health of the data being replicated from primary to secondaries. Figure 15.4 shows a typical set of PerfMon counters monitoring a SQL Server instance.

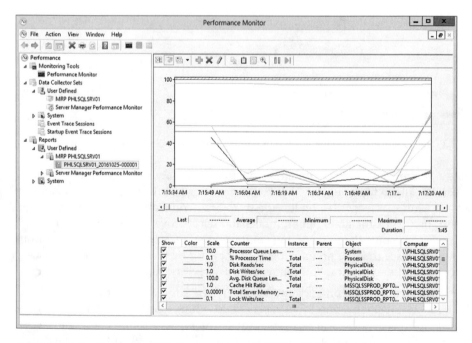

FIGURE 15.4   Monitoring SQL Server high availability with PerfMon counters.

The following are PerfMon counters you typically need to set up for SQL Server and AlwaysOn availability groups (where PROD_DB01 is the name of the SQL Server instance):

Counter Group	Counter
Memory	PageFaults/sec
Memory	Available Kbytes
MSSQL$PROD_DB01:Availability Replica	Bytes Received from Replica/sec
MSSQL$PROD_DB01:Availability Replica	Bytes Sent to Replica/sec
MSSQL$PROD_DB01:Availability Replica	Flow Control Time (ms/sec)
MSSQL$PROD_DB01:Availability Replica	Flow Control Time/sec
MSSQL$PROD_DB01:Availability Replica	Resent Messages/sec
MSSQL$PROD_DB01:Availability Replica	Sends to Replica/sec
MSSQL$PROD_DB01:Database Replica	Mirrored Write Transactions/sec
MSSQL$PROD_DB01:Buffer Manager	Buffer Cache Hit Ratio
MSSQL$PROD_DB01:Databases	Transactions/sec
MSSQL$PROD_DB01:Databases(tempdb)	Transactions/sec
MSSQL$PROD_DB01:General Statistics	User Connections
MSSQL$PROD_DB01:Locks	Lock Wait Time (ms)
MSSQL$PROD_DB01:Locks	Lock Waits/sec
MSSQL$PROD_DB01:Memory Manager	Total Server Memory (KB)
MSSQL$PROD_DB01:Plan Cache	Hit Ratio
Physical Disk	Avg. Disk Queue Length
Physical Disk	Reads/sec
Physical Disk	Writes/sec
Process	% Processor Time
Process(sqlservr)	% Processor Time
System	Processor Queue Length

The other HA configuration types (for example, replication, mirroring, snapshots, log shipping) have their own PerfMon counters available once you enable or configure the HA solution. You can add them to your PerfMon collection accordingly and set up thresholds to get alerts when issues arise.

You can also use the AlwaysOn High Availability dashboard in SSMS, which is continuously refreshed and shows the overall health of your HA configuration. As you can see in Figure 15.5, the high availability configuration is up and running, fully synchronized, and performing well (all green checkmarks!). Just right-click the AlwaysOn High Availability node in SSMS to launch this dashboard.

15

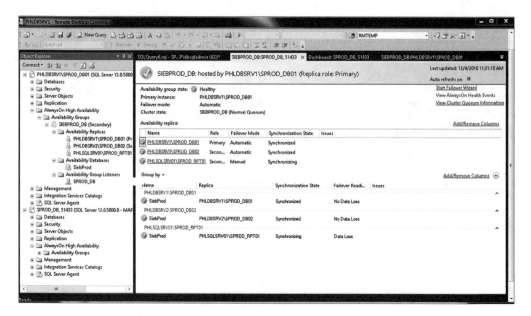

FIGURE 15.5   AlwaysOn High Availability dashboard monitoring in SSMS.

For some HA deployments, you might want to use cloud-based monitoring services, such as New Relic, and create a synthetic transaction concept that can be sent through the primary to secondary replicas on a set frequency. This seems to be one of the best ways to verify that your replication is running successfully, that it is replicating reasonably quickly, and that your application is truly available.

TIP

A little word to the wise: Do not turn on your HA configuration until you have set up full monitoring. We think you understand why.

Summary

Upgrading to a viable HA configuration can be fairly easy, depending on the HA options you are choosing. With SQL Server 2016, the process has certainly become streamlined quite a bit. Upgrading often involves replacing or upgrading your hardware and software stack to a much higher level to support more advanced HA solutions. You should also go through a full HA assessment exercise so that you can determine exactly which HA solution is the right one for you. You can then plan the infrastructure upgrades, get the upgrades configured, upgrade your SQL Server platform to SQL Server 2016, configure the right SQL Server HA configuration for your needs, and migrate to that well-tested environment. Gone are the days of month-long migrations to HA. On average, I can migrate a pretty large SQL Server HA configuration in about 3 days, including fully testing the application, testing all failover scenarios, and coming up on a disaster recovery SQL Server instance.

CHAPTER 16

High Availability and Security

The subjects of security and high availability are rarely considered in the same breath. However, as I have built numerous (and varying) types of high availability solutions, I have noticed that one Achilles heel is always present: security. It is crucial to properly plan, specify, manage, and protect the security-related portions of high availability solutions.

Time after time, I have seen application failures and the need to recover an application from a backup related to security breakdowns of some kind. In general, nearly 23% of application failures or applications becoming inaccessible can be attributed to security-related factors (see http:www.owasp.org). The following are some examples of various security-related breakdowns that can directly affect the availability of an application:

▶ Data in tables are deleted (updated or inserted) by users who shouldn't have update/delete/insert privileges on a table, rendering an application unusable (unavailable).

▶ Database objects in production are accidentally dropped by developers (or sysadmins), completely bringing down an application.

▶ The wrong Windows accounts are used to start services for log shipping or data replication, resulting in SQL Server Agent tasks not being able to communicate with other SQL Servers to fulfill transaction log restores, monitor server status updates, and process data distribution in data replication.

▶ Hot standby servers are missing local database user IDs, resulting in the application being inaccessible by a portion of the user population.

Unfortunately, these and other types of security-related breakdowns are often neglected in high availability planning, but they often contribute to large amounts of unavailability.

Much can be done in the early stages of planning and designing a high availability solution to prevent such issues from happening altogether. You can take a general object permissions and roles approach or an object protection approach, using constraints or schema-bound views. Even more thorough testing of your applications or better end-user training on their applications can reduce data manipulation errors on the database that the application uses. One or more of these methods can be used to directly increase your applications' availability.

The Security Big Picture

Looking at things from a bigger security and compliance point of view will help you better understand the many layers involved in a broader security enforcement approach. Figure 16.1 shows many of these layers, starting at the top with solid guidelines, policies, and compliance reporting capabilities. You must start with these to guarantee that you are aware of what must be done and have a way to show that you are doing what the policies outline.

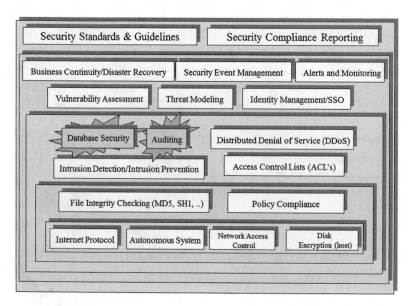

FIGURE 16.1   Security enforcement layers and components.

Next, you must define and create other aspects of security and compliance, such as security event management, alerting and monitoring, complete threat models, and vulnerability assessment objectives. These types of things must also reach into and be enforceable across major events such as disaster recovery (to ensure business continuity) and continue to support what you have deployed in the way of identity management and single sign-on.

The next inner layer is where your database security is defined, along with any database-level or database instance-level auditing you put in place. It is also this layer where messy things such as SQL Injection can occur and things such as denial-of-service attacks often surface. Getting some type of intrusion detection and prevention scheme into place is essential. Clear access controls are also essential. A bit later in this chapter I describe some basic SQL Server–based auditing at the database level. Figure 16.1 highlights two critical areas: database security and auditing.

Moving further down the layers of security, you find file integrity checking, secure Internet protocols, disk-level encryption, and other security-enhancing items. These all work together to bring you what should be a more secure (and compliant) place to deploy your applications.

With SQL Server 2016, you are essentially out-of-the-box ready to do absolutely *nothing*. In other words, Microsoft has taken the policy to "allow nothing" and you must explicitly grant any access, execution, or other action. Believe it or not, this is the right thing to do. This approach ensures that all objects and accesses are explicitly declared, and are, by definition, fulfilling security and many compliance regulations. The Open Web Application Security Project (OWASP; see www.owasp.org) lists the following as the top 10 application vulnerabilities:

▶ SQL Injection

▶ Cross-site scripting

▶ Broken authentication and session management

▶ Insecure direct object references

▶ Cross-site request forgery

▶ Security misconfiguration

▶ Failure to restrict URLs

▶ Unvalidated redirects and forwards

▶ Insecure cryptographic storage

▶ Insufficient transport-layer protection

To guard against any type of unauthorized access or untimely data manipulation that affects the data integrity of your application, you should have in place the usual precautions: firewalls, antivirus software, and a complete and well-orchestrated user ID and permissions scheme. Most applications are now tied into LDAP directories (like Active Directory) that are able to authenticate and authorize use of both data and functionality via roles and other properties. You must make sure the antivirus software profiles are up to date, keep the LDAP directory in sync with your database-level permissions, and ensure that no other points of failure (or points of corruption) exist in your environment. These basic protections directly affect your system's availability!

Using Object Permissions and Roles

The first line of defense for making sure someone doesn't drop (or alter) a table, view, stored procedure, or other object accidentally is to create an administrator user ID (like MyDBadmin) other than sa and then explicitly grant specific CREATE permissions (such as CREATE TABLE, CREATE VIEW, and so on) to that ID. By doing this, at a minimum, you will be able to tightly control object creations by a small set of authorized users. You can create an administering user ID, or you can assign the appropriate roles to individual Windows logins (for better audit tracking and less sharing of passwords). These approaches translate directly into reducing errors of this kind.

Securing via a Specific User ID or Windows Account

An following is an example of granting object rights to an individual login/user ID:

```
GRANT CREATE TABLE TO [MyDBadmin]
```

This MyDBadmin user (which can be a Microsoft SQL Server login or an existing Microsoft Windows user account) can now create and drop tables in the current database. Any user in the dbcreator or sysadmin server roles can also create and drop tables. Your company's group responsible for object maintenance in production will only be given the MyDBadmin user ID to use, not sa. To get a quick verification of what grants exist for a user, you can run the sp_helprotect system stored procedure, as shown in this example:

```
EXEC sp_helprotect NULL, 'MyDBadmin'
```

You get a result set like the following:

Owner	Object	Grantee	Grantor	Protect Type	Action	Column
.	.	MyDBadmin	dbo	Grant	CONNECT	.
.	.	MyDBadmin	dbo	Grant	Create Table	.

Securing via Created Roles

Another approach is to create a role, assign an object permissions to this role, and then add a user ID to this role. For example, you could create a role called ManageMyDBObjects, grant the CREATE TABLE permissions to this role, and then add a user ID as a member of this role, as follows:

```
EXEC sp_addrole 'ManageMyDBObjects'
GRANT CREATE TABLE to ManageMyDBObjects
EXEC sp_addrolemember 'ManageMyDBObjects', 'MyDBadmin'
```

This will have the same net effect as granting to an individual user ID, but it is much easier to manage at the role level. You can look at the protections for all statement-level permissions in the current database by using the sp_helprotect system stored procedure:

```
EXEC sp_helprotect NULL, NULL, NULL, 's'
```

You get a result set like the following:

Owner	Object	Grantee	Grantor	Protect	Type	Action	Column
.	.	dbo		Grant		CONNECT	.
.	.	ManageMyDBObjects	dbo	Grant		Create Table	.
.	.	MyDBadmin	dbo	Grant		CONNECT	.
.	.	MyDBadmin	dbo	Grant		Create Table	.

Securing via Fixed Server Roles or Database Roles

You can tap into the fixed server roles, such as `dbcreator` or `sysadmin`, or you can use the database role `db_ddladmin`. When you create a user ID in SQL Server (or want to use any Windows account), simply grant that user (or Windows account) the role you wish the user to have. For example, you could grant the `MyDBadmin` user ID the fixed role `sysadmin` as shown here:

```
EXEC sp_addsrvrolemember 'MyDBadmin', 'sysadmin'
```

As you may know, the ability to grant and revoke permissions via the GRANT and REVOKE commands depends on which statement permissions are being granted and the object involved. The members of the `sysadmin` role can grant any permission in any database. Object owners can grant permissions for the objects they own. Members of the `db_owner` or `db_securityadmin` roles can grant any permission on any statement or object in their database.

Statements that require permissions are those that add objects in the database or perform administrative activities with the database. Each statement that requires permissions has a certain set of roles that automatically have permissions to execute the statement. Consider these examples:

▶ The CREATE TABLE permission defaults to members of the `sysadmin`, `db_owner`, and db_ddladmin roles.

▶ The permissions to execute the SELECT statement for a table default to the `sysadmin` and `db_owner` roles, as well as the owner of the object.

There are some Transact-SQL statements for which permissions cannot be granted. For example, to execute the SHUTDOWN statement, the user must be added as a member of the `serveradmin` or `sysadmin` role, whereas `dbcreator` can execute ALTER DATABASE, CREATE DATABASE, and RESTORE operations.

Taking a thorough, well-managed approach to permissions and access (user IDs and the roles they have) will go a long way toward keeping your systems intact and highly available.

Object Protection Using Schema-Bound Views

Another easy-to-implement method to prevent tables from being accidentally dropped in production by developers or system administrators is to use schema-bound views. This is accomplished by creating views on all production tables that you don't want dropped accidentally, using the WITH SCHEMABINDING option. The net effect is that a table cannot be dropped until the view is dropped first. This behavior results from the dependency that you are explicitly creating between the view and the table (the WITH SCHEMABINDING option). This is a nice safety net that is easy to use and manage.

Basic Schema-Bound Views with Primary Key Column Only

The easiest way to create a schema-bound view to help prevent accidentally dropping tables in production databases is to create a basic view for each table that has the table's primary key column only. The following is a sample table that can be created in the AdventureWorks database (or any other database) in SQL Server:

```
Use AdventureWorks
go
CREATE TABLE [MyCustomer] (
    [CustomerID] [nchar] (5) NOT NULL ,
    [CompanyName] [nvarchar] (40) NOT NULL ,
    [ContactName] [nvarchar] (30) NULL ,
    [ContactTitle] [nvarchar] (30) NULL ,
    [Address] [nvarchar] (60) NULL ,
    [City] [nvarchar] (15) NULL ,
    [Region] [nvarchar] (15) NULL ,
    [PostalCode] [nvarchar] (10) NULL ,
    [Country] [nvarchar] (15) NULL ,
    [Phone] [nvarchar] (24) NULL ,
    [Fax] [nvarchar] (24) NULL ,
      CONSTRAINT [PK_MyCustomer] PRIMARY KEY CLUSTERED
                 [CustomerID]
   ON [PRIMARY]
) ON [PRIMARY]
go
```

This table has no outright protection to prevent it from being dropped by any user ID that has database creator or object owner rights (such as sa). By creating a schema-bound view on this table that will reference at least the primary key column of the table, you can completely block a direct drop of this table. In fact, dropping this table will require that the schema-bound view be dropped first (making this a formal two-step process, which will drastically reduce failures of this nature in the future). You might think this is a pain (if you are the DBA), but this type of approach will pay for its built-in overhead time and time again.

Creating a schema-bound view requires you to use the WITH SCHEMABINDING statement in the view. The following is an example of how you would do this for the just created MyCustomer table:

```
CREATE VIEW [dbo].[NODROP_MyCustomer]
WITH SCHEMABINDING
AS
SELECT [CustomerID] FROM [dbo].[MyCustomer]
```

Don't worry, you will not be creating any grants on this view because its sole purpose is to protect the table.

If you now try to drop the table:

```
DROP TABLE [dbo].[MyCustomer]
```

you will be rudely prohibited, as this example shows:

```
Server: Msg 3729, Level 16, State 1, Line 1
Cannot DROP TABLE 'dbo.MyCustomer' because it is being
referenced by object 'NODROP_MyCustomer'.
```

Here you have effectively and painlessly added an extra level of protection to your production system, which will directly translate into higher availability.

To look at all objects that depend on a particular table, you can use the sp_depends system stored procedure:

```
EXEC sp_depends N'MyCustomer'
```

As you can see, it shows the view you just created and any other dependent objects that may exist:

```
Name                    Type
dbo.NODROP_MyCustomer   view
```

Keep in mind that this initial method does not prohibit other types of changes to a table's schema. (That can be done by using an ALTER statement.) The next section describes how to take this approach a bit further to embrace schema changes that would also cause an application to become unavailable.

Full Table Structure Protection (All Columns Specified in the Schema-Bound View)

Building on the schema-bound view approach a bit further, you can also protect against many table structure changes by listing all columns in the base table in the SELECT list in the schema-bound view. This essentially provides column-level schema binding, which means that any changes to the bound columns will be restrictive. This, in turn, prevents the alteration of any schema-bound column in a table (either the datatype, nullability, or dropping of the column). It does not prohibit you from adding a new column, though— and you need to understand this from the start. The following is an example of creating a schema-bound view that lists all columns in the referenced table:

```
CREATE VIEW [dbo].[NOALTERSCHEMA_MyCustomer]
WITH SCHEMABINDING
AS
SELECT [CustomerID], [CompanyName], [ContactName], [ContactTitle],
       [Address], [City], [Region], [PostalCode], [Country],
       [Phone], [Fax]
FROM [dbo].[MyCustomer]
```

Then when we try to change the datatype and nullability of an existing column, this operation fails (as it should):

```
ALTER TABLE [dbo].[CustomersTest] ALTER COLUMN [Fax] NVARCHAR(30)
NOT NULL
```

This is the failure message that results:

```
Server: Msg 5074, Level 16, State 3, Line 1
The object 'NOALTERSCHEMA_MyCustomer' is dependent on column 'Fax'.
Server: Msg 4922, Level 16, State 1, Line 1
ALTER TABLE ALTER COLUMN Fax failed because one or more objects access
this column.
```

If you try to drop an existing column from the table

```
ALTER TABLE [dbo].[CustomersTest] DROP COLUMN [Fax]
```

you get a similar message:

```
Server: Msg 5074, Level 16, State 3, Line 1
The object 'NOALTERSCHEMA_MyCustomer' is dependent on column 'Fax'.
Server: Msg 4922, Level 16, State 1, Line 1
ALTER TABLE DROP COLUMN Fax failed because one or more objects access
this column.
```

This is a fairly safe method of protecting your applications from inadvertent table alterations that can render your application useless (and effectively unavailable). All these schema-bound methods are designed to minimize the human errors that can and will take place in a production environment.

Ensuring Proper Security for HA Options

Aside from the common infrastructure security protections that have been discussed already, there are often security breakdowns and other miscues directly associated with the major high availability options. As you will see, each HA option has its own set of problems and areas to consider from a security point of view. A good example of possible security miscues is not specifying the correct startup service account (Windows login/ domain account) for the SQL Server Agent that is needed to distribute transactions for data replication. The following sections highlight and reinforce these types of issues and considerations so that you can head them off before you attempt to build any of these complete HA options.

SQL Clustering Security Considerations

As you know, SQL clustering is built on top of Microsoft failover clustering, and SQL Server is cluster aware. This means SQL Server and all related resources can be managed as resources within failover clustering and to fail over as needed. For this reason, all the security setup and configuration that you have done for failover clustering must be done *before* you start installing a SQL clustering configuration.

As part of building up a viable failover clustering configuration, you must make sure that you have done one of the following:

▶ Identified (or defined) a domain to be a member of

▶ Configured all nodes that will be part of the cluster to be domain controllers in the same domain

▶ Created a domain account that will be used by cluster services (for example, `Cluster` or `ClusterAdmin`) with appropriate permissions

To configure the cluster service on a Windows server, the account you use must have administrative permissions on each node. In other words, this is the domain user account that will start the cluster service and is used to administer the failover cluster. You should make this account a member of the Administrators local group on each node of the failover cluster.

All nodes in the cluster must be members of the same domain and able to access a domain controller and a DNS server. They can be configured as member servers or domain controllers. If you decide to configure one node as a domain controller, you should configure all other nodes in the same domain as domain controllers as well. It is not acceptable to have a mix of domain controllers and member servers in a cluster. Then, there is only one more security-related item that needs to be set up to successfully install SQL clustering: You need to create domain user accounts for SQL Server and SQL Server Agent services. SQL Server Agent will be installed as part of the SQL Server installation process and is associated with the SQL Server instance for which it is installed.

During the process of installing the virtual SQL server, you must be prepared to identify the user account that will be starting the services associated with SQL Server (SQL Server itself, SQL Server Agent, and, optionally, SQL Full Text Search). SQL Server service accounts and passwords should be kept the same on all nodes, or the node will not be able to restart a SQL Server service. You can use Administrator or, better yet, a designated account (such as `Cluster` or `ClusterAdmin`) that has administrator rights within the domain and on each server (that is, is a member of the Administrators local group on any node in the cluster).

Log Shipping Security Considerations

Log shipping effectively replicates the data of one server (the source) to one or more other servers (the destinations) via transaction log dumps. By definition, this means that more than one SQL Server instance will be potentially used as the primary database server. Effectively, each of these source/destination pairs should be equal (from a security point of view at the very least). In order for log shipping to work well, you need to do a few things during the setup and implementation:

▶ Copy the source SQL Server user IDs to any destination SQL Servers securely.

▶ Verify the login being used to start SQL Server Agent for each SQL Server instance.

▶ Create the appropriate network share on the primary server for log shipping files.

▶ Make sure to create the `log_shipping_monitor_probe` login/user ID that will be used by the monitor server (unless you are using Windows authentication).

▶ Create cross-domain log shipping trusts.

The user IDs and the permissions associated with the source SQL Server database must be copied as part of log shipping. They should be the same at all servers that will be destinations for log shipping.

Make sure the source and each destination SQL Server instance have their corresponding SQL Server Agent running because log shipping and monitoring tasks will be created on each SQL Server instance and won't get executed unless their SQL Server Agent is running. The login that you use to start the MS SQL Server and SQL Server Agent services must have administrative access to the log shipping plan jobs, the source server, and the destination server. These accounts are usually the same account and are best created as domain accounts. The user who is setting up log shipping must be a member of the SYSADMIN server role, which gives that user permission to modify the database to do log shipping.

You need to create a network share on the primary server where the transaction log backups will be stored. You do this so that the transaction log backups can be accessed by the log shipping jobs (tasks). This is especially important if you use a directory that is different from the default backup location. Here is an example:

```
"\\SourceServerXX\NetworkSharename"
```

The log shipping monitor server is usually (and is recommended to be) a separate SQL Server instance. The `log_shipping_monitor_probe` login is used to monitor log shipping. Alternatively, Windows authentication can also be used. If you use the `log_shipping_monitor_probe` login for other database maintenance plans, you must use the same password at any server that has this login defined. What is actually happening is the `log_shipping_monitor_probe` login is used by the source and destination servers to update two log shipping tables in the MSDB database—thus the need for cross-server consistency.

Very often, the network share becomes unavailable or disconnected. This results in a copy error to the destination transaction log backup directory (share). It's always a good idea to verify that these shares are intact or to establish a procedure to monitor them and re-create them if they are ever disconnected. After you have reestablished this share, log shipping will be able to function fully again.

Make sure your logins/user IDs are defined in the destination server. Normally, if you intend the destination to act as a failover database, you must regularly synchronize the SQL Server logins and user IDs anyway. Double-check that each login has the proper role that was present in the source database. Syncing the logins causes many headaches during a primary role change.

Last but not least, if you are log shipping a database from a SQL Server in one domain to a SQL Server in another domain, you have to establish a two-way trust between the domains. You can do this with the Active Directory Domains and Trusts tool, under the Administrator Tools option. The downside of using two-way trusts is that it opens up a pretty big window of trusting for SQL Server and any other Windows-based applications. Most log shipping is done within a single domain to maintain the tightest control possible.

Data Replication Security Considerations

The security considerations in the different data replication models can be a bit complex. However, using a standard approach for replication can all but eliminate any issues you might ever have.

Start by thinking through the entire data replication flow from publisher, to distributor, to subscribers. When you first start setting up your replication configuration for high availability, you will likely use the Replication Tools option within Enterprise Manager (as opposed to just the replication system stored procedures). Microsoft assumes that you will start here and has proactively started to plot your future actions. It starts by actively querying what account is being used to start up the SQL Server Agent service. This is a built-in check to verify that you have the right login with the correct authorization at every step of the way. Microsoft is trying to get security started off on the right foot. It is your job to answer the call by supplying the right scheme to your replication solution—and it's not really very difficult.

In general, the following are the causes for concern from a security point of view for data replication:

▶ SQL Server Agent service startup accounts on each node of a replication topology

▶ All replication agents functioning with proper accounts

▶ All replication setup and grant authorizations

▶ Correctly authorized data and schema transfers for data synchronization/snapshot processing

▶ Logins/user IDs synchronized between publisher and subscriber (if used as a hot spare for failover)

As described earlier, Enterprise Manager looks at what account is defined to start the SQL Server Agent service. This is critical because all replication agents are initiated via the SQL Server Agent service. If it is down or has not been started with the appropriate account, replication doesn't occur.

You need to make sure that a duly authorized account that is a member of the `sysadmin` server role is used.

The best approach for data replication is to use one designated account for all replication-oriented setup. This should be an account named `Repl_Administrator` that is defined on each SQL Server instance that will be involved in the replication topology and that is a member of the sysadmin server role. Then, another account named `SQL_Administrator` (not `sa`) should be created that is used for the overall SQL Server Agent processing and startup, and it should also be a member of the sysadmin server role. Create this same `SQL_Adminstrator` account in all SQL Server instances and use it to start SQL Server Agent consistently. In fact, this is best done as a domain account. This way, you can have pretty tight account and password control at the SQL Server Agent services level and at the detail replication agent level. Remember that the SQL Server Agent is used for many things in SQL Server land, and you don't want to use a login that is just oriented toward replication to start it. However, you will want to use the `Repl_Administrator` account (domain account) as the owner of all replication agents in your topology. If you ever undo replication, you can also remove the `Repl_Administrator` account to guarantee that replication won't work; this is a nice undo safety net.

Keeping in mind that from the time of setting up remote distributors, enabling publishers and distributors, registering subscribers, and eventually subscribing to a publication, there are numerous security interactions that must work perfectly. Each interaction will require a login and password as part of its execution parameters and, in turn, creates agents (and tasks that an agent will execute). All agents should be configured to be owned (and executed) by the `Repl_Administrator` account.

Taking this simple and standardized account management approach makes replication really work in an environment and creates a stable high availability result.

Database Snapshots Security Considerations

With regard to database snapshots, several things need to be highly managed: snapshot sparse file size, data latency corresponding to your users' needs, the location of the sparse files within the physical deployment, the sheer number of database snapshots you are willing to support against a single database instance, and the security and access needs of users of database snapshots.

By default, you get the security roles and definitions that you have created in the source database available to you within the database snapshot—*except* for roles or individual permissions in the source database that are used for updating data or objects. Rights inherited from the source database are not available to you in a database snapshot because a database snapshot is a read-only database! If you have specialized roles or restrictions that you want to be present in the database snapshot, you need to define them in the source database, and you get them instantly. You manage from a single place, and everyone is happy.

AlwaysOn Availability Group Security Considerations

As you also know, AlwaysOn availability groups is built on top of Microsoft failover clustering. This allows SQL Server and all related resources to be managed as resources within failover clustering. Most of the basic failover clustering security considerations already mentioned in this chapter apply here as well. Enabling AlwaysOn availability groups requires membership in the Administrator group on the local computer and full control on the failover cluster.

Security is explicitly inherited from the failover cluster. Failover clustering provides two levels of user security granularity: read-only access and full control.

AlwaysOn availability groups need full control, and enabling AlwaysOn availability groups on an instance of SQL Server provides full control of the failover cluster (through the SSID).

You cannot directly add or remove security for a server instance in the Failover Cluster Manager. To manage failover cluster security sessions, you use the SQL Server Configuration Manager or the WMI equivalent from SQL Server.

Each instance of SQL Server must have permissions to access the registry, cluster, and a few other components:

▶ Creating an availability group requires membership in the sysadmin fixed server role and either CREATE AVAILABILITY GROUP server permission, ALTER ANY AVAILABILITY GROUP permission, or CONTROL SERVER permission.

▶ Altering an availability group requires ALTER AVAILABILITY GROUP permission on the availability group, CONTROL AVAILABILITY GROUP permission, ALTER ANY AVAILABILITY GROUP permission, or CONTROL SERVER permission.

▶ Joining a database to an availability group requires membership in the db_owner fixed database role.

▶ Dropping/deleting an availability group requires ALTER AVAILABILITY GROUP permission on the availability group, CONTROL AVAILABILITY GROUP permission, ALTER ANY AVAILABILITY GROUP permission, or CONTROL SERVER permission. To drop an availability group that is not hosted on the local replica location, you need CONTROL SERVER permission or CONTROL permission on that availability group.

NOTE

The transport security for AlwaysOn availability groups is the same as for database mirroring. It requires CREATE ENDPOINT permission or membership in the sysadmin fixed server role. It also requires CONTROL ON ENDPOINT permission.

TIP

It is a good idea to use encryption for connections between server instances that host AlwaysOn availability groups replicas.

SQL Server Auditing

SQL Server auditing enables you to audit server-level actions such as logins and/or database-level actions such as CREATE TABLE events and individual actions against database objects, such as SELECT, INSERT, DELETE, or UPDATE, and even execution of stored procedures. I strongly encourage you to enable some level of auditing so you have full visibility to all changes on your highly available SQL Server platforms.

An *audit* is a combination of several elements into a single package for a specific group of server actions or database actions. The SQL Server Audit feature produces an output that is called an audit.

The SQL Server Audit feature is intended to replace SQL Trace as the primary auditing solution. SQL Server Audit is meant to provide full auditing capabilities, and only auditing capabilities, unlike SQL Trace, which also provides performance debugging.

SQL Server Audit is also tightly integrated with the Windows operating systems and can push (write) its audits to the Windows application or security event log. With SQL Server Audit, you can set up auditing of just about any event or execution within SQL Server, and it can be as granular as you need (right down to the table or operation level). This is huge because not only can you track all these events, you can use this auditing capability to fulfill application and database audit compliance and look for patterns of misuse—or even specific "hot" objects that contain the most sensitive data in your database. With SQL Server 2016, more filtering is possible to help focus on specific items and reduce unnecessary audit clutter.

As you can see in Figure 16.2, there is a branch under the SQL Server instance node called Security, which contains several of the common security-related options that you know and love (Logins, Server Roles, Credentials, and so on). The Audits node allows you to specify audits and audit specifications. You can have SQL Server–wide audit specifications and audits as well as database-specific audit and audit specifications. You can have as many specifications as you want, and they can be at varying levels of granularity.

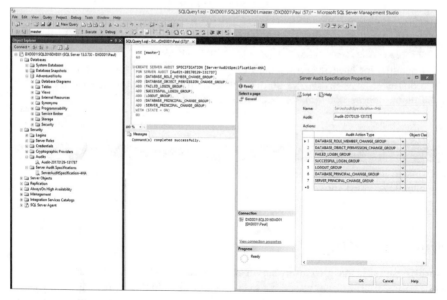

FIGURE 16.2   Audit and audit specifications in SSMS.

As you can see in Figure 16.3, there are three main objects that describe audits in SQL Server 2016:

▶ **Server Audit**—This object is used to describe the target for audit data, as well as some top-level configuration settings of the audit. The audit destination can be a file, the Windows event log, or the security event log. The Server Audit object contains no information about what is being audited—just *where* the audit data is going and server-/instance-level information of this audit. Multiple Server Audit objects can be defined, with each object independent of the others (that is, they can each specify a different destination).

▶ **Server Audit Specification**—This object is used to describe what to audit at the server instance level. A Server Audit Specification object must be associated with a Server Audit object in order to define where the audit data is written. There is a one-to-one relationship between the Server Audit Specification object and the Server Audit object.

▶ **Database Audit Specification**—This object is used to describes *what* to audit at a specific database level. Where the audit data is written is determined by the Server Audit object it is associated with. Each Database Audit Specification object can be associated with only one Server Audit object. A Server Audit object can be associated with Server Audit objects for multiple databases but only one Database Audit Specification object per database.

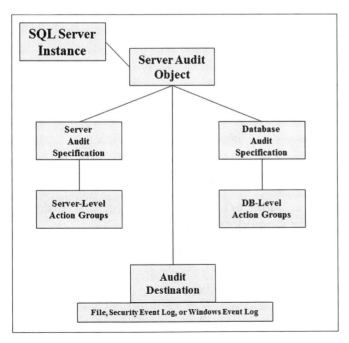

FIGURE 16.3   Audit objects, specifications, server/database action groups, and audit destinations.

After you create these objects, you can enable them by right-clicking each one and selecting Enable. As soon as the Server Audit object is enabled, it begins auditing and writing audit records to the specified destination.

You can review the details by right-clicking the Server Audit object and selecting View Audit Logs, or if you are auditing to the Windows application or security event log, you can open the Windows Event Viewer directly. One of the advantages of opening the audit log from within SSMS is that is automatically filters it to show only SQL Server Audit object events. Figure 16.4 shows the Log File Viewer open for a Server Audit object using the Log Viewer option (which you get by right-clicking the Server Audit object).

FIGURE 16.4   Log File Viewer showing the audit events of a Server Audit object.

It's up to your security and audit team to decide how to use these audits. It is recommended that you create your audit specifications with scripts so that you can easily manage them and not have to re-create them via SSMS dialogs.

General Thoughts on Database Backup/Restore, Isolating SQL Roles, and Disaster Recovery Security Considerations

In general, you should make a concerted effort to ensure that you can back up and recover your databases on a moment's notice. Very often (and usually at 3 in the morning, it seems), a system administrator is asked to restore a database because of some type of failure or database corruption. This system administrator's ability to recover can be dependent on whether he or she has the rights to recover a database. It is your job to make sure the mechanisms for database backup and recovery are well tested and are completely up to date. This should include having system administrator accounts created as members of the `sysadmin` fixed server role or, at a minimum, have created an account that has the `db_backupoperator` database role so that your system administrators can back up a database.

Many organizations isolate different SQL Server accounts for specialized purposes. The following are some examples:

▶ **Managing server logins**—Must be a member in the `securityadmin` fixed server role

▶ **Creating and altering databases**—Must be an account that is a member of the `dbcreator` fixed server role

▶ **Performing any activity in SQL Server**—Must be a member in the `sysadmin` fixed server role, whose permissions span all of the other fixed server roles

▶ **Adding and removing linked servers and executing some system stored procedures, such as** `sp_serveroption`—Must be a member in the `serveradmin` fixed server role

▶ **Adding or removing Windows groups and users and SQL Server users in the database**—Must be a member in the `db_accessadmin` database role

▶ **Managing roles and members of SQL Server database roles and managing statement and object permissions in the database**—Must be a member in the `db_securityadmin` database role

▶ **Adding, modifying, or dropping objects in the database**—Must be a member in the `db_ddladmin` database role

▶ **Performing the activities of all database roles, as well as other maintenance and configuration activities in the database**—Must be a member in the `db_owner` fixed server role, whose permissions span all of the other fixed server roles

From a disaster recovery point of view, you should make sure you can completely re-create and resynchronize your security from the ground up (including Active Directory, domain accounts, SQL Server logins/passwords, and so on). This includes making sure that someone has access to the `sa` password if necessary. This is called *security resynchronization readiness*. And, as part of this readiness, you need to completely test this recovery (one or more times a year)!

Summary

This entire chapter is devoted to security considerations and how security affects high availability. Lessons are often "hard lessons" when it comes to systems that are highly available, and you can avoid much anguish if you give enough attention and planning to the security ramifications up front. This chapter outlines the key security points that can become mismanaged or broken for each HA option presented in this book and a few general security techniques that can be applied to all your production implementations.

Many of the security techniques described in this chapter are commonsense methods such as preventing tables from being dropped in production by using a schema-bound view approach. Others are more standards and infrastructure oriented, such as using domain accounts for clustering and common SQL accounts for data replication or starting SQL Server Agent services. Together, they all add up to stability and minimizing downtime. Getting these types of security practices in place in your environment will allow you to achieve or exceed your high availability goals much more easily.

Remember that security risks appear due to architectural problems or holes in applications (such as with SQL Injection). The main aim of security for software is to just fail safely and carefully and to limit the damage. I don't want to read about your failing in the newspaper or on Twitter.

CHAPTER 17

Future Direction of High Availability

The next time I update this book, I will only be talking about 100% high availability solutions (not five 9s). For many, this is already a reality. But for still way too many, this is not possible yet due to backward compatibility, budget restrictions, security concerns, and a host of other factors.

The advancements that Microsoft and the rest of the industry have made in the past 5 years in terms of high availability options are nothing short of staggering. Having been a part of the Silicon Valley high-technology industry for all of my 30+-year career, I've always been at the forefront of these types of advancements. I spent many years architecting global solutions for multi-billion-dollar corporations that had some of the most severe high availability requirements that have likely ever existed. But today, mere mortals can easily reach stratospheric high availability levels without even breaking a sweat. Am I out of a job? Actually, it would be incredible if high availability architects weren't needed anymore. Likely this is exactly what the future has in store. (I have other skills, I'll be fine, not to worry!) The industry is truly headed toward being out-of-the-box highly available and at staggering levels of availability. A more modern way to express this future trend might be to say that high availability will become a service that you merely enable—high availability as a service (HAaaS).

High Availability as a Service (HAaaS)

As I talk to various industry service providers, such as Microsoft, VMware, Salesforce, Cisco, and many others, a common theme is providing services that are *never* unavailable. Whether it is on-premises virtualized server images, IaaS, PaaS, SaaS, DRaaS, or any of the many other as-a-service offerings, they are all pushing the envelope to become 100% highly available. The world is demanding this level of availability. Many factors are diving this demand. Today, although device technologies such as mobile phones have become immensely popular, more than half the world is not yet online. However, Facebook and Google have massive projects to provide Internet to the world, so that is changing rapidly. In addition, the costs of hardware (storage and compute) and constantly decreasing. It is only a matter of time before most places on the planet have access to systems and data globally—and they will likely not know where their services are coming from. A worldwide thirst for instant gratification of data and applications will bring with it an equal thirst for all of those being highly available—and *always* available.

Yes, HAaaS is starting to emerge in many ways already. It is disguised as basic architectures such as Hadoop clusters, geo replication, failover clusters, hot server failover of VMs, and many others. However, most of these existing architectures must be configured or built out separately or in layers. The HAaaS I speak of will insulate you from all this configuration and layer build-out. It will just be a service option of whatever IaaS, SaaS, PaaS, or even on-premises VMs you choose to purchase. Turn it on, and—voilà!—you have 100% availability. Of course, there will be a cost for this service, but, you have learned in this book to calculate your downtime cost per minute, and you will see that your HA downtime cost will rapidly justify this type of service. And, as Moore's law dictates, this service cost will also go down over time (likely very rapidly, just as compute and storage costs continue to go down). Before too long, look for Microsoft (both in its virtualization and in Azure) and Amazon to announce this type of HAaaS option. It will likely take the shape of a service level agreement option and have a price associated with it. Others will follow. The key will be that you won't have to do anything to get it other than turn it on and pay for it.

100% Virtualization of Your Platforms

One of the biggest steps any organization can take to lower costs and achieve more flexible HA capabilities is to become 100% virtualized. In other words, you can use commodity hardware in a server farm that is constantly being rotated according to the life expectancy of every hardware component. Then, on top of that compute, network, memory, and storage layer, you can virtualize it all into varying virtual compute resources at your disposal. Oh, then you have to move all your applications and databases to these virtualized platforms—which is not so easy. However, the payoffs are huge in regard to utilizing commodity hardware, and you can basically expand horizontally to meet any processing need your organization can muster.

One global company for which I consulted started out being 100% on specialized and super-expensive servers with an annual cost of $25 million in annual hardware purchases of some really big iron from Dell and HP. Within about 18 months, it had dropped to an annual cost of $1.5 million in annual hardware purchases of commodity hardware with an average failure rate of less than 5%. The company's compute power quadrupled, and its storage quintupled. So, why haven't you done this yet yourself?

Figure 17.1 illustrates what will further advance in the on-premises virtualized platforms you create. Basically, the VM providers (such as Microsoft and VMware) will get to a point where they will manage all the components related to being highly available (along with performance). You will just turn a simple dial in your VM manager to the HA level you'd like to have. The VMs will be replicated, configured, rotated, and distributed automatically to achieve your HA level, based on what is available to the VMs to work with. System administrators will just have to watch a dial; they will not have to configure clusters and so on. The HA services will determine the best way to use the VM resources. There will be no easy way to do that type of thing if you stay on raw iron.

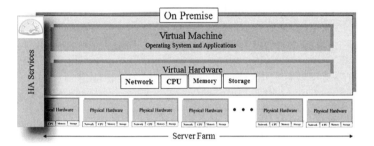

FIGURE 17.1   HA as a service or as an option in the on-premises virtualization world.

As Figure 17.2 shows, this extends naturally to any IaaS platforms you might also be using for your infinite computing platforms. In this case, you don't worry about the commodity physical server farms, which are insulated away from you at the providers (Azure, Amazon). However, HA services will automatically expand or configure these layers without you being involved in any way. Just turn the HA dial up—how about at 100% available?

17

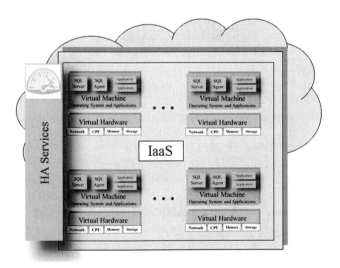

FIGURE 17.2   HA as a service or as an option in the IaaS world.

The same type of HA dial will also appear with PaaS and SaaS providers as well (for a cost, of course). Most PaaS and SaaS providers don't offer 100% SLAs yet, but when they get there, it will likely be turned into an HAaaS offering and monetized.

Being 100% in the Cloud

Most organizations that have been around a long time take a very slow path to the cloud. It starts out as an experiment of some minor application or capability and then starts to be a whole business function (like CRM, HR, or financials). Some companies just move their existing application to an IaaS platform, others convert to an SaaS provider that gives them the same service but in the cloud (like going from Siebel CRM on-premises to Salesforce CRM SaaS).

These days, many newer organizations simply leap to the cloud from the very beginning and never have an on-premises footprint—ever. As you can imagine, a lot of folks are in between as well, using some cloud, some on-premises. They use the cloud more opportunistically to fit specific needs but want control of some of their applications and keep this close to them (hence, on-premises). Remember that if part of your application is on-premises and part is in the cloud, your availability is only as good as the combined SLA. For example, if your on-premises application is using a third-party SaaS data aggregator as a critical feed to your application, your total application availability is dependent on both what you can deliver on-premises of the application itself *and* the availability of that SaaS provider. If the provider goes down or becomes unavailable (for whatever reason), you are effectively down as well, even though your on-premises application was never down.

However, more and more CIOs have been given a mandate to get off their on-premises footprints and get to the cloud with "everything." This worldwide trend is picking up massive steam. With the movement to the cloud, the emphasis of high availability shifts to the cloud. It also shifts to the things needed to get to the cloud—like networks and the Internet itself. The SLAs (especially availability) of each cloud provider becomes paramount. For a CIO to calculate her company's high availability, she will have to work a jigsaw puzzle of the combined application SLAs the company has subscribed to, as illustrated in Figure 17.3. This means that IT organizations as we current know them will rapidly diminish in size. The IT organization of the future will likely be mostly business analysts, architects, a financial analyst, and a few techies thrown in for good measure. Gone will be the infrastructure groups, the software development groups, the data warehouse groups, and so on. It will all be just SaaS applications and PaaS capabilities done by a collection of providers. Some organizations around the globe are already there. When they got there, they went from 500 IT employees down to about 25 IT employees in 24 months and didn't miss a beat in providing the company's needs. As for the high availability of those that are 100% in the cloud, in general, all have increased their applications' availability significantly over what they were delivering with their on-premises footprint. Now you see why this is catching on.

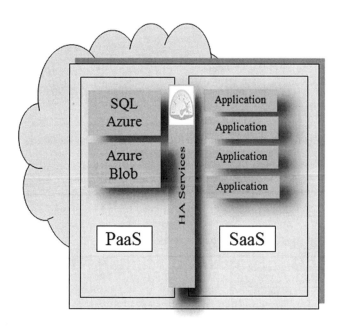

FIGURE 17.3   HA as a service in the 100% cloud-based world.

Advanced Geo Replication

A very strong emergence of many new PaaS providers is helping to move companies to the cloud more quickly. Examples of PaaS providers and PaaS capabilities are Microsoft's SQL Azure (SQL Server as a service) and Microsoft's Blob storage. With SQL Azure, you basically get all the SQL Server capabilities but really don't have to do anything to build it out. All you need to do is define what you want to put there and use it. Microsoft provides this PaaS capability with some basic HA services already by virtue of SLAs on the PaaS itself, data redundancy within a single region, and geo replication of the primary database's data to up to three other regions, as shown in Figure 17.4. One region becomes a failover for high availability but with some data loss (because the replication is asynchronous, not synchronous).

As Microsoft invests to get faster pipes between its regions, look for an increase in the number of geo replication sites to a very high number. In addition, geo replication to other regions will become synchronous—and likely to more than one region synchronously—as predicted in Figure 17.5. This will increase this core PaaS capability to 100% availability out of the box (but, for a charge, of course).

17

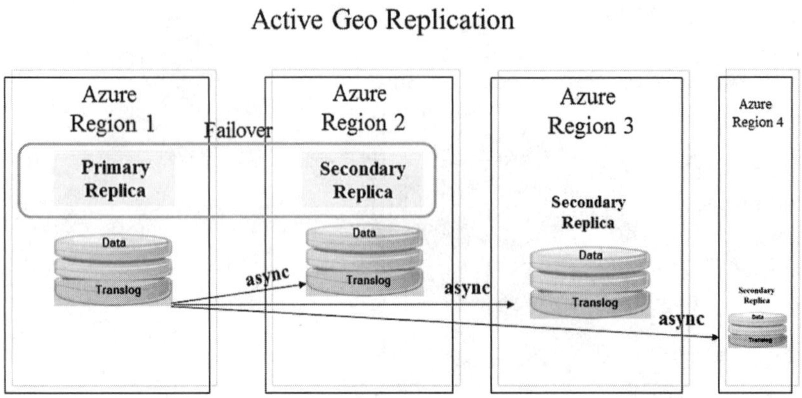

Active Geo Replication

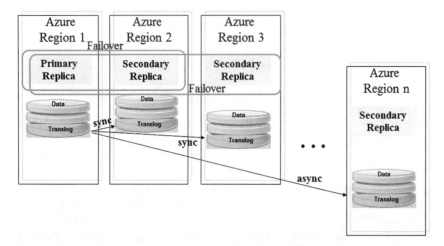

FIGURE 17.4   Current HA configuration of SQL Azure across regions.

FIGURE 17.5   Azure possible advancement with advanced geo replication.

Disaster Recovery as a Service?

Providers have already started advertising their new disaster recovery as a service (DRaaS) offerings. Yep, this is here now. Basically, DRaaS will allow a separate service to be plugged into your IaaS, PaaS, SaaS, and even your on-premises footprint and to receive all critical applications and data needed to operate the company in case of major failure of all those services. DRaaS will essentially consolidate all of your company's critical applications and data into a single cloud location that is kept hot in case of catastrophic failure. Could this happen? Perhaps...in the event of a war, a major natural disaster, destructive breaches, evasive viruses, and even a massive DDoS attack across a broad part of a continent. Many organizations want the ease of just plugging into a DRaaS capability to have a place to recover to just in case. Vendors like Microsoft are already providing services like Azure

Site Recovery with customizable recovery plans; these are the first stepping stones toward DRaaS. Figure 17.6 shows how a DRaaS would simply plug into your current IaaS, PaaS, SaaS, and on-premises footprints and provide the needed business capabilities in case of major failure.

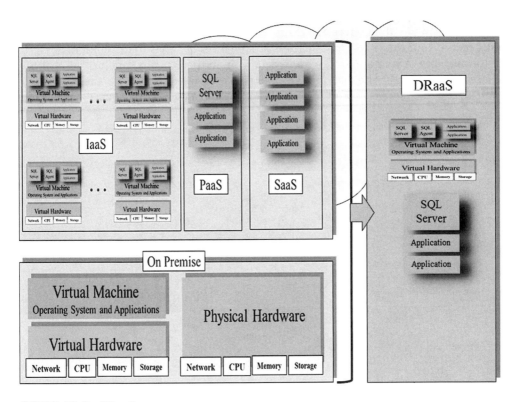

FIGURE 17.6   DRaaS.

Summary

High availability depends on laying a fundamentally sound foundation that you can count on when failures occur. Then you need to determine how much data loss you can tolerate, how much downtime is possible, and what the downtime costs you. That's the reality right now. However, emerging quickly are services like HAaaS and DRaaS that will change the way you think about enabling your business to be 100% available for every application you have. Granted, this will require many years of migrations for organizations that have much invested in their current infrastructure and application portfolios. But, they will get there; costs will drive them there.

Conclusion

I often talk about *global risk mitigation*, which involves spreading out your business capabilities and data across the globe to mitigate against loss at any one place (for example, if a region or a data center fails). This could even be a mitigation strategy for small, local companies. As the pipes get bigger and the applications or services become globally aware and able to distribute themselves out across resources in many parts of the world, you greatly reduce your risk of loss and increase your chances of survival. In addition, you gain 100% availability of your applications and data with, in theory, zero data loss. All that is left for you to do is keep the dial on 100% and enjoy the warmth of living the HA life.

Index

A

Active Geo Replication, cloud computing, 270–271

Active Geo replication, disaster recovery (DR), 330

active multisite DR pattern, 319

active/active configuration, failover clustering, 82

active/active DR sites pattern, 318–319

active/passive configuration, failover clustering, 81

active/passive DR sites pattern, 316–317

activity logs, clusters, 295

Add a Failover Cluster Node Wizard, 109

Add Node Rules dialog, 110

adding, HA elements, to development methodologies, 76–77

advanced geo replication, 395–396

Agent History Clean Up: distribution, 213

ALTER_DATABASE command, 180, 186

ALTER ANY AVAILABILITY GROUP permission, 385

AlwaysOn

    availability groups, 21, 39–40, 54, 122

        availability group listeners, 124

    Azure, 43–45

    configuring, 95–96

        disaster recovery (DR), 124

        endpoints, 125

    failure, 369

        investment portfolio management scenario, 145–147

        modes, 122–123

        read-only replicas, 123

    security, 384–385

    cloud computing, 265–268

    dashboard, 143–144

    FCI (failover cluster instance), 120–122

    multinode AlwaysOn configuration, 125–126

        backup up databases, 130

        connecting with listeners, 141

        creating availability groups, 131–132

        enabling AlwaysOn HA, 129–130

        failing over to secondary, 141–142

        failover clustering, 126–128

        identifying replicas, 133–135

        listeners, 138–140

        preparing database, 129

        selecting databases, 132–133

        SQL verifying Server instances, 126

        synchronizing data, 135–138

    use cases, 119–120

    WSFC (Windows Server Failover Clustering), 87–88

Amazon Web Services (AWS), 273

Apache Hadoop, 273

Apache Spark, 280

Apache Storm, 280

application clustering, 45–46

application data values, 322

application resiliency, 11, 349

application service providers (ASPs), 18

    SQL Server clustering, 114–117

application service providers (ASPs) assessments, 57–64

application types, availability, 10

applications

    assessing existing applications, 16–17

    isolating, 34

articles, data replication, 200–201

    filtering, 201–205

AS SNAPSHOT OF statement, 160

B

R

S

triggers, data replication, 213

two-node SQL Server failover clustering configuration in active/passive mode, 101

U

United States, DDoS (denial-of-service) attack, 258

unplanned downtime, 4, 5

unplanned outages, 1

upgrades

  performing, 368

  planning, 367

upgrading, deciding what to upgrade to, 363–364

uptime, 4

uptime requirement, 10, 348

use cases

  AlwaysOn and availability groups, 119–120

  big data use cases, Azure, 300–301

user IDs, security, 376

user requirements, data replication, 213

V

variables

  availability variables, 10–12

  gauging HA primary variables, 348–349

  HA primary variables, gauging, 52–53

vendor agreements, 25

verifying SQL Server clustering, 126

@@VERSION, 332

vertical filtering, 201–202

View Synchronization Status option, 228–229

virtual machines (VM), 303

  backing up, 308–310

  live migration, 307–308

  Microsoft Windows 2012 hypervisor virtual machines, 304

virtualization, 100% of your platforms, 392–394

VM (virtual machine, 303

VM snapshots, 310–311

vulnerabilities, 375

W

warm standby, switching over to, 226–227

Windows 2012 hypervisor virtual machines, 304

Windows accounts, 376

Windows Performance Monitor, 230–231

Windows Server 2012 R2, live migration, 308

Windows Server Failover Clustering. See WSFC (Windows Server Failover Clustering)

Windows Server Manager, installing, failover clustering, 89–94

WITH SCHEMABINDING option, 377–378

witness database servers, 171

witness roles, database mirroring, 172

wizards

  Add a Failover Cluster Node Wizard, 109

  Cluster Validation Wizard, 83

  Database Mirroring Wizard, 173

  Install a SQL Server Failover Cluster Wizard, 101

  New Availability Group Wizard, 132

  New Publication Wizard, 217

worldwide sales and marketing

  assessments, 64–68

  business scenarios, 19

  data replication, 233–235

WSFC (Windows Server Failover Clustering), 21, 36–37, 82–86, 120

  AlwaysOn, 87–88

  extending, with NLB, 86–87

  installing, SQL Server clustering, 100–113

  SQL clustering, 80, 87–88